THE
REDISCOVERY
OF JOHN WESLEY

George Croft Cell

UNIVERSITY
PRESS OF
AMERICA

LANHAM • NEW YORK • LONDON

University Press of America,™ Inc.

4720 Boston Way
Lanham, MD 20706

3 Henrietta Street
London WC2E 8LU England

Library of Congress Cataloging in Publication Data

Cell, George Croft, 1875–1937.
The rediscovery of John Wesley.

Reprint. Originally published: New York : Holt,
c1935.
Includes index.
1. Wesley, John, 1703–1791. I. Title.
BX8495.W5C4   1983   287'.092'4   83–6505
ISBN 0–8191–3222–5 (pbk.)

Reprinted by arrangement with
Holt, Rinehart and Winston
New York, New York

To

the future leaders of the Christian
Church throughout the world

PREFACE

The Rediscovery of John Wesley is the outcome of a literary
project and the solution of a problem which has occupied my time
once and again for the past twenty-five years. The radical revision of the tradition about Wesley outlined in these essays has
been therefore in the first place an event in my own experience.
The long prevalent and still current anti-Calvinist interpretation
of Wesley's message and ministry was abandoned under compulsion of the facts upwards of twenty years ago as equally false
to the truth about John Calvin and to the truth about John
Wesley. Analysis of the content of John Wesley's preaching made
it perfectly clear that for fifty-three years he said as extremely
little about the human side of saving faith, except man's dire
need of it, as he said extremely much about saving faith as God's
work for us in Christ and in us by the Holy Spirit. Further, the
Wesleyan doctrine of the Holy Spirit, so conspicuous and controlling in the Wesleyan theology, simply stood for and summed
up the true objectivity and reality of our communion with God.
It was indeed something of a surprise from the standpoint of the
Arminian tradition about Wesley to discover that he had consistently and categorically denied the doctrine commonly referred to him, namely, that a man can of himself by the powers of
his free will produce or generate this faith in his own mind;
rather, since man is by nature evil and incompetent both to think
and do good, it is altogether necessary that saving faith as the
first principle of all Christian experience should be wrought in
him by the Holy Spirit. True genuine Christian faith is in its
totality the gift and work of God.

The radically anti-Calvinist representation of Wesley was
displaced by the thesis that the individuality and religious energy
of the Wesleyan Reformation lay not in any deviation from the

faith of the first Reformers, but in the rediscovery and the re-affirmation of that faith. Protestantism in its three principal formations, which refer to Luther, Calvin and Wesley respectively, ceased to be a loose, unprincipled collection of religious groups, large and small, and began to appear in virtue of this insight once more in its truer light as an essential unity of faith. Most Protestants are too keenly conscious of the many superficial differences to perceive the deeper dynamic unity. The affiliation of the Wesleyan Reformation with the work of Luther and Calvin as the key to Wesley's position in the Protestant evolution occupied from the first the conspicuous position in the University lectures. It continues to do so in this review of Wesley's religious understanding of the Gospel.

The special investigations which have been directly tributary to *The Rediscovery of John Wesley* open with three years (1904-1907) of research at the University of Berlin, carried on chiefly in the scientific and philosophical movements of the eighteenth century in connection with the writing of a dissertation for the doctorate in philosophy which was submitted and accepted in 1907 by the University of Berlin.

The second period (1910-1912) made the religious movements of the eighteenth century the subject of special investigation and laid the foundation for my University lectures on *The Revival of Protestant Christianity in the Eighteenth Century*. The subject matter of these lectures and the main conclusions reached twenty-five years ago have been checked up again and again at the original sources. The lectures have been considerably modified and enlarged in the interest of accuracy and completeness. But the main thesis of the lectures, won before they were written, that the essentials of the Wesleyan Reformation represent the deeper and dynamic unity of Protestantism and not any one of its thousand and one diversities, has endured the test of every re-examination.

A sociological study of the Wesleyan movement, begun in 1921, yielded in 1923 results that were set forth under the caption, "The Decay of Religion." Here for the first time the deeper kinship of Wesleyanism with West-European Protestantism was pushed into the foreground and stressed. It was now clear that the kinship of Wesleyanism and Calvinism greatly exceeded their common affiliation with Luther. The data analyzed seemed then and still more now to demonstrate beyond reasonable doubt that the Wesleyan ethic of life was in respect to its ascetic temper (Puritanism), its concept of the vocation, its religious, non-mystical evaluation of activity in the world, and the exclusive orientation of its Christian ethic in the idea of divine grace, essentially and thoroughly Calvinistic.

A fourth period of research preceded and attended the writing in 1925-1927 of the "History of American Thought" for the twelfth and last edition of Ueberweg's *Grundriss der Geschichte der Philosophie,* and accumulated the materials in part for the course of lectures given since 1926 on "The History of American Thought" with diminishing attention to speculative questions and increasing attention to political and social subjects vital to the work of the Church.

The fifth period (1931-1934) of special research in the eighteenth century has been devoted entirely to the investigation of the creative and controlling religious ideas of the Wesleyan Reformation. The first volume of Curnock's monumental Standard Edition of Wesley's Journal in eight volumes appeared in 1909 and the eighth in 1916. Telford's Standard Edition of Wesley's Letters, a fresh and exceedingly rich source of information, appeared in 1931. Scholarship was, after these publications, in possession of practically all the important means of information and the time had come for subjecting the entire tradition about Wesley in the secondary sources to a thoroughly critical investigation and a comparison with the original sources and after that for a fresh synthesis of results. This monograph is therefore the result, at once a record and résumé, of extensive research in the origins, character, and consequences of the Wesleyan Reformation or in historically related subjects.

He who turns from the secondary writing about John Wesley in which the parsimony of genuine scholarship is overmatched by the enormous amount of copying, goes back to the original sources, and steeps himself in them will, I am persuaded, be compelled to revise radically the whole tradition about Wesley essentially along the lines of this monograph. If then the investigator brings to his mastery of sources thorough discipline in the history of Christian thought and in the movements of modern Christianity, he may reach the conclusion that John Wesley has made a contribution to theology no less important than his contribution to practical Christianity. Indeed the one may be the secret of the other.

The findings of a master of essential Christianity on the meaning of God in Christian experience is the golden thread of fire that runs through this report. It is not a general statement of the Christian teaching, but a special investigation of John Wesley's pioneer work toward the New Protestantism and his triumphant reaffirmation in the Age of the Enlightenment of the historic Christian faith against "the worship of humanity." It undertakes to trace the principal stages of his progress through an experiment in religion which yielded negative results and terminated in his evangelical reaction against the humanistic Arminianism of his own Church, to the experiment in the faith of the first Reformers which is the principal source of everything important in his career as preacher, promoter, and general superintendent of the Revival.

The lack of uniformity in the several editions of Wesley's sermons has made it necessary for purposes of reference to reprint the sermon titles according to the third London edition in fourteen volumes compiled by Thomas Jackson and published in the years 1829-1831. To this reference will always be made in the footnotes. This key will enable the reader to use any of the current editions of Wesley's writings. All references to Wesley's Journals and Letters are to the Standard Edition of the Journal by Curnock and of the Letters by Telford. Wesley's other writings are referred to by title. It is to be hoped that a Standard Edition of these miscellaneous writings and sermons uniform with Journals and Letters may soon complete the technical work of heuristic in the field of *Wesleyana*. This would do much to facilitate the use of the original sources, which we may safely assume are for the purpose of a knowledge of Wesley's doctrinal ideas now complete.

It was not the custom of the best writers of the eighteenth century to litter their discussions with continual references to other writers until their books had degenerated into a series of book reviews. The great advantage of that method is that it enables an author to do a much larger amount of writing on a smaller margin of information. But it certainly does not facilitate intelligent reading nor is it serviceable to a deeper insight into the subject. Professor Sedgewick of Oxford University used to tell his classes in philosophy of a certain island whose inhabitants spent all their time washing each other's clothes. This method accounts for too much philosophical and theological writing. I have been influenced by eighteenth-century models in choosing to abide by the orientation of the arguments and the conclusions in the original sources.

This procedure in a critical exposition and appraisal of Wesley's religious principles is dictated by two further considerations. The conception of the problem in this monograph has no predecessors. Many of the facts and features of Wesley's theology have long been subjects of valuable comment by numerous writers. But with rare exceptions, this writing exhibits a monotonous lack of historical objectivity and critical power, and a constant neglect of the original sources. The radical developments in Wesley's doctrine of Christian experience have rarely been traced genetically, and in no case thoroughly. That peculiar element in Wesley's theology which made him at once the consummator and conqueror of the humanistic religion of his age has been ignored and no attempt has been made to define accurately the deposits in his doctrine of religious experience from the culture of the Enlightenment. Even more fatal is the general failure to bring the categories, to be won alone from adequate discipline in the history of Christian thought, to bear in understanding and appraising Wesley's possible contributions to Christian thought.

He dipped deep into the general stream of Christian thought, so that the regnant doctrinal ideas of his preaching must be historically discerned.

The principal reason however for the energetic concentration of attention upon the original sources of information and the exclusive orientation of the general view of Wesley in them lies in the notable fact that no other great expounder of doctrinal and exponent of practical Christianity has left posterity so careful and complete a picture of the essential elements and inner development of his own thought as well as the daily routine of his active career from his ordination in 1725 to his coronation in 1791. Wesley's journalistic and epistolary record of the inner developments in his doctrinal ideas in conjunction with the extensive and formal expositions of his understanding of the Gospel in the epoch of his maturity is absolutely unique in Church History. This fact may indeed make the work of historical criticism in this field much more onerous and difficult, but all the more a duty. Additional reasons for the appeal from the Wesley of the secondary to the Wesley of the primary sources are advanced in the opening chapter on "The Crisis of Religion."

Several of the chapter titles used are of Wesleyan coinage or usage. "Saints of the world" and "a religion not more than human" are the characteristics which Wesley gave to the humanistic religion of the Age of the Enlightenment. "The very edge of Calvinism" was used to indicate that his own understanding of the Christian faith was very much closer to the faith of the first Reformers than to the Arminian teaching and preaching of his own Church. "From 1738 to this time" indicates Wesley's habit of thought in referring to the origin and progress of the Revival. "The infinite distance" refers to the endless ethical difference between the perfect holiness of God and the sin-stricken state of man. "The gate of religion" is his appellation for justification by faith. "The entire work of God" indicates that saving faith, which is, all of it, the work of God, underlies the progress no less than the beginning of Christian experience. "A continual sense of total dependence on God," also a formula of Wesleyan coinage, at any rate usage, is clearly enunciated as the essence of all religion as experience. It is hoped that this fidelity to Wesley's language as well as thought may add to the objectivity of this Rediscovery of John Wesley. Originality is a poor compensation for objectivity and intuition is a poor substitute for information; *no documents or the failure to use them, no history,* is the first law of historical criticism.

An author who has foraged over the whole field of Wesley writing for a period of twenty-five years will have contracted a thousand obligations of a general nature which he is unable to identify or acknowledge in any detail. Since the conclusions herewith submitted have all been checked up at the original sources and the arguments are drawn directly from them, I am satisfied to let that fact speak for itself. To Lewis Oliver Hartman who has for many fruitful years occupied the editorial chair once held by Abel Stevens, the first historian of Methodism and a writer unsurpassed in his mastery of things Wesleyan, I owe more than I can say for his unfailing encouragement, counsel, and co-operation. Likewise I am deeply indebted to John W. Langdale's constructive interest in this reinterpretation of John Wesley for the future leadership of the Christian Church. It is altogether owing to his initiative that I finally harnessed myself during the past quadrennium to the task of writing *The Rediscovery of John Wesley* for which I began to gather the materials a quarter of a century ago. The slow progress of the writing has been caused not only by the inherent greatness and difficulty of the subject and the conscientious research which it exacted, but also by other duties, academic and literary, which would not be denied or delayed. I now send the book forth in high hope that the substance of the deeper, richer understanding of the Gospel which has accrued to the writer under the tuition of John Wesley may also accrue to the reader.

G. C. C.

Boston, Massachusetts
Thanksgiving, 1934.

CONTENTS

Chapter I. *The Crisis of Religion*

Chapter II. *The Last Oxford Sermon*

Chapter III. *Religion as Experience*

CONTENTS

CONTENTS

Chapter XIV. *Love's Categorical Imperative*

Chapter XV. *The Entire Work of God*

Chapter XVI. *The Decay of Religion*

Part I

CONTENTS

CHAPTER I

THE CRISIS OF RELIGION

The Wesleyan Reformation is the necessary bridge between the Old Protestantism of the sixteenth and seventeenth centuries and the New Protestantism of the eighteenth and nineteenth centuries. We are now well into the fifth century of Martin Luther's path-finding experiment in the Christian faith, his epoch-making rediscovery of the knowledge of a living and saving God in the Gospel, that is, in the person and work of Jesus Christ, his Ninety-five Theses, and his ever memorable, "Here I stand, I can no other." It is an even four centuries since John Calvin's conversion to Protestant principles and his flight from Paris to Strassburg, Basel, and Geneva, where he devoted himself, confessedly under Luther's tuition, to the teaching and preaching of the Word of God and to deep, brooding, systematic thinking over the majesty of the divine purpose and the tenderness of Jehovah's electing love, slowly moving down the ages. Midway in the vista of intervening events between the foundations laid by the first Reformers and our own parlous times in travail of we know not as yet what new birth, stands the figure of John Wesley, master mind of the Revival of Protestant Christianity in the eighteenth century and the principal historical link between the Old and New Protestantism.

The life of John Wesley (1703-1791) spans the eighteenth century; his constructive influence, the modern world. He is an epitome of the religious conflicts of the last two centuries. He tried out and transcended the humanized Christianity of the Age of the Enlightenment. He summed up in his thought and experiments in religion a thorough trial of its decadent Christianity, the evangelical reaction against its superficial liberalism, and the origin and progress of the Revival for half a century. The Christian centuries know no greater adventurer of the Christian faith and propaganda. His daring thought of the World for a parish has been measurably fulfilled in the world-encircling influence of the Wesleyan Reformation. The verdict of history, based on the long perspective and revealing logic of events, is that "he has wielded a wider constructive influence in the sphere of practical Christianity than any other man who has appeared since the sixteenth century."[1] His resourcefulness in Christian enterprise set up its own standards. Recognized by all as a religious genius of the first order, rated by some "one of the most powerful and most active intellects of England," traversing every vital phase of the Christian movement, he lifted the decadent Christianity of his time out of the ruts and cut new channels for its reawakened doctrinal and practical energies.

However great his resources in natural gifts, education, and practical technique, however much they were multiplied by the inspiration of the Gospel and whatever the boundary of his vast achievement, the true kernel of his greatness is wrapt up in the fact that he consecrated every moment and every faculty of his being in utter simplicity to the Jesus-way of going about and doing all the good he could. He had one absolute: to preach the universal love of a living and saving God in the glad tidings of salvation by faith in Jesus Christ and to spread scriptural holiness over all the lands of the earth. Though versatile in interests and many-sided in his activities, he had "one, only one end to regard on earth, one, only one business to pursue."[2] It is summed up in the one word, religion, which he conceived to be the highest practical concern of mankind. It was given to him to see life and see it whole in prospect as well as in retrospect. He felt himself to be in the light of the eternal "a creature of a day passing through life as an arrow through the air." He was conscious of standing on "the little isthmus of life between two boundless oceans." He foresaw and felt at the sunrise of

[1] Lecky, *England in the Eighteenth Century*, II, 558, 631.
[2] From the Preface to Wesley's Edition (1735) of *The Imitation of Christ*.

his career what the common run of men realize first at the sunset of life; any day is short when it is over; any time is brief when it is done. Over the very door of his life-work he wrote the inscription: "Leisure and I have taken leave of each other." His biographer well may add, "never to meet again." Wesley's endless pilgrimages of Gospel passion and his colossal industry in the Christian propaganda recall Pauline standards. But the time-span of his active Christian ministry was lengthened to just double the years of St. Paul's apostolate. The magnitude and intensity of Wesley's sustained industry in the Gospel are alone enough to invest his two great experiments in the Christian faith with a unique and perpetual significance.

The sixty-six years of his active career were spent in working and augmenting the institutions and resources of the Christian Church for the redemption and improvement of humanity. The great and steadfast churchman in him, never for one moment doubting or despairing of the Christian Church, sank at length from sight, as it were, in the greater humanitarian. It was his way to go deeper and to ask what the Church is for? "Is it not to bring souls from the power of Satan to God and to build them up in His fear and love? Whatever in the Church Visible answers these ends is so far valuable. Whatever answers them not, is nothing worth." [3]

Wesley first appears in the modern Church in the thick of an experiment in the Christian faith, undertaken in the fulfilment of his call to the Christian ministry. This experiment first discovered to him the spiritual bankruptcy of the current Christianity of his age. The negative results of his first experiment, lasting thirteen years, drove him further in the search for power and ripened him for another experiment in the Christian faith which wrought a revolution in his religious principles and in the content of his preaching, shifted the center of gravity in his personal Christian experience, changed the character of his century, and forms an epoch in modern Christianity. It was by these two experiments in personal and practical Christianity that

[3] Letters, II, 77 f.

he was first qualified to summon "the whole Christian world back to religion as experience in the face of a dead theology and a dead ceremony." The nature and the results of Wesley's two experiments in the Christian faith indicate the main subject of these investigations. *The Rediscovery of John Wesley* is submitted as a report of findings. It will be made evident in the progress of the report that John Wesley in overcoming the humanistic Christianity of the Enlightenment succeeded in capturing and carrying into his doctrine of Christian experience and program of practical Christianity the creative idea of the Enlightenment: the spirit of experimental science. In a very true and sound sense he was, in spite of the many appearances to the contrary, both the fulfiller and the conqueror of the humanistic religion of the Enlightenment.

So radical and revolutionary were the changes through which the Western world, more especially the Protestant peoples of Western Europe, passed concurrently with "the religious revolution begun in England by the preaching of the Wesleys and Whitefield," that able thinkers have begun to consider seriously whether the Middle Ages did not in fact come to a close first in the eighteenth rather than in the sixteenth century. It is hardly more than a truism of history to say that every century belongs in a very clear and sound sense both to the past and to the future and is transitional. The evolutionary view of history must with open mind consider the cancellations, the continuities, and the creations of development. There are in every age some things that are going out, some that abide, and still others that are coming in. But this general character of all ages does not deprive any period of its special characteristics and true individuality. Now the men and women of eighteenth-century England began to do so very many unprecedented things of lasting importance to the race as to make it the period of great new departures in human thought and action and of bold pioneering on every front of human interest. More concisely it has impressed the historical mind as the revolutionary century.

But in whatsoever view of that unique century the unresting

thought of man may tarry for a time, this much we know: The advancing scientific control of natural forces and the dominant rôle of the scientific movement in the modern world; the beginnings of the Industrial Revolution and the commencement of material progress over wide areas, going forward by leaps and bounds, never before experienced by mankind; the reappearance of the social question in a new form fixed by the Industrial Revolution; the birth of the spirit of self-government and the beginnings in America of the world's greatest experiment in democracy; the transfer of the electric fires of democracy and nationalism from the New World to the oppressed peoples of the Old World; the culmination of the rising modern spirit of emancipation, progress, democracy in the French Revolution; the rise of a social conscience calling for the socialization of the benefits of the Industrial Revolution; the rapid and radical swing from purely traditional thinking to critical, progressive, experimental thinking on all subjects, religion and economics included; finally and perhaps the most perfect symbol of the century, the birth of the gospel of human progress, material and moral, through man's conscious, forethoughtful effort; these are all certainly among the powerful movements contemporaneous with the second vital phase of the Protestant Movement, namely the Wesleyan Reformation. The life work of John Wesley which was built solidly on foundations laid by Luther and Calvin constitutes therefore in this historical setting an essential part of the real bridge out of mediæval into modern Christianity.

Wesley's constructive work on both doctrinal and practical Christianity belongs essentially to the real bridge out of the Old into the New Protestantism, not alone by reason of the magnitude of his constructive influence in the sphere of practical Christianity, but also by reason of the method which he pursued to discover and demonstrate the truth-values of the Christian faith. He began on a scale never before carried into practice to put every issue of the Christian faith into the test-tubes of experiential thinking and to try out every question of theology in the laboratory of applied Christianity. How far he was prepared to go in his theology of experience, evidenced in many ways, may be gathered from the fact that he made it an object of inquiry to ascertain whether the Christian experience of God is in its structure and indications truly Trinitarian. In submitting thus the Christian conception of God in its entirety to the tests of experiential thinking, he has submitted in principle all questions of Christian doctrine. Farther than this the theology of experience cannot go. Thus the line where theology has ceased to be Biblical, experimental, and practical fixed for Wesley the limit of all theology.

The inner genius of Wesley's theology may be provisionally indicated by a question which he put to himself and those with him at the outset of his Evangelical Ministry and by an observation of similar import which he made toward the close. The principle involved was a factor, often avowed, in all his work.[4] In one of his early conferences which he resolved into a seminar on Christian doctrine, he faced the question as to how much experiential data is required to sustain a conclusion on any question of faith and morals? How can we reason soundly on religious subjects in terms of experience? Then once and again throughout his career he reverted to the principle that dogmatic opinions which clash with the realities of Christian experience must yield. He reacted in the first ten years of his ministry as a graduate and resident Fellow of Lincoln College (1725-1735) very strongly against the dogma of predestination and became so strongly Arminian that he felt himself in duty bound, as he put it, "to oppose predestination with all his might as a dangerous mistake subversive of the very foundations of Christian experience." Thirty years later, this species of anti-Calvinism was openly renounced as "mere bigotry." Wesley then confessed that he could not reconcile his early position with his mature theology of experience and so abandoned it. He had come to know many believers in predestination whose "real Christian experience" could not be doubted. "This fact stares me in the face," so runs the candid thought of our first "Theo-

[4] Letters, II, 298.

logian of Experience," and "is clear proof that predestination is only an *opinion*, not subversive of the very foundations of Christian experience, but compatible with a love to Christ and a genuine work of grace. Yea, many hold it at whose feet I desire to be found in the day of the Lord Jesus."

Twenty years later another of his dogmatic prejudices went down before this same theological empiricism. He then widened his doctrine of Christian experience, after reading a life of Thomas Firmin, to include Unitarians.[5] He was "exceedingly struck" to discover from that good man's life that one of his dearest theological tenets had been refuted by facts. "But I cannot argue against matter of fact." In short, the verdicts of experience are for theology final. The great churchman and the outstanding religious individuality of the eighteenth century who experienced a profound evangelical reaction against its humanized Christianity and had begun "to preach by the grace of God," as he put it, "the faith of the Gospel, of the primitive Christians, or of our first Reformers," [6] is also the theologian who introduced the experimental method of reasoning into religious subjects and entrusted the future of the Christian Church to the free interaction of man's entire personal life with the historic Christian faith. Now Wesley's constructive work in the whole sphere, but above all on the frontiers, of practical Christianity is a great but open book, well written, known, and read of all men. But his consciousness that the rise of criticism and the collapse of all systems of infallibility had created the necessity of a new apologetic for the Christian faith and his contributions to the foundations of a theology of experience is a relatively unexplored subject.

The conception of Wesley's position in the Protestant evolution and of his significance for modern Christianity which I have ventured to call *The Rediscovery of John Wesley*, promises something radically different from the traditional interpretations of the Wesleyan Reformation. These have hitherto paid little or

[5] *Arminian Magazine*, Vol. IX.
[6] Secker-Wesley Correspondence, Moore's *Life of Wesley*, II, 475.

no attention to Wesley's power of constructive thought on the
Christian faith. It has been assumed on the contrary that he
"has no title to be regarded as a great thinker." [7] It has been
asserted of him that "the influence of men bears no kind of
proportion to their intellects." The author of these two remarks
about Wesley has nevertheless confidently rated him "one of the
most powerful and most active intellects of England." [8] But we
might well ask where, outside the sphere of Christian thought
and action, would Wesley give evidence of any, to say nothing
of the highest, intellectual force? The contradiction might be
resolved by denying his mastery of essential Christianity or his
ability to find in terms of modern thought any formula adequate
to his understanding of the Gospel, while recognizing and affirm-
ing his world-wide constructive influence in the sphere of practical Christianity. This inconsistent way of recognizing Wesley's
intellectual force shows at any rate more respect for the facts
than is to be found in the all too common *a priori* banishment of
the Revival from the progress of Christian thought. "It is useless to look to the evangelical movement, in any of its forms,
for any theologian who directly advanced the progress of Christian thought." [9] This *a priori* assurance that no influential idea
in modern Christian thought, making for progress, could have
come out of the Evangelical Movement was possible perhaps
fifty years ago. Its corollary has been the assumption that it is
necessary to make a detour through German speculative philosophy and liberal theology in order to find out what Christianity
is.[10] There is no other way to learn the essentially experiential
nature of religion and the wider meaning of God in the experi-

[7] Matthew Arnold, no enemy of faith, but a disenchanted lover, an agnostic,
with a much quicker, keener sense of intellectual force from the negations than
from the affirmations of faith, pronounced Wesley a third-rate intellect.

[8] Lecky, *England in the Eighteenth Century*, Vol. II, pp. 558, 629, 631.

[9] Allen, A. V. G., *Continuity of Christian Thought*, 1884. Chap. VI, "Renaissance of Theology in the Nineteenth Century," pp. 373-438.

[10] It is instructive to note that this question was raised and became an issue
already in Wesley's time; see his Journal, Vol. I, p. 492 f. He could learn from
German sources without falling into servile dependence on German theology.

ence of humanity. Later research in the Wesleyan Reformation has rejected this *a priori* banishment of the Evangelical Movement from the history of Christian thought.

It is never useless to look at the facts. Instead of dogmatizing on what Wesley could not have done, it may be more informative to consider what he has done. Without prejudice either for or against any other source of light or leading, least of all against the great masters of liberal theology in German Protestantism from Schleiermacher, the regenerator of theology in central Europe, to Ritschl, Harnack, Hermann and Troeltsch, it is simply proposed to investigate from the ground up Wesley's doctrine of Christian experience.

Wesley has not written thick volumes on theology and that sits hard with his reputation among the schoolmen. But if he did not display "great speculative power in theology," it might be due simply to the fact that in a century which turned radically from all speculation to investigation and poured its best thought into scientific research, Wesley, in active sympathy with the spirit of the new science, has the distinction of introducing the experimental method of reasoning into religious subjects. He may not have "speculated magnificently" precisely because he had deliberately forsworn it. "I, of set purpose, abstain from all philosophical speculations" in expounding "the essentials of true religion." There is an ancient and deep-seated prejudice that only an elaborate, scholastic theology can reveal the power of a great thinker on religious subjects. Thus Jesus will have no title to be regarded as a great thinker on religious subjects; that goes to the scribes. Thus Luther will have no title to be regarded as a great thinker in theology; that goes to the scholastics before or after him. Thus Wesley will have no title to be regarded as a great thinker on "the essentials of true religion"; that goes to the later philosophical theology of the German mind. But Harnack, whose authority on the history of Christian thought is the highest, informs us that every reformation of Christianity, every great forward movement in the history of the Christian Faith, has been marked by a return to simplicity in theology. And this puts us in some doubt about the scholastic standards of a great thinker on religious subjects.

Wesley accepted at the outset his inevitable responsibility for both the doctrinal guidance and the pastoral oversight of the Evangelical Movement. The credentials for his extensive discipline in the historic Christian faith and his solid work in doctrinal guidance are impressive. Although he preached on the average eight hundred sermons annually, his itinerant ministry exacted of him a relatively small stock of new sermons, so that he had far more free time for constructive work than the average local pastor of our time. He conducted more than one seminar on Christian doctrine for his preachers.[11] The enormous extent of his life-long reading and writing bears witness to his free time as well as to his colossal industry. Plus extensive general reading, he mastered on the average one solid book in divinity monthly. He knew ten languages [12] and made good use of them. His published works as author, editor, translator, passed the four hundred mark. His own distinctive writings fill upwards of twenty-five massive volumes. He records the fact that he examined minutely every word of the Greek text of the New Testament. He made an independent translation of the New Testament, the true merit and importance of which have never been explored and appreciated. He mastered the literature of mysticism, reading the principal mystics in the originals. His discipline in historical theology was extensive. He read widely in the Patristics and in the masters of Protestant theology, especially Luther, Calvin, Arminius, Episcopius and the Anglican divines. The religious writers of his own age, in particular the deists, did not escape his careful attention. These few references will not begin to give a full account of the range, variety and vigor of his intellectual interests; but they indicate the fact that he foraged very widely in the fields of Christian thought.

[11] See Green's *Bibliography of Wesley's Works*, p. 156.
[12] Arabic, Hebrew, Greek, Latin, French, Italian, Spanish, German, Dutch, English.

Incidentally he made short shift with preachers who despised intellectual industry.

In the course of his constructive work for the doctrinal guidance of the Revival, Wesley drew up in the eleventh year of the movement a list of three questions as guide-posts for constructive doctrinal thinking. It is a project for a new Christian apologetic and was submitted to one of the foremost deistical writers of the time. To the deistic demand that historic Christianity be put to the test of pure reason, Wesley opposed, not the appeal to the infallible voice of the Visible Church, nor to the "inspiration of every word of the Bible," as Lecky and other writers represent him, but he proposed simply to put the historic Christian faith to the tests of experiential thinking. The principal difference then between a Middleton and a Wesley in their theory of religious knowledge or test of truth-values in religion is that the former referred traditional Christianity exclusively to the test of pure reason while Wesley appealed to the free interaction of the historic Christian faith with man's entire personal life.

The questions propounded were:

1. Who is a Christian indeed?
2. What is real, genuine Christianity?
3. What is the surest and most accessible evidence to know that it is of God?

(Letters, II, 375-388.)

Attention is directed first of all to Wesley's strikingly modern way of putting the question. The second of these questions, somewhat abbreviated, is the title of the late Adolph Harnack's lectures which were given in 1900 at Berlin University and were designed for "a short and plain statement of the Gospel and its history." In sending his *What is Christianity?* through the gates of the press, Harnack paid his respects to theologians who do no more than "treat of the Gospel in the recondite language of learning and bury it in scholarly folios." If now this putting of the question was not original with Wesley, it was certainly adopted and consistently used by him a full century before its adoption in German Protestant thought.[13]   Prior to the Reformation the doctrinal question always was, What is the faith of the Visible Church?   Early Protestantism asked, What is the revelation of the Bible?   Wesley's contemporaries began to ask, What is religion within the limits of reason alone?   Although Wesley reasoned at times in the spirit and in the letter of the early Protestant theory of inspiration, still he never asked any of these questions.   In some way or other he turned his back on all of them and came by a putting of the question that is supposed to be born of the critical, developmental, historical understanding of Christianity.   But whatever its source and significance for him may have been, he belongs by his way of stating the question and by his method of seeking the answer not to the Old but to the New Protestantism.

Wesley observed with great acumen as early as 1749 that the critical movement, then called deism, was driving traditional Christianity out of its misplaced confidences and exposing its general bankruptcy.   He wished the critics success. ' "Go on and prosper!   Shame these nominal Christians out of that poor superstition which they call Christianity.   Reason, rally, laugh them out of their dead empty forms, void of spirit, of faith, of love."   Current Christianity seemed to him, then, a "poor superstition" ripe for destruction!   Did Voltaire say anything worse about it?   And Wesley directed attention to the fact that the negative work of the critical movement was clearing the ground for a reconstruction and revival of genuine Christianity.   He pointed out further that criticism was proving a blessing in disguise in that it had laid upon Christian thought the inescapable necessity of turning to the scientific method in religion.   And this would of course amount to a theology of experience.   It will not abandon the appeal to tradition, nor neglect any other source of insight; but henceforth experience and its indications will be the citadel of Christian apologetic.   All the other arguments may either fail or remain but half effective.   But the fact that Christianity can

---

[13] Troeltsch, *Gesammelte Schriften,* Bd. II, ss. 391-401.

be and continues to be experienced by free souls is the "strongest evidence and constitutes a stream which will never dry up."

After the Age of the Enlightenment the question, What is the authoritative teaching of the Visible Church? was no longer admissible. "I could not," said Wesley, "at the price of implicit obedience be a member of any church." Likewise he got clear for all practical purposes of the question, What is the teaching of an infallible Bible? If he did not adopt the critical position in principle but reverted in some cases to the early Protestant theory of inspiration, he certainly has adopted the critical position and rejected the early theory of inspiration in practice. "The Old Testament," he asserted roundly, "is not the standard of Christian experience." He revised the Anglican Prayer Book for American Methodism with sovereign freedom, striking out "many Psalms, and many parts of others, as being highly improper for the mouths of a Christian congregation." He did not believe any of the Apostles ever had any right to implicit obedience. He called attention in his New Testament notes to the fact that the words "out of Egypt have I called my Son" (Matthew II, 16) were originally spoken of Israel. He lays down the rule: "A passage of Scripture whether prophetic, historical or poetical, is in the language of the New Testament, fulfilled when an event happens to which it may with great propriety be accommodated." [14] A comparison of Wesley's exegetical judgments with those of his supposed master, the foremost New Testament scholar and lower critic of Wesley's time, Bengelius, reveals in the diciple far more critical freedom than is exemplified by the master; and then did not Wesley in a crucial case require "something more, namely, experience," to certify even the New Testament? Finally Wesley did not ask after the fashion of the desolate theorizing Christianity of his age, "What is the teaching of an infallible reason?" He denounced a religion within the limits of reason alone, which was the dearest idol of the Enlightenment, to be at best only "Painted Fire." The fundamental, practical conviction of his message and ministry

[14] Wesleyan New Testament, 13, 14.

was that the free, full interaction of the historic Christian faith
with our entire personal life is all the authority we need. So
long as we are free to explore and trust Christian experience and
its indications, we have no need of an infallibility of any kind.
Wesley in the epoch of his maturity therefore simply asked, What
are the reactions and indications when traditional Christianity
is put into the test tubes of experience and life? He belongs
therefore both by reason of his modern way of putting the question and his modern way of finding the answers, that is by the
standpoint and principles of his theology of experience, far more
to the New Protestantism than to the Old Protestantism.

The voice of the Age of the Enlightenment is therefore distinctly perceptible in Wesley's doctrine of Christian experience.
It assumes in relation to any other man or group of men the
complete autonomy of the human spirit in deciding religious
issues. Every significant response to the Gospel must spring
freely from man's own inner life. The reference of the entire
religious question to experiential thinking is the keynote. This
principle is strongly accented in the doctrinal minutes of the
earliest conferences. They assert that where the Church canons
can not be observed with a safe conscience, the canons must
yield. Wesley expanded this thesis in his Journal to read, "I
could at the price of implicit faith or obedience be a member of
no church under heaven. For I must insist on the right of private
judgment. I dare call no man Rabbi. I can not yield either
implicit faith or obedience to any man or number of men under
heaven." [15] The following year (1747) the principle laid down
in the first Conference and expanded in the Journal was given a
full precise formulation and reenacted by the Conference. "Can
a Christian submit any further than his conscience permits to
any man or number of men on earth? It is undeniably plain
he can not either to pope, council, bishop, or convocation. And
this is that grand principle of every man's right to private judgment in opposition to implict faith in man on which Calvin,

[15] Journal, III, 243.

Luther, Melanchthon and all the ancient Reformers,[16] at home and abroad, proceeded. *Every man must think for himself,* since every man must give an account of himself to God." These words, every man must think for himself and can not resign that function or surrender that right to any man or number of men on earth, regardless of their rank and station or their ecclesiastical authority, define the first principle of the Enlightenment. Immanuel Kant (1724-1804), a contemporary, twenty-one years Wesley's junior, made, a generation later, the autonomy and essential activity of the human spirit the keynote of his critical philosophy. But the principle harks back, as Wesley pointed out, to the Reformers themselves. *Sapere audete!* said Melanchthon in his first address at Wittenberg (1520). Have the courage of your own insight! *Intellectum exercere audemus!* said Luther. Let us dare to think for ourselves! It is hardly necessary to add that this is the central idea of the Renaissance and the great and durable truth of humanism; no theological weapon forged against it shall prosper.

But Wesley's doctrine of Christian experience further fulfills the principle of the Enlightenment by making the reference to experiential thinking in religion comprehensive of the free interaction and response of man's entire personal life, not simply the intellectual function, to the historic Christian faith. The doctrinal master of the Revival always trusted out moral and volitional responses as our deepest organ of communication with God. Here he transcends the narrow rationalism of his age in religion by according the primacy in religious experience to feeling and the will. Moreover, the theologian of the Revival who kept the deepest truth of humanism, reacted strongly against the humanistic Arminianism of his day and went clean over to a theocentric doctrine of Christian experience. But this fact about Wesley has been thrown into total eclipse. What now, we ask, is the barrier that prevents our seeing in Wesley's theology what he always regarded as of vastly greater significance than the corrective it offers for ultra-Calvinism?

[16] In Wesley's list, Calvin's name commonly comes first.

Perhaps the most universal tradition about John Wesley as preacher, pastor, superintendent of the Revival, above all, as its doctrinal guide, has been that he was the arch-foe of Calvinism, root and branch. His doctrinal convictions are supposed to have been in their origin and development a *radical Arminian reaction against the influence of Geneva in English Christianity*. He is therefore the true historical successor and finisher of the work begun by Archbishop Laud (1573-1645) who found the Anglican Church saturated with the doctrines and practises of Geneva and set himself to redeem the Church of England from the influence of Calvinism. He undertook to break the blood-bond between the Reformation and English Christianity and to restore the Catholic tradition. Laud's anti-Calvinism passed through the Wesleys into the structure of Methodism. Wesley's influence in the Modern church has done more than anything else to discredit Calvinism.

This is in bold outline the historical account generally given of the origin and essence of Wesley's theology. It is scarcely necessary to point out that this radically anti-Calvinist view of Wesley holds undisputed sway in the secondary sources and is in most recent interpretation of Wesley almost axiomatic. What exposition of Wesley does not begin, continue, and end with his anti-Calvinism? This bias reaches the limit of paradox in the assertion that Methodism has no particular theology except opposition to Calvinism and that Wesley's teaching was at all points the antithesis of Calvinism. He can not be pictured in history as standing on the shoulders of Luther *and Calvin*. It is now quite the fashion to represent him as originally, i.e., from 1738 onward, the antithesis of Calvinism, as thinly affiliated with Luther, but deeply rooted, grounded, and steadfast in the Catholic tradition of the Anglican Church. This total reversal of the facts reaches then a limit in the recent attempt to represent Wesley as a reaction against genuine Protestantism and at heart a High Churchman not far from the Catholic fold. He did indeed say of himself that he had been, prior to 1738 without knowing it, a Catholic humanist; but he has also said that he found himself out and broke radically alike with the Catholic conception of the Church and with the humanist conception of faith.

The thesis of this monograph is that the Wesleyan Revival was in its origin and earliest stage (1) negatively a powerful reaction against Arminian Anglicanism in the doctrine of Christian experience and against High Church principles in the theory of Church institutions and the exercise of the pastoral office; and (2) positively a return to the faith of the first Reformers. Moreover, the Revival retained in spite of the Calvinistic controversy, in which it was involved, its original character so long as Wesley's hand was at the helm. There is in the birth of the Evangelical reaction, as summed up in Wesley, no traceable consciousness of any antagonism, much less of polemic, against the faith of Luther and Calvin. That element in the theology of Luther and Calvin which Wesley later withstood was in the Spring of 1738 entirely crowded out of his consciousness and banished from his attention by his fiery interest in that part of the Reformation faith which he then first found out and accepted. There is no trace or sign in Wesley's thinking at the point where he crossed his Religious Rubicon of the least interest or concern to correct or oppose Calvinism, either all of it or any part of it. The issues which soon after arose from that source were in the Spring of 1738 simply outside his field of vision. His mind was fixed at the religious turning point of his life, not on any danger of ascribing too much to God in our experience of faith, but on the total failure of the humanist version of faith. Is saving faith the figment of creative imagination which a man puts over on himself or is it actually the gift and work of a living and saving God? The reality of our communion with God was the issue, then as now.

Wesley's conversion-experience is then in no sense to be construed as a reaction against Calvinism. It was in its origin and principal character a reaction against the current religion of the Church of England. The facts are that Wesley, as we shall see in due course, not only rejected the Arminian divines of the

Anglican Church as untrustworthy expounders of Christianity, but he arraigned them as "betrayers of the Church, sappers of the foundations of the faith and miserable corrupters of the Gospel of Christ." He saw in their doctrines a common apostasy from "the fundamental doctrine of all the Reformed Churches." He brought under this condemnation not only most of the living teachers of the Anglican Church but also "the general stream of writers and preachers." "Indeed very few can we find who simply and earnestly teach and preach the faith of the first Reformers." He cited in his sermon on "True Christianity Defended" (significant title!), written June 1741 to be preached at Oxford, the greatest Anglican divines of former times, Tillotson, Bull, as examples of this Arminian apostasy from the Reformed faith. He seems to have had this situation in mind when a little later he remonstrated against "running away from Calvinism as far as ever we can," when as a matter of fact "the truth of the Gospel lies within a hair's breadth of Calvinism." For of Calvinism's three points, two of them, the essentials, are evangelical and fundamental to Christian experience.

The comprehensive issue between Wesley and Arminian Anglicanism, after he perceived its fatal gravitation toward humanism, experienced his evangelical reaction against its intellectualism, moralism, mysticism, and went back to the faith of the first Reformers, was, as Wesley himself has stated it, the idea of a God-given faith in Christ or the work and witness of the Holy Spirit as the first principle of all Christian experience. What then was the opinion formed in the first decade of the Revival concerning Wesley's position by the general stream of writers and preachers, by the living teachers and leading minds of the Anglican Church, by the highest voices in the convocations, in the pulpits, and in university circles? Did his preaching impress them as moving securely in the Arminian paths their feet were accustomed to? Was there no other issue between Wesley and the Church of England in 1738 save only the most unusual manner and method of his ministry? Did they feel that he was in harmony with the Arminian mind and spirit of

Anglican teaching and preaching? Or did he impress them as one of the leading bishops who always spoke of Wesley with respect, never with rancor, said: "You have gone back into the old and exploded Calvinistical expositions of the Christian faith." He told Wesley he was rejecting the counsel and guidance of the Modern or present Anglican Church which was Arminian in spirit and understood the faith in the Arminian sense and was going back to the Church of England when it was Calvinistic in spirit and understood the faith in the Calvinistic sense. Here we come upon a fact of great, perhaps decisive, importance. The mass of writing and public utterance against Wesley from Anglican sources, ranging from a mild to a militant opposition, all shares the opinion that Wesley's message was a radical reaction against the Arminian sense and spirit of current Anglican teaching and preaching. How can these things be? It is also quite remarkable that Wesley never refers to the Anglican Arminians in support of his own position but only to Arminius himself who, as Wesley observed, very largely agreed with Calvin, taught two of his three points in terms as strong, clear, express as John Calvin himself, so that in respect to original sin and justification by faith both parties fully agree, that is, all evangelicals do, and "There is not a hair's breath difference between Mr. Wesley and Mr. Whitefield." He also believed that the evangelicals were divided only on matters of opinion, whereas the Arminians were divided on the essentials of Christian experience. Wesley clearly appears to concur with his Anglican critics as to his closer doctrinal affiliation with the Calvinists than with the Anglican Arminians. This is passing strange!

Hitherto the judgment of Wesley's contemporaries has not been drawn upon as a valuable source of information concerning his position in English Christianity and therewith in the Protestant evolution. It is now universally agreed that the primacy accorded to religious experience was at once a principal work of Wesley's theology and a source of power in the entire Wesleyan movement. "John Wesley brought the whole Christian world back to religion as experience in the face of a dead theology and

a dead ceremony." [17]   At the same time he taught the whole
Christian world by a supreme example of Christian thought and
action that in religion, experience and reality come to the same
thing. Now for Wesley the Christian Faith is the highest form
of religious experience so that the substance of his theology is
not pared down to the meaning of God in human experience nor
even in religious experience, but rises to the higher levels of
Christian experience. Moreover, he explored the Christian experience of the individual not as if an isolated phenomenon, but
as a fact within the whole gravitational field of Christ and his
Church. Within this sphere the individual experience of saving
faith can alone arise and gain its limits. For beyond all doubt
Christian experience is historically mediated and conditioned.
Wesley's perception of this basal fact is never feeble nor obscure.
But with Wesley the first and the last word about Christian expe-
rience is never the human receptivity nor the historical mediation.
It is always the divine gift; It is always the work and witness
of the Holy Spirit. Christian experience is the experience of a
God-given faith, of the immanent activity of the Holy Spirit.
No other exponent of the Gospel has surpassed him in the clarity
of his apprehension and the cogency of his exposition of the
Pauline principle, "No man can say Jesus is Lord, but by the
Holy Spirit." In this plenary sense he called it "the very foundation," "the essence of Christianity" and "the main doctrine of
the Methodists" [a term he tolerated only from necessity and
never conquered his dislike of it!]. Now this principle which
meant for him the true objectivity of the Christian faith as
experience summed up all the issues between the faith of the
first Reformers on which he took his stand and the current
religion of the Church of England which he undertook to reform.

The Wesleyan Revival seen as a whole and in its full historic
setting passed, in the period while Wesley's hand was at the
helm, through two major conflicts: the first conflict was in Wesley's judgment of major, the second, of minor doctrinal impor-

---

[17] I am indebted to the late George A. Gordon of Old South Church, Boston,
for this sound and illuminating generalization.

THE CRISIS OF RELIGION 21

tance. He viewed the former as a conflict of first principles between the *humanistic* Arminianism of Anglican teaching and preaching and the *evangelical* Arminianism of his own position, which he consciously derived from and confidently referred to Arminius himself. This conflict dominated roughly the first half of Wesley's evangelical ministry, and is quite understandable if the Wesleyan movement was in its origin and early development an evangelical reaction against humanistic Arminianism.

In the twenty-fifth year of the Revival we find Wesley doing his utmost to form an Evangelical Alliance of all clergymen "who agree in these essentials:

1. Original Sin;
2. Justification by Faith;
3. Holiness of Heart and Life;

provided their life be answerable to their doctrine." Full latitude of opinion was guaranteed in his proposals touching absolute decrees on the one hand and perfection on the other. These, it may be observed, were the points at which the Calvinistic and the Arminian Evangelicals clashed. But the fact of maximum significance is that Wesley's conception of the Alliance included all Evangelicals alike, Calvinists and Arminians, who would agree to think and let think on Predestination and on Christian Perfection, but positively excluded the humanistic Arminians. To this period of Wesley's life and project of an Evangelical Alliance belongs his immortal saying, "I desire a league offensive and defensive with every soldier of Jesus Christ." Wesley's conception of an Evangelical Alliance is obviously the key to the universal opinion entertained by the Anglican Arminians that he stood much closer to the Calvinists than he did to them; and Wesley always thought so too. Not until Whitefield's death in 1770 did the consciousness of unity in evangelical principles pass under a cloud. Not till then did the fires of fierce controversy break out. And the outbreak then was due chiefly to the fact that no masterful leader appeared among and for the Calvinistic branch of the Revival who was Wesley's equal in the spirit of toleration. The aloofness of the very small group of

Evangelical Anglicans and the intolerance of the ultra-Calvinists, timid institutionalism and overweening dogmatism, defeated Wesley's purpose of a league offensive and defensive with every soldier of Jesus Christ.

The last half of Wesley's evangelical ministry was marred and scarred by the bitter Calvinist controversy. There is no occasion here to retell the wearisome and unedifying story. This provisional reference to the two major conflicts of Wesley's career has been made solely for the purpose of pushing into the foreground of the investigation the fateful fact that the last, and in respect to its doctrinal importance the lesser, conflict between the Arminian and Calvinistic Evangelicals has been as assiduously remembered by his ardent followers as the earlier and in the judgment of John Wesley far more significant doctrinal conflict between humanistic and evangelical Arminianism has been quite forgotten and as much neglected in the interpretation of Wesley's Theology.

The net result of this lack of historical insight and perspective has been that Wesley's anti-Calvinism has been made the principal, if not exclusive, historical key to his position in English Christianity and in the Protestant evolution. The inference is that Wesley's theology is the radical and inclusive antithesis of Calvin's theology. This is also the true parentage and lineage of the generally accepted theory that the Wesleyan Revival was already in its origins and always in its development an Arminian reaction against Calvinism. The fact is that the Wesleyan movement was in origin and development and in its inner motivation an evangelical reaction against the dominant Anglican Arminianism, so persuasive and powerful that Wesley was at his own word carried by it to "the very edge of Calvinism," until he stood "within a hair's breadth" of the third point of Calvinism. So powerful was his first reaction against Arminianism that he actually scrupled for a time to admit that faith is even the condition of salvation. Faith in that sense is noticeably omitted from the first manifesto of the Revival. All the emphasis is on the divine initiative. It is not surprising therefore that he later confessed his leaning too much at first toward Calvinism. Which way the theological wind was blowing for him is evident from a proposition laid down in the doctrinal minutes of the second Annual Conference of 1745 called "Conversation II." No interest whatever in correcting ultra-Calvinism is manifested. But those who "run from it as far as ever they can," rejecting the first and second points of Calvinism which contain "the truth of the Gospel," because they do not quite agree with all of it, are severely censured as "altogether foolish and sinful." Now these doctrinal minutes define Wesley's reaction and reply to Bishop Secker's first letter which was received just before the Conference met. The doctrinal point of the letter was that Wesley had in his Revival manifestoes abandoned the Arminian teaching of his own church and was going Calvinistic; not so far, to be sure, as Whitefield, but still he was headed in the same direction and going strong. Wesley in defining his position though he refused to be identified outright with Whitefield, did not, strange to say, deny but affirmed that he had gone back to the faith of the first Reformers. He then turned on his critics and censured them as "altogether foolish and sinful for running away from Calvinism as far as ever they could."

Why this warning (sinful is a strong term!) against too much anti-Calvinism? Wesley's interest is plainly an anxious concern not to correct Calvinism but to recover and bring back Arminianism to evangelical principles. These principles, he said, consisted (1) In ascribing all good to the free grace of God; (2) in denying all natural free-will, and all power antecedent to grace, and (3) in excluding all merit from man; even for what he has or does by the grace of God. The reader who has any interest in the subject and is surprised, if not shocked, to find Wesley among "the deniers of all natural free-will and all power antecedent to grace" will have to reckon further with the fact that John Wesley never was, that is after 1738, an Arminian in the current semi-humanist or semi-Pelagian sense of the term. For him too, as for Luther and Calvin, in the thought of salvation by faith, God is everything and man is nothing.[18]

This is, of course, not at all the conception of Wesley's theology in the secondary sources. They commonly represent him as the radical negation, right from the start, of Calvinism, root and branch, and at the same time an ardent advocate of Arminianism. These sources also derive Wesley's Arminianism direct from Anglicanism and identify it with the Anglican variety. Thus Wesley's refusal in the words of one of his fairest Anglican critics to "go such unwarrantable lengths as Whitefield did" and his care and caution to safeguard the evangelical reaction and the return to Reformation principles from a relapse into ultra-Calvinism have been singled out as if the only fact of importance in defining his theological position. The fact that Wesley and Whitefield as representatives of the Evangelical Reaction both alike went back to the faith of the first Reformers and that Wesley went a long distance with Whitefield in that direction has received little or no consideration. The Jesus-Paul critique of legalism is undoubtedly the historical key to their message and ministry. Is Wesley's negative on Predestinationism in the same sense the key to his doctrine of Christian experience? The secondary sources say Yes; the original sources say No. The fact is that a radical critique of humanism in all its variations was for Wesley, as the critique of work-salvation was for Luther and Calvin, as the critique of legalism was for Jesus and Paul, the master-key to their religious principles. Likewise the exclusive orientation of man's entire higher spiritual life in the idea of divine grace is equally characteristic of them all.

Wesley's measures to safeguard the evangelical reaction, conceived as a radical reaction against the religion of humanity, from running into ultra-Calvinism must therefore in any sound historical interpretation of his doctrine of Christian experience be thoroughly and consistently subordinated to the Evangelical Reaction itself and to the energetic measures taken to bring

[18] As this question is the special subject of Chapters IX and X, there is no reason to pursue it further here.

Anglican teaching and preaching back to evangelical principles. To place these two conflicts, the first with the current religion of the Anglican Church and the second with ultra-Calvinism, in their true historical perspective and proportion, to show how Wesley as his main work transcended the humanization of the Christian Faith in the decadent Christianity of his day without falling back into Predestinationism and to restore to its rightful preeminence the gage of battle which he threw down to the humanistic Arminianism of Anglican teaching and preaching as the master-key to his position in English Christianity and in the Protestant evolution is the principal undertaking of this monograph.   The facts will make it abundantly clear that the Wesleyan Movement was very much evangelical in the early Reformation sense and very little Arminian as that term was taken and accepted in the Anglicanism of Wesley's time or as it is taken and accepted in the Methodism of our time.   Indeed, the facts carry with them a still more drastic conclusion: Wesley in the epoch of his maturity never was an Arminian as that term is now more commonly taken and accepted.   Wesley would reject as decisively the current Arminianism of Methodist theology today as he rejected the current Arminianism of Anglican theology in his own time and for the same reasons.   As he saw it, Anglican theology, decidedly Arminian, had "run from Calvinism as far as ever it could," whereas "the truth of the Gospel lies within a hair's breath of Calvinism."   Anglican teaching and preaching had in its anti-Calvinistic animus broken so radically with the religious principles of the Reformation that it had simply ceased to be evangelical.   It no longer had a gospel to preach, certainly not one which is the power of God unto salvation to every believer.   Wesley, therefore, after exploring this Arminian theology for over ten years, concluded that it was a byway of spiritual despair and futility, not a highway of saving faith and Christian perfection and went back in his search for power to the Luther-Calvin idea of a God-given faith.

The religious ideas which a deep, clear thinker on the essentials of Christianity chooses to emphasize in teaching and preaching may be acquired strictly from historic Christianity or may represent more or less new departures in Christian thought. But the choice and the emphasis, the way and the manner in which a Wesley has acquired, constructed, and put into practise his understanding of the Christian faith will always represent the interaction between his own incommunicable individuality and the climate of opinion which he breathed or the tides of thought in the midst of which he lived and labored. If now it avails little to know Wesley through the parsimonious scholarship of most recent writing about him, then it avails much to know him by his own words and deeds. But even these alone are not enough; it is just as necessary to look at Wesley through the eighteenth century as to look at the eighteenth century through Wesley. It is just as important to know the impression which Wesley made on the Churchmen of his day as to know his reaction to the Christianity of his age. The judgment of Wesley by his contemporaries is an indispensable source for a knowledge of Wesley as well as of his century.

Wesley's last Oxford sermon in 1744 was his public answer to public strictures upon his theology by those accounted the pillars in church and university. We cannot ignore the target and still appreciate the marksman. Anti-Methodist literature has been much abused and often cited to illustrate the works of the devil, but seldom if ever used, as it can and must be, to learn the truth about John Wesley. There were in fact among Calvinists who wrote against Wesley able and good men who insisted that he was in his doctrine of Christian Perfection more Catholic than Protestant; and Wesley's defense was, What is there wrong about that? And there were also good men among Anglican leaders, the ablest among the living teachers of that Church, all strongly Arminian, who insisted that Wesley was a much better Calvinist than Arminian. And the import of Wesley's defense was, What if I do think on original sin and justification by faith exactly as John Calvin does! What if on the fundamentals of Christian experience I do not differ from Calvin a hair's breadth! I am not going to give up evangelical prin-

ciples to get rid of predestinationism. I am not going to part
with the truth of the Gospel to keep clear of the "Decrees." I
take my stand on Arminius himself, who largely agreed with
Calvin, thought and taught exactly what Calvin did, on Sin and
Salvation by Faith. It appears from this résumé that the Calvinists may have had a true impression of Wesley's Catholic
leanings in the doctrine of Christian Perfection as the Anglican
Arminians may have had a true impression of his Calvinistic
leanings in the doctrine of sin and salvation by faith.

Certain writers have of late made the great discovery that
Wesley has seldom, if ever, referred, apart from the single Journal
entry for May 24, 1738, to the fact that he once "felt his heart
strangely warmed." And they have jumped at the conclusion
that the conversion-experience was therefore a negligible quantity in his evangelical message and ministry. This humanist
prejudice voiced recently by an able Catholic scholar and writer
on Wesley, is finding already echoes in Wesleyan circles. There
seems to be much haste to hang an adverse opinion of Wesley's
conversion on a very slender fact. What if Wesley never let the
warm heart become a memory but tended the fires of Christian
experience so well that it remained a present reality! The intuition of the grace of God was always present in his preaching
in all of its strangely quickening power. Why then refer to the
starting of a fire twenty years ago in proof of its reality if
it is still burning? Wesley may indeed have said little or nothing
later about his conversion-experience in the Spring of 1738. But
before drawing a negative we must first know that there was no
serious falling out between Wesley and the Anglican authorities
prior to 1738 over either his message or his methods; whereas
the revolution in the content of his preaching which marked
his conversion-experience changed his hitherto feeble, fruitless,
preaching into preaching that, he said, "ran as fire in dry
stubble." It was after 1738 that friendly critics in church circles
first began to think him "a not quite right man" and some
of them "heartily prayed God to stop the progress of this lunacy," while hostile critics in a chorus passed upon him the sen-

tence of enthusiasm, the worst thing that could in eighteenth-century parlance be said of a gentleman and a scholar. If there were no Journal narrative of the conversion-experience in the Spring of 1738, the facts would compel us to invent one.[19] The admitted fact of Wesley's meticulous reticence about his conversion-experience as a purely private and personal matter easily deceives the unwary. Here the stream of clamorous criticism poured upon him after 1738 by friends and foes is the true source of information and demonstration that he crossed his religious Rubicon in the Spring of 1738. After this crossing he preached in the full-orbed consciousness of the fact that he was planting his feet identically in the footprints of Luther and Calvin and had made his own their idea of the sovereign saving significance of a God-given faith in Christ. "It is the faith of our first Reformers which I by the grace of God preach." [20]

The conclusions reached and submitted in this monograph on Wesley's doctrine of Christian experience, as they were acquired from, so they rest throughout the exposition upon, the original sources and claim no other authority. New positions impose corresponding burdens of proof. This fact explains and justifies, I trust fully, the large amount of quotation, citation and reference to Wesley's writings. No other master of essential Christianity has left to posterity so full and vivid a moving picture of the workings of his own mind. And no pains have been spared and no labor has been accounted too much to let Wesley speak for himself at every turn of the road in the argument and the exposition. Even the repetition is vital to the plan and is, I hope, not excessive for the purpose. The danger of too much re-iteration of Wesley's thought, though real, is not half so great as the danger of a subjective reconstruction and interpretation of Wesley's doctrinal convictions. I have not been overly anxious about the first. I have been extremely solicitous to avoid even the appearance of subjectivity. The historian may not retouch his "negatives" in accord with his own ideas. The wise maxim

[19] Of this subject much more later in Chapters II and VII.
[20] Quoted from Wesley's last letter (1748) to Bishop Secker of Oxford.

of the Church historian Gieseler, that no age is rightly understood until it is heard to speak for itself, is doubly true of our
subject.

This conscientious orientation in the original sources is specially necessary in the present crisis of Christian thought. A
historical representation and just appraisal of the doctrinal convictions that were the source of power in Wesley's preaching and
underlay his exercise of the pastoral office may drive us to raise
the question whether we still possess and carry in our teaching
and preaching the essentials of Wesley's doctrine of Christian
experience or have actually lost the elements of its power which
we never intended and can never afford to lose. Moreover, since
Wesley went back to the faith of the first Reformers, took deep
draughts at Reformation springs, and made the faith of Luther
and Calvin central in his preaching, it raises an equivalent question for all Evangelical Churches—a question that is now being
asked all over the Protestant world today. If Protestant teaching and preaching continue on their present downward road in
humanistic paths, has the Protestant Church a future? The
judgment of the Wesleys that "unless we return to the principles
of the Reformation" the future of English Christianity is hopeless, has come back to life again and presses hard upon us today.
It is once more an inescapable question. Wesley called a Godless, Christless Christianity a "poor superstition," mistaking fiction for fact. It was a flight of ideas away from the realities
of religious experience. The worship of humanity proved out
in the eighteenth century to be for practical religious purposes
only a vagrant flight of notions! The epitaph which forethoughtful sceptics wrote for the historic Christian faith was used for
other purposes. They failed to reckon with the inexhaustible
resiliency of the Christian faith.

If now we but knew *a priori* that all changes in Christian
doctrine since the time of Wesley, since that of Luther and
Calvin, registered pure progress and unalloyed improvement, we
of the Protestant Churches would today certainly be living on
the mountain tops of optimism. But what critical thinker will

be forward to submit his mind to this fallacy of modernity any sooner than he would to the fallacy of antiquity? If the right and duty to submit the historic Christian faith to free, experiential thinking terminate in empty negations, we are not richer but poorer. Freedom of the mind is not yet freedom until the mind is just as free to think with historic Christianity as to think otherwise. That may be only a truism, but it needs now to be thundered from the housetops. It is necessary to be emancipated from the narrow dogma of much modernism that dissent from the historic Christian faith is in religion the only possible form and positive meaning of intellectual freedom. The path of progress from false religion to true religion seems to lie through the temporary negation of all religion. But the negation can not last. Humanity does not live on negations in anything, least of all in religion.

These considerations and this sense of crisis in Protestant thought underlie this attempt to rediscover the source of power in the Wesleyan Reformation, to follow Wesley back to the first source of the Reformation, and to reorient Christian preaching afresh in their understanding of the Gospel. A revisitation of the historical sources of Protestantism is an urgent necessity in these melting and testing times. A fresh study of how a Wesley halted the drift two centuries ago toward the worship of humanity with a mighty summons, born out of the faith of the first Reformers, to return to the worship of God in the Christian sense comes very close to the present crisis of religion. It is in this spirit that the conclusions here offered which are in the nature of the case always subject to revision, are submitted as strict inductions won by analysis of the content of Wesley's teaching and preaching in comparison with the faith of the first Reformers, by analysis of the impression which he made upon contemporaries, foes no less than friends, hostile critics as well as ardent disciples, and by analysis of the main lines of his deep and durable influence upon modern Christianity.

The slogan, "Back to the sources," always the very alphabet of historical research, has right now another compelling reason.

It is no longer possible to be sure about Wesley's religious principles from the secondary sources. John Wesley seen through the drifting clouds of tradition and John Wesley seen in the clear light of the original sources are two radically different individualities. The thought-patterns of teaching and preaching in the Wesleyan branches of the Christian Church are no longer Wesleyan. We have kept something, lost something and no doubt learned much these last two centuries (1738-1938). But whatever the gains or the losses may be, the first fact to be faced is that Methodism today resembles in its teaching and preaching much more the humanistic Anglicanism which John Wesley challenged than the evangelical Methodism which he created. Methodism has drifted in its essential message away from the religious principles of John Wesley as Anglican teaching and preaching in his time had gone away from the faith of the first Reformers. American Methodism has in its theology run about as far away from the idea of a God-given faith as it can. It has been caught and carried far away from the course charted by its founder, by the powerful humanist currents in religion. The question is inescapable: Is this humanization of the Christian faith a positive development of or is it a radical departure from the religious principles of John Wesley as well as of the first Reformers?

The humanistic thought-patterns of teaching and preaching in American Methodism have supplanted the religious principles of John Wesley. Let us in a purely preliminary way put this thesis to the test of a few questions. Who could ascertain from the secondary sources that John Wesley was one of the best informed men on the literature of mysticism and with that knowledge was a life-long militant foe of the mystics? Where is there a hint that his understanding of the Gospel is, with the possible exception of John Calvin, the most radically, it can even be said, ruthlessly, anti-mystical among the great religious leaders and individualities of the Modern Church? It may all be most natural, if the facts are unknown, for "the modern chorus of voices in praise of mysticism," to claim everything in sight, including

Wesley, as an example of mysticism. But by what anarchy of religious thought is a Wesley, whose life-long attacks on the mystics had a certain element of ruthlessness in it, still classed and claimed as a mystic? [21] Again who would surmise from the secondary sources that it was the entrance of the Luther-Calvin idea of a God-given faith in Christ into his understanding of the Gospel that wrought a revolution in his personal experience and in the power of his preaching; that this idea was the pivot of his evangelical message and ministry; and that he virtually single-handed challenged the living teachers of the Anglican Church for their neglect of, if not apostasy from, the Luther-Calvin idea of faith? Who could gather from these sources that Wesley consciously, expressly joined together again in his doctrine of Christian experience what had been sadly put asunder in the decadence of Christianity that preceded and in the conflicts which attended the Reformation, namely, the Protestant teaching concerning the nature and force of saving faith and the Catholic teaching concerning the nature and force of Christian Perfection?

A critical investigation of the Evangelical reaction as summed up in the person and work of a Wesley against a religion of humanity can not but be of maximum value to a generation which has itself experienced again the grave sickness of religion in Wesley's time. The religion of humanity in that age had a deistic birth-mark in contrast to the riotous pantheism of recent religious thought. The eighteenth-century mind did not so much lose God in the universe; that is the grave sickness of religion in our time. Deism conducted God to the back door of a finite universe and bowed Him out. When confidence in traditional Christianity was completely undermined, the attempt was made to find all the values of religion exclusively in considerations of natural reason. The net result, as Wesley defined it, was to cancel Christ out of Christianity and God out of religion. But

---

[21] Rattenbury's chapter on "Methodism and Mysticism" in his able book on *Wesley's Legacy to the World*, 1928, has done much to redeem the situation. But his concessions seem to me out of tune with an objective representation of Wesley.

men and women did not for one moment cease to hunger and thirst for a power infinitely higher and better than humanity to enter in and possess it. A few adventurous spirits persuaded themselves that the idolatry of Human Reason offered a full equivalent for the worship and trust of "The Heavenly Father and the Father of our Lord Jesus Christ"; and this happened two centuries after Martin Luther first clearly, forcefully taught the Christian Church that the idea of a Christ-like God is the pulse and power of the Christian faith and the heart of all Christian thinking about God.[22] But the net result for practical religion and the general effect on the life-principle of the Christian faith is all one whether God is banished from.the universe as in deism or is lost in the universe as in recent pantheism and in the confusion is represented as stricken with finitude, impotently, hopelessly sharing in its processes of good and evil.

It was Wesley's mature judgment that the God who is revealed to us in the Gospel is so transcendent that "beside Him the universe is nothing," and so immanent that "He is the soul of the universe." And he judged the case of religion which either had cancelled God out of our experience-world or had ceased to believe that the God who is immanent in our experience-world is God the Father Almighty, to be "neither better nor worse than atheism." Athanasius told the church of the fourth century that "polytheism is atheism." In strange but striking agreement with David Hume, Wesley told the church of the eighteenth century that deism is practically atheism, that a God in whom we do not live and move and have our being, and is not accessible to real communion, is as good as none at all.

It remains to be seen what the verdict of the Christian consciousness, which is the highest court of appeal, will be on a riotous pantheism which leaves God stricken about with finitude and pictures his own inner life in a constant state of insurrection on account of his own sinful nature. Wesley believed that God in his holiness is infinitely distant, not spatially but quali-

---

[22] I am indebted for this observation to a statement in one of Harnack's Lectures heard thirty years ago.

tatively distant, from every touch of evil. In fact, he laid down
as the primordial element of Christian experience, not the experience of the immature, but of the mature, "a deep sense of
the distance between man and God" (the same Wesley who
summed up all Christian experience as "the life of God in the
soul of man") "so great that man must regard himself in the
sight of God as less than nothing." As the second element of
mature Christian experience he placed "the continual sense of
total dependence on God" and insisted in season and out of season
that there is in man no originality of moral goodness or of Christian perfection whatsoever distinct from the feeling of total dependence on God.

Philosophy in the eighteenth century as in all centuries knew
nothing, thought a little, and said a lot, as Wesley phrased it, "on
the mighty question, *Unde malum?*" (Whence then is evil?)
Writers on religious subjects in that age, taking their cue from
thence, busied themselves much with this subject. Their writings threw many into perplexity, among them Wesley's father,[23]
although this recrudescence of second-century Gnosticism did
not enlighten or help anybody. For philosophy, the first source
of evil in our experience-world can, said Immanuel Kant, never
be anything but a vain question. Hume, profound analyst and
merciless dissector of natural religion or of a religion reduced
to considerations of natural reason, showed conclusively [24] that
a strictly inductive theism or a strictly cosmological religion
must abridge either God's power or deny his good will and, if
really consistent, both alike, in order to rationalize the reality
of evil. Another of Wesley's contemporaries, William Law, a
mystic, very widely read and followed by the clergy, including
Wesley for a time, made God himself the main problem of religion by subjecting Him to "the sinful properties of nature"
which subjection set a "boundary alike to His power and to His
justice."

The Christian Church, if once, then often, has been summoned

[23] Letters, I, 64, 67.
[24] Calling Hume an infidel does not quite answer his argument.

to surrender its conviction that it possesses in the person and
work of Christ and in the general stream of Christian experience
that has flowed from the Christian revelation, the highest knowledge beyond comparison of a living and saving God. The first
source and mainspring of the Christian consciousness is to think
more and better of God than of this present good and evil world.
To do so is to follow the light of revelation, to keep true to the
higher range of Hebrew and Christian thought, and above all to
keep the very pulse of life in Christian experience. There never
was a religion worth its salt which refused or failed to think
more and better of God than of the world. Augustine teaches
us that God is most nearly like the best that we can know,
think of, or experience. But He is also so much better than our
best that we blush to compare him at all with our best. This
imperious ethical feeling of the divine transcendence, the feeling
that when we have done our utmost to think of what God is
most nearly like, He is still infinitely better than the highest in
our knowledge, thought or experience, though in power always
"nearer than breathing, nearer than hands and feet," is original
and fundamental in the Prophetic-Christian idea of God. They
never can be, at any rate, never have been divorced. It was
just this conviction that prompted Wesley to pass the extremely
severe sentence on Law's mystical pantheism which wound the
strings of finitude around the being of God, denied his essential
holiness, abridged His justice no less than His power, set up
matter as an original, inescapable drag on the mind and will of
God and sunk the Christian religion in cosmology, until the
thought of God no longer had the least relish of salvation in it.
Of this riotous pantheism, Wesley said sternly, "The Doctrine I
utterly abhor, as I apprend it to be totally subversive of the very
essence of Christianity." Even if this were only Wesley's individual reaction it would be weighty enough. But if it be also
the normal and necessary reaction of the Christian consciousness
it will command profound attention. It had as its necessary
corollary in Wesley's theology the conviction that "Christ is not

only God above us which may keep us in awe but can not save; but he is Immanuel, God with us and in us."

There is nothing new of course in the thesis that the Christian faith requires both transcendence—"Beside Him the universe is nothing" and immanence—"He is the soul of the universe." But then there is also nothing new in rival views, unless it be, as Wesley acutely observed, the illusion of originality which commonly attends their periodic reappearance. Hume pointed out that the abridgment either of God's power or His justice or both alike on account of evil is very ancient; "Epicurus' old questions are yet unanswered." "Is he willing to prevent evil, but not able? Then is he impotent. Is he able but not willing? Then is he malevolent. Is he both able and willing? Whence then is evil?" Since Epicurus sharply defined a problem which inductive theism has never been able to master in any beneficial way, and, since outside the main stream of Prophetic-Christian thought at its best, every possible point of view among considerations of natural reason has been many times discovered, forgotten, and discovered again, there can be no longer any merit of originality but the rival theories to the Christian faith simply have to content themselves with reweaving the shoddy of outworn and rejected speculations.

We simply face the very old but ever new question whether there is anything, old or new, ancient or modern, able to rob the intelligent Christian of the knowledge of God to be won only from the Gospel. Harnack, who knew his Luther, tells us "In one thing only was Luther great, gigantic, arresting, irresistible, victorious, the strong man of his times, transcending a thousand years of history in order to thrust his age out of the ruts of tradition into new paths. His superlative greatness all lay in the knowledge of a living and saving God rediscovered in the Gospel, that is, in Jesus Christ." Now the Christian faith that brings victory over the world always has been the truest source of power in the world. But a philosophy or theology which knuckles to the ambiguous impression which the mixture of good and evil in our experience-world inevitably makes upon us and knows nothing better about God than to read his character, purpose, power in terms of this naturalistic ambiguity, does not unlock the resources of a great faith in us but simply delivers our Christian faith up into the hands of Mr. Giant Despair. The Cross never was for Jesus a question of God's power, but only of God's purpose. "Abba, Father, all things are possible to Thee. Take away this cup from me: yet not what I will, but what Thou wilt." The assimilation of the Cross to the good, acceptable, perfect will of God, the Father Almighty, is the meaning of Christ's victory in Gethsemane and the source of his power at Calvary. To die on a Cross could not break his trust in God the Father Almighty. And I think it a sound judgment on Wesley's part that any conception of God that will not let us build an absolute trust upon the total attitude of Jesus toward God is the end of the Christian faith. Jesus' trust in God is the one perfect mirror we have of who and what God is.

Adolph Harnack (1851-1930), unrivalled master of historical theology and one of the soundest exponents of liberal Christianity, unforgettable to those who sat under him, said in substance, if not in so many words, exactly twenty-four years ago: "The paramount issue of Christian thought today is neither miracle nor science, but the question whether this personal life of ours has an eternal value which distinguishes it from all else, whether moral goodness is only a conventional product and provincialism of this planet or a life-principle of the spirit in absolute control of the universe and whether there be a living and saving God or not." It can safely be said after a quarter of a century that the issue is today even more sharply defined; but with a difference! The tide has turned; we stand at the end of an age of humanism in religion that is going out and on the threshold of a revival of genuine Christianity that is coming in. A fresh and earnest study of Wesley's force as a thinker on the nature of religion and of his findings on the meaning of God in Christian experience promises to be in every way and in the highest degree serviceable to such a renaissance of Christian faith. May it be so!

CHAPTER II

THE LAST OXFORD SERMON

On St. Bartholomew's Day, August 24, 1744, Friday morning at ten o'clock, after the academic procession to the University Cathedral, a young preacher robed in full canonicals stood in the historic pulpit of St. Mary's the Virgin at Oxford. The cathedral was crowded to hear him. The Official University preacher on this occasion was John Wesley, a graduate since 1725 of Oxford University, elected March 17, 1726, Fellow of Lincoln College, and promoted February 14, 1727, to the degree of Master of Arts. Obligation to Statute required of him as a clergyman, holding a Fellowship and the degree of Master of Arts, to preach before the University once every third year, just as the University was bound by the same Statute to give him an audience. It was said very significantly of John Wesley on this occasion that "as no clergyman can avoid his turn, so the University can refuse none; otherwise Mr. Wesley would not have preached." He had preached in the course of his eighteen years as Fellow of Lincoln College six times before the University; this was to be his seventh and last time.

The three sermons preached at Oxford in the years 1738, 1741, 1744, respectively, are in contrast to Wesley's preaching prior to 1738 in a class by themselves. They are Revival manifestoes. They assailed boldly the dead theology and decadent Christianity of Oxford circles and of the Church at large. They depicted the current religion as a "nominal Christianity," no better than "the faith of a devil and the life of a heathen." Its adherents were called "Saints of the World," or "baptized heathen" whose religion is only a "poor superstition" or "mean pageantry." This nominal Christianity is handed over as the lawful prey of a de-

structive criticism. But at the same time these Revival manifestoes do much more than picture the decay of religion; they
raise the standard of reformation. They are sure "a return to the
principles of the Reformation" can alone avert national disaster.
They culminate in the prayer, "Be glorified in our reformation,
not in our destruction!" Wesley saw in the Revival "God's
design, not to form any new sect; but to reform the nation, particularly the Church; and to spread scriptural holiness over the
land."[1] If these sermons are depressed with the decay of religion, they are resilient with the hope of revival. In words that
gave his University audience "an universal shock" and impressed
them as "full of presumption and of seeming imprecation," he
demanded of them: "In the name of the Lord God Almighty,
what religion are ye of?" And again, "Shall scriptural Christianity be restored by young, unknown and inconsiderable men?"
As if to say, Are leaders in Church and University going to evade
their responsibilities in this crisis of religion and leave it to men
outside officialdom to raise the standards of reform? And then,
with uplifted eye, he cried, "It is time for Thee Lord to lay to
Thine Hand! . . . Lord, save or we perish! . . . Yet not as we
will, but as Thou wilt." The meaning can not be mistaken.
There will be difficulties; there may be martyrs; there must be
reformation!

Twenty-seven years after his last Oxford sermon Wesley wrote
for the purposes of a history of the Revival this terse account
and interpretation of the event: "Friday, August 24, St. Bartholomew's Day, I preached for the last time before the University of Oxford. I am now clear of the blood of these men.
I have fully delivered my own soul. And I am well pleased that
it should be the very day on which, in the last century, near two
thousand burning and shining lights were put out at one stroke.
Yet what a wide difference is there between their case and mine!
They were turned out of house and home, and all they had;
whereas I am only hindered from preaching, without any other
loss; and that in a kind of honourable manner: it being deter-

[1] Quoted from early Conference Minutes.

mined, that when my next turn to preach came, they would pay another person to preach for me. And so they did twice or thrice; even to the time that I resigned my Fellowship." Thus John Wesley has identified himself beyond recall with the history of Nonconformity in England.

St. Bartholomew's Day was a day of black memories for the Protestant faith. It recalled the blood-baptism in 1572 of the Protestant faith in France. It recalled the ejection in 1662 of Nonconformist Ministers in England, among them John Wesley's grandfather, John Westley, "from house and home and all they had," by which "near two thousand burning and shining lights were put out at one stroke." These memories haunted Wesley on that high occasion. And he afterward confessed his joy over standing even in a small way in this apostolic succession of heroic Protestantism. Did he also recall and ponder any time at Oxford the ineffable thrill of moral victory in the midst of utter physical defeat, experienced by Latimer on the 16th of October 1555, as he and Ridley were led to the stake at Oxford? "Be of good comfort, Master Ridley, and play the man. We shall this day light such a candle by God's grace in England as (I trust) shall never be put out."

Moreover had Wesley not anxiously watched for three years past the rising violence of mobs and magistrates against every voice of the Revival. The ill winds of violent opposition blew fiercely. This violence of mobs, the hostility of magistrates, and the provocative antagonism of many of the clergy were inescapable facts. Moreover Wesley did not have two centuries of growing toleration back of him to quiet his mind. It is now clear that the first six years of the Revival were in respect to its inner development and its outer situation critical years. This Wesley well knew and became more clearly conscious of his mission as a reformer. This consciousness of his vocation as a reformer is the granite on which the Three Oxford manifestoes of the Revival are built. The inevitable leader and spokesman of the Revival had not come to Oxford to weave before their eyes a sermonic garment of polite and pious platitudes; he came to proclaim the day of doom and redemption for the decadent Christianity around him. He therefore preached this sermon in the bold spirit of the prophets, of a Martin Luther and John Knox, to a generation which was in the habit of saying to the real seers, "See not," and to the genuine prophets, "Prophesy not unto us right things; speak unto us smooth things"; and for the most part it had its wish. There is a tragic note of seriousness in Wesley's comment on his last Oxford appeal for a revival of genuine Christianity. "I preached, I suppose, the last time at St. Mary's. Be it so. I am now clear of the blood of these men; I have delivered my own soul." He had nailed his reformation theses to the door of a decadent Christianity. And the official reactions of Church and University to these stirring Revival manifestoes constitute in the light of history the first in a series of events which put the Wesleyan Movement in the course of ultimate separation from the Church of England.

Among Wesley's forty thousand pulpit utterances over a period of fifty years, no other brought down so much wrath on his head. He had intended to preach this sermon three years sooner, but was dissuaded from his purpose by the Countess of Huntingdon to whom he submitted the discourse for judgment. Regardless of the way John Wesley came by it or whether we may concur with his convictions about it, he carried a transcendent vocational consciousness into his work. The consciousness of his vocation as a reformer is very strong in the Oxford Revival manifestoes. So far as I know the suppressed sermon on "True Christianity Defended" is the only case in Wesley's career where in a matter vital to the fulfillment of his vocation he allowed himself to be moved from his purpose. He yielded, after reading it on June 28, 1741, to Lady Huntingdon, to her influence, laid it aside, and wrote another sermon—much less militant. Over this retreat from the outspoken attack on the doctrine and practise of the University, Wesley carried for three years an uneasy conscience. Then in 1744 "the Word of the Lord" came to him again to go and tell this people. He wrote the sermon on "Scriptural Christianity." He did not submit it this time to anybody. He preached it on St. Bartholomew's Day. It assumes that "the faith of a Devil and the life of a heathen make up what most men call a good Christian" in Oxford. In indicts Oxford circles as so remote from the way, the truth, the life of genuine Christianity, that any talk of it outside the pulpit was insufferable, while the reference in the pulpit to the Work and Witness of the Holy Spirit, as the essence of all Christian experience, was resented as either hypocrisy or enthusiasm. So far from finding in Oxford circles a strong center of active Christian learning, the student body was just a generation of triflers without the semblance, much less the substance, of anything Christian. And Wesley was bold enough to ask how many of those set over them to teach and preach had any living epistles to certify the genuineness of their work? "And how many of you in authority are yourselves strangers to the Gospel? Where is scriptural Christianity then? Is this a Christian city? Is this a Christian nation? It is time for Thee, Lord, to lay to Thine hand!"

Such was the spirit and in part the language of the last Oxford sermon. There is no effort to placate the audience or to abate the darkness of the portrait of current Christianity. The sermon moves inflexibly on to its goal. It has a model in the Apostle Stephen's defense of true religion before the Sanhedrin, excoriating the stiffnecked and uncircumcised reactionaries who always resist the Holy Spirit of truth and progress in the Kingdom of God. After preaching this reformation sermon and in the spirit of a man who had in the spirit of the ancient prophets or the early Reformers simply given, as if under the constraint of a higher authority than any human will, to man the Word of God that came to him, Wesley wrote the comments, "I preached in St. Mary's, I suppose, for the last time. Be it so. I am now (!) clear of the blood of these men. I have delivered my own soul." He had three years before in deference to human rank hushed up the Word of God. He had this time in deference to his vocational consciousness declared openly the Word of God.

The active resentment which the authorities felt while listening to this reformatory blast was perfectly natural and justifiable.

The moderation, forbearance, and leniency of their procedure is quite remarkable. It is hardly necessary to observe that this utterance can have a worthy significance only to whose who have a measurable sympathy with Wesley's consciousness of his vocation "to reform this nation, in particular the Church and to spread scriptural holiness over the land." Nor does the objective significance of his utterance hang on the strict objectivity of his representation of the state of the Church and the University and of the decay of religion; though his tragic concern over the decadence of Christianity is in general abundantly sustained by competent witnesses who were indifferent or even hostile to his message and ministry. The appeal for reform was confined to the last part of the sermon. "It was not my design when I wrote ever to print the latter part of the sermon," said Wesley, "but the false and scurrilous accounts of it which were published almost in every corner of the nation," made it necessary for him to send this message also through the gates of the printing press; and so it was put into circulation to pass through several editions with many reprints of each edition. It is second in significance only after the first Oxford manifesto on "Salvation by Faith."

The last Oxford sermon was Wesley's public answer to the growing public censure of both his message and of his entire ministry by the prelates of the Anglican Church. He sensed the hour of decision. Once and again throughout the first six years of his conversion-experience (1738-1744) and even before, though less often, his Journal has this entry: "At these churches likewise (!) I am to preach no more." This was a recurrent experience. Charles Wesley allowed that churches, able to stand what his brother preached, were sure of a blessing. Very few stood it. Oxford stood it as long as they could. But after 1744 whenever Wesley's official turn came round, as it did in 1747 and again in 1750, the authorities appointed another preacher, denying Wesley his turn and fee of three guineas rather than suffer another of his reformatory blasts. Then in 1751 Wesley, with marriage intentions, resigned the Oxford Fellowship. The pillar authorities of Church and University, smarting under the 1744 fulmination,

were minded at first to make an example of him. On further
thought they decided "to punish him by a mortifying neglect,"
our informant being no less a man than Blackstone, then a Fellow
of All Saints, later commentator on the Laws of England as well
as Judge of the Realm.

The idea of punishing him by "a mortifying neglect" was
probably Blackstone's inference from the event, though it may
well have been the feeling of most of the authorities. But the
change of purpose from that of an official censure to one of silence
and forbearance may safely be referred to the intervention and
counsel of the good Bishop of Oxford who approved of Wesley's purpose and labor "to bring all the world to solid, inward,
vital religion" a great deal more than he disapproved in Wesley
"some errors in doctrine, some mistakes in conduct and some
excess in zeal." And it is quite plausible, indeed highly probable,
that he formed the purpose at that time of writing Wesley the
six able, anonymous, and conciliatory letters which he began to
write nine months later to put Wesley right. He did not want
to lose but hoped to retain so great and good a man as he saw in
John Wesley steadfast in the service of the Anglican Church.

The repudiation of his preaching by Oxford officials came then
as no surprise to the preacher. "The beadle came at once after
the sermon, sent by the Vice-Chancellor, to bring the preacher's
notes." Wesley "sealed up and sent them without delay, not
without admiring the wise providence of God. Perhaps few men
of note would have given a sermon of mine the reading if I had
put it into their hands; but by this means it came to be read,
probably more than once, by every man of eminence in the University."

At a distance of two centuries when the sermon is again read
the reader, with the reaction of the authorities in mind, can only
say to himself with continual surprise—"What was there about
that to set an Oxford audience by the ears?" But there is a key
for every lock. John Wesley was too much in earnest about
Christianity to suit an age when Christianity in University circles
was more laughed at than investigated. And where it was still a

subject of inquiry, the custom was to explain it as little more than a compound of superstition and fanaticism and let it go at that. Wesley was for thirty years closely identified with Oxford University. He was for twenty-six years officially a member of the Oxford University staff. He was always proudly conscious and highly appreciative of his University connections. He therefore lacked nothing of the highest intellectual stimulus from academic associations. He wrote some of the most important doctrinal deliverances of the Revival primarily for University constituencies. Wesley never ceased to be in love with Oxford.

Nevertheless these weighty deliverances were invariably prophetic, never apologetic. They reverberated the "Thus saith the Lord" of Scripture and experience. The prophet did not accommodate what he had to say or the way he said it to "the superiority of the Intellectuals." They confronted every man alike, whether doctor of philosophy or coal-digger, with the "Thus saith the Lord" of the Christian revelation in Scripture and in experience. Wesley told his Oxford audiences precisely what he told the tinners of Cornwall, the colliers at Kingswood, the keelmen at Newcastle, the drunkards of Moorefields and the harlots of Drury Lane, that man is a sinner in need of a savior, without any merit of his own, nothing but "an undone, helpless, damned sinner," with no resource but the grace of God. Men who had achieved distinction, academic or otherwise, with quantities of stored-up self-respect were not likely to listen complacently to any such terribly humbling, if not insulting, doctrine. An exordium and an application which insinuated that salvation is specially for the outcasts, the riffraff, the untouchables and that the rich, the well-born, the cultured, the intellectuals really stand in no such utter need of a savior as do "the common wretches that crawl the earth," is much more palatable to human nature.

The conflict between Wesley's theocentric doctrine of Christian experience and the humanized Christianity of his age can be read between the lines of all his later Oxford addresses on religion. "We (who preach the Gospel) are simply told that salvation by faith only ought not to be preached as the first doctrine, or, at least, not to be preached to all. . . . For 'He came not to call the righteous but sinners to repentance.' Why then, if any, we are to except the rich, the learned, the reputable, the moral men. And true it is, they too often except themselves from hearing; yet we must speak the Words of our Lord." [2] And "as the Lord liveth, whatsoever the Lord saith unto us, that we will speak." He did not hesitate then in preaching before the University to put the joint-witness of Scripture and experience into the category of revelation and to call it the Word of God. That made his preaching different.

Wesley began no Oxford sermon with fine, smooth words—how perfectly natural it is to be religious and how perfectly sufficient human reason is to be the architect of virtue and righteousness. Threescore years later the great Schleiermacher began his appeals to the Intellectuals of Germany with a diffident apology for bringing the subject of religion to their attention and a candid confession that he had no particular reason to expect success even in winning their applause for his endeavors and still less in winning them over to his point of view in religion. He does deftly insinuate that they had been so busy and successful in making themselves comfortable in this world that "the idea of God had been fattened out of them." No man may speak save only in profound respect of Schleiermacher's special religious apology to the educated, among whom religion had ceased to be an object of thought, much less a subject of personal concern; even though he may be fully convinced that apologetic at its best is the feeblest form of Christian propaganda. For it is religion itself as experience that alone creates and sustains churches.

Presupposing the essential values and admitting the epoch-making importance of Schleiermacher's undertaking to rehabilitate religion in the intellectual respect and personal concern of the educated, but without attempting to expound his theory of religion even in outline, it will be at least serviceable, if not essential, to our subject to have in mind certain important dif-

---

[2] From the *Fifth Oxford Sermon*, but the first of the Revival, on Salvation by Faith.

ferences between his conception of religion and Wesley's doctrine
of Christian experience.   The former represented religion as
essentially the voice of the universe in the human consciousness
proclaiming itself.   This seems on the surface very much like
Wesley's representation of true, Christian saving faith as "the
voice of God in the heart proclaiming itself."   And it could be,
commonly has been, mistaken for its exact full equivalent.   There
is a kinship; but the identification is at once forbidden by Schleiermacher's obvious efforts, as his thinking matured, to reorient
his theory of religion much more in historic Christianity, much
less in speculative philosophy.   There is a real progress traceable
in his thought away from a purely philosophical and psychological construction of the essence of religion and a corresponding increase of emphasis on the inner structure and real genius
of historic Christianity.   Whether now we choose to call it an intelligent or a blind adherence to the church-form of Christianity,
the fact is that the full appreciation of the historic Christian
faith from which Wesley sets out and on which his doctrine of
Christian experience is securely built, remains the unattained goal
of Schleiermacher's effort in theology.

The ideas of religion as worked out by these two outstanding
but widely differing individualities, one of them a master of the
historic Christian faith, correlating experimental and practical
theology closely with the teaching of Scripture and the voice of
the Christian Church, the other linking up experimental theology
closely with speculative philosophy, do still have something important in common.   They agree in the primacy accorded to religious experience in the theory of religion.   But while the boundary of the experiential view of religion was for one the limit
of all theology, the experiential view of religion was for the other
hemmed and hedged in and corrupted by his rational and speculative line of thought.   The truth-values of the Christian faith
were staked on the ability to prove that the feeling of absolute
dependence is the highest stage of human self-consciousness.   But
this line of thought runs into the humanist impasse and is fatal
to the revelational interpretation of Christian experience.   The

fact is that this interpretation of the feeling of absolute dependence as the highest form of human self-consciousness is of the
nature of a final intuition of religious experience of which no
further account can be given. It can and should be trusted; it
can not be rationalized by deducing it from anything else. Here
the constructive work of Schleiermacher is foot-bound with an
outmoded rationalism.

These two great religious individualities, if we choose, one a
master of practical, the other of intellectual Christianity, further
agree as to the essential objectivity of religious experience.
Schleiermacher's focalization of religious experience in "the feeling of absolute dependence" was certainly never intended to
mean "a religion not more than human." The objective reference
to a reality of a higher order is for him the decisive and essential feature of religion. This feature alone, no more, no less,
justifies and differentiates in his system the feeling of *absolute*
in distinction from the other feelings of *partial* or *relative* dependence along with that of personal *freedom*. The former alone
carries in itself the reference to a transcendent God. Yet even at
its best it must in all candor be said how dimly, feebly the objectivity of religious experience is apprehended in Schleiermacher's
theory of religion in contrast to Wesley's full, forceful, all-
pervasive apprehension of the true objectivity of Christian experience!

The philosophical premises, approach, and method of Schleiermacher's reconstruction of religion is therefore answerable for
the fact that the Gospel is drawn in his theory of religion into an
entangling alliance with German Idealism. Under this entangling
alliance, the curve of metaphysical speculation since Kant has
been a constant source of corruption and interference with the
experiential and revelational interpretation of religion and a
menace to the real genius of the Christian faith. It can not be
denied that the Christian doctrines of Schleiermacher are at many
points foot-bound with outmoded philosophy.

Again, the feeling of absolute dependence, as Schleiermacher
has deduced and expounded it, is in spite of his earnest protest

against a cosmological religion still too much of the nature of cosmic, too little of the nature of Christian feeling. Wesley's formula for the nature of religion also was "the continual sense of total dependence," [3] which not only obviously anticipates in conception but also greatly surpasses Schleiermacher's half-developed experiential theory of religion. For Wesley always found the meaning of total dependence in the first Beatitude and in the Christian self-estimate according to the standard of grace. He did not exclude the creaturely feeling of physical dependence and the feeling of finite nothingness which overtakes any man who reflects in the midst of cosmic vastness; [4] but these impressions which the universe makes on man by the gateway of the senses are at once and always subordinated to the normal responses in man's entire personal life which arise from his free interaction with the historic Christian faith.

The deep insight into the nature and the large place given to the voice of religious experience are admittedly the principal values in Schleiermacher's theory of religion. It is not the reference to German Idealism, but the reference to religious experience in his work that has made it so attractive and fruitful to Protestant theology. There is growing consensus that the former is the weakness as the latter is the strength of his theory of religion. Now the Father of German liberal theology and of much more acquired his experiential insight into the nature of religion ultimately from his own personal experience in the Moravian brotherhood. This identifies it as a deposit of his own Christian experience and proves that it came to him out of historic Christianity. And he has called himself a Moravian of a higher (intellectual) order, which carried the inference that his theory of religion was a derivative of historic Christianity; it is then a philosophical reconstruction of the Christian idea. It is not at all difficult to perceive the kinship between his idea of religion as the feeling of absolute dependence on God and Wesley's idea of saving faith as in its totality the gift and work of God. It is

[3] Sermons 16, 21, 28, etc.
[4] Letters, II, 373.

also made evident from the fact, hitherto much neglected, if not entirely overlooked, that Wesley already has and uses Schleiermacher's formula, "the continual sense of total dependence on God," *as the equivalent of utter trust in the grace of God in Christ,* and of that saving faith in Christ which objectively is in its totality the gift and work of God and subjectively the essence of all Christian experience. Here clearly the two are treated as equivalents; and so are they in the main in the theory of Schleiermacher. His theory of religion is still always the voice of historic Christianity which the hands of speculative philosophy can not quite conceal.

It was in a sense inevitable that Schleiermacher's thinking, in view of its starting point and orientation in a religious experience which drew from the living stream of historic Christianity, should show a progressive emancipation from philosophical modes of thought and a steady approach to the real genius of the Christian faith. The goal of his thinking was the complete ascendency of the free interaction of man's personal life with the historical Christian faith over cosmic feeling in its myriad forms. We can read it in his remonstrance that external nature is the outermost court, not the holy of holies of religion. Neither fear of nature's awful powers, nor the feeling of nothingness which overtakes man in the midst of cosmic vastness, nor the happy enjoyment of the blissful aspects of the natural world can unlock the door into religious experience. So in the last analysis, as Wesley put it, "God is a consuming fire," until we come to the knowledge of a living and saving God to be won only from the Gospel.[5]

Whatever the values and advantages may be of taking the Christian compass in hand and starting from the opposite pole to the Christian faith, and of exploring the various ways back to the heart of things, the fact remains that the goal of Christian thought for the speculative theologian—namely, the church-form of Christianity—was the starting point for the essentially historical, practical experimental doctrine of Christian experience, as it was thought out and wrought out by John Wesley.

[5] Journal, I, 464.

We could hardly expect to meet, and certainly do not find, in the skillful, supple apologist of Christianity before the Intellectuals of Berlin the prophetic boldness and power of the mastercraftsman of the Revival at Oxford. Here lies the essential difference between the pulpit and the chair. This prophet of the living Word of God therefore preached with the fear of a Holy God, high and lifted up, inhabiting eternity, not at all with the favor of man, the rich, ruling, cultured class before his eyes. He began not with ideas of the divine immanence and the natural goodness and gravitation of all men toward God, all of which he admitted and took for granted, but with man's sinful separation and the radical discontinuity between man and God.

His preaching brought every man alike to his knees in the dust and ashes of repentance. The leveling implications of this doctrine of sin and salvation gave very great offense.[6] Instead of toning down his essential teaching to avoid offense, he estimated the merit of his sermons by the amount of offense they gave.[7] His prototype is not the fencing apologetic of the schoolmen, but the majestic moral earnestness of the major prophets and of a John the Baptist of whom Jesus said that he could not be moved from his convictions by the seductive but shifty winds of handclapping, much less by the patronage of those who own large estates and live in fine mansions.[8] The Prophet of the Living God dwells in a castle of moral security high above the fickle winds of popularity or the fawning and flattery of slick apologetic which too often corrupt the message of those who cultivate the rich and powerful.[9]

Wesley has drawn a very dark picture of the prophetic office of the church in his time. We might well hesitate to accept it without corroboration. But all the witnesses, and they are numerous and competent, agree that the beginning of Wesley's century saw the lowest levels of prophetic quality in Christian

[6] Lecky, *England in Eighteenth Century*, II, 617.
[7] Journal, I, 440.
[8] Matthew XI, 1-30.
[9] Letters, VII, 148-151.

preaching. The prophetic function of the Church was nearly extinct. In the midst of many fox-hunting, hard-drinking, dicing clergy, the living epistles of the Gospel could not avail to stem "the tide of immorality which overspread the land as a flood." Then too, the evangelical truths of early Protestantism were seldom preached. Wesley diagnosed the whole sickness of Christianity in the eighteenth century as an acute secularization of the Gospel. The prophets themselves entrusted with warning seemed to him "conformed to this world" both in their mode of living and in their message. His words, "I answer, Ten thousand wise and honorable men . . . these are false prophets in the highest sense of the word," indicate his conception of the abject levels of much Christian preaching around him. He lamented that there was little or nothing distinctively Christian either in their message or mode of life. He said bluntly that commentators construed away the text; philosophy corrupted the meaning of the Gospel; preaching softened its unpleasant truth and reconciled the spirit of Christ and the spirit of the world. And why such preaching? Wesley gave the official expounders of the Gospel, many of them, a sinister character. He used—one thinks of Hus in his little Bethlehem chapel pointing his finger at the magnificent episcopal mansion with its luxurious appointments just across the river in Prague—the terms "luxurious, sensual, covetous, ambitious." He saw in current Christianity little else than a spirit of compromise, accommodation and conformity with the world. The Church had nearly lost the power of resistance to the world, to say nothing of reformation.

The last Oxford sermon was preached in the sixth year of Wesley's conversion-experience. The young Franciscan scholar, Piette, in his able monograph on *La Réaction de John Wesley dans l'Évolution du Protestantisme* (1927), came to the conclusion that the total significance of "the official Wesleyan legend" about "the great Conversion of 1738" was no more than a flare of religious feeling and hardly exceeded the contingent fact that Wesley as a matter of routine recorded the incident in his Journal. Now in general concerning the objective significance of

Wesley's conversion-experience we submit (1) that the whole question has been involved in needless psychological obscurity by the attempt, contrary to Wesley's example, to find the significance of the experience in its purely private and personal aspects; (2) that the concurrent humanist and hierarchical disparagement of its significance rests, not on the mature Wesleyan view of Christian experience, but on a special definition of conversion that simply begs the question; (3) that Wesley's meticulous reticence about the purely private aspect weighs nothing against his fixed habit of thought, pervading all his writing. For he always defined the progress of the Revival in terms of his conversion-experience. He always referred the origin of the Revival to his return in his public preaching and personal faith to the faith of the first Reformers, and he has consistently deduced the power of the Revival from the religious energy of Reformation principles. These considerations would probably carry the conclusion with them for most readers. But the manifold reactions, often violent in their nature, to Wesley's preaching which attended and followed the revolution in its religious principles, constitute an entirely distinct, and for most readers easier, line of argument.

The Luther-Calvin idea of the sovereign saving significance of a God-given faith in Christ impressed the Arminian Wesley himself at first as "a new doctrine" and "a strange doctrine," and excited his strong opposition and resistance. *It clashed with his Arminian theology.* "My soul started back from preaching it." But the Luther-Calvin idea of faith excited the strongest opposition also in the Oxford circle formerly in active sympathy with Wesley as well as among all his other friends and associates. It aroused the ire of his brother Charles, who bluntly told him he did not know what mischief he was doing by talking thus. It was "very shocking" to him. He records that he was "much offended at his [brother's] worse than unedifying discourse." John Wesley's deduction of the possibility of "instantaneous conversion" from the Luther-Calvin idea, mediated to him by Böhler, at once ran amuck on deep-seated prejudices against any such doctrine of

Christian experience. Wesley did not indeed argue for its strict necessity; he always admitted gradual conversion. The new idea simply was that "God *can* (at least, if He *does* not always) give that faith whereof cometh salvation in a moment, as lightning falling from heaven." In the last analysis the real issue was the dynamic practical religious implications of the idea of a God-given faith. The doctrine of saving faith then prevailing was not developed in the spirit of a true experimentalism or in terms of Christian experience and its indications but rather the doctrine of Christian experience was itself narrowly circumscribed by *a priori* naturalistic and humanistic prejudices. These were being sprung by Wesley's roomier views of Christian experience.

The cleansing of the early dogmatism out of Wesley's doctrine of Christian assurance is a parallel, if indeed it is not at bottom the same, case. In his mellower and riper years, after the fiery zeal of his first conversion glow had toned itself down into a wider tolerance and a wiser patience, he ceased to teach and preach the realities of Christian experience in terms of the absolute and was well-content to build faith more simply on the joint sanctions of Scripture and experience and to subject it to the laws of growth and development. In this vein he remarked (1788) to Melville Horne, "When fifty years ago [10] my brother Charles and I, in the simplicity of our hearts, told the good people of England that unless they *knew* their sins forgiven, they were under the wrath and curse of God, I marvel, Melville, they did not stone us! The Methodists, I hope, know better now: We preach assurance as we always did as a common privilege of the children of God; but we do not enforce it, under the pain of damnation, denounced on all who enjoy it not." It is plain to see that this latest putting of a most precious truth-value of the Gospel is a very great improvement over the absolutism of his first statement of the doctrine. Nevertheless, even the absolutism of his earlier teaching had a big point to it as a protest against an atheistic humanism, which had banished the reference to ex-

[10] Wesley has in hundreds of cases like this dated the origin of the Revival in 1738! See Chapter VII.

perience altogether from the teaching and preaching of the Christian faith. Even his eldest brother, Samuel, recoiled from the least reference to religious experience, from any talk of indwellings, experiences, getting into Christ, etc., etc., as so much cant, disorder, lunacy, all of which that age lumped together as enthusiasm. Enthusiasm was in eighteenth century parlance the evil genius of religion. But he who put any trust in the voice of experience was sure to "fall into enthusiasm" and to "do a world of mischief." [11]

The return to Christian experience as the life principle of Christianity was not likely after such a drought to be a gentle shower; it was a cloudburst. The main point for note is that Wesley, in the final statement of his doctrine, refused to budge from his position that assurance is a common privilege of the children of God and should be so preached. And this was the real issue between Wesley and his age. All else is beside the point. To the charge of extravagance or enthusiasm in religion Wesley retorted: What could be more extravagant or worse enthusiasm than a barren choice between a dead theology and a dead ceremony or else atheistic humanism! This inane choice has no more substance than a flight of ideas away from the solid realities of Christian experience. Who then are the enthusiasts? [12] Those who build their trust on Christian experience and its indications? Or those who distil their conception of the nature of things from the misplaced confidences of traditional Christianity?

Similar reactions took place in the minds of virtually every member of the Wesley circle. All were much perplexed, some deeply distressed, and a few greatly provoked by the new doctrine. From the Hutton Home in College Street, a chief center of the rising tides of Christian faith, a letter went from Mrs. Hutton to Samuel Wesley: "Your brother John seems to be turned a wild enthusiast, or fanatic, and, to our great affliction, is drawing our two children into these wild notions by their

[11] See the relevant citations in Southey's *Life of Wesley*, I, 101 f., 178 f.
[12] This remarkably effective *ad hominem* was often used.

great opinion of Mr. John's sanctity and judgment." And she warned the elder brother that "when you hear his teaching, you will think him a not quite right man." The elder brother evidently thought so too; for his letter in reply, dated June 17, 1738, has much to say in the same vein, in particular this: "In the meantime I heartily pray God to stop the progress of this lunacy." [13] Not the least illuminating feature of this Hutton letter and the reply of the elder brother is the fact that the correspondents knew no other way to reason about or to define the meaning of conversion except in terms of baptism. They could therefore hardly be expected to understand a revolution of principles that shifted a man's spiritual birthday from his baptism to his conversion.

Wesley on May 28, 1738, took the breath of the Hutton circle away by standing up in the presence of a great number of people gathered in the Hutton library and solemnly asserting that "five days before (i.e., as late as May 23rd) he was not a Christian" and knew it as surely as he knew he was in the room. This evoked sharp protests. It was "despising the benefits received by the two sacraments." Wesley was bluntly told that "he was an enthusiast, a seducer, and a setter-forth of *new doctrines.*" Wesley was not yet conscious of the break with Anglican theology implicit in his conversion-experience. It was his critics who first opened his eyes to the fact. Twelve years later he said that "some of the clergy judge us heterodox, maintainers of strange opinions. And the truth is, *the old doctrines of the Reformation are now quite new in the world.* Hence those who revive them can not fail to be opposed by those of the clergy who know them not." The protest reveals clearly the bondage of Christian thought in the Wesley circle which till then knew no other way to reason about Christian experience but in terms of the two sacraments. But the retort, always quoted with great approval by the whittlers at Wesley's doctrine of Christian experience, came from Mrs. Hutton who in all simplicity and sincerity remonstrated, "If you have not been a Christian ever since I knew

<hr>

[13] Tyerman, *Life of Wesley,* Vol. I, p. 189 f.

you, you have been a great hypocrite, for you made us all believe that you were one." From either the High Church or the humanist point of view, this sensible remark puts a quietus on the "official Wesleyan legend"—as if the manifestly erroneous negative implications of Wesley's much too narrow definition of the term, Christian, could demonstrate that he had not actually, experientially thought his way through to a profounder understanding of the Gospel, one that wrought a revolution first in his own preaching and personal faith and then started a religious revolution in England. Wesley as noted retracted this all too narrow definition of conversion. But he never ceased to think about the origin, progress, and power of the Revival in terms of his acceptance and proclamation of the Luther-Calvin idea of a God-given faith.

But every doubt or denial of the objective significance of the conversion-experience must then reckon further with the monumental fact that the pillar authorities in Church and University from the year 1738 closed virtually all of the pulpits to Wesley, and then after 1744 twice paid out of the University treasury the regular fee of three guineas to another in order to keep Wesley out of St. Mary's, Oxford.

There were two reasons for the hostile reactions of the Anglican Churches to Wesley's preaching: the content of the preaching and the unwonted crowds. The former came from the clergy, the latter from the laity. "Some clergymen objected to this *new doctrine*, 'Salvation by Faith,'" but the far more common (and indeed more plausible) objection was, "the people crowd so that they block up the church and leave no room for the best of the parish." [14] The best of the parish! The people crowd! What right had the commons to inconvenience their betters in the house of the Lord? The smug complacency of fashionable well-to-do Church-goers was much upset on arriving at the church door to find the House of God already crowded with "the common wretches that crawl the earth." That was an offense against the proprieties too grievous to be borne. An insatiable curiosity

[14] *Short History of Methodism.*

about America, as Wesley realistically observed, had in the Spring of 1738 much to do with the size of his audiences. The laity knew little and cared less about theology so long as the preaching was high-toned and impersonal. But Wesley was tremendously realistic and personal. It was next to impossible for any auditor not to forget himself and his surroundings, while Wesley preached, and he was made to feel that he was actually on trial before the Supreme Judge of the universe. There spoke in Wesley's sermons, as one of his episcopal critics described him, not only "a natural knack of persuasion," "much awakening warmth and earnestness," but also a transcendent vocational consciousness, an intellect keen as a Damascus blade, an imperious will to bring every soul into captivity to Christ, a personal life as sensitive and responsive to all the greatest thoughts of the Christian Faith as a delicate instrument could be to the hand of the expert musical genius. He did not indeed, as one auditor observed, have the torrential eloquence of some preachers. But, when most sermons were hard to remember, many of his were hard to forget.

It is then a certainty that both his message and manner of preaching were factors in the following cases with Journal comments from Part II or the Conversion document. Why indeed are they crowded so closely around the Conversion-experience?

1738, Feb. 4., St. John the Evangelist. "I was afterwards informed many of the best in the parish were so offended that I was not to preach there any more."

Sun. 12. St. Andrews, Holbein. "Here too it seems I am to preach no more."

Sun. 26. At six, St. Lawrence's, at ten in St. Katherine Cree's, in the afternoon at St. John's, Wapping. "I believe it pleased God to bless the first sermon most because it gave most offense."

May 7. St. Lawrence's, St. Katherine Cree's. "I was enabled to speak strong words at both, and was therefore the less surprised at being informed I was not to preach any more in either of these churches."

May 9. Great St. Helen's. "My heart was so enlarged. . . . Afterwards told, 'Sir, you much preach here no more.'"

May 14. St. Ann's, Aldersgate; Savoy Chapel. "I was quickly apprised that at St. Ann's likewise I am to preach no more."

Fri. 19. St. John's, Wapping; St. Benet's, Paul's Wharf. "At these churches likewise I am to preach no more."

May 28. St. George's, Bloomsbury; Chapel in Long Acre. "The last time (I understand) I am to preach at either."

Sept. 21. At Newgate, St. Ann's, twice at St. John's, Clerkenwell. "I was enabled to speak strong words so that I fear they will bear me there no longer."

Oct. 8, Sun. "I preached at Savoy Chapel (I suppose the last time)."

Nov., Sun. 5. "I preached in the evening to such a congregation as I never saw before at St. Clement's in the Strand. As this was the first time of my preaching here, I suppose it is to be the last."

1739. Feb. 4. Sunday at St. Giles'. "How was the power of God present with us! I am content to preach here no more."

Sun. 18. "Desired to preach morning and afternoon at Spitalfield Chapel." (He planned a sermon in two parts. He succeeded with the first part and then) "I was not suffered to conclude my subject" (II, 142).

Sun. 25. St. Katherine's near the Tower; at Islington afternoon. "Many here were *as usual* deeply offended."

May 7, 1739. "Our minister having been informed you are beside yourself does not care you should preach in any of his churches."

Tues. 8. "At Bath I was not suffered to be in the meadows where I was before" (II, 193).

The last Oxford sermon simply marks the climax in this rising hostility of the Church to Wesleyan principles just as it was Wesley's boldest utterance in his capacity as Oxford Fellow. He was conscious of an inevitable conflict between his conception of Christianity and the spirit of his age. As he observed elsewhere of two sermons: "I believe it pleased God to bless the first sermon most, because it gave most offense." He was not depressed but took heart from the hostile reactions of his age. One must accede to his extraordinary vocational consciousness and heed the singular harvest of results or else account him a madman who sets up, as Wesley has done, the amount of the offense as the measure of merit in the sermon. We who belong to a tamer race of toilers can only stand in awe of him very much as those who knew him first-hand, including his enemies, generally did.

Even if the acceptance wholeheartedly of Luther's understanding of the Gospel in terms of *salvation by faith only* had made no appreciable difference to Wesley himself, it did so change the content and quality of his preaching—and since it sprang from experiential thinking was not that Wesley himself— as to make an immense difference to the church authorities. For a time they opened their pulpits to this self-appointed rector of the world. Over in Bristol Bishop Butler shut every pulpit to Whitefield and the Wesleys. Whitefield, not to be denied, turned to jail preaching. But ecclesiastical authority pursued him into the jail and soon put an end even to his jail preaching. With everything from churches to jails shut against him, Whitefield turned to the open fields and chose God's out-of-doors for his Gothic. Wesley followed him into the open fields. This is the origin of field preaching.[15] It is not at all hard to conjure up considerable sympathy with the responsible local pastors and their Bishops. After their conversion, the preaching of these roving evangelists unlocked vast reservoirs of power. They started real problems.

Writers of the older school of Methodist orthodoxy were pretty well satisfied as their apologetic for Whitefield and the Wesleys simply to represent the Anglican authorities as the Apostle Stephen in his defence has represented the authorities of the Jewish Church. The spirit and tactics of bishops like Lavington and Warburton seem to want a single defender. Their words and their. deeds moved on a level beneath the dignity of the episcopal office. One turns with a sigh of relief from their words and ways to consider worthy bishops like Butler, Secker and Horne, who did not add malignity to misunderstanding. Even so,

[15] The priority of Whitefield in this move is undeniable. Letters, II, 133.

the course of events and the reactions to Wesley's preaching, pastoral and superintending activities is not explained by a simple reference to "the Onfall of the Bishops" and to Anglicanism as "the church of missed opportunities." The analogous expulsion of Christianity from Judaism, of Protestantism from the Roman Catholic Church, of Methodism from the Anglican Church have other and deeper, less circumstantial and more positive meanings. After prolonged spiritual drought, the floods came and the winds blew with such force and fury that old channels could not endure them. But the arbitration of this complicated question is not essential and has the special disadvantage of every attempt to be wiser than history. Any theory must face the fact of the Revival and its strange propulsive force. It is the key to this force that we seek to ascertain. The issue between Wesley and the Church, as commonly stated by the Bishops, was "the pretension to an extraordinary inspiration and inward feeling of the Holy Spirit." By this was meant neither more nor less than Wesley's incessant preaching of the sovereign saving significance of a God-given faith in experiential terms.

Turning back from the analysis of the hostile reactions due to the preaching of Wesley to the Wesleys themselves, we must consider that John Wesley with all his talent and finished technique preached thirteen years with negligible results; after 1738 he preached with extraordinary power; he revised every one of his earlier sermons which he continued to use on account of his conversion-experience (a fact overlooked by Piette and others); and the conversion-experience furnished the celestial fire for the hymnology of the Revival in both the Calvinistic and Arminian branches. This new era of Christian song, unsurpassed in the history of the Christian Faith, reached its climax after, not before, "John Wesley began to bring the whole Christian World back to religion as experience." It was chiefly songs of Christian experience that Wesley had selected and translated out of the treasury of German hymnology. Finally in the very beginning of his deeper insight into "the nature of saving faith," Wesley began to be irked by his bondage to the printed forms

of prayer (a prophecy of the future course of the Revival!)—and
to break away from them. Both the Wesleys experienced at this
time a similar emancipation from their bondage to manuscript in
their preaching. In the strength of these considerations we need
not hesitate to refer even to events recorded by Wesley in the
more private and personal aspects of his conversion-experience.
A sense of boundless power in preaching, flashes forth again and
again after 1738, not before. He records with utter candor that
he felt in one of his Bristol sermons "as if he could shake the
universe"—a rhetorical extravagance for the strange power of
the new doctrine over himself no less than over his auditors.
But probing a little deeper he records as touching himself that
"before 1738 I was sometimes, if not often, conquered; now I
was always conqueror." [16] From all these considerations the
reader can readily try conclusions for himself whether Wesley,
the inner circle of his friends, his audiences, and the public authorities were all alike entirely deceived about the tremendous difference between a humanistic and a theocentric doctrine of
Christian experience. The great revivals of the Christian religion have had their first birth in a return to the knowledge of
God revealed in the Gospel. Everything important in Wesley's
evangelical ministry is rooted and grounded therein. If there
were no account of the conversion-experience in this simple inclusive sense to be found in the Journal, the facts would make it
necessary to invent one. The humanistic version of the Revival
collides with the facts and breaks down of sheer excess.

The four Oxford sermons, three by John Wesley, "Salvation
by Faith," preached 1738, "The Almost Christian," 1741, and
"Scriptural Christianity," 1744, and one by Charles Wesley
preached 1742, are all fresh studies of the nature of Christianity,
of the facts of Christian experience and above all of the meaning of God in Christian experience. They are the fruit of a re-
examination of the thought of God and the nature of faith in the
light of the whole gravitational field of Christ and his Church

[16] Journal, I, 477; see the all-important letter to his brother Samuel: Letters,
I, 262.

within which alone Christian experience can take its rise and gain its limits. They all represent religion as experience. The first Oxford sermon after the conversion-experience represents salvation as the progressive experience of divine grace. The sentence "If any man die without this faith and love, good it were for him that he had never been born," in "The Almost Christian," comes out of the travail of Wesley's spirit over the decadent Christianity of his age,[17] and is a sentence not of dogmatic theology but of Wesley's conversion-experience. The generalization from his own experience may have been too sweeping; but it was deeply sincere and genuine. The sermon culminates in the prayer, "May we all thus *experience* what it is to be *altogether Christians*." The whole point to the last Oxford sermon is the experiential nature and reality of the work and witness of the Holy Spirit. Christian experience issuing forth in Christian activity and in building a Christian world is the meaning of Christianity from center to circumference. And all this is true because Christian experience is the experience of God. In this sense these sermons all accent the conversion-experience and in so doing represent Wesley in the epoch of his maturity.

And he has said so: "Forty years ago I knew and preached every Christian doctrine which I preach now."[18] This draws the line sharply at 1738, the year of the first Revival Manifesto, and defines the epoch of his doctrinal maturity.

In the last Oxford discourse we come then upon another of the great vital doctrines of Wesleyanism, or more truly, just another way of stating the one great systematic thought of his message. It is his doctrine of the *Witness of the Spirit*. It affirms that all the major truths of the Gospel admit of continual verification in experience and life. It enforces the essentially experiential nature of religion. But this doctrine provoked instant hostile criticism when it was first preached in a humanist climate and has done so ever since. On humanist premises in particular, a thousand and one logical difficulties—mostly gratuitous—swarm about it.

[17] Sermon 2.
[18] Journal, Sept. 1, 1778.

But if the doctrine of the Witness of the Spirit really means the witness of experience, if in religion experience and reality come to the same thing, why did Wesley so consistently call it the work and witness of the Spirit, and not rather simply the witness of experience? To ask this question is on Wesleyan principles to answer it. He did so precisely because the constant overwhelming emphasis in all his preaching falls, not upon the human side of salvation save only man's utter need of it and utter dependence on God, but always upon the divine initiative. It is the witness of experience to the divine initiative in all Christian experience. Undoubtedly every true, simple focalization of the Christian faith opens a door into the ineffable mystery of Christian experience, like the sense of a far sail dipping on the horizon of the rolling sea, of the azure blue of a sunlit sky, of the immensity of the star-strewn spaces. So it is in all our communion with God.

What then is this work and witness of the Holy Spirit more or less but the meaning of God in Christian experience, first of Jesus, then too, of ours. Now in that experience there must be both mystery and manifestation. The men and minds of Wesley's generation commonly shut God out of both the cosmic and Christian picture. Wesley had a quarrel with his age about that. He thrust the thought of God earnestly into everything. He thrust the truth about God into the life of all sorts and conditions of men. He announced to all men alike his own discovery of God and promised every man as much. True Christianity always begins with the announcement of the discovery of God. His age was too fastidious to stand for that. It had a way of letting God, though he is nearer than breathing, nearer than hands or feet, very much alone beyond the confines of the universe. But Wesley lived in the very thought of God and in the actuality of his presence. He taught with militancy that the witness of the spirit was no specialty of Apostolic Christianity, but is common to all Christianity and is the mark of its genuineness. It simply cancels Christianity to deny that "the inspiration of the Holy Spirit, the indwelling Spirit of God, is the common privilege of all believers, is the simplest blessing of the Gospel, is the unspeakable gift, the universal promise, and the criterion of a real Christian." What is there else beside in Christianity?

Wesley's statements and uses of the "Witness of the Spirit" were, it may be granted, liable to many imperfections and defects of suitable expression. But once the truth of his central teaching has been seen and felt, none of these real difficulties count very much nor do they seriously hinder. His several sermons on this topic, the fruit of experiential thinking and of prolonged meditation, offer ample opportunity to study the development and variation of his thought. But the great essential is not to miss in the process of criticism the truth that was the power of the Wesleyan Reformation. After analyzing the friendly yet impressive debate on this subject, in the correspondence between Bishop Secker and Master John Wesley, it is clear the advantages are not all on one side. But Wesley was rightly steadfast in declining any description of Christian experience which failed or refused to ground it all in divine agency. A thousand and one intellectual difficulties, even if real and not, as most of them are, purely imaginary, are not enough to abandon the strongest position of Christianity. No man can say believingly *Jesus is Lord* but by the Spirit. Such confession and faith must be at once revelational and experiential. "For in the scripture language to say, or to believe, implies an *experimental* assurance. The sum is, none have the Holy Spirit but Christians: all Christians have this Spirit." [19] This position must never be dissociated from the fact that Wesley affirmed there had been and could be and will be revelation outside the Christian sphere of influence. But he never allowed a quibbling rationalism to obscure for him the supremacy of the Christian revelation.

The Bishop of Lichfield (1730-1749) took it upon himself to censor and frown upon the central thesis of Wesley's preaching, namely, the work and witness of the Holy Spirit or the continuous verifiability of the truth of the Gospel in Christian experience and life. He delivered in 1741 and published in 1744 a charge to

[19] *Wesleyan New Testament*, p. 433.

his clergy which maintained that the witness of the Spirit referred only to the miracles and extraordinary gifts of the Apostolic age. He denounced the Wesleyan type of teaching as "pretense of our modern enthusiasts" and the Methodists are called "a new sect of enthusiastical seducers among us." The Anglican prelates sought in several cases to fasten on Wesley the odium of enthusiasm, and to close the mind of the people against him. The eighteenth century mind was pretty much sealed to what men stigmatized as enthusiasm—the reality of God in human experience. Wesley too disavowed, thus paying tribute to this climate of opinion, all enthusiasm. But as above noted he identified the real enthusiasts with those who confounded the outward conformities of Christianity with the inward realities of Christian experience. That was the bad enthusiasm.

This view of Wesley through his last Oxford sermon may conclude with the important accounts of the event by the preacher himself and by three eyewitnesses, namely Charles Wesley, Benjamin Kennicott and William Blackstone. The Journal of Wesley has this to say: "I set out with a few friends for Oxford. On Wednesday my brother met us from Bristol." Friday, 24 (St. Bartholomew's Day): "I preached, I suppose the last time, at St. Mary's. Be it so. I am now clear of the blood of these men. I have fully delivered my soul. The Beadle came to me afterwards and told me the Vice-Chancellor had sent him for my notes. I sent them without delay, not without admiring the wise providence of God. Perhaps few men of note would have given a sermon of mine the reading if I had put it into their hands; but by this means it came to be read, probably more than once, by every man of eminence in the University. I left Oxford about noon, preached at Wycombe (twenty-five miles south-east of Oxford) in the evening; and on Saturday, the 25th, returned to London." [20] His *Short History of the Methodists* (1781) then placed this experience at Oxford more definitely in the history of Nonconformity in England.

[20] This account in the Journal should be compared with that in the *Short History*.

The first account of an eyewitness is taken from Charles Wesley's Journal for Aug. 23rd and 24th: "I went to Christ Church prayers with several of the brethren, who thought it strange to see men in surplices talking, laughing and pointing, as in a play-house, the whole time of service. I got two or three hours' conference with my brother; and found the spirit which had drawn us formerly in this place. I preached to a multitude of brethren, gownsmen and gentry from the races (it was the Oxford race-week) who filled our inn and yard. The strangers that intermeddled not with our joy seemed struck and astonished with it, whilst we admonished one another in psalms and hymns, &c. O that all the world had a taste for our diversion!! Friday, Aug 24.—I joined my brother in stirring up the Society. They did run well, till the Moravians turned them out of the way of God's ordinances. At ten I walked with my brother and Mr. Piers and Meriton (two clergymen who had just taken part in Wesley's first Conference in London) to St. Mary's, where my brother bore his testimony before a crowded audience, much increased by the racers. Never have I seen a more attentive congregation. They did not let a word slip them. Some of the Heads stood up the whole time, and fixed their eyes on him. If they can endure sound doctrine like his, he will surely leave a blessing behind him. The Vice-Chancellor sent after him, and desired his notes; which he sealed up and sent immediately. We walked back in form, the little band of us four, for of the rest durst none join himself to us. I was a little diverted at the coyness of an old friend, Mr. Wells, who sat just before me, but took great care to turn his back upon me all the time, which did not hinder my seeing through him. At noon my brother set out for London, and I for Bristol." [21]

The second word of an eyewitness is by Benjamin Kennicott then twenty-five years of age, later a Fellow of Exeter, who became one of the most eminent Hebrew and Oriental scholars in England: "On Friday last, being St. Bartholomew's Day, the famous Methodist, Mr. John Wesley, Fellow of Lincoln College,

[21] Journal of Charles Wesley, Vol. I, pp. 380 f.

preached before the University; which being a matter of great curiosity at present, and may possibly be greater in its consequences, I shall be particular in the account of it. All that are Masters of Arts, and on the foundation of any College, are set down in a roll, as they take their degree, and in that order preach before the University, or pay three guineas for a preacher in their stead, and as no clergyman can avoid his turn, so the University can refuse none; otherwise Mr. Wesley would not have preached. He came to Oxford some time before, and preached frequently every day in courts, public-houses, and elsewhere. On Friday morning, having held forth twice in private, at five and eight, he came to St. Mary's at ten o'clock. There were present the Vice-Chancellor, the proctors, most of the heads of houses, a vast number of gownsmen, and a multitude of private people, with many of his followers, both brethren and sisters, who, with funereal faces and plain attire, came from around to attend their master and teacher. When he mounted the pulpit, I fixed my eyes on him and his behavior. He is neither tall nor fat; for the latter would ill become a Methodist. His black hair quite smooth, and parted very exactly, added to a peculiar composure in his countenance, showed him to be an uncommon man. His prayer was soft, short, and conformable to the rules of the University. His text, Acts IV, 31: 'And they were all filled with the Holy Ghost.' And now he began to exalt his voice. He spoke the text very slowly, and with an agreeable emphasis. His introduction was to prove that the word *all* in the text was meant, not only of the apostles and those who received the extraordinary, but of others who received the ordinary influences (only) of the Holy Spirit; and that of such there were many in the infancy of the Gospel, persons who had no business to perform besides the reformation of their own lives, and therefore wanted the ordinary divine influences only, to refresh them in their conversion and complete their Christianity. And this he chose to do because, if the Holy Ghost was necessary for men as private persons at first, it must be so in all ages. His division of the text was, first, to show the influence of Christianity in its infancy on individuals;

secondly, in its progress from one period to another; thirdly, in its final completion in the universal conversion of the world to the Christian faith. Under these three heads he expressed himself like a very good scholar, but a rigid zealot; and then he came to what he called his plain, practical conclusion. Here was what he had been preparing for all along; and he fired his address with so much zeal and unbounded satire as quite spoiled what otherwise might have been turned to great advantage; for as I liked some, so I disliked other parts of his discourse extremely. Having, under the third head, displayed the happiness of the world under it—complete final reformation—'Now,' says he, 'where is this Christianity to be found? Is this a Christian nation? Is this a Christian city?'—asserting the contrary to both. I liked some of his freedom; such as calling the generality of young gownsmen 'a generation of triflers,' and many other just invectives. But, considering how many shining lights are here that are the glory of the Christian cause, his sacred censure was much too flaming and strong, and his charity much too weak in not making large allowances. But so far from allowances, that, after having summed up the measure of our iniquities, he concluded with a lifted-up eye in this most solemn form: 'It is time for Thee, Lord, to lay to Thine hand'—words full of such presumption and seeming inprecation, that they gave an universal shock. This, and the assertion that Oxford was not a Christian city, and this country not a Christian nation, were the most offensive parts of the sermon, except when he accused the whole body (and confessed himself to be one of the number) of the sin of perjury; and for this reason, because, upon becoming members of a College, every person takes an oath to observe the statutes of the University, and no one observes them in all things. But this gave me no uneasiness; for in every oath the intention of the legislator is the only thing you swear to observe; and the legislators here mean that you shall observe all their laws, or upon the violation of them submit to the punishment if required; and this being explained in the statute-book given to every member, does, I think, solve the whole difficulty. Had these things been omitted, and his censures moderated, I think his discourse, as to style and delivery, would have been uncommonly pleasing to others as well as to myself. He is allowed to be a man of great parts, and that by the excellent Dean of Christ Church, (Dr. Conybeare); for the day he preached the dean generously said of him, 'John Wesley will always be thought a man of sound sense, though an enthusiast.' However, the Vice-Chancellor sent for the sermon and I hear the heads of colleges intend to show their resentment." [22]

The third is from the pen of the celebrated William Blackstone, who at the age of twenty-one was chosen a Fellow of All Soul's and later rose to fame as the author of the *Commentaries on the Laws of England* and a Judge of the Realm. In a letter dated August 28, 1744,[23] he says: "We were last Friday entertained at St. Mary's by a curious sermon from Wesley the Methodist. Among other equally modest particulars he informed us, 1st That there was not one Christian among all the Heads of Houses; 2dly, that pride, gluttony, avarice, luxury, sensuality and drunkenness were the general characteristics of all Fellows of Colleges, who were useless to a proverbial uselessness. Lastly, that the younger part of the University were a generation of triflers, all of them perjured, and not one of them of any religion at all. His notes were demanded by the Vice-Chancellor, but on mature deliberation it has been thought proper to punish him by a mortifying neglect."

Thus all the accounts agree that the preacher spoke with reformation boldness to his distinguished auditors. Charles thought "if they could stand such doctrine, they were sure of a blessing." Kennicott detected in the deliverance a "sacred censure much too flaming and strong," and a conclusion in "words so full of presumption and seeming imprecation that they gave an universal shock." If he had but left out "his plain practical conclusion" that was from the first so obviously his goal, his discourse would have been," as to style and delivery, "uncom-

[22] See *Methodist Magazine,* Jan., 1866.
[23] See Hurst's *History of Methodism,* Vol. II, p. 602.

monly pleasing" to everybody. Blackstone called it "A curious sermon from Wesley the Methodist" containing a modest (!) bill of indictment against Heads of Houses, Fellows of Colleges and the student body generally. Perhaps the most revealing of all these facts is the picture drawn by Charles of "the little band of us four," after the academic procession that preceded the service, "walking back in form, for of the rest durst none join himself to us." The two Wesleys and two clergymen, Piers and Meriton, all members of the first Methodist Conference, a little band of four, walked in form alone!

Twenty-odd years later, it was in the early sixties, William Blackstone, then at the height of his power as Lecturer on Laws at the University of Oxford and a rising practitioner in the courts, and at the time when he was working away on his *Commentaries on the Laws of England,* the first volume of which appeared in 1765, took it upon himself to make an examination of the preaching in all the leading London pulpits. After doing so he reported that he could not find in any one of the sermons audited any more of Christianity than could be found in the writings of Cicero; nor could he make out from the content of the preaching whether the preacher was a disciple of Confucius, Mohammed or Christ. Thus historic Christianity appeared to be obsolete. There were wise men who were sure the Church was done for, and some of the brightest were even beforehand in writing the epitaph of both the Church and historic Christianity. It was against this decadent anarchic Christianity, armed with his rediscovery of the Luther-Calvin idea of the sovereign saving significance of a God-given faith in Christ, that John Wesley measured himself.

CHAPTER III

RELIGION AS EXPERIENCE

The investigator who turns from the literature of religion in the eighteenth century to examine the works of John Wesley will be struck with the appearance of a new term in theology: Experience. If the investigator comes to his subject with adequate discipline in the history of Christian thought, he will receive a similar but stronger impression. Before John Wesley the word "experience" does not occupy the conspicuous position in the preaching, teaching, writing of any master of doctrinal and practical Christianity. The reference to experience does occupy for the first time in the history of Christian thought the conspicuous position in the Wesleyan understanding of the Gospel. In fact the appeal to experience is so pervasive and powerful as to determine its historical individuality. It is a theology of experience. It rests, to be sure, on two pillars: Scripture and experience. These are, however, taken and accepted not as alien and antagonistic, but cognate and congenial principles. The early Reformers, Luther and Calvin, introduced the principle of private judgment into Biblical theology and assumed the active mind to be essential to the practical religious use of the Scriptures. But owing to well-known circumstances the free activity of the mind on the subject matter of the Scriptures was in the sixteenth century hemmed and hedged within the narrowest limits. Two centuries later the reference to experience in theology, implicit in Protestantism, emerged in the midst of a great age of scientific discovery into power in the Wesleyan understanding of the Gospel. It is safe to say that no other teacher of the Christian Church and preacher of the Gospel ever laid upon experience so heavy a burden of responsibility for discerning and

confirming the truth-values of the Christian faith. In respect
to the primacy accorded to religious experience, the extent to
which he made experiential thinking his principle of method
and the results of his researches into the meaning of God in
Christian experience, it can truly be said that Wesley started
theology on the paths in which today religious thought moves
increasingly.

There came about the same time, not quite ten years ago,
from one of the foremost preachers of American Protestantism
and from the pen of an able young Franciscan scholar in Bel-
gium, two fresh and intelligent appraisals of the inner genius and
historical significance of the whole Wesleyan movement. The
first defines its significance in the sphere of practical Christianity, while the second also takes into consideration its contribution to the development of Christian thought. The first of
these was an utterance from the pulpit of Old South Church,
Boston, February 1, 1925, by the late George A. Gordon on the
subject of "Religion as Experience." "Let it be said once for
all that Wesley brought the whole Christian world back to religion as experience in the face of a dead theology and of a dead
ceremony; he made religion a living, creative, glorious reality,
and the thought and determination and affirmation of Wesley
have gone round the world." "Consider Charles Wesley's hymn,
'Jesus, Lover of my Soul.' . . . It does not differ very much
from Toplady's [1] theology, but you can see working through it
the living soul of a religious person. . . . The words of this
hymn are all terms of experience. There is religion, one great
surging experience creating its forms of belief; and therefore its
forms of belief represent spiritual reality, and they are forms of
living truth and living experience wherever they go."

These are weighty words. As a general judgment on the genius
and historical significance of the Wesleyan Revival they go
straight to the heart of the matter. *Wesley brought the whole
Christian world back to religion as experience; in religion, experience and reality come to the same thing.* A certain variety

[1] Toplady was a strong Calvinist.

of terms, such as experience, religious experience, Christian experience, and the witness of the Spirit, is characteristic of Wesley's exposition of the doctrine. Viewed objectively, Christian experience is the witness of God's Spirit, viewed subjectively, it is the witness of our own spirit.[2] Wesley well knew that his doctrine of Christian experience was, with reference to the Church of his day, something new under the sun. It was new, radically new, at any rate in respect to the central place and importance given to the doctrine of the witness of the Spirit and to the tremendous emphasis put upon it. The Secker-Wesley correspondence fixed upon it as the supreme issue between Wesley and the Arminian teaching of his own Church. Both parties were agreed as to what the issue was. Wesley asserted again and again that it is "one grand part of the testimony which God has given Methodists to bear to all mankind." But he roundly denied that the doctrine is anything new from the standpoint of historic Christianity or that it was any peculiarity either of the Wesleyan or of Protestant teaching. It is also shared by many Catholics. Wesley had an instinctive repugnance for theological provincialisms. He always endeavored, and largely succeeded in his endeavor, to think in terms of historic Christianity. It was an exact transcript of his own case and experience when he wrote: "It is by God's peculiar blessing upon them (Wesley and those with him) in searching the Scriptures, confirmed by the experience of His children, that this great evangelical truth has been recovered which had been for many years well-nigh lost and forgotten."[3] Great evangelical truths well-nigh lost and forgotten for many years; great evangelical truths rediscovered by scriptural and experiential thinking and brought back to life and power again—that is an epitome of the decadence and revival of Christianity in the eighteenth, and also very much in all centuries.

In striking concurrence with the general estimate in Gordon's sermon on "Religion as Experience," a young Franciscan scholar,

[2] Sermons 10, 11.
[3] Letters, III, 137; V, 21.

Piette, in working out the requirements for his degree at the University of Louvain, very creditably undertook to trace more specifically the radical influence of the Wesleyan theology of experience upon modern religious, and especially upon modern Protestant, thought. The conclusion which he reached is thus forcefully stated in the Preface: [4] "On all sides Methodism from a doctrinal point of view occupies in every way *a unique position, by reason of the primacy which it has accorded to religious experience;* it is a reaction against the antinomianism of the Lutherans; it is a reaction against the absolute decrees of Calvinism; it is a realization of free research within the limits of a single powerful organization of discipline. It is a forerunner in theology of Schleiermacher's theory of religion." He observes further that "the Wesleyan theology of experience has exerted an uncontestable influence upon the theories of liberal Protestant theology from Friedrich Schleiermacher to William James." Perhaps the most notable fact about Piette's incisive revision of the traditional view of Wesley, backed as it is by honest research, is that the expounders of John Wesley within the denominational fold had to be told by a Roman Catholic scholar that the master-mind of the Revival belongs inevitably in the history of Christian thought and must be recognized as a principal founder of the theology of experience. As to Piette's conception of Wesley's position in Protestant Christianity, the question will have to be well weighed whether he has not mistaken theological mole-hills for mountains in magnifying the admitted differences between the theology of John Wesley and that of Luther or Calvin, while ignoring the fundamental unity of faith among the three great masters of Protestant Christianity. But this has to do with the definition, not the recognition, of Wesley's inevitable place in the history of Protestant thought.

The character backgrounds and vocational control of Wesley's earliest research into *the nature of Christianity* are of con-

---

[4] *La Réaction de John Wesley dans l'Évolution du Protestantisme,* 1925, Second Ed., 1927.

siderable importance. In a college constituency where idleness
was nearly universal and industry most unusual, where blasphemy, profanity, gambling, drunkenness, etc., were regarded by
the student body as no offense at all and by the University
authorities as "most venial offenses." [5] This opinion is supported
by numerous reliable witnesses, including Adam Smith and
Edward Gibbon. Wesley, by the discipline of his meagre resources
and by methodical industry in the things of the mind and spirit,
won great distinction and scarcely less unpopularity. He later
made himself "more vile" by taking his Christian calling very
seriously, pursuing it with an energy of will, power of intellect
and a strictness of method that started a nickname which has
become historic.

About the time of his graduation from Oxford in 1724, being
then at the age of twenty-one, he chose the Christian ministry
for his life-work. In addition to the native force of his religious
genius and strong personal predilection, he was almost, if not
altogether, predestined to it by his antecedents on both sides
of the house and by the strong direction given him by home
forces, in particular the masterful influence of his incomparable
mother. Soon after his ordination in 1725, he entered the service
of the Anglican Church. Six months after ordination, he received an appointment (March 17, 1726) as Fellow of Lincoln
College, Oxford, which provided sufficient fixed income, "sixty
pounds a year," [6] to give a frugal Wesley enough and to spare,
and so set him free either to become "a mere saunterer *inter
sylvas academicas*," [7] or in obedience to his genius and divine
calling to execute "the work I came into the world for." [8] The
Oxford Fellowship removed every barrier and set no boundary
to Wesley's activities and influence save only the measure of
his genius, the strength of his purpose and the opportunities of
his vocation. Moreover, the ordination vow and terms of the
fellowship, as construed by the ordaining bishop, left Wesley
entirely free to carve out his own career and to choose his field

[5] Lecky's *England*, II, 613.   [7] Letters, II, 68.
[6] Letters, I, 38.   [8] Journal, I, 88.

of service as well as the method of fulfilling his vocation. Many of the established clergy, including some of the bishops, annoyed by his intrusive activities, felt that he had taken ill advantage of his Oxford Fellowship and had presumptuously appointed himself rector of the world.[9] One of the bishops remonstrated with him that he had really taken upon himself "the Apostolate of England."[10] Wesley demurred not at all to this startling idea but only to his being limited to the Apostolate of England. "Wherever I see one or a thousand men running into hell, be it in England, Ireland or France, yea, in Europe, Asia, Africa or America, I will stop them if I can." This was written just ten years after he penned the words inscribed on his tablet in Westminster Abbey: "I look upon all the world as my parish." Wesley had in him the grandeur of conception that is the distinction of extraordinary minds.[11] Where many, perhaps most, of the Oxford Fellows saw leisure and often lived in "luxury and idleness," Wesley saw only labor and a summons to world service.

In response to his vocational awakening and the great decision, Wesley entered into himself more deeply and began to discipline himself soul and body rigorously, relentlessly for his lifework, until as a slave of the Gospel he should be able to do with himself what he would. A Francis of Assisi repels us more than our feelings can stand by his reckless contacts with lepers; but at least he could do with himself what he would in striving to be another Christ even to the print of nails in hands and feet. A Francis or a Wesley is one man in millions. So everything in Wesley's career, including even the strange vacillations in his five love affairs, his persistence for over twenty-five years in a homeless career in the face of choice opportunities and the keenest heart-hunger for a woman's love, find their sufficient explanation in his transcendent vocational consciousness and the necessity of keeping the Oxford Fellowship which forbade marriage in order to its fulfilment. He sacrificed everything on the altar of his

[9] Journal, I, 216 f.
[10] Letters, II, 137.
[11] Journal, I, 88, 460; Letters, I, 123, 208, 286, 322; II, 137; V, 15.

vocation. Moreover, if genius is infinite capacity for taking pains in purposeful thought and action, it was his above measure. His mother sent him, as a kind of ordination beatitude, these words: "Henceforth happy you are if you shall make of religion the business of life." The grey dawn of the Industrial Revolution in which Wesley set out upon his career summoned men of enterprise to the lists of great adventure, most of them to make a religion of their business, but a chosen few to make a business of their religion. Wesley had in him the genius of the projector. Born master of men, with rare organizing talent, he could have been a great captain of industry and amassed a large fortune. He chose rather, like St. Francis, whom he most resembles, to shun riches as if deadly poison to the highest in man, became the founder of a church against his will and after giving away for years all of an income that ran into thousands of pounds, died a voluntary pauper. Such was the genius of the man who set himself to create a new empire for the Gospel of Jesus Christ.

His decision to enter the service of the Christian Church raised major issues. What is the nature of the call to the Christian ministry? But above all, *What is the nature of Christianity?*—a new putting of the question that was consistently used by Wesley a full century before its adoption and use in German Protestantism.[12] Letters were at once exchanged between Epworth and Oxford on these subjects. They are valuable as indicating how far away Wesley then was from the mastery of evangelical principles which makes the epoch of his maturity. They also mirror the current Christianity of that age which was at best a hybrid of devout rationalism and blind traditionalism. But the tradition of religion in the circles to which Wesley himself belonged oscillated between the new rationalism and the old traditionalism.

Of the home forces that moulded the mind and character of Wesley, the influence of his mother is easily first; her influence subordinated all others to itself. She was unquestionably the

[12] Journal, I, 122, 422.

principal whetstone of his precocious mind and his chief mentor
in the formative period of his life on all religious and moral subjects. It was in sweet communion with his Mother Monnica
that Augustine scaled the heights of the ecstasy divine.[13] What
Monnica was to Augustine, his chief mentor in the things of the
mind and the spirit, all that Susanna Wesley was to her gifted
son. Samuel Wesley, the father, was a man of ability, character, and the courage of his convictions. But like Patricius,
the father of Augustine, Samuel Wesley is a vague and shadowy
figure in Wesley's spiritual biography. Wesley sometimes consulted his father on practical matters. But the correspondence
with the mother reveals a kinship of spirit and fellowship of
religious thought on the highest questions of faith for which
there is no equivalent in the paternal letters. Beyond the native
talent of the mother, her relation to John Wesley must be understood from the fact that she was to him entirely in the place of
the public school and of the Sunday school until he was eleven
years of age. All the evidence shows that the father resigned
rather than shared this educational responsibility. And after he
went to Charterhouse and then to Oxford the mother continued
to be his chief counsellor in Christian doctrine. It was the
Oxford graduate who wrote, "I am, therefore, at length come
over entirely to your opinion." [14] The debt of the leader of the
Revival to his incomparable mother has not been overestimated.

Wesley's mother has recorded in her own hand that she was
brought up in the midst of "good books and ingenious conversation, early initiated and instructed in the first principles of
the Christian religion." She was a very able thinker, well-read
in theology, with strong leanings for a season toward rationalism
in religion. To this reference is made in one of her private meditations: "Married to a religious orthodox man: By him first
drawn off from the Socinian heresy and afterwards confirmed and
strengthened by Bishop Bull." In her violent, youthful reaction
against Nonconformist theology, its extreme Calvinism, she

[13] *Confessions*, Bk. IX, Ch. X.
[14] Letters, I, 25, 39.

landed in humanism. Although she did not abide in this position
but returned to the highways of the historic Christian faith, still
the leaven of liberalism continued to be a factor in her own
thinking and was passed on to her gifted son. Lord Acton, after
a study of Wesley, in particular in his Journals, got the impression that Wesley had made a progress in religious liberalism such
as Gladstone had made in political liberalism. Wesley printed
"an extract from the life of Mr. Thomas Firmin" in the *Arminian
Magazine* for the year 1786. To the extract he prefixed this note:
"I was exceedingly struck at reading the following life; having
long settled it in my mind that the entertaining wrong notions
concerning the Trinity was inconsistent with real piety. *But I
can not argue against matter of fact.* I dare not deny that Mr.
Firmin was a pious man, although his notions of the Trinity were
quite erroneous. J. W." Firmin was a devout Unitarian. "I
can not argue against matter of fact!" Wesley introduced the
experimental method of reasoning into religious subjects and
pursued it until it became a settled habit of thought. Across a
period of half a century he proclaimed, "We break with no man
for his opinion. We think and let think." [15] Slowly but surely
the dogmatic shell around many traditional opinions was dissolved. One by one theological prejudices were overcome. Wesley to be sure did not by any means clear himself of all useless
theological encumbrance nor outgrow all the prejudices. But he
did outgrow enough of them to make him for all time a shining
example of progressive theological thinking.

But this ultimate trust in experience and its indications, this
emancipation from the dead hand of tradition represents Wesley
in the epoch of his maturity, not the graduate student of Oxford.
The graduate student was for a brief season carried far along
with the prevalent rationalism. How very like his age to say
(1725), "I call faith an assent upon rational grounds. . . . Faith
must necessarily at length be resolved into reason." [16] But this
unbounded trust in reason as the highest court of appeal on all

[15] Journal, III, 178.
[16] Letters, I, 23.

issues raised by the religious consciousness and as the ultimate test of truth-values in the Christian faith, was short-lived. Wesley's talent for logic is attested by his appointment, 1726, Lecturer in Logic. It took less than four months for his logical acumen to discover the fallacy in this shallow rationalism. He had mistaken and substituted one element of faith, the intellectual function, for the response of man's total personal life to the truth-values of the Gospel. "I am therefore," so he again wrote his mother,[17] "at length come over entirely to your opinion that saving faith (including practice) is an assent to what God has revealed because He has revealed it and not because the truth of it may be evinced by reason." For a brief season then, as was only natural to a young collegian, Wesley traveled the *via rationis* or way of reason in religion but quickly abandoned it for the *via auctoritatis* or way of external authority, by which all the truth-values of the Christian faith come down to a direct, unqualified inference from the Scriptures.

The prevailing tendency of Wesley's age was either to repudiate all reference to religious experience or else to confine the Christian consciousness within the intellectuality of faith. But Wesley early abandoned the way of reason for that of authority and broke radically with all intellectualism in religion. He never went back. On the contrary, he worked his way through to a doctrine of Christian experience which, while it takes up into itself the truth of rationalism, completely transcends it. Of no less, perhaps of greater, importance is the fact that his doctrine of Christian experience completely transcended and dispensed with every appeal to external authority in the traditional sense. It seems passing strange in view of Wesley's flat refusal in his maturity to submit his theology to an external authority of any kind, in view of his open unqualified repudiation of the authoritarian way of discovering and deciding the truth-values of the Christian faith, in view of his extensive and constant practice of a different method, that he should ever have been represented as "thinking or professing to accept the faith on the old author-

[17] Letters, I, 25.

ity." [18]   This opinion about Wesley has no foothold in the facts.
The interpretation itself appears not to have been won from a
study of the original sources, but to be only an inference from
the preconceived notion that "it is useless to look to the evangelical movement in any of its forms, for any theologian who
directly advanced the progress of Christian thought."

According to Wesley's earlier position, which alone gives a
handle to this false conception of his theological method, the
mind is supposed to submit itself immediately, without any further operation of critical thought, without rational or *any other
kind of insight,* simply to what the Bible says, as if that were
always perfectly simple and self-evident, solely because it is in
the Bible.   And such intellectual assent was for a season given
the lofty title of saving faith!   In reality such assent is a species
of that "implicit obedience" which Wesley in his maturity (1738-
1791) strongly repudiated.   Thirteen years after thus committing
himself to *the direct inference from Scripture* without any intervening factor, Wesley, on the basic question, *What is saving
faith?* openly and positively refused to abide by the argument
from even the New Testament, although he admitted it to be in
the premises perfectly plain and entirely conclusive.   He laid
down the principle in a crucial case that the teaching of the New
Testament must be sustained and vouched for by the facts of
experience before we can build a final trust upon it.   What led
him to transfer his final trust from the way of reason and that
of traditional authority to *experiential thinking* upon the truth-
values of historic Christianity chiefly along the lines of New
Testament teaching?

Wesley indeed did not in solitary fashion make this great
epoch-making transition for theology; nor was it for him simply
or primarily a borrowed idea.   It was a century peculiarly prolific in just such significant new departures in human thought.
Ideas create climates of opinion.   All men breathe it.   Thus the
two foremost philosophical critics of the eighteenth century,
Hume of Scotland and Kant of Germany, referred, the former

[18] Allen, *Continuity of Christian Thought,* 1884, p. 375.

to a *reformation in the natural sciences*,[19] the latter to a *revolution in the thought-habits of the sciences*,[20] as having in it *the seed-thought for a similar reformation or revolution in every other department of human thought.* They undertook just such a reformation or reconstruction in all reflective thought on the highest themes of existence by making *experience and its indications* the first principle of method. The highest authority for the first principles of thought is our experience of their reality. Existential thinking is experiential thinking. These thinkers also began to widen and deepen the principle of thought as an organ of communication with the nature of things, to include not simply the logical use of intellect but also, and essentially, *experiential thinking* and to confer upon it the highest authority.

Wesley and these thinkers who in surpassing measure exemplified both the critical principle and *the return to experience* in philosophy were contemporaries. It would seem impossible to imagine minds at more opposite poles of religious thought than these exponents of critical rationalism and the leader of thought and action in the Revival. Wesley recoiled from Hume's icy criticism, where it touched Christianity, as sheer intellectual insolence. He called Hume "the most insolent despiser of truth who ever appeared in the world" and thought that Beattie was more than a match for Hume's intellect. This was the same Beattie of whom Immanuel Kant said that he did not have critical acumen sufficient even to know what Hume was driving at. He had beautifully missed the whole point to Hume's question by proving with a great flourish of victory what Hume never doubted, but had failed to discern the most significant question ever submitted to the philosophers. In spite of Wesley's repulsion by Hume's critical objectivity, we venture to submit the question, and we believe here for the first time, whether there can not be clearly traced in the work of Wesley on Christian doctrine a revolution in the whole approach to the interpretation of the Gospel and in the whole method of theology quite com-

[19] *Treatise of Human Nature,* Ed. G. & G., Vol. I, p. 308.
[20] *Critique of Pure Reason,* Preface to Second Edition.

parable in importance and closely analogous in significance to what his philosophical contemporaries set themselves to do in their own field, namely, to substitute experiential thinking for the purely logical use of the intellect. At any rate, that is precisely what Wesley succeeded largely in doing in his style of Christian doctrine.

The fact then of major importance for Wesley's entire reexamination of Christian doctrine and still more for its leavening influence in modern Protestantism was the entrance of the leaven of experimentalism into his work and the revolution wrought in his doctrinal thinking in the thirteen years between his graduation in 1725 and his conversion-experience in 1738. Now the superiority of the argument from experience over all other considerations in the understanding and decision of moral and religious questions began to take possession of his mind while a student at Oxford. A reference here to the traditional empiricism of the English mind would be entirely in order. Taxed with disobedience to his calling as well as to the wishes of his parents and hard pressed to marry himself to local parish work, Wesley defended himself with spirit for cleaving to the resources and freedom of the Oxford Fellowship and to the opportunities thus afforded to carve out his own career in the service of the Gospel. He took his stand in his labored defense of his "course of life" on the principle that "for the proof of every one of these weighty truths experience is worth a thousand reasons."

Moreover, it was not the Moravians, as commonly supposed, but Wesley who first insisted when the truth-values in the doctrine of Justification by Faith were being put to the test, and after having been strongly urged upon his acceptance by the Moravians, that the argument from the plain teaching of the New Testament could not alone carry the conclusion with it but must first be vouched for by the argument from Christian experience.[21] It was Wesley, not the Moravians, who prescribed the dual test of "Scripture and Experience" and took an appeal

[21] Letters, I, 166-178; Journal, I, 465-472.

from the unmistakable verdict of Scripture to the further trial of experience. Finally the idea of religious experience, while not entirely absent, is certainly not pronounced or conspicuous in the written reports made by Wesley of the sermons heard and the conversations held with the Moravian leaders. In particular, the sermon by Linner, "a first planter of the Moravian Church" on "The Ground of Faith" contains in Wesley's résumé no reference to Christian experience. And later in the conflict with (English) Moravian extravagances, Wesley opposed his doctrine of Christian experience to Moravian dogmatism which did not stop short of implicit obedience. It appears then that the historical sources of Wesley's theology of experience lie elsewhere.

First of all, we know an open, active mind can not escape a climate of opinion even though we can not define exactly what was taken from it. It is very difficult to sense or imagine the empire which scientific thought swiftly won over the imagination of men in the century after Sir Isaac Newton threw the net of his gravitation formula around every atom in the universe. The founding of the Royal Society in 1662 opens "a great age of scientific discovery in England." Newton discovered the law of gravitation in 1666 and gave his *Principia* to the world in 1687. The next half century, says the historian Green, saw an outburst of "wonderful activity of directly scientific thought." The experimental temper began to tell upon every phase of man's thinking. For the first time in the history of Western Europe men were entirely free to be scientific in method and began a serious attempt to bring religious thought also into harmony with reason and experience. The introduction of the experimental method of reasoning into every subject became the passion as well as the standing order of the age. In view of this powerful climate of thought in which Wesley did his work in its formative stage, in view of his way of keeping all the windows of his mind wide open to every source of truth, finally his unfeigned admiration for celebrated scientists like Dr. Stephen Hales, in whom Wesley noted that "science and religion so well agreed," [22] the historical derivation of his idea of religious experience can not safely be pinned down to Moravian influence. The latter had in fact little, if anything, to do with Wesley's epoch-making insight [23] that, since the advent and negative work of criticism, the argument from Christian experience must henceforth become the citadel of Christian apologetic. It is entirely safe to say that the subordination of traditional Christianity to an experimental and pioneering spirit in Christian thought and practice is not only distinctive of Wesleyanism but as a conscious and constructive method it appears to be largely Wesley's own new departure in theology. He sensed enough of the significance of the scientific movement and inherited enough of the Nonconformist trust in the voice of religious experience before him, to introduce the experimental method of reasoning into theology. He perceived the general significance of criticism for Christian apologetic and laid down the principle in his reply to Conyers Middleton, that inasmuch as criticism had exposed the misplaced confidences of Christian apologetic, henceforth the historical and experiential approach, purified by criticism, to the question, What is Christianity? must supersede the old system of external authority. And further, as between the evidence of tradition and the evidence of experience, he submitted that while the former will always be important, the latter must henceforth be the principal resource of Christian apologetic. For the evidence of experience is a "stream which time will never dry up."

Instead, therefore, of searching far and wide in remote places for the sources of Wesley's theological empiricism, we must start with the fact that he acquired it in the formative period of his religious thought from many sources. The whole stream of modern religious thought is surcharged with transcendental empiricism. Wesley collected in the year 1735 materials from various modern writers for the preface of his own translation of *The Imitation of Christ*. It contains the strongest references to experience. "The understanding of divine truths is to be sought

[22] Journal, IV, 73.
[23] Letters, II, 375-388.

for in the paths of obedience and *experience, and by carefully observing the workings of the Holy Spirit in the soul."* And again "the great practical truths of religion, the mysteries of the inward Kingdom of God, can not be fully discerned but by those readers who have *read the same thing in their own souls.* These truths of religion can not be clearly known but by those who derive their knowledge *'not from commentaries, but experience.'* Thus alone may we attain to *an inward, practical, experimental, feeling knowledge of God."* The standpoint of the Wesley preface is frankly experiential. We further find in the Arminian Secker's lengthy debate with Wesley exactly ten years later that a threefold test of truth is there proposed by the Bishop of Oxford: "(1) Experience; (2) the Word of God; and (3) the nature of the thing." And the bishop has given precedence to the argument from experience, though he may possibly have taken his cue from Wesley's ordering of the arguments.

Undoubtedly Wesley's experiential approach to religion was one in principle with his Arminianism. The chief difference at this point between Secker and Wesley lay in their doctrine of experience. Secker saw the whole significance of religious experience in "the slow steps of ratiocination," "rational assent," and "a full practical assent to truth." This was in humanist terms "the nature of faith." To this Wesley had a double rejoinder: True Christian saving faith implies *abundantly more* than this. First, subjectively, the idea of Christian experience must be widened and deepened to include the progressive response not simply of the human intellect but also and far more the response of man's entire personal life to the truth-value of the Gospel. Then, objectively, the entirety of Christian experience must be subsumed under the Work and Witness of the Spirit. There is then perhaps a certain concurrence between the two minds in the primacy accorded to religious experience, but there is a vast difference in their doctrines of Christian experience.

Reference has been made to Stephen Hales' probable influence on Wesley. The relation of John Wesley to Dr. Stephen Hales, who presided at the meeting of the Board of Trustees for the

Colony of Georgia, at the meeting on February 22, 1738, when Wesley made his report and responded to certain complaints filed against him, calls for more than a passing notice. Hales' influence upon Wesley was important not only as a shining example to Wesley of the compatibility of scientific pursuits with genuine Christian faith, but also for specific directives given to Wesley's thinking. Hales' pioneer inductive studies of the alcohol question with reference to its effect upon the structure and functions of the human body and also its social consequences as a cause of poverty, disease, and crime gave a permanent directive to Wesley's thought and interest. He read Hales' monograph on the *Drink Question,* published anonymously in 1734, while en route to Georgia—Hales was a Trustee of the Georgia Colony—in 1735, and began at once to try out on himself Hales' reckless theory that a man's health would not be ruined, as everybody believed, but really benefited by total abstinence. Six days after the *Simonds* sailed down the Thames, Wesley records, October 20, 1735, that "my brother and I wholly left off the use of flesh and wine." Five years later he bracketed into the record the fact that it is "a diet which has agreed with us hitherto perfectly." But a much stronger comment appears in the Journal for February 5, 1736, where, as the long voyage of 114 days was ended, there stands written alone on a blank page of the Journal these words: *Nos tres proponimus Deo juvante neq carnem neq vinum gustare, ante Diem Dominicum.* "We three resolved by God's help to taste neither flesh nor wine, except on the Lord's Day (Communion)." [24]   Now according to received habits of thought and well-established principles of diet and health in that age this result was a miracle. Wesley should have died of total abstinence from wine. Wesley's versatility in experiments looking to the betterment of mankind and his prophetic boldness in antagonizing and arousing opinion are a source of continued astonishment. He it was who branded human slavery as "the sum of all villainies." He it was who denounced those who make and market "all that liquid fire,

[24] Journal, I, 146.

commonly called spirituous liquors, as poisoners general, who murder . . . by wholesale. Why, there would be very little place for spirituous liquors even in medicine but for the unskillfulness of the practitioner." [25]

Finally, in addition to the leavening influence of the scientific and critical spirit upon every phase of human thought, in addition to a climate of opinion whose powerful moulding influence no mind could escape,[26] attention is directed to parental influence as an immediate source for Wesley's return to experience in theology. This trust in experience is clearly traceable in the weighty letters on the Essentials of Christianity exchanged by Wesley with Bishop Secker of Oxford. The attempt was made to persuade Wesley to subordinate his vocational consciousness to Church order and to tone down, if not to abandon, his strenuous emphasis on the objectivity of Christian experience. But Wesley was not to be dissuaded from either his call to world service nor his exposition of the Christian faith. As for the doctrine of the Work and Witness of the Spirit as the unique essence of Christian experience, he disclaimed all originality of doctrine. But he refused to budge in his conviction that this doctrine is the deepest, richest, most durable truth-value of the Gospel. "I heard my father say more than once . . . 'The inward witness, Son, the inward witness, that is the proof, the strongest proof of Christianity.' " The inward witness means, of course, as Wesley has it in his Sixth University Sermon, "the sure testimony of experience." The inward witness is a summary term for all those final and important intuitions of the Christian consciousness of which no further genetic account can be given. They are our deepest and ultimate human responses to the truth-values of the Gospel.

Still more important information on the parental sources of Wesley's theological empiricism is furnished by Whitehead, one of Wesley's executors and his first official biographer who, as such, had access to all the Wesley manuscripts. Every inter-

[25] Sermon 43.
[26] Green, *History of the English People,* Vol. III, pp. 331-339.

preter of Wesley's antecedents gives major attention to his incomparable mother. Before Whitehead lay "great numbers of religious meditations in Mother Wesley's own handwriting." They reveal an intellect of the highest order. "To know God only as a philosopher; to have the most sublime and curious speculations concerning his essence, attributes and providence; to be able to demonstrate his Being from all or any of the works of nature, and to discourse with the greatest propriety and eloquence of his existence and operations *will avail us nothing unless at the same time we know him experimentally*. Nothing less than the same Almighty power that raised Jesus Christ from the dead, can raise our souls from the death of sin to a life of holiness. *To know God experimentally* is altogether supernatural." [27]

Evidently Wesley's mother, who was his principal mentor in religion, was not wholly in the dark about the essentially revelational and experiential nature of the Christian Faith. Both of Wesley's parents had become strongly Anglican in their attachments. But the conviction that experience is the stronghold of the Christian apologetic points unmistakably to their Nonconformist antecedents where in the nature of the case, external authority being reduced to a minimum, the higher significance of inner experience of necessity was pushed into the foreground of Christian doctrine. It was in the Nonconformist branches of English Christianity that the appeal to experience had its strongest and richest, though not exclusive, development. The Quaker disparagement of the Visible Church and means of grace moved Wesley to say once of the Quaker movement that on this account he would as soon "commence Deist as Quaker." Nevertheless he was not the least intimidated when Secker rightly pointed out the consanguinity of his doctrine of Christian experience with Quakerism. He refused in 1746 to commit himself on this doctrinal kinship but said simply, "If the Quakers hold the same with me, I am glad." "I have," he said, "not studied the writings of the Quakers enough (having read few of them beside

[27] Whitehead's *Life of Wesley*, I, 38.

Robert Barclay) to give an opinion." It is the mark of an
educated mind on such premises not to have an opinion! But
two years later, having evidently gone into the matter, he drew
up a full account of the agreements and differences, as he saw
them, between Quakerism and Christianity and positively identified much of their teaching, "The Spirit is our first and principal leader"; "It is by the Spirit alone that the true knowledge
of God hath been, is, and can be revealed," as also his own. And
so he came out clearly in his fifth letter (1748) to Bishop Secker:
"If you speak to the purpose, if you mean the inward Witness
of God's Spirit, I maintain it always as well as they." There
are other references like this a-plenty to establish that Wesley
took much from the Nonconformist stream of Christianity in
England. But instead of divorcing the Witness of the Spirit
from the historical objectivity of the Word of God in Scripture
and the Means of Grace, he tied them together closer than ever.

Wesley always defined the whole Methodist economy, which
was his special handiwork, as a system of expedients subject to
perpetual revision. But some of his conservative followers could
"not understand this changing one thing after another continually." [28] To which Wesley replied: "This is not a weakness or
fault, as you imagine, but a peculiar advantage which we enjoy.
We thus declare our whole system of expedients, in the Methodist
economy, to be merely instrumental. We prevent, so far as in
us lies, their growing formal or dead. We are always open to
instruction; willing to be wiser every day than we were before
and to change whatever we can change for the better."

When Wesley traced the origin of Methodism as a unique
system of expedients for carrying on "the work of God," his mind
often reverted to the radical influence of the frontier on his
principles. He took along with him to the New World a lot of
theology and High Church notions that never came back. For,
"By my experience in the New World God taught me better."
In the melting pot of frontier life, and on the anvil of utterly
new conditions, the necessity was thrust upon the young col-

[28] Letters, II, 298.

legian of inventing and forging out methods new and very strange from the standpoint of tradition.   Deeply conservative in religious feeling, he quickly imbibed the practical spirit of the frontier and was gradually transformed into one of the boldest and most progressive pioneers among the great leaders of the modern Church.   The leaven of experimentalism and the virus of American pragmatism entered his blood.   He came back from his frontier experience to live his life on the frontiers of doctrinal and practical Christianity and to blaze new paths both in the interpretation and practical application of the Gospel.

But, some one may ask, how far was Wesley willing to go in the application of his experimental and practical principles? Did he not stop short of the institutions of historic Christianity? Did he not exempt the Church order and system received from the past and sanctified by the ages?   The answer is also given in his letter to Bishop Secker of Oxford: "Methinks I would go deeper.   I would inquire what is the end of all ecclesiastical order?   Is it not to bring souls from the power of Satan to God and to build them up in fear and love?   Order, then, is so far valuable as it answers these ends; and if it answers them not, it is nothing worth." [29]   Farther than this Wesley could not go save only to bring Christian doctrine itself to the test of experience.   This also he has done.

Inasmuch as it is the major interest of this monograph as a whole to set the conversion-experience of John Wesley, what led up to it, what was involved in it and what issued forth from it, in the strongest possible light of all the salient facts, it must suffice here to refer simply to the conversion-experience as the master-key to his mature doctrine of Christian experience.   The experiential confirmation in 1738 of the highest truth-value of the Gospel, formed and informed henceforth his theological method.   His understanding and exposition of "the Essentials of True Religion" moved increasingly in experiential paths. Every sermon he preached hangs on the appeal to experience. And several of his ablest discourses are devoted to a direct ex-

[29] Letters, II, 77.

position of the basic truth that in religion experience and reality come to the same thing. Of course Wesley always developed his doctrine of Christian experience, not on the low level of sense empiricism but in the higher form of transcendental empiricism. He also made the entirely sound distinction between the Christian assurance that is inferential and that which is intuitive, immediate. He appreciated both kinds but militantly opposed the reduction of the whole human response to the Gospel to the intellectual function and still more, to the purely humanist interpretation of religious experience. All Christian assurance he assumed and asserted is given in "experience or inward consciousness." Thus religion lives and moves and has its being in immediacy. "By the testimony of the Spirit, I mean an inward impression on the soul whereby the Spirit of God immediately and directly witnesses to my Spirit that I am a child of God; that Jesus Christ hath loved me and given himself for me; that all my sins are blotted and I, even I, am reconciled to God." This he said in 1746. "After twenty years further consideration, I see no cause to retract any part of this." [30] Most of the difficulties with Wesley's doctrine of Christian experience arise from the failure to give it a right historical setting and to understand and appreciate it as a protest against, an emancipation from, and a corrective of the poverty-stricken results of the philosophical reconstructions of religion in which his century was most prolific. It has been said that the best element in the work of Kant was that he started philosophy on the road to a better doctrine of experience. There might be some question about that; there can be no question that John Wesley's answers to the question, *What is Christianity?* took the form of an inquiry into the meaning of God in Christian experience, that his theology found out and followed increasingly experiential paths and that he started Christian doctrine on the right road to a better doctrine of Christian experience.

[30] Sermon 44.

CHAPTER IV

THE REACTION AGAINST MYSTICISM

The Wesleyan Revival of Christianity and reformation of the church took its rise from Wesley's thorough trial of the humanistic approaches to religion, whether along intellectualistic or moralistic or mystical lines. The experiment was marked throughout by systematic reflection upon the poverty-stricken results of every humanistic reconstruction of the Christian faith. The Wesleyan Revival and reformation combined therefore a profound reaction against naturalistic humanism with a definite reaffirmation of early Reformation principles. Moreover, Wesley was in the epoch of his maturity and throughout the fifty-three years of his conversion-experience increasingly conscious of his close affiliation with the early Reformers. He believed that he too, like them, must build an absolute trust upon the Word of God verified in experience.

Experiential thinking in religion, the insight into the necessity of a personal and inner religious experience, the principle that the ultimate meanings and truth-values of the Christian faith must be forever sealed to a man who has not himself experienced it, supplies the master-key to the great Reformer's commentary on St. Paul's Epistle to the Romans and therewith to his religious understanding of the Gospel. This truth, moreover, is implicit in all of Luther's Biblical interpretations and breaks forth at the crucial points of his theology in the significant appeal to experience. The reference to personal experience —(*cum experientia testetur ; ita mecum pugnavi ; sola experientia cognosci possit*)[1]—is in fact the deepest, richest element in Luther's Biblical work. When the Apostle Paul affirmed that

---

[1] From Luther's *Commentary on Epistle to the Romans* IV, 7; XII, 2.

the experiential knowledge ("to know by sure trial") [2] of the truth-values of Christian revelation and all insight into what the good, acceptable, perfect will of God is, comes out of a radical and renewing transformation of all our experiential thinking, he indicates, quoting Luther, "something deeper than anything traditional by letters or learning, something that defies tradition, something ultimate that is knowable only by experience." "And so I have said that unless the highest truth-values of the Gospel (this is the meaning of the term, *voluntas dei,* which Luther used) are known experientially and practically, they will never be known at all." [3]

The starting point, driving power, and undergirding principle of the Protestant Reformation was a great Christian faith given in actual experience. It was from Luther's experience as a believing Christian that the Reformation took its rise. It was an experience in the soul of a man before it became a quickening force in the life of many nations. Luther always recognized in saving faith the ultimate mystery of Christian experience. Above all, he recognized from first to last that faith of this kind is a direct gift from God. This divine gift was to him the core and center of the Christian religion. The experience itself does not admit of exact definition. A God-given faith carried for Luther a self-evidencing quality in itself and required no other credentials beside the experience of its reality. This transcendental empiricism is too deep for either pure reason or external authority. Faith of this kind can not be made to order, either by objective reasoning or by a fiat of authority, but as the gift of God more often overtakes the subject of faith like a thief in the night. Only when a man-made faith is dissolved into a God-given faith does it rise to the Luther pattern. In these and like thoughts by Luther and what they clearly suggest, we come upon his basic idea, namely, the unique essence of Christian experience. The meaning of a God-given faith which gathers up in itself every resource of Christian experience and living is

---

[2] *Wesleyan New Testament,* 396.
[3] From Luther's *Commentary on the Epistle to the Romans.*

precisely what first Wesley, then Schleiermacher, defined as "the continual sense of total dependence on God." This is the root thought of Wesley's entire doctrine of Christian experience.

Thus Luther has put before us the forever open and inexhaustible book of Christian experience as far and away the best commentary on the Word of God in the Scriptures. But the development of this basic idea by Luther was hindered by immovable barriers. Wesley in a far freer climate of thought and action renewed Luther's limited appeal to the joint witness of Scripture and experience, gave it a richer, fuller development and shifted much more of the burden of proof from the plain sense of Scripture to the "sure testimony of experience." Wesley also found a precedent in Calvin's preeminent reference to religious experience in his interpretation of the Divine Word, which in his system is organically related to the work and witness of the Holy Spirit. It was clearly a renewal of the Pauline teaching about the Witness of the Spirit as the objective principle of all saving faith and all Christian experience. This doctrine was sharply defined in Wesley's first principle: "True, genuine Christian experience is the manner wherein the Holy Spirit ever did and does at this day work in the souls of men." [4]

The doctrine of Christian experience as formulated by Wesley in terms of a God-given faith is the necessary premise and approach to an investigation of his hostility to every mystical reconstruction of Christianity. It is customary in the anarchic state of current religious thought to identify mysticism outright with Christian experience. But we find in Wesley a thoroughgoing, experiential understanding of the Gospel combined with a militant opposition to mysticism of every name and nature. Harnack in his great *History of Dogma* defends with energy the thesis as a sound induction from the history of Christian thought that mysticism can never be made Protestant without doing violence to history, to Catholicism, and to Evangelical principles. Does the example of Wesley confirm or refute this thesis?

[4] Sermon 41.

The reaction of Wesley against naturalistic humanism in religion, whether the philosophical, the moralistic or the mystical variety, was radical, deep, complete. The Wesleyan doctrine of faith does recognize and retain the truth-values in humanism; but it utterly transcends every primarily intellectualistic, moralistic or mystical version of the Christian faith. A religion of ideas and feelings, whose primary reference is to the subject of faith, a religious experience whose primary trust is in considerations of natural reason or floats on the changeful tides of emotion or limits its confidences to a round of good works, is not the Wesleyan type, but its antithesis. Considerations of natural reason and systems of opinion, codes of conduct and work-righteousness, the wind and weather of subjective states and feelings, are radically subordinated therein to the objectivity of Christian experience and the Christian faith, to that of revelation and the atonement. The reference in Christian faith to a living and saving God is what really counts. All else is emptiness. An egocentric religion might have everything for sinful humanity but the power of saving faith and moral goodness in it.

What now was John Wesley's personal and official attitude toward *the particular variation of humanistic religion known as mysticism?* What significance has his judgment for us? For among the conspicuous leaders of the Modern Church, John Wesley, a master of essential Christianity and probably the best informed evangelist in the history of the faith, is a radical and thoroughgoing opponent, a life-long, militant opponent, of every mystical reconstruction of the Christian faith. His numerous judgments of mysticism are never clouded or wavering. His indictments of mysticism are always clear, strong, steadfast, relentless.

Wesley explored historic Christianity far and wide to discover its truth-values. It was while at Oxford, having read some of the writings of William Law, a pronounced mystic, that Wesley sought him out personally, and very soon began to follow him as "a sort of Oracle" on religious subjects. Somewhere then in the early thirties Wesley, under Law's influence, took probably

his first plunge into mysticism. This experiment was not entirely
due to Law's influence. Much rather Wesley's mode of life and
experience gave him just then a strong affinity for Law's monastic
mysticism. It is a just historical observation that the monastic
communities have been the natural nurseries and principal sources
of mysticism in Occidental Christianity. But what psychological
affinity could Wesley have had at any time for monastic mysticism? Practically all who have traced Wesley's religious interests in his Oxford period have emphasized his pronounced
ascetic temper and trend. But he himself knew and said that
"he lived, while at Oxford, almost like a hermit." [5] For he
then believed activity in the world to be incompatible with the
nature of Christianity. He supposed a contemplative religion of
salvation to be of the nature of Christianity. But "God taught
me better in America by my own experience." My own experience! Wesley's singular ability to reason about Christianity in
terms of experience is thrust upon the attention at every point
of his work. It was then in the spirit of the hermit that at
Law's suggestion Wesley turned to the literary gardens of the
mystics to learn the psychological secrets of union with God.
He later confessed to his total fascination for a few years with
"the noble descriptions of union with God and internal religion
made by the Mystic Writers." [6] He thus acquired from the
mystics "an entire new religion," although in his later critical
judgment "it was nothing like the religion which Christ and His
Apostles lived and taught."

Wesley's emancipation from mysticism, if we look through his
own eyes at his psychological emergence from its fascinations,
appears to have been an obscure and gradual process, but in any
event, the reaction was profound and lasting. Soon after he
fell under the influence of Law's mysticism he offered himself
to teach the Georgia Indians the Nature of Christianity and went
from England to the Colony of Georgia in order to find in its
frontier life a better, certainly a very different, laboratory to

[5] Letters, VI, 292; especially, Journal, I, 416.
[6] Journal, I, 420; Letters, I, 207.

test his theology. He thus exchanged the religion of a hermit for that of a frontiersman. For it was amid the realities of frontier life with their irresistible human incentives to creative practicalness and in an environment which presented the highest conceivable contrast to the dreamy stillness and moral passivity of life spent amongst books or in a lonely monastic cell, the natural nursery of mysticism, that John Wesley cleared and quit himself of the mystical mood in religion. The iron of American pragmatism entered his blood. After his return to England he rode too much on horseback ever to be much of a typical mystic.

Wesley's primary reaction against mysticism is recorded in an important letter to his elder brother Samuel, dated Savannah, November 23, 1736: "I think the rock on which I had the nearest made shipwreck of the faith was the writings of the Mystics; under which term I comprehend *all and only those who slight any of the means of grace.*" The first count then in Wesley's critique of mysticism is the fact that, with their bias toward a *contemplative* religion of salvation, the mystics cut themselves off from the collective consciousness of the followers of Christ, dissociate themselves from "the means of grace" and claim when the active side of man's personal life is sufficiently abandoned and he has entered fully into the passive state, that he is then one with God and is a deified man. Exactly seven weeks after this letter, Wesley, on the return voyage to England, made a profound analysis and wrote down in order the results of his whole experiment with the three variations of humanistic religion. He concluded this analytic review with another even stronger indictment of mysticism: "Only my present sense is this; all the other enemies of Christianity are triflers; the mystics are the most dangerous of its enemies. They stab it in the vitals; and its most serious professors are most likely to fall by them. May I praise Him who hath snatched me out of this fire likewise, by warning all others that it is set on fire of hell." The realistic comparison of his rescue from mysticism to his rescue from the burning Epworth rectory gives a tragic meaning to his judgment that the mystics are "the most dangerous enemies of Christianity." [7]

Now this is for us a hard saying; who can receive it in our climate of opinion where every turn and trend of thought goes rather to cancel the historical individuality of the Christian faith and to level Christianity down to the lower levels of some sort of vague universal religious consciousness? It is nowadays just about enough to be mystics. It is not so important, much less necessary, that we be definitely Christian. The truth-value of Christianity is now sought for not in its historical individuality on the principle of revelation, but in some common denominator or weird mixture of all religions and in some vague, primitive often unethical, awareness of God. The truth-value of Christianity is thus reduced to the universal mysticism of natural religion. It is reducible to the results of the primitive seeking, feeling after and finding, if perhaps! dubious hope at any rate in the judgment of St. Paul! if perhaps there may be some finding of God by man's own effort.

How often in the crises of history has the Christian Church been summoned to surrender its basic belief that there was and is an infinite difference as touching the religious question between what a St. Paul brought with him to the intellectual and artistic capital of the Mediterranean World and what he found there. The Christian Church had its first birth and has the abiding principle of its existence in the belief that it possesses now as always in the person and work of Christ the incomparable revelation of a living and saving God. And it has hitherto resisted every reductive rationalization from the standpoint of the mysticism of natural religion. The ambassador of the Gospel is not therefore an ambassador of Christ because he knows by experience what mysticism is and may even begin the construction of his missionary message with the fact of a universal seeking after, the feeling after God, which is given in the very structure of man's personal life. He does indeed know himself to be a sharer to the uttermost in all of that; and he knows that it is

[7] Journal, I, 420.

common ground for Christianity and for all other religions. But he is the ambassador of the Gospel solely and precisely because he is the competent announcer of a great discovery and the qualified witness of revelation. It may in the spirit of St. Paul be said: "The living and saving God whom you worship only in the fumbling, groping obscurity of humanity's own best efforts I know, not indeed by my own efforts, for that yielded no better results in my experience of work-righteousness than your own vague mystical awareness of God. I know the one true God only because he in his infinite grace has revealed himself first in Jesus Christ, and then his Son in me. I bring you this knowledge of a living and saving God, to be won only from the person and work of Christ, only from the Gospel."

Wesley's criticism of the mystics was thoroughgoing. The starting point was the radical conflict which he discovered between mystical principles and his religious evaluation of the Church. "Under the term, Mystics, I comprehend all and only those who slight any of the means of grace." It was Wesley's deep feeling as a churchman that was first wounded by the mystics. But this deep churchly feeling was abundantly more than blind attachment to an institution. It sprang from early perception and growing insight into *the practical dependence of the basic Christian experience upon the Church and the means of grace.* Saving faith simply does not arise without the influence of and some form of interaction with the believing community. Wesley's doctrine of Christian experience accepted the church-form of Christianity as fundamental. Now Wesley early reached the conclusion that the mystics cancelled out of the doctrine of Christian experience the idea of all mediation in religion. All intermediaries are to be set aside and excluded. But this cancels out of religion the idea of the Church and means of grace and finally undermines even the mediatorial office of Christ. Wesley's idea that all and only those are mystics who *slight any of the means of grace,* points not simply to a logical consequence but also to the actual fact that mysticism by its very nature impugns the essentially historical and social character of Christianity and collides with the Christian idea of saving faith as given by the reconciling ministry of Christ and the Church.

But is Wesley's demarcation of the mystic writers as all and only those who slight any of the means of grace a sound and serviceable definition? Is depreciation of historical revelation and of the actual historical Church a good mark of mysticism?

It is indeed hardly more than a truism of the science of comparative religions to say that Christianity of course shares to the full in the universal mysticism of all religion, or more accurately in *the mystical traits and tendencies implicit and present in all religion.* Such a reference to the universal, structural and functional significance of religion in human life is doubtless made in Tertullian's dictum: "The soul is naturally Christian." It shines out more clearly in Augustine's heart-warming words, "Thou, Lord, hast made us for Thyself!" And the human spirit knows nothing of true peace or power until it finds both in God. This also is the law of man's spiritual graviation as enunciated by St. Paul. This universal human search for God, the seeking, feeling after God is itself already a mystical awareness of the reality and presence of God. But while Christianity thus shares in full measure in the universal mysticism of all religion, this common ground does not at all reveal nor does it describe the historical individuality of the Christian faith. The historical individuality of Christianity begins precisely at the point where it transcends the universal mysticism of all religion.

But this use of the term mysticism as the virtual, if not actual, synonym of religion and of all religious experience, is very loose and careless. Such a use, though all too common, is too utterly innocent of all sound historical and experimental reasoning, which is the only possible basis of any profitable exchange of ideas on religious subjects. Since the entrance of the human spirit into right relationship with God is, along with all their differences in the thought of God, the goal, the supreme objective of every religion, since this goal is commonly, and in the higher religions, chiefly represented as salvation, it would be far better, indeed terminological conscience clearly demands, that the term mysticism be reserved for *the way and manner characteristic of the historical varieties of mysticism,* in which the right relationship—salvation, communion, union with God, has been and is to be sought and found, possessed and enjoyed. An idea without a boundary is useless. Such a historical definition would give the idea of mysticism a boundary and render the definition at once intelligible and useful. On this premise then the common ground of all religions could be usefully described or defined as the mystical traits and tendencies implicit and present in all religion. With some such bounding of the idea, clearly prescribed alike by its greater serviceableness and demanded by the historical and experiential method in theology, there would be some hope at least of mutual understanding on the subject of mysticism.

The mystical traits and tendencies common to all religions, Christianity included, are clearly recognized as fundamental by St. Paul, for example, in his Athens "Lecture of Natural Divinity." [8]   He assumed that in these respects the religion of the Greek and Hebrew peoples, of all peoples, finally also of Christianity, have something important as common ground. "I perceive you (Men of Athens) are greatly addicted to the worship of invisible powers." So the Wesleyan New Testament translates the address in the Areopagus. Moreover, the Apostle to the Gentiles chose here for once to begin with natural religion and ideas of the divine immanence. "God need not be sought afar off. For he is very near us! in us! only perverse reason thinks Him afar off." The Apostle began then at Athens not with the infinite estrangement of man from God by the fact of sin, but the natural nearness of God and he first directs attention to *the universal effort of man,* to a universal element in religious experience, namely, man, seeking as it were blindfolded, to detect the presence of Him in whom we live, move and have our being, as the starting point for his interpretation of the Christian revelation. But thanks to the restless imagina-

[8] *Wesleyan New Testament,* 325.

tion, the free curiosity, and the strenuous rationalism of his audience, the Apostle never really got round to his subject. The hearers stumbled and fell at the very threshold of the Christian faith. There was no transition for them (Is there for us?) from the ideas of natural religion to the idea of a world brought to judgment on account of sin. Some mocked; the rest were evasive but polite enough to say they would like to hear him again. But in any event the intellectualist-mystical representation of Christianity as the continuation and supplement of natural religion fell still-born among those whose chief pride and passion it was to know the very latest. It is not clear that the Apostle ever again preferred the ideas of natural religion to the facts of historical revelation, as the first foundation of his message. Soon after his futile Athens experiment he recognized no other foundation nor introduction to saving faith but Jesus Christ the Crucified,[9] or again prophets, apostles, Jesus Christ,[10] or again revelation in history and in experience.[11] Religion is man seeking, feeling after God. Revelation includes religion but is not comprehended by it. Revelation transcends religion.

If now the sole and sufficient criterion of the whole truth-value of the Christian faith and revelation is supplied by ideas of natural religion, by ideas of immanence, by ideas of mystical awareness, we might allow, indeed have to allow, that religion as man's effort to find God and historical revelation as God's discovery of himself to man are nothing different. If our best thought of God and that of the world simply come to the same thing, if all we may justly, wisely, savingly think about God must be derived strictly from and patterned exactly after what we now know about the behavior of nature and of humanity, if God is neither stronger nor weaker than the actual universe, neither better nor worse than the strange mixture of good and evil in our human world, we might have to dwell forever in the tents of natural reason and religion and the Christian con-

---

[9] I Cor. II, 2; III, 11 f.   [11] Rom. I, 1-17; Gal. I, 15 f.
[10] Eph. XI, 20.

sciousness might have to be reduced to the mystical traits and tendencies common to all religions.

But if we dared to believe that the highest truth-values in St. Paul's Areopagus address lay not in the considerations of natural reason and religion with which it begins, lay not in the worship of an unknown God on the low level of mystical awareness, furbished and polished by philosophic and moralistic manners, confounding creator and creature, ignoring the transcendence of God and passing by the feeling of infinite distance interposed by man's sin between man and God—if the major truth of Christianity is not in mysticism, then we might well hesitate to live on the husks of mysticism. The entire force of revelation, all the higher energies of religion lie in our ability and duty to think more and better of God than of the world. God is indeed most nearly like the best we can experience or think of. Yet the Christian consciousness which begins with and never strays from the true humility, the poverty of spirit, the feeling of total dependence on God that is the nature of Christian experience is stricken with shame even at the thought of comparing God with the best in man. The qualitative difference between a holy God who inhabiteth eternity and a creaturely sinful being such as man, is in the language of the Christian consciousness simply immense. God is indeed by his power always "nearer to us than breathing, nearer than hands or feet." But the difference between two persons under one roof may in terms of moral goodness be infinite. Then beside the gulf of sin, what is man as creature before the Infinite but dust and ashes.[12] His body is only a bit of the earth which itself is in turn only a pin-point in cosmic vastness and his earthly life is less than a tick of the clock in the immensity of cosmic time. Nothing short of final trust in the essential righteousness, infinite grace, and perfect compassion of the creator could give a sinful man so much as courage even to lift up his downcast eyes and turn his face Godward.

Perhaps enough has been said to arouse the suspicion that

[12] Gen. XVIII, 27.

considerations of natural reason and religion simply do not permit the unique essence of the Christian revelation and experience to shine through.   Natural religion simply shunts the unique revelational and experiential nature of the Christian faith out of the picture.   St. Paul used two ideas to change the point of view from natural and humanist religion, which begins with the idea of immanence, to historical revelation which begins with God's holy judgment of sin revealed in his work of condescending grace.

The first and worst barrier to the reception of the Christian revelation which St. Paul undertook to remove was and is a religion of pure immanence.   He therefore set himself at the very threshold of his message to correct a religion of pure immanence by subjecting it to the idea of a God who is incomparably greater than his world, needing nothing from it, or from any creature in it; a God who, if indeed he is immanent, is also transcendent.   The comment in the Wesleyan New Testament on the Areopagus address is most illuminating.   Although his annotation of the New Testament for pulpit guidance is professedly a translation and abridgment of Bengelius' *Gnomon of the New Testament,* and so very largely agrees with it, still his comment on the Mars' Hill discourse deviates radically from that of Bengel.   For Bengel, the essentials of the Pauline message lay in St. Paul's concurrence with rather than *his corrective of a religion of pure immanence.*   But Wesley saw in the *corrective* the main point and purpose of St. Paul's message.   Bengel wrote: "The one God, true, good, different from his creatures, and manifest in his creation."   Wesley rewrote: "The one true, good, God; *absolutely different from the creatures, from every part of the visible creation.*"   Wesley had a clear perception of the fact that a religion of pure immanence can have no relish of salvation in it.   A consistent religion of pure immanence leaves God himself in a dubiously salvable state, stricken with finitude.

It is St. Paul's meaning that since God transcends beyond compare all creation, we ought so far as in us lies always to think more and better, never to think the same, nor less and worse of

God, than of his creatures. At least since he is infinitely above man, how inept, perverse to liken him to what a man can make. For every sincerely cosmological religion is of necessity idolatrous; it can not think more and better of God than of the world; it can only patronize God in the creature instead of worshipping God above the creature. But now and henceforth all this haphazard groping and unethical vagueness of philosophical and mystical religion, grown rank with the idolatry of creature-worship was in the mind of St. Paul confronted by the fact of Jesus Christ. God's patience with it all was at an end. He has commanded repentance and fixed a day of judgment by a man of his own choosing, with the resurrection for a credential. But even after this ingratiating introduction by St. Paul the best of the Gospel had to be left unsaid. For we have in the Christian revelation and nowhere else the knowledge of a living and saving God. Not a word was on this occasion said about that; there is no reference to faith as the all-inclusive first principle of Christian experience. The Apostle to the Gentiles certainly intended to say more.

After nineteen centuries we Christians confess that we too must have a religion; it is nature's categorical imperative; but we know that because of the incomparable superiority of the Christian revelation we can bear no other. For the Christian faith utterly transcends the mystical traits and tendencies common to all religions, surpasses the truth-values of "natural religion." In this light it would be hard to decide which is the worse—the orthodox blindness of bygone days which refused to recognize the truth-values in other religions, or the humanist blindness of these days which refuses to recognize the incomparable superiority of the Christian faith. Likewise the nonchalant and ever-recurring prediction that Christianity is destined to be superseded by a better religion—a prediction whose best credential appears to be a total disability to think of anything better than Christianity—is on the brink of intellectual insolence. In flat opposition to this levelling-down logic Wesley affirmed [13] that

[13] Sermon 16.

"Christianity begins just where heathen morality ends and that the very first point in *the religion of Jesus leaves all pagan religion behind.*" "Christianity is not one religion among many; it is religion. He who does not know this religion, knows none, and he who knows it and its history, knows all" (Harnack).

Considerations of natural reason and religion may therefore conceal rather than reveal the unique essence of the Christian revelation and experience. St. Paul seems to have drawn some such conclusion. Wesley noted the fact that nowhere else had St. Paul less fruit than at Athens. The cause lay in the fact that Athens was "a seminary of philosophers who have ever been the pest of true religion." [14] Reflecting upon the meager results of the Athens experiment, St. Paul made up his mind en route to Corinth to have done with the philosophical and mystical approach to the Christian revelation. He decided, as if something very important had been learned, to begin hereafter not with considerations of natural religion and ideas of the divine immanence, but with historical revelation and the factual side of the Gospel. "I determined not to know anything among you Corinthians save Jesus Christ, the Crucified." There is no extant Pauline Epistle to any Christian Church at Athens. But the message of the Cross at Corinth, utterly disengaged from philosophical and mystical modes of thought, was attended with the demonstration of the spirit and power.

The *Wesleyan New Testament* observes that the whole effect of St. Paul's Corinth preaching, its one vast resource, lay in its plain historical, experiential presentation. It reversed the customary laws of logic and persuasion in philosophical circles on religious subjects. It did not mingle the Gospel with but deliberately avoided "the depths of philosophy and the charms of eloquence," so that the word of revelation which is the testimony of Christ [15] and the testimony of God,[16] verified in the experience of the preacher, stript of all accessories, should speak straight to the experience of the hearer. Wesley says: *"And they* (who open

---

[14] *Wesleyan New Testament,* 324.   [16] I Cor. II, 1.
[15] I Cor. I, 7.

their minds) *experience* that Christ is the power and wisdom of
God." So then his dynamic preaching at Corinth in contrast to
his humanistic preaching at Athens began with historical revelation, proceeded with the witness of the spirit and concluded with
an appeal to the trial of personal experience. To the miracle-
mongering mind, the Cross is a spectacle of weakness beneath
contempt. To the rationalizing mind it is a "silly tale." But
to the historical and experiential thinker, aware that revelation
and experience hold the key to the nature of Christianity, the
doctrine of the Cross, summed up in an objective revelation, an
objective atonement and objective Christian experience, may well
appear to have been the creative principle of the Christian
Church. When St. Paul says that "God has revealed to us (Wesley says "to *experienced* Christians") by his Spirit" what utterly
transcends humanistic religion, the seeing eye, the hearing ear,
the free fancy, and that "the Spirit searches even the deep things
of God," he means that religious experience is of unique essence
and is final. He means that the highest reason we can give for the
truth of the Gospel is our experience of its reality. He means
that Christian experience itself is revelation—"So the things of
God also knoweth no one but the Spirit of God." In these
thoughts St. Paul is still our most dynamic contemporary to
warn us that the strength of Christianity rests not in the effort
of man, but in the revelation of God.

The deductions here made from the evident contrast between
the fruitless intellectual-mystical interpretation of the Gospel at
Athens and the fruitful historical-experiential interpretation at
Corinth are identical with the contrast drawn by St. Paul himself between a faith whose resource is only considerations of natural reason and a faith that springs forth from revelation and
sends its roots down into Christian experience, whose truth-value
runs back to the fact that God has revealed the things beyond
the human effort, to us by his Spirit, which fathoms everything
even the depths of God himself. So then the objective principle of
Christian experience, namely, the Spirit that comes from God—
transcends all the mysticism of man's natural ascent to an im-

mediate and unmediated union with God. Revelation is the first truth of Christian experience both as to its possibility and meaning. Finally, whatever of truth-value we may choose to put upon the mystical traits and tendencies in all religion, one thing is certain: they denote and they are, the soil, not the seed, of the Christian consciousness.

We do not, therefore, improve the Christian faith by robbing it of its historical individuality. We would only beat a historical retreat from its infinite superiority into the inferiorities of a so-called universal mysticism. The experience of gnostic and mystical syncretisms through which the Christian Church once passed, safely to be sure, but not unscathed, in the second century of the Christian era is being now repeated on a vaster scale in the twentieth. The individuality of the Christian faith is challenged, again on trial. Just so the eighteenth century rethought its Christianity downward until the inane remnant was beneath serious consideration. We have gone far in the same direction. In this climate of syncretistic opinion, Wesley's radical repudiation of the mystical reconstruction of the Christian faith cuts deep, straight across one of the powerful drifts of the age. And it is of first and last importance that we undertake afresh to understand all our problems once more in the searchlight of Wesley's very strong reaction against mysticism, his return to evangelical principles, and his masterful doctrine of Christian experience. We must go back again and again to the principal fountains of historic Christianity, not at all to abide there, but to reorient our thinking, renew our strength, and resume the march of Christian progress.

CHAPTER V

THE INDICTMENT OF MYSTICISM

The mellower judgment of the mature Wesley receded far enough from his first total veto of mysticism to appraise it for its positive values as well as a valuable corrective to the Church system which prevailed in the day and generation of the great mystics. "As almost all of them lived in the Romish Church they were lights . . . in a dark place." [1] Wesley's acute observation that all mysticism on Christian premises belongs essentially, by its origin and development, in the history of the Roman Catholic system of Christianity has received strong support from historical criticism. Albrecht Ritschl and a large number of modern scholars have justified the apprehension of mysticism as Catholic piety. Harnack states the thesis incisively: "A mystic who is not a Catholic, is a dilettante." And again, "Mysticism can never be made Protestant without giving history and Catholicism a slap in the face." Denifle, Catholic scholar, incomparable master of the facts concerning Christian life and thought in the Mediaeval Church, has confirmed it by his "epoch-making" (Harnack) researches, showing how completely Eckhart, the mystic, was a disciple of Thomas Aquinas and took from him all the best he had. The case is representative and the relation is typical.

Moreover the faith-state of the soul, as described by the mystic writers, is never genuinely evangelical, never a simple product of the Gospel. If the idea of the new birth is prominent in some of the mystic writers, the idea of the forgiveness of sin is much more conspicuously absent from all of them. The mystics explored inner religious experience with sharp eyes and made many valuable observations. But the supreme mystery of Christian

[1] Letters, VI, 43.

experience in the evangelical sense remained for the most part hidden. It is the commonplace paradox of Christian faith in the evangelical sense that a man can become in the progress of Christian experience only what in faith, that is its creative significance, he already is; and this faith, like the forgiveness of sin, is God's gift unto men. The sovereign significance of saving faith in the Lord Jesus Christ remains in the mystic writers a faint and flickering light.

This observation, if true, is important; on this account it ought to be put to a test. We choose for the purpose the most loved and widely read classic of mystical and monastic piety—according to the title in Wesley's own edition, *The Christian's Pattern or a Treatise of the Imitation of Christ, by Thomas à Kempis.* This reference has maximum value for our purposes inasmuch as *The Christian's Pattern* is universally regarded as the fairest flower plucked from the garden of monastic mysticism. Wesley has the distinction of making an excellent edition of it with an independent translation from the original Latin. The Wesley edition is a fine piece of scholarship and may have been done in partial fulfillment of the obligations arising out of his Lincoln College Fellowship. The edition was published in 1735 by C. Rivington, London. Of the five articles which make the preface, four were extracted from standard authorities on the subject. The fifth is original with Wesley. No other classic of the Christian faith stands closer to Wesley's conception of religion in his pre-evangelical period (1725 to 1738) or gives us so clear an insight into the workings of his mind. Although he emancipated himself finally from its dominant influence and rejected his early extravagant estimate of it, still he always cherished it, put a positive value upon its teaching, and required his assistants in the Revival to study it.

Wesley rightly saw in *The Christian's Pattern* an earnest apprehension and an excellent exposition in monastic terms of the idea of Christian holiness or evangelical perfection as the innermost kernel of the Gospel and the Christian ethic of life. The Wesley Preface is built around the idea that "the whole Treatise on the

Imitation of Christ is a complete and finished work, comprehending all that relates to Christian perfection." It is said to expound "the essence of Christian perfection, the ways and degrees by which it is attained, and the means or instruments of it." The scope of the Treatise is said to be "that perfection which every Christian is bound to aspire to." The meaning of Christian perfection is said to be "the resemblance of God who is the first and supreme excellency, and the imitation of Christ who is the effulgance of his glory, the most perfect pattern of all holiness." "Described in the most experimental manner and as a great practical truth of religion, knowable 'not from commentaries, but experience,' the whole essence of Christian perfection consists in love which unites the soul to God."

Here we come upon several facts of major importance. First we observe Wesley already in his Oxford days, long before he met a Moravian, earnestly striving to think through the great practical truths of religion and the mysteries of the inward Kingdom of God in experiential terms and saying the full meaning of the Christian faith and life can not be fully discerned from commentaries but *by experience alone.* The search for the understanding of divine truths and the hope of attaining to a more full and inward knowledge of Christ must follow "in the path of obedience and experience." "He that willeth to do his will shall know of the doctrine." "Oh, taste and see that the Lord is good." The superiority of the pragmatic test and of experiential thinking as the key to the truth-values of the Christian faith is already implicit and actively present in Wesley's work on *The Christian's Pattern.*

But far more important is the strong light thrown on the historical orientation of Wesley's doctrine of Christian perfection. Wesley's doctrine of Christian perfection has been inadvertently stigmatized as a theological provincialism of Methodism. Here we discover that Wesley originally acquired his interest in the doctrine of holiness or Christian perfection from his intimate perusal of this most widely read and loved classic of mystical and monastic piety. He was fully convinced, chiefly under its influence, that the doctrine of Christian perfection is the inner-most kernel of the Christian ethic of life and that it is thor-oughly rooted and grounded in New Testament teaching and in the teaching of historic Christianity. In proof of the latter con-viction he has cited in his Preface fifteen passages from the Gos-pels and Epistles of the New Testament and two passages from the Church Fathers, one from Augustine, the other from Ber-nard. These references to the teaching of the New Testament and of the Church Fathers "relate," he says, "to the substance of this Treatise." The interest thus acquired in the doctrine of sanctification was never lost and from the conviction then formed Wesley never deviated,—but of this much more later.

Turning from this early and thorough grounding in the historic doctrine of Christian perfection to its religious orientation at Wesley's hands, it is very remarkable in the light of his later prin-ciples that neither in the Preface itself, nor in the Scriptural passages cited, nor in those from the Church Fathers, does the word, "faith," occur. The idea of a God-given faith as the fountain of all Christian perfection and the undergirding prin-ciple of all Christian experience and of the Christian ethic of life is conspicuous therein solely on account of its absence. In its place we find an ethical maxim of self-denial with the usual monastic specifications, and the admonition, "labor to work your-self up into a temper correspondent with what you read." What we have then in the main is the Gospel ethic of life without the Gospel dynamic. Is this the key to Wesley's cryptic remark, fourteen years later, that he was "for ten years fundamentally a Papist and knew it not"? I think so. True it is that "the grace of God" is formally recognized in the Wesleyan Preface as "above all and in all the chief instrument or means of Christian perfection." And it is there assumed that the grace of God carries in itself the power of sinless perfection. And this insight looks surely, steadfastly in the direction of evangelical truth. But we vainly search alike the Wesley Preface and *The Chris-tian's Pattern* itself for a perception of the necessary unity of the Gospel and saving faith (*Evangelica fides,* a combination first found in a Fourth Century Commentary and the oldest extant in Latin, on the First Gospel). There is no apprehension nor appreciation, at any rate it is not adequate in the mystic writers, of the necessary dependence of the experience of saving faith upon the preaching of the Gospel and all the means of grace, that is upon historical revelation.

The Christian's Pattern, as Wesley read it, does see in the nature of Christian perfection the possible meaning of God in Christian experience, first in that of Christ and then of all Christians. But this is nowhere properly connected with a distinctly religious understanding of the Gospel. Such an understanding of the Gospel always comes down to the sovereign saving significance of a God-given faith in the Lord Jesus Christ as a perfect revelation of God and a complete atonement for sin. It is clear from this brief glimpse into what Wesley took from one of the foremost classics of mystical and monastic piety that the sovereign saving significance of a God-given faith in Christ remains therein a faint and flickering light. And it is impossible by any fair reading of the documents of mysticism to find therein the peculiar religious element in the Luther-Calvin-Wesley understanding of the Gospel. Wesley never abandoned the conviction formed thus early about the importance of the doctrine of Christian perfection. But he added to it, in the progress of his experiential thinking, something tremendously important, namely, insight into the nature of saving faith. What this progress was has been sharply defined by Wesley himself. The Wesleyan Reformation began with "the return to *the old paths of salvation by faith alone,* after wandering many years in *the new paths of salvation by faith and works.*" The breach then with a semi-humanistic faith and the return to the Luther-Calvin idea of a God-given faith as the sovereign principle of all Christian experience defines the epoch of Wesleyanism.

On these premises alone can we appreciate the significant fact, pointed out by the great psychologist William James, that Evangelical Protestantism has, as history shows, abandoned the method of mysticism. "It is odd that Evangelical Protestantism should

seemingly have abandoned everything methodical in this line."
And then "Protestant mystical experience appears to have been
almost exclusively sporadic." [2] Thus the judgment of the facts
by the great psychologist agrees unwittingly with that of the historian: "A mystic who is not a Catholic is a dilettante." But
there is nothing "odd" about the facts. Historical judgment won
from adequate discipline in the history of thought runs that it
belongs to the genius of evangelical Protestantism to abandon,
precisely as it belongs to Catholic piety to pursue, the method of
mysticism. Historical theology thus strongly sustains Wesley's
judgment of mysticism as of the nature of Catholic piety. It is
worth noting also that James planted his feet, unwittingly of
course, exactly in the footprints of Wesley,[3] in the observation
that the mystical doctrine of religious experience was extrava-
gantly individualistic. Wesley said, "The Mystic writers describe
not our *common Christianity,* but you will find as many religions
as books." James observes that "the mystical Catholic books represent nothing objectively distinct. So many men, so many
minds." Moreover if the best in mysticism totally transcends
common Christianity and is accessible to very few, it follows that
the mystic experience is high and lifted up far above the plain
truth of the Gospel. Wesley had little patience for aristocracies
of any name or nature; least of all in religion. If once, then a
hundred and a hundred times Wesley stoutly disclaimed anything
in his own Christian experience that did not belong to common
Christianity and in all and every Christian experience. He
taught in season and out of season that the truth-values of the
Gospel are accessible to all Christian experience.

But while Wesley later corrected his extreme views, and
acknowledged the "excellent things in most of the mystic writers,"
even called them "providential lights in time of darkness," nevertheless his indictment of mysticism as essentially, radically unsound was never retracted, frequently reiterated, and steadfastly
sustained. His opposition to the doctrine of predestination was

[2] *Varieties of Religious Experience,* p. 406.
[3] Letters, VI, 44.

a very mild thing in striking contrast to his militant denunciation of both antinomianism and mysticism in religion. Among
all of Wesley's antagonisms in religion the opposition to mysticism is easily the strongest, deepest and most conspicuous of his
career. The depth and force of his opposition can be sensed best
in the characters he has given to the mystics and to their teachings. Here is a partial list: "The grand delusion; the plague; the
superessential darkness; high-sounding nonsense; the offspring of
hell; set on fire of hell; grand error; the spawn of Mystical
divinity; a dark pit, apparently deep only because dark; bane
of brotherly love; bane of true religion; the Mystic or the
Popish purgatory; one of those fundamental mistakes which
run through the whole Mystic divinity; the prime fallacy of
all the Mystics; my tracts against Deists, Papists, Mystics
'strike at the apple of their eye'; Mystical notions stand in full
opposition to plain Old Bible divinity; the Mystic divinity was
never the Methodist's doctrine; a whole army of Mystics are
with me nothing to St. Paul; I can not but bewail your vehe-
ment attachment to the Mystic writings; Mystic writers abound
among the Roman Catholics; the snare of the fowler; Behmen's
writings are 'most sublime nonsense, inimitable bombast, fustian
not to be paralleled'; Mysticism is not the Gospel of Christ;
Mystic divinity is a snare of the devil; the same poison of Mysticism; odious and indecent familiarity with our Maker; no conception of church communion; the reading of those poisonous
writers, the Mystics, confounded the intellects of both my
brother and Mr. Fletcher and others." One of the last of Wesley's letters, it was to a Quaker, contains this: "O be content!
I love you well; do not constrain me to speak. I do not want
to say anything of George Fox but I hope he was stark mad when
he wrote that medley of nonsense, blasphemy and scurrility
styled his 'Great Mystery.'"

These characters of mysticism as drawn by Wesley are not
confined to any one period of his life, but are found in all of his
writings, sermons, Journals, Letters, Monographs, in every period
of his ministry from 1736 to 1791. In 1789 he revised and pub-

lished "five volumes of my brother's Hymns." In doing so, although they had been revised seven times by Charles Wesley in the space of twenty years, John Wesley "corrected or expunged those that savour a little (!) of Mysticism." He did his best to cleanse the Wesleyan message of the leaven of mysticism. Herein then is summed up over half a century of consistent and fundamental opposition. There is indeed no more curious phenomenon in the history of Wesleyan thought than the fact that Wesley's fundamental, life-long, militant opposition to the mystical reconstructions of Christianity has been in our time so far forgotten that he is now currently classed as himself fundamentally a mystic who did no more than oppose certain extravagances in contemporary mystics.

How fundamental and far-reaching his opposition was can be gauged by the swift and radical change in his estimate of even Luther the moment he discovered in the great Reformer's teaching what seemed to him not only "the taint of mysticism," but also "a handle for the antinomian doctrines." The fervent eulogy of Luther in the "Sermon on Salvation by Faith," natural enough and just in the premises, gave place three years later to a decidedly critical reserve in general and to a positive reaction against his unbalanced Solifidianism and the aid, comfort, and support which the Moravian mystics extracted, apparently not without cause, from some of his teachings. He opened Luther's famous book on Galatians on June 15, 1741, with a deep sense of personal debt to the author, and with the highest praises of the book in his mind. But as he read, Wesley was disappointed, shocked, and "utterly ashamed" of himself, that hitherto he had given Luther such uncritical credence, and had in a sense "followed him for better or for worse." Now Wesley never retracted nor qualified his conscious agreement with Luther on the great principle of justification by faith. But from this time forth he became more critical. He translated in the eleventh year of his conversion-experience a *Life of Luther,* still appreciating Luther "as a man highly favored of God and a blessed instrument in His hand," but deploring his "rough, untractable spirit and bitter zeal for opinions and want of a faithful friend to rebuke him at all hazard for the things so greatly obstructive of the work of God." [4]

Reference is here made to Wesley's critical judgments of Luther not to subscribe unreservedly to them, but to indicate the psychological depth and force of his reaction against the companionate strains of mysticism and antinomianism wherever they appeared in Christianity, even in that of a Luther. What a debt he owed to the Moravian disciples of Luther! He never forgot or failed to own that debt. But he was adamant against their mysticism. It is conceding too much to say, as some do, that the issue between Wesley and the Moravians was "almost infinitesimal." A mysticism that cancels the idea of the church out of the doctrine of Christian experience, and was also in Wesley's judgment a dissolvent of all soundness in doctrinal and practical Christianity, raised for him at least anything but a trivial issue. He called predestination, never mysticism, only an opinion. Wesley stood ready and even sought after reconciliation and union with the body of Moravians which, in spite of antinomian quietism in the English branch, counted in its numbers, as he put it, "the best Christians in the World." But he would not allow on any terms the leaven of mystical antinomianism free course in his societies. "This issue," said Wesley, "can not be buried in oblivion." St. Paul was lenient with the Corinthian doubters, but stern with those who would not even try to live worthy of the Gospel. The function of the Gospel is to save men, not *in sin* but *from sinning*.

In view of the well-informed, solidly reasoned and inflexible character of Wesley's life-long opposition to mysticism, well may we ask whether there is in theological writing such a thing as *terminological conscience?* Can the primary historic concepts of theology have anything durable in their meaning? Is it the privilege of every writer on theological subjects to play the anarchist with historic meanings? Evidently we have been interpreting Wesley by our present predilections. If these collide with

[4] Journal, III, 409.

the facts, so much the worse for the facts. Whether or no Wesley's critical judgment of the mystical reconstructions of Christianity, though he certainly knew his subject and his discipline in the whole literature of Occidental mysticism was extensive, adequate, profound, is to be partly or wholly taken and accepted, there is at any rate no exegetical hocus-pocus by which his attitude toward mysticism—the historical varieties no less than his contemporaries, can be construed into even the remotest approval in principle. The Ritschlian theologians of Germany were much noted for the vigor of their opposition to mysticism. If militant opposition in principle to every mystical reconstruction of Christian faith and morals makes a Ritschlian, Wesley is the foremost master of them all. His critique of mysticism was far more thorough, profound, militant.

Wesley's original judgment of mysticism, based on his analysis of the writings of the mystics, was later much confirmed by his experience as preacher, pastor, and superintendent of the Revival. To his wide discipline in the literature of the subject was added his comprehensive experience as pastor. He represents in his own personal life the elements of feeling, thought, will, each in full, well-rounded, equal development and in well-balanced harmony. As an evangelist among evangelists he stands in the whole history of the Church without a peer in respect to the extent of his solid general information. He brought to his work as preacher, pastor, superintendent a natural sensitivity to and highly cultivated appreciation of the most delicate religious feelings. He added to a precocious talent for reasoning trained expertness in logic. To incessant activity of body and mind he added distinct genius for the practical. In particular his free time in the Oxford-Georgia period, 1730-1738, apart from pulpit and parish activities and essential health exercise, was crammed full of research in the literature of religion and of reflection upon its highest themes. There was a continual ferment of seeking and finding. A bare catalogue of his varied studies ranging from the soaring idealism of the mystics to the sheer unethical realism

of Machiavelli [5] makes a tremendous impression. It was in this
period that he read deeply and reacted strongly against the writings of the mystics. Now his judgments are not wanting in the
blood of passion. It is hard to say which reaction is stronger,
whether that against the flight of ideas in the mystics away from
historical, organized Christianity on the one hand and from a
social, open, active Christianity on the other, or that against the
fiendish politics of pure force in Machiavelli. The soaring religious idealism of the mystics is "set on fire of hell" while the
deadly destructive politics of Machiavelli is "the first-born of
hell."

Wesley's judgment of the nature and bearing of mysticism on
genuine Christianity was therefore acquired before his contacts
and conflicts with Moravian "Stillness" or "Quietism." He rejected mysticism prior to his conversion-experience in 1738. He
first met Moravian mysticism after it. Interpreters of Wesley
with a predilection for mysticism commonly and conveniently
assume, contrary to the facts, that his judgment was either in-
adequately grounded in the literature of the subject or else that
it was formed chiefly with reference to a degenerate species.
Neither argument is relevant. The Modern Church knows no
better-read mind in the literature of mysticism. With ten languages at his command he could and, as his Journals prove, did
read the mystic writings in the original. The deduction of Wesley's view on mysticism either from the supposed inadequacy of
his historical knowledge or from his experience with Moravian
Quietism is a clumsy evasion of the authority of his judgment.
His well-informed and well-reasoned anti-mystical doctrine of
Christian experience is the root, not the fruit, the cause, not the
effect of his doctrinal and pastoral conflicts with Moravian and
all other mysticism. His opposition to mysticism was fundamental, not circumstantial. It was acquired and sustained by
solid historical and experiential reasoning.

The events which issued in the complete separation of Wesleyan
Methodism from Moravian mysticism are briefly as follows: At

[5] Letters, I, 313; Letters, I, 213.

a watch-night meeting of the original society of the Revival, called by Wesley "our lovefeast in Fetter Lane," held Jan. 1, 1739, attended by about sixty-seven, seven of them leaders, Whitefield, the two Wesleys and others, those present were conscious about three in the morning of overpowering religious feelings that are reminiscent of Pentecost. The seven leaders held a conference five days later at Islington on many things of importance. They met to plan their work, to agree on a field of activity and parted with a full conviction that "God was about to do great things among us." [6] Whitefield, not an organizer and a freelance in his methods, did most of the initial trail-blazing for the Revival. It was agreed at the Islington conference that Whitefield should go to Bristol while Wesley was to remain active in the London and near by religious societies. But toward the end of March, Whitefield and others sent Wesley "the most pressing call to Bristol" to assume pastoral oversight of the Revival. "Many are ripe for the bands [the technical Wesleyan term for group meetings]. I leave that entirely to you." Whitefield already had a clear perception of Wesley's pastoral genius. On April 1, Wesley opened his Bristol Ministry by expounding "our Lord's Sermon on the Mount," which, he observed, was a case of field preaching. He was conscious of "entering upon this new period of my life," yet that it was also the natural issue of his vocational principles which gave him the world for a parish. While active in Bristol and absent from London, a certain Molther, a sincere and worthy Moravian missionary and a radical mystic, arrived in London, joined the Fetter Lane Society and began at once to win its members over from the Wesley-Whitefield evangelical teaching to his "mystical" Christianity. Wesley at once, having learned the facts even before he came back to London, wrote and preached the sermon on the "Means of Grace" as a corrective to this mysticism.

A struggle began in November between the Moravian and the Wesleyan element in the Fetter Lane Society for leadership and control. While Wesley was on the ground, Molther was no

[6] Phillip's *Life of Whitefield*, Ch. IV.

match for his genius. Wesley was in surpassing measure master of men. But he was too much absent and active in other places. The Moravian doctrine of "Stillness" therefore gradually gained ground and finally got the upper hand. On July 20, 1740, Wesley and about eighteen, seeing the breach was inevitable, formally withdrew after a declaration of principles, and united themselves with another society at the Foundery. This secession and union is the origin of the United Foundery Society. Thus a radical reaction against Moravian mysticism which, true to the genius of mysticism, took from Christian faith every historical foundation, every social restraint, every pragmatic test and set it adrift upon a boundless sea of pure subjectivity, is the birthmark of the first foundation, or at least, the foremost among the first foundations of the Wesleyan Reformation. For in spite of the fact that the First United Body at Bristol was formed a little over a year before,[7] and that the Wesleyan movement acquired its first piece of property and defined its property system and policy in connection with the New Room at Bristol, the London Foundery Society has strangely enough enjoyed an undisputed historical primacy as the First Society of the Wesleyan Reformation. Actually the Bristol Society clearly appears to be the first foundation of "the people called Methodists." But since the Bristol United Society was the joint work of Whitefield and John Wesley, primarily that of Whitefield's evangelism, while the Foundery was exclusively a Wesley project, and since the Foundery Society came to be easily the central and most significant United Society during Wesley's lifetime, it is easy to see why the title to the first foundation has had to yield to the title to the foremost foundation of the early Wesleyan Reformation. But whether the first or foremost of Wesley's foundation or both, it stands written that opposition to mysticism is an original and constituent factor of the Wesleyan Reformation. The Wesley spirit of church co-operation could overlook the issues raised by the doctrine of predestination, but not the issues raised by mysticism and antinomianism. The principle of toleration

[7] Whitefield's Journal, July 11, 1739.

as he conceived it included predestination, but excluded the anti-church, anti-social and anti-ethical tendencies implicit in mysticism.

The first volume of Standard Sermons (1-12) wrestle throughout with the first principles of Christian experience. It opens with the Oxford discourses on *saving faith* and closes with a sermon on *the means of grace*. The latter sermon, in spite of strong whiffs in some of the paragraphs of a dogmatism that Wesley later openly disavowed, stands second to none in importance. The great inclusive subjects treated in all these sermons are: God; his grace in Christ our all; The Standard of the Christian Ethic of grace is Christ; the Atonement is primarily and wholly God's work; it has boundless efficacy in moral goodness, in holiness of heart and life; all Christian experience is the work and witness of the Holy Spirit; Christian experience rests ultimately and forever upon historical and continuous revelation; saving faith with all its holy potentialities which is "the mystery of Christian experience" can not begin or continue without the Church and the means of grace. We can sum up in four terms: (1) God, (2) his Grace in Christ, (3) in his Church and (4) in Christian experience. For Wesley's doctrine of Christian Faith begins with the church-form of Christianity and does not depart from it. The life principle of this form of Christianity is the idea of the grace of God. But in order to do justice to Wesley's doctrine of faith we shall have need of another idea which is like unto the doctrine of grace. It is the idea of the Kingdom of God, of God actively ruling, actively regnant in our entire human experience-world. The second idea receives its richer, fuller development in the thirteen Expository Sermons based on the résumé of the Teachings of Jesus in the Hillside Teaching.[8] Now these two ideas, each comprehensive of Christianity, are treated by Wesley not as conflicting principles, but as one and inseparable. For while his Christian ethic is in the most thoroughgoing sense an ethic, not of human freedom but primarily of divine grace, it never terminates for Wesley in a mystical

[8] Matthew V-VII.

quietism but always in a world-transforming, practical activity, in a social, open, active Christianity, comprehending personal and social life in its totality. Nothing in our human experience-world is exempt from or lies outside the application of the Christian principle. The perfect circle of Christian truth has two foci or centers: absolute trust in the grace of God; the active doing of God's Will among men.

In all these discourses, in particular that on *the means of grace* which unfolds Wesley's religious evaluation of the Church, Wesley reveals as a thinker his synthetic grasp of great subjects, —as a theologian his judicial balance and deep understanding of the general experience of the Christian Church, as a preacher his deep insight into the realities of Christian experience, as a pastor of souls his consummate wisdom and power with men.

The Wesleyan indictment of mysticism has four counts against it:

(1) It cancels out of the doctrine of Christian experience the idea of the Church as the fellowship of the redeemed which refers its origin and existence with all of its revealing and redeeming activities to the person and work of Christ. Instead of recognizing the necessary and total dependence of Christian experience upon historical revelation in the person and work of Christ and upon the continuation of his revealing and redeeming activities in the Church as the body of Christ, mysticism seeks, that is the nature of mysticism, to attain to union with God by escape from every historical, social or empirical condition of Christian experience. The Wesleyan view is that the door of Christian experience swings wide open only to him who is met and mastered by the Word of God. Now the testimony that alone can awaken faith must proceed from the believing fellowship of Christ. Only by active participation in its quickening life can any one confess experientially, that is by the Holy Spirit, that "Jesus is Lord." But the Church and the means of grace, taken in the most comprehensive and dynamic sense, are for typical mysticism at best a superfluity, essentially a hindrance and at worst an insurmountable barrier to the mystic experience.

Wesley, who could read in many languages, having read the

mystic writers widely and searched them out earnestly for their deeper motivation and meaning, complained that he could find in none of them a proper conception of the mediatorial office and activities of Christ and his Church, nor a proper appreciation of the indispensableness of the preaching and personal study of the Word of God, of the living witness of the Church, of all the means of grace not only as the necessary source but also as the sustaining ground of Christian experience. He agreed with A. H. Francke, a historical reference of the highest importance for Wesley, that "every mystic has *a religion of his own*. They do not describe *our common Christianity*." "It is very true," observed Wesley, that "if you study the mystic writers, you will find as many religions as books; and for this plain reason, each of them makes his own experience the standard of religion." [9] Now Wesley's radical reaction against mysticism in principle followed hard upon and was intimately associated with his intensive study of Francke and was therefore probably caused in part, perhaps chiefly, by it. Wesley's words are: "That wise and good man, Professor Francke, used to say of the mystics, etc.," and what he used to say "is very true." The reference points to a primary historical source of his anti-mystical doctrine of Christian experience.

Wesley was by no means the slave of traditional Christianity, nor did he ever inculcate or exemplify a purely passive mind toward even the teaching of Scripture, much less that of the visible Church; nevertheless he believed that the great common convictions of Christendom were and are, and must be for every Christian thinker, at least the beginning of wisdom in the understanding and interpretation of the Gospel. He was entirely free from the desolate, shallowing, poverty-stricken conceit of modernism which measures the degree of any man's intellectual freedom in religion by the amount of his dissent from historic Christianity. Experience is indeed the standard of religion. But it is not the experience of an islander who with a minimum knowledge of the Christian faith to begin with has also lost all further contact or communication with the main lands of historical Christianity. The only trustworthy experience becomes progressively normative by a maximum of instruction, inspiration,

[9] Journal, I, 116, 124; Letters, VI, 44.

orientation, enrichment out of the general Christian experience. Traditional Christianity must of necessity submit to progressive experiential thinking. No less does the fruitful experiential thinking of any Christian continuously depend for its birth and bread on historical Christianity.

(2) The mystical reconstruction of the Christian faith is in principle and largely in practise a religion of defeat and retreat in utter despair of the Kingdom of God among men and of the social application of the Gospel. "The flight of the alone to the Alone" cancels Christian sociology. Wesley's critique of monastic mysticism from this point of view [10] is incisive, searching, profound. There and elsewhere he stoutly maintains that a solitary Christianity is an experiential contradiction. "Christianity is essentially a social religion; to turn it into a solitary religion is indeed to destroy it." Wesley's insight into and deliberate emphasis on the necessary social character not alone of all the activities of the Christian spirit, but also on the necessity of the Christian fellowship for the origin and vigor of true Christian feeling, received early and definite expression in the Hymn Book of 1739. The Preface first repentantly confesses that some of the hymns are tainted with mysticism and then it indicts mystical divinity for its essential humanism; it is egocentric salvation; it refers salvation to man's effort and not to the Christian atonement. And it is also a "Solitary religion." But "the Gospel of Christ knows of no religion but social, no holiness but social holiness. Faith working by love is the length and breadth and depth and height of Christian perfection."

(3) Mysticism of the historic varieties isolates the religious consciousness too much from the free, earnest, active use of intellect in religion; very often it must be admitted as a justifiable reaction against or necessary compensation for a desolate and barren theorizing Christianity. It has often disparaged therefore the theology of the intellect and that of the will for that of the feelings. Mystical religion is not seldom indeed a sort of natural revenge upon institutionalism or intellectualism or moralism in religion. Subjectively considered, the truth of religion must be both seen and felt and put into practise in order to realize in full its truth-value. We have now in Wesley's

[10] Sermon 19. Journal, I, 420.

doctrine of Christian experience a magnificent model of experiential thinking which includes alike the theology of the intellect, of the will, and of the feelings, enlists alike head, hand and heart and allows to each its full right in Christian experience and its interpretation.

(4) Mysticism of the historic varieties exhibits a fatal gravitation toward disreputable sentimentality. It has indulged, as Wesley put it, in "an odious and indecent familiarity with the Deity." There are three things in religion that Wesley loathed: One is a desolate theorizing Christianity, a skeleton religion, starved, emaciated, reduced to the bloodless categories of the intellect. Another is a Christianity which traffics with the pure, free, almighty grace of God in terms of good works. But, if possible, he hated still more the sensuous sentimentality of certain types of religion, in describing the union of the soul with God as if it were the mating of sexes. The mystical descriptions of union with God often revel in the most realistic imagery of the sex-relation. It has portrayed communion with God in the loud colors of suppressed sexuality as in the monastic orders—the natural nurseries of mysticism in religion. Witness the strange inordinate fondness of the mystic writers for the amorous language, realistic sex-imagery and strong emotional word-pictures of the Song of Solomon, a sensuous Oriental love-song. For a test out of numerous cases, consider a hymn by the great Spanish mystic, St. John of the Cross, rated one of the greatest, who in his book, *The Dark Night of the Soul,* has said "all the best that mysticism had to say." The mystic pictures a dark night in which the soul, stripping herself of everything, goes forth to meet her Lord, and "secretly, seen of none," Lover and Beloved meet, unite, in a "night far sweeter than the dawn"; "with his fair hand he touched me lightly on the neck"; and the picture closes with the soul "lying quite still in sweet abandonment." Yet this picture, reeking and dripping with sex suggestion, is rated "the great hymn of mysticism," and is supposed to be religious. But let any one turn from the great hymn of mysticism to the great hymns of Methodism; let him sense the tone and trend of Charles Wesley's "Wrestling Jacob," in which the story of Jacob at Peniel is transmuted into an epic of the inner life wherein the soul in the Dark Night is overtaken by and wrestles in fear and

trembling with the unknown and terrible fate-God, until this awful God is revealed in the mystery of Christ as a friend-God whose name and nature is redeeming love. There is simply an infinite moral distance between the soft sensuous amorousness of the choice hymn of mysticism and the heroic, victorious ethical activity of the great hymns of Methodism. The love-dalliance of the former and the moral daring of the latter hymns simply represent lower and higher levels of the religious consciousness. The hymn of the great mystic knows nothing of the sin and self-despair or of the righteousness that is rooted in the sovereign significance of saving faith, of the total dependence on God, that are the very soul of Charles Wesley's "Wrestling Jacob," and of the whole Wesleyan message. To this may be added the lines characteristic of what has been called the Marseillaise of Methodism, "A charge to keep I have," with its magnificent vocational idealism and its challenge to translate an ethic of divine grace into a strenuous life of pure Christian service.

This fact alone of a chronic preference for the soft, amorous language of the Song of Solomon in describing communion with God over the vigorous religious and ethical teaching of an Isaiah or a Jeremiah or of Jesus in the Synoptic version, of the interpretation of Christ by St. Paul or in the Fourth Gospel, so indicative, revealing, symptomatic of the spirit and genius of mysticism, is alone enough to give any thinking Christian an arresting pause before committing himself to this intricate phenomenon in the history of the Christian faith as the best pattern of Gospel interpretation.

CHAPTER VI

THE GATE OF RELIGION

The Wesleyan doctrine of Christian experience retained the truth in Anglican Arminianism. It assumed that "man is not entirely passive in the business of salvation"; it asserted that the human receptivity of the Gospel is an act of self-determination and is of radical importance. For it is a necessary condition, always present, never absent from the experience of saving faith. And all this is one in principle with the recurrent reference to experience in Wesley's theology. At the same time the humanist standpoint in Anglican Arminianism was radically subordinated to the early Reformation idea of a God-given faith. The latter attained to complete supremacy in Wesley's teaching and preaching. Now Wesley's exit from mysticism was as deeply involved in this reconstruction of the doctrine of Christian experience as was the trial and rejection of the intellectualist and moralist approach to religion.

The experiment with what Wesley called work-righteousness and his reaction against it is well known. Bishop Secker thought Wesley's protest against "salvation by works" was quite out of date and no longer useful. But is human nature ever out of date? Wesley confessed, "I am one who for twenty years used outward works . . . as commutations instead of inward holiness. . . . Nor did I ever speak close to one who had the form of godliness without the power but I found he had split on the same rock. Look into the facts; you will surely find it is the very thing which almost destroys the (so called) Christian world."[1] He is referring to Anglican Arminianism in his confession that he "had wandered many years in the *new path* of sal-

[1] Letters, II, 59, 73; Twenty years: 1718-1738.

vation by *faith and works*." He is referring to the faith of the
first reformers when he continues, "about two years ago it
pleased God to show us the *old way* of salvation by *faith only*."
After wandering in Anglican Arminianism many years, he rediscovered "the true Christian saving faith," which he represented
variously as "the root of Christianity," as "the door or the gate
of religion."

Intellectualistic religion, whether the unbelieving sort of deistic
naturalism or the believing sort of traditional, ecclesiastical theology, is given a very low rating in Wesley's doctrine of Christian
experience.   Orthodoxy is rated a poor credential of genuine
Christianity.   He pronounced "orthodoxy at best but a very
slender part of religion." [2]   "Religion does not consist in orthodoxy, right opinions." "They are not in the heart but in the understanding." "A man may be orthodox in every point, assent to
all the creeds, be almost as orthodox as the devil . . . and may
all the while be as great a stranger as he to the religion of the
heart." [3]   "Of all religious dreams, trust in orthodoxy is the
vainest, which takes hay and stubble for gold tried in the fire."
Wesley's writings abound in anti-intellectualistic utterances of
this character.   Although he believed and practised the maxim
that "true religion is the highest reason," he did not expect to
find spiritual grapes growing on intellectualist thorns.   Only
when the truth-values of the Gospel are committed to experiential
thinking which goes to the bottom of the heart, do they make a
difference.

But even more important for our investigation of Wesley's radically anti-mystical doctrine of Christian experience is the fact
that his final no to an ego-centric salvation was a comprehensive
veto alike of intellectualism, moralism and *mysticism* in religion.
Their common root, as he understood and experienced them, is
the primary reference of the highest truth-values of Christian
experience to the human subject.   The essence of religious experience in humanist terms is comprised in the striving and effort

[2] "Plain Account of People called Methodists," 1748.
[3] Sermon 7.

of man, not in the revelation and condescension of a gracious God. Christian experience is a tall mountain piercing the clouds, lifting its head into the light of eternal sunshine. Humanism of the intellectualist, the legalist and the mystical kind tells us that we may expect to meet God only at the summit when the climb is done, not in the valley before it is begun. The Christian faith revolutionizes all that. The prophetic-Christian idea of God puts the divine initiative first. "We love him because he first loved us." The inner nature of Christian experience is the personal trust of the justified sinner in *the father-love* of a personal, all-powerful, eternal, holy God, which father-love is revealed to us in the person and work of Christ and is assured to us by our inclusion in the believing community of the justified and thus in the God-consciousness of Jesus. The deepest and dominant intuition of Christian experience is that saving faith is the gift and work of God. Any reference in salvation to the human subject raises the whole issue of good works. But this reference is dominant in the intellectualist, moralist, and mystical theory of religion. They are all variants of humanistic religion.

The importance of this insight for the Wesleyan Reformation can be tested and traced better than anywhere else in his emancipation from mysticism. The Journals for the Georgia Mission [4] from mid-October 1735, through January 1738 depict and interpret the varied experiences of these twenty-seven and a half months, over five of them on the two voyages, in the light of the Pauline comment on another experiment that failed: "Because they sought righteousness not by Faith but, as it were, by the Works of the Law." [5] Wesley has prefixed a Scripture passage to each of the principal stages in his Journal which he intended for the interpretative key. Accordingly he looked back over his long preconversion period, thirteen years, of ardent seeking and finding. He saw in it a slow but sure pilgrimage from the town of Legality to the foot of the Cross. We out of whose Christian consciousness the idea of the Cross was nigh unto van-

[4] Journal, I, 104-424.
[5] Rom. IX, 30, 31.

ishing away may want the very alphabet of Wesley's doctrine of Christian experience. What can an experiential pilgrimage from the town of Legality to the foot of the Cross mean? Moreover the term, Legality, accents the moralistic reduction of the Christian faith. But Wesley's trial of the humanistic approaches to religion was much more radical and comprehensive. It took in intellectualism and mysticism. But who would venture to identify the self-sufficient humanism of our time with the irreligious spirit of the ancient town of Legality from which Wesley, like Christian, escaped? Who would suspect that the current confusion of tongues, as to what Christianity really is and what its bearing on the problem of life could be, has any connection with our man-built towers of self-improvement rising to the very gates of heaven? Our towers are machines and the scientific control of natural forces. Why should the modern man be concerned at all to have God in his thinking? Man is self-sufficient! Nevertheless signs are not wanting that Paul, Luther, Wesley will be yet again far more our contemporaries than we of the past generation have been thinking.

On the return voyage from America Wesley, on nearing England, "wanting but one hundred and sixty leagues of the Land's End," records January 24, 1738, the fact that "My mind was now full of thought, part of which I writ down as follows." What he wrote down was the results of a stern stock-taking analysis of his thirteen-year-long experiment with an idea of the Christian faith that failed. The account of an experiment that yielded chiefly negative results begins with intellectualism and concludes with mysticism. Between the attempt to reason himself into saving faith and the attempt to emotionalize himself into it, came the exclusive efforts to do enough to be sure of the grace of God, that is, to earn it by the discipline of the will. The entire humanistic scheme was tried out to see if it could unlock the door into Christian Assurance and Christian Holiness, into saving faith and moral goodness, by an energetic self-discipline of the intellect, the will, the feelings. Intellectualism, moralism, mysticism are therefore, according to Wesley's suggestive analysis, the three primary variations of the humanistic approach to Christian experience. But they are in the judgment of Wesley, which was derived from and based on experience, all of them alike failures precisely because they are humanistic, precisely because, as Wesley acutely observes, "they are refined ways of *trusting to my own works.*" These ego-centric confidences—whether considerations of natural reason, or codes of activity in really good works, or the intensive discipline of the feelings and the self-rapture of the soul into union with God—fail utterly in the judgment of Wesley to rise to the levels of Christian experience. Here we may perceive the fundamental unity in Wesley's critique of intellectualism, moralism, mysticism in religion. They are ego-centric, humanistic. And Wesley informs us that he was "not a little surprised" over the poverty-stricken results of his explorations of all these humanistic approaches to religion.

Wesley admitted that throughout the experiment he had not yet discovered the fact that "he had been all this time building on the sand." Not until he changed radically his entire point of view from work to faith, from nature to grace, from man to God, from a humanistic to a theocentric doctrine of Christian experience, focussing thought and fixing attention upon "God in Christ reconciling the world unto himself," did the Gospel finally yield up to him its sublimest secret of peace and power. "I was," he said, "not without short anticipations of the life of faith." "But still I fixed not this faith on its right object. I meant only faith in God (mysticism), not faith in and through Christ (Christian experience). Again I knew not that I was wholly void of this (Christian) faith; but only thought I had not enough of it." So that when Wesley was confronted by the Moravians with Luther's profoundly religious understanding of the Gospel which deduced salvation from a God-given faith in Christ, he "was quite amazed and looked upon it as a new Gospel." [6] But he agreed to submit the whole question to the decision,—as a matter of fact he demanded that *"the dispute be put upon the issue of Scripture and experience."* Böhler eagerly

[6] Journal, I, 471.

consented. Then Wesley notes significantly, "I first consulted the Scripture." Being for himself a crucial test, it had to be a thoroughgoing examination. When it was done, Wesley found that the New Testament "all made against me." Well, now if the teaching of Scripture is infallible and if the meaning of the New Testament is thus plain, unmistakable, as Wesley admitted, why cling any longer to the human No; why not let belief take final hold of intellect, feeling, will and surrender? For Wesley the last obstacle was simply this: *Scripture alone is not enough;* it lacks something. Now this is for us, as it was for him, the most significant hesitation of his entire career, of his entire research into the nature of Christianity. We are face to face with the most modern as well as the most radically significant issue Wesley ever faced. "I was forced," he confessed, "to retreat to *my last hold.*" "My last hold!" The humanistic No of distrust and unbelief had one final stronghold, as Wesley still confidently supposed. What was it? *"Experience!* would never agree with the *literal interpretation* [the italics are Wesley's] of those scriptures. Nor could I therefore allow it to be true, till I found some living witnesses."

This was a test case of maximum importance both in the personal experience of John Wesley and in the historical development of Protestant Christianity. It was plainly the crucial decision in Wesley's career. Moreover in the procedure agreed upon and carried out, we come upon a new system of discovering and demonstrating the truth-value of the Christian faith. The principle of method was at least new in the clearer apprehension of it, new in the more thorough application of it, and new in the absolute trust built upon it. The plain teaching of Scripture is by itself not enough. It requires an additional credential to establish its truth-value. It must be made authentic by "the sure testimony of experience." "The Oracles of God" require "the sure testimony of experience" to carry any conclusion about the truth-value of the Christian faith and to command the full, free consent of mind and heart to the plain teaching of the Scriptures. *So the Word of God in the Scriptures must be identified—this is final, as the Word of God in experience.* The highest reason which we can give for the truth-value of the Christian faith is the experience of its reality. Thus the procedure defined and applied by Wesley in accepting the basic truth of the Protestant Reformation, *Salvation by faith only,* became a paradigm of theological method for Wesleyanism precisely as Luther's personal religious experience molded for a time the theological method of Early Protestantism. This is evidently a primary and principal historical source of the theology of experience.

The Wesleyan procedure was as follows: First came the examination of the New Testament. For Wesley positively denied that the religious experience described in the Old Testament, though rich in its anticipations, could be "the standard of Christian experience." [7] If then the sense of Scripture is not plain to the inquirer, he may consult the best helps, Wesley says, "The experienced." But the inquiry and judgment must be his own. Secondly, the sure testimony of experience must, by listening to "the experienced" and above all to the Voice of God in one's own personal life, be taken. Accordingly the joint-witness of Scripture and experience is the regulative idea of Wesleyan theology. Wesley in a very few cases pairs Scripture with reason instead of experience. But in such cases—they are rare—the term reason may be a hang-over of a rationalizing theology or, what is more likely in Wesley's case, it is a metonym of experience. For it is not even open to question that Wesley consciously, deliberately used the term *experimental* in preference to the term *rational* and considered it incomparably more significant in getting at and expressing the truth-values in Christian doctrine. We find him often using two seemingly disparate tests of truth-values: (1) Scripture is the most decisive of all proofs; [8] (2) experience is the strongest of all arguments.[9] But these are, as active principles, correlative, interactive and in substantial agreement, so that the Word of God in Scripture and in experience is not a house divided against itself but is invested by their con-

[7] Letters, IV, 11.   [9] Letters, VII, 129; Sermon 15.
[8] Letters, VI, 245.

currence with the highest truth-value for the religious consciousness. Now this regulative idea of Wesleyan theology has been
clearly stated in the Preface to the Standard Sermons: The Scriptural, experimental religion, no more, no less, is the true religion.
Thus the agreement of Scripture and experience is taken and
accepted as the highest truth-mark of Christianity. Wesleyan
theology is therefore in its original conception, and also in its
actual development, a theology of the Word of God that is in
the most radical sense a theology of experience and a theology of
experience that is in the most thoroughgoing sense a theology
of the Word of God. To complete the description we need one
more term: The Wesleyan theology is never speculative, but
first, last and always practical theology.

The question comes here whether it would be safe to follow
Wesley in building so extensive a trust upon Christian experience
and its indications in the discovery and interpretation of the
Word of God. Are "the Oracles of God" not thus very unequally
and most dangerously yoked together with "the sure testimony
of experience"? If we allow that the Oracles of God must receive an experiential verification and that the acceptance of the
plain teaching of the Bible must be held in suspense until the
witness of experience is taken, and even then that the truth
learned must be confirmed in the personal religious experience
of the inquirer, do we not thus expose the Christian faith to
the wind and weather of modernism? The answer is we do and,
what is more important, also that the Christian faith must be
able and is in fact well able to stand all the wind and weather
of modern thought. It is perfectly safe to strike a match in
God's universe. Moreover this Wesley attitude toward the Christian faith, this Wesley way of getting at its truth-value is alone
scientific. For the test—*Try me and know my nature*—is now
not only scientific in nature but it is also the Gibraltar of the
Christian apologetic. We have, in the language of St. Paul, been
shut up to this way by the discovery that there is no other
thoroughfare.

Wesley then refused, in making this crucial test, to be too easily persuaded. He stood his ground. Scripture is not enough. Bring on the living witness. It is not enough that we have a written record of the fact that God has spoken by the prophets, or even by his Son. That is only history. He is the God of the living. He must be able to speak to us now. "Faith is the voice of God in the heart proclaiming itself." "Religion is the life of God in the soul of man." Christian experience is the dynamic presence of the living God. Now this view of faith may seem to be the very stuff of mysticism. And if it is truly the soul of Wesleyanism, how could he consistently oppose mysticism?

The portals by which Wesley entered into the experience of saving faith is not the way of mysticism. The disciples of Luther's religious understanding of the Gospel stormed, in the Spring of 1738, the last citadel of the humanistic No, by confronting Wesley with the living witness. Five disciples of Luther's doctrine of faith "all testified of their own personal experience that a true, living faith in Christ is inseparable from a sense of pardon for all past and freedom from all present sins." They added with one mouth that "this faith is the gift, the free gift of God." Wesley summed up the net result of this unprecedented appeal from the New Testament to the authority of experience with the admission: "On Sunday, April 23d, I was beat out of this retreat too, by the concurring evidence of several living witnesses. . . . Here ended my disputing. I was now thoroughly convinced."

We are indebted to Peter Böhler for other essential facts. "I took," he says, "four of my English brethren to John Wesley. They told one after another what had been wrought in them. Wesley and those that were with him were as if thunderstruck at these narratives. I asked John Wesley what he then believed. *He said four examples were not enough.* I replied I would bring eight more here in London. After a short time he stood up and said, 'We will sing that hymn:

Hier legt mein Sinn sich vor dir nieder.' "
(My soul before Thee prostrate falls.)

Since the voyage in the Winter of 1735-36 to Georgia, Wesley had
mastered and made his own, with an intimacy of feeling peculiar
only to himself, many hymns of Christian faith and experience
in the German emanating from Pietistic circles. They were in-
tensely evangelical. Some of them seem to have gained rather
than lost in their religious quality by his translation of them.
The hymn Wesley asked for mirrors a soul deep in the valley of
humiliation and despair, overripe to resign all trust in man,
made ready by a long inglorious experiment in self-salvation, to
build an absolute trust upon the grace of God in Christ. We
are indebted to Peter Böhler, his chief mentor at this time on
"the faith whereby alone we are saved," for an important detail
which the meticulous and consistent reticence of Wesley about the
purely private and personal aspects of his conversion-experience
barred from the Journal. Böhler informs that Wesley—we may
be sure he was watched with eagle eye—"during the singing of
the Moravian version often wiped his eyes." Here then was
something more than an active and powerful intellect, also a
man of deep, rich, strong feeling. Soon after this hearing of
these testimonies, Wesley in his own room declared to his mentor that he was now satisfied about the nature of saving faith
and was done with any further doubt or questioning. Wesley has
confined his narratives to the objective significance of his conversion-experience. This he always read in terms of the principles involved and the results produced, and not in terms of
the extremely variable psychological concomitants of their experiential apprehension. The one exception is in the clause "I
felt my heart strangely warmed," and "I then testified openly
to all there *what I now, May 24th, first felt in my heart.*" But
this passage stands solitary, unique in Wesley's autobiography
and among the multitudinous accounts of the origin of the Revival. This extraordinary objectivity of Wesley about religious
matters pertaining to himself explains the fact that in his several

accounts of the origin of the Revival he has seldom referred to the days, Sunday, April 23rd, and Wednesday, May 24th, which especially marked progress in his own personal apprehension, insight, assurance as to the nature of saving faith, but he has given instead the day, Monday, March 6th, on which *"I began preaching this new doctrine of salvation by faith alone, though my soul started back from the work."*

But this strict objectivity of Wesley in tracing the course of the Revival in terms of the history of preaching rather than the purely private aspects of his religious experience has greatly deceived the unwary in respect both to the essential facts and their relative importance. The three major steps in Wesley's conversion were: First his conviction that the doctrine of salvation by faith alone was the teaching of the New Testament and of the Church of England. Secondly, the demonstration of the living witness that this doctrine is clothed with the authority of present experience. Third and last, the discovery that the idea of a God-given faith in Christ unto salvation on which the Moravians insisted as the first principle of Christian experience also comes to us vouched for by the personal experience and authority of the great Luther; and then, and first then, the full and final Yes—"the Everlasting Yea," of Wesley's own experience.

It could not be plainer that the indeterminate point with which Wesley wrestled was the nature "of that faith whereby alone we are saved." This resolved itself into two questions: *How is the experience of saving faith given?* and *What are the fruits (again in terms of experience) of living faith?* This crisis of his faith was precipitated on March 5, 1738, at Oxford. "I was on Sunday the 5th clearly convinced of unbelief, of the want of that faith whereby alone we are saved." The next day he "began preaching this new doctrine." The crisis therefore lasted full eighty days, through the months of March, April and May, that is, if we stick to May 24th as Wesley's *Aufklärungszeit*. Seven weeks were spent in digging up the roots of doubt and in gathering the arguments to satisfy Wesley's "active and powerful intellect"

(Lecky). That the doctrine "Salvation by Faith alone" was decidedly strange to Early Oxford Methodism is demonstrated by the shock which it at first gave to every member of that circle Wesley included, as well as in all other circles. But this transition from a humanist to a theocentric doctrine of Christian experience was carried forward by powerful forces and was at the end of seven weeks clear of all prejudicial barriers. Ripe for conviction, Wesley, it could be truly said, then waited still another month for word, the decisive word, the authoritative word, from Martin Luther.

It is generally agreed that the vital part of Luther's faith, the experiential element whose "adequacy to the deeper parts of our human mental structure is shown by its wild-fire contagiousness when it was a new and quickening thing" (James) was renewed and continued in Pietism. "There is in Pietism something of the original impulse of the Reformation. The subjective religious life (the insistence on conversion, on the personal turning to God in Christ) asserts itself against religion objectified in Church doctrine and ordinance,—Luther rebels against Lutheranism." To this direct influence of Pietism, Paulsen has referred Immanuel Kant's deep respect for the religious view of life and the world.[10] It is also known to be a principal source of Schleiermacher's interpretation of the nature of religion. Its influence has touched and quickened every vital phase of modern religious thought. Ritschl's unfortunate disparagement of Pietism has been entirely overcome and reversed by recent thought. A constructive view—it is well stated by Troeltsch,[11] now prevails and rates the positive influence of Pietism not only very high in its effects but also far more appreciatively in its quality. But exactly threescore years before Schleiermacher is said to have introduced the leavening influence of Pietism into modern theology, which is revealed in the primacy which he accords to religious experience in his conception of the nature of religion,[12]

[10] Paulsen, *Immanuel Kant* (Eng. Tr.), pp. 12-21, 27-29.
[11] *Kultur der Gegenwart, Die Christliche Religion*, 407-423.
[12] Wobbermin, *The Nature of Religion* (Eng. Tr.), 1933.

John Wesley created a new system of doctrinal and practical Christianity whose alpha and omega is *the meaning of God in Christian experience.*

The impulse came to Wesley also in part from German Pietism, as a continuation of the most vital part of Luther's faith and the original impulse of the Reformation. These are precisely the ideas of Christian faith which made Wesley's doctrine, acquired in the Spring of 1738, seem "new, strange, shocking, scandalous," first to Wesley himself and those with him and then to his Anglican contemporaries.

These ideas of saving faith and its sovereign significance find expression in the evangelical hymn which Wesley asked the little circle to sing at the moment when he was first thoroughly convinced of the truth of *Salvation by faith alone.* This hymn emanated from a circle under the influence of "the wise and good Professor Francke." [13]   It is from the pen of Richter, one of Francke's helpers, and it is still found in the Lutheran Hymnal, (No. 355). Wesley's felicitous translation is found unabridged in the very earliest Methodist hymnals.

If now Wesley began during this crisis of his faith to bear down hard in private conference and in public preaching upon "instantaneous conversion," "believing in a moment" and gave henceforth a conspicuous position in his message to the proposition "that God *can* (at least, if He *does* not always) give that faith whereof cometh salvation in a moment, as lightning falling from heaven," it must fairly be understood in the light of the fact that he was not for one moment either then or later enforcing the uniform necessity of such a conversion, but was simply blasting out of the humanized Christianity all around him the dogma of its impossibility. And he destroyed this dogma, root and branch, using as his principal weapon the scientific formula that the best argument for religion is religion, that the highest verification of the truth-values of the Christian faith is experimental and that the surest discoverer of its richest meanings is experience itself. Ninety-nine percent of the misunderstanding

[13] Letters, VI, 44.

and objection to Wesley's doctrine of conversion arises from the failure to relate properly his insistence that a man need not take forever to make up his mind, that God *can* give saving faith in a moment, to the dominant humanism of his age with its negative dogmatism toward all the major realities of Christian experience. The real and only issue between Wesley and his age was not instantaneous conversion, but any kind of conversion. Most of the haggling about instantaneous conversion only hides a humanist prejudice against admitting anything objective in Christian experience. Lifting the question then out of the psychological obscurities, the real issue was whether the meaning of God in Christian experience has anything positive and objective in it whatsoever.

After the emancipation of the Christian faith from the *a priori*, dogmatic denials of an atheistic humanism has been assured, after its emergence into the full, comprehensive freedom of a true experimentalism has been accomplished, Wesley could and did have no further interest in instantaneousness. On the contrary, right from the rupture on July 20, 1740, of all further relations with the Moravians for their insistence on instantaneity and totality as essential to conversion and for excluding Christian experience from the law of development, Wesley began to safeguard the doctrine of Christian experience not only from the negative dogmatism of atheistic humanism, but also from the psychological extravagances into which untutored minds so easily run. He did this by the general rule which anticipates William James that "there is an irreconcilable variability in the operations of the Holy Spirit on the souls of men more especially in the manner of justification (conversion)." [14]   A capital statement of his doctrine, both of conversion and sanctification, is found in the correspondence with Lady Maxwell. Writing in the 27th year of his own conversion-experience, Wesley observes: "It may please him to give you" Christian assurance, that is faith and the witness of the spirit, "by almost insensible degrees like the dawning of a new day. *And it is all one how it began, so you*

[14] Letters, V, 175; VII, 298; VIII, 110.

do but walk in the light.   Be this given in an instant or by degrees, hold it fast." [15]

The fact is, when a true balance is struck, that Wesley had
no predilection whatever for the violent types of conversion.
He also had no prejudice against them; for his consistent teaching was that "God works in different ways" and "there is great
variety," "an irreconcilable variability" in Christian experience.
In other words, he was well-versed in "the varieties of religious
experience" and joined with it the profoundest insight into the
meaning of God in Christian experience.   This keen analyst of
the facts also noted not only that in individual experience "God
works in very different ways," but that there are real differences
between the different ages of the Church.   Looking back over
his large and long experience, Wesley in the 47th year of his
conversion observed that the number of those who in the late
Revival had experienced "the overwhelming power of grace" was
perhaps greater than in any other age since the times of the
Apostles.

Out of the crisis of his own faith there emerged a new conception of the almighty grace of God and a new and continual
sense of total dependence upon it.   And he acquired a new and
lasting assurance of the moral efficacy of the atonement which
took complete possession of his mind and the old leaven of
humanism was washed clean out of his doctrine of salvation.
There was now room in that doctrine for only a God-given,
justifying, saving faith, "a full reliance on the blood of Christ
shed for *me;* a trust in Him as *my* Christ, as *my* sole justification, sanctification and redemption."

Now for Wesley in this new view of salvation by faith, man
had ceased to be the author of saving faith in himself, had become only the subject and the beneficiary of the grace of God in
Christ.   It must indeed invariably be received by an act of man's
self-determination.   But the whole emphasis henceforth fell upon
what is received by the faith that is itself a work of divine
grace.   Henceforth he insisted, "What have we that we do not

[15] Letters, IV, 308.

receive?" Whatever in our experience, above all faith itself in its vast and sovereign significance, all that has any relish of salvation in it, has its exclusive original source in the grace of God. Here the entire objectivity and efficacy of Christian experience, of revelation, of atonement is summed up in one word: God—the God whom Jesus trusted even unto the death of the Cross, and who still reveals himself unmistakably to us in all our experience of saving faith. And since the mystical reconstruction of Christian faith as Wesley understood it was a species of humanistic religion, that too was swept away in this revolutionary transition from a humanistic to a theocentric doctrine of Christian experience.

A master mind of practical Christianity like Wesley, who was thus made keenly, absolutely conscious in revising his doctrine of faith, first of his dependence upon the historical objectivity of revelation, upon "the Word of God in the Scriptures," and upon "the Word of God" in the living witness for his *discovery*, and then secondly of his utter dependence upon the Means of Grace and the living witness for his own *experience* of the truth, i.e., the reality of this religious understanding of the Gospel, was certain to acquire a new point of resistance to the mystics, in none of whose writings could he ever find a proper conception either of historical revelation or of the Christian communion. He now knew not only from reading and observation, but also by his own experience as never before that the Christian Church and the means of grace, all the redeeming and revealing activities of the believing community, above all *the living witness,* had become the indispensable basis for his whole doctrine of Christian experience. The Church in this sense had become a vital part of his understanding of the Gospel. Wesley's life-long resistance to the separation of his societies from the Anglican Church was therefore dictated by something far more significant than a blindly tenacious conservatism. It was dictated by an intelligent religious appreciation of the Christian Church as the means of grace. It was rooted and grounded in a profoundly *soteriological* evaluation of the Church. If we think only of the Church as the believing community of the justified, it is then preeminently true that apart from the Church there is no such thing as Christian experience. This is the basic truth expounded in the sermon on "The Means of Grace," which was intended to be a strong antidote to mysticism.

A sound doctrine of Christian experience must teach and train every person who as such is "a sinful being called to perfection," "neither to neglect nor rest in the means of grace." For Christian experience can not arise in any personal life without the means of grace. These are chiefly the hearing and reading of the Word of God, prayer, the sacrament, the witnessing of faith, the fellowship of faith. The collection of live coals on the altar is at once the secret of the origin and of the continuance of saving faith. From the altar fires a live coal may be taken; but if kept from the altar, it soon loses all its distinctive quality unless it is used at once to light the fire of faith in another experience. Fire alone kindles fire. That is the mystery of Christian experience. That is the interlocking and interaction of all Christian experience in the means of grace. On the other hand, the means of grace as such must never be our first or final trust. All our trust is alone in God. This is the mature view of Wesley.

And here a great truth—let us call it a first principle—clearly appears. The Christian consciousness can brook no rival to an absolute trust in the grace of God. This is the crucial point in Wesley's steadfast definition of religion as *the continual sense of total dependence on God,* and also later in Schleiermacher's cognate conception of religion as the feeling of absolute dependence. Now to inject into the Christian consciousness the feeling of freedom or any reference to man's own effort, as if anything distinct from the grace of God, as if the equal or in any degree a rival or a competitor of the feeling of dependence, as if the sign of any human independence of the grace of God, simply spoils, clouds, weakens, disrupts, contradicts the purity and power of the Christian consciousness. For the Christian consciousness, as it is described by Wesley, the feeling of ethical freedom, while no illusion but tremendously real and significant, belongs nevertheless within the totality of our dependence on God. We are made neither free nor holy by refusing to acknowledge and to surrender to the Holy Will of God above us but only by doing so. And further, the Christian consciousness is precisely most imperative and insistent at the point of acknowledging that all our power of response and conformity to the divine will is the pure gift and grace of God. There is nothing of good outside the network of the almighty grace of God. Hence Wesley's principle: Use therefore industriously the means of Grace; trust only and always in the Grace of God. This is the idea of Christian experience developed by Wesley to illumine and to enforce the indispensableness of the Church and the means of grace. We are to seek and find the presence and awareness of God, a living and saving God, not in the total absence, but in the utmost use of historical revelation and the means of grace.

Now on these Wesleyan premises, Wesley's historical and critical judgment of mysticism combines a warm appreciation of the deeper reasons for the mystical reactions against a formal and enfeebled Christianity and also a high appraisal of the practical religious significance of the mystical reactions relative to their own age. For at the bottom the causes of these reactions and the causes of reformations are one and the same. Their common spring is the necessity once and again of a return to personal experience in religion, precisely Wesley's objective.

But at this point the idea of mysticism and the idea of reformation involve totally different methods. For the mystic in utter despair of the Church, as if unseaworthy, is for taking to the life-boats even in mid-ocean. The reformer, knowing that Christian faith can not survive the Church and that the Church can and will survive a thousand storms, is for standing by and repairing the ship, if need be, and for battling the storms and bringing the vessel into port. He knows also that this is not the last voyage. But the mystics were at least partly right in their objectives, even if utterly wrong in their methods: "Many of them," said Wesley, were "burning and shining lights, experimentally acquainted with true inward religion," whose major concern we may well believe was "no more *at first*, than to show that outward religion is nothing worth without the religion of the heart." Thus Wesley saw in the mystical reactions that have occurred along the highway of Church history a profound and sound protest against a *purely institutional Christianity* on behalf of a *personal religious experience*. He has thus identified the motivation of the mystical reactions with the basic idea of Luther and with the purpose of his own work. It is summed up in the recurrent necessity of a return to personal and inner religious experience as the essence of Christianity. In so far then as the mystics may be credited with a perception of the experiential character of the Christian faith and so of all religion, in so far as they sought to find the unique essence of religion in personal experience, Wesley could as little join issue with the mystics, as he could or did with Luther or St. Paul. He approved whole-heartedly and put into practise in epoch-making fashion precisely such a return to inner religious experience.

Nevertheless Wesley, who also read the nature of religion, and saw the whole meaning and reality of the Christian faith summed up, in "the mystery of Christian experience" joined issue squarely with every species of mysticism. He too lived in an age when Christianity had once more been so objectified in the institutional, as to have nearly lost "the life of faith." He knew exactly what it was that so deeply troubled the Molther-Moravian wing of the Fetter Lane Society, the original society of the Revival, when they sought to sever all connection with the Anglican Church and so began to teach that "the way to faith is to wait on Christ and be still, to leave off using the means of grace, to leave off running to church and sacrament and praying and singing and reading either the Bible or any other book." Manifestly this species of mysticism cancelled outright the historical objectivity of the Word of God and cast out the whole principle of revelation and mediation from religion. But if this is the true way of Christian experience, how then is it true that there is one mediator between God and man, the man Christ Jesus? If this be true, what can we make of St. Paul's question: "How shall they call on Him in whom they have not believed? And how shall they believe in Him of whom they have not heard? And how shall they hear without a preacher?" The historical objectivity of the Word of God is of absolute importance to Christian experience! Augustine, after moving round the whole structure of Christian faith and after probing Christian experience to the bottom, likewise identified bedrock in these words: "My faith, O Lord, calls upon thee which *thou has given me,* which *thou has inspired in me* even by the humanity of thy Son and by the ministry of thy preacher."

Now the fact that these Moravian mystics obviously appear to be and were very extreme is for our purposes a wholly minor and trivial consideration. For Wesley confessed after the widest reading in and reflection upon the writings of the mystics that he could not anywhere find a proper conception of Church communion or appreciation of the means of grace in any of them. But that lies in the very nature of mysticism. For mysticism— I speak of the historical varieties, not of a made-up sort by special definition—thinks it can attain to right relationship with God by denying one and all the intermediaries of a finite and temporal character, and so disregards the elemental conditions of all Christian experience. The cautious Wesley, fully aware how deceitful Universals are, said, "Though it is God only changes hearts, yet He generally doeth it by man." And this he said against mysticism.[16]

Mysticism is a contemplative religion of salvation. One of its greatest exponents, Origen (185-254), master-mind and premier theologian of Greek Christianity, a soaring genius, a Christian Gnostic who probably never felt an impulse to limit his speculations, trusted the logic of mysticism far enough to suppose there will come a stage, the final one, which is the beatific vision of God by the soul, when even the Son of God will be a superfluity. We are not concerned with Origen's rash speculation which the

[16] Sermon 19.

Reformers soundly renounced,[17] save only to illustrate the vitiating fallacy in all typical mysticisms. Wesley allowed that predestination was only an opinion, not subversive of the foundations of Christian experience.[18] His adverse judgment of mysticism for its basic fallacy—namely, the cancellation of the idea of the Church as a believing community, with the means of grace out of the doctrine of Christian experience, its idea of a completely unmediated relationship to God—is made of sterner stuff. He judged it to be subversive of Christian experience.[19] And in this matter he has deliberately used very strong language: "Mysticism strikes at the root of Christianity, spoils it, stabs it in the vitals." Right or wrong, his meaning seems clear enough. We submit, after long exploration of the experience of the Christian Church, that Wesley's judgment after we get his point of view and understand his meaning seems to us entirely sound. There is nothing to be gained, there is everything to lose by exchanging Wesley's doctrine of Christian experience for the vague term mysticism, which incurably shies away from the real genius of the prophetic-Christian religion. Moreover Wesley, an adept in the historical and experiential understanding of the Gospel, with his unusual penetration into the realities of the Christian consciousness, was quick to discern that the basic religious feelings: (1) that of total dependence on God; (2) the quiet, steady joy of an ever-deepening Christian assurance, and (3) the progressive satisfaction of the yearning after evangelical perfection by a steady progress in Christlikeness, are twisted and distorted beyond recognition in the mystical reconstruction of the Christian faith. He perceived many points of agreement between what he called Bible Christianity and Mystical Christianity. But his last word was that the difference is radical. We, too, I think, must take our choice.

But we will never gain entrance into the deeper reason for Wesley's antagonism to the mystics by reflecting only upon the

---

[17] *Origenes nimium philosophatur.*
[18] Letters, IV, 298.
[19] Sermons 12, 19; Letters, I, 207; VI, 431, etc.

inevitable clash between the abysmal subjectivity of the mystic way into right relationship with God and Wesley's idea about the integrity of the Church and the efficacy of the means of grace as the basis of Christian experience. The conflict includes all this, but it goes deeper. We shall find the clue in Wesley's deep reaction against all reference to the human subject in the interpretation of the Gospel as an unholy intruder upon the purity of the Christian consciousness. He perceived in mysticism too much refined self-salvation. He identified it as work-righteousness and so as humanistic. Forty years after his first definite reaction against mysticism he wrote: "This refined religion of Mysticism gives a delicate satisfaction to whatever of curiosity and self-esteem lie hid in the heart." This observation on the nature of mysticism is in entire accord with his earlier analysis of mysticism given in the review of his life. There it stands written that "the mystic writers zealously inculcated this refined way of trusting to my own works and my own righteousness." "Now mental prayer and the like exercises were in truth as much my own works as visiting the sick or clothing the naked; and the union with God thus pursued was as really my own righteousness as any I had pursued under another name." [20] Wesley therefore sincerely believed the mystic way and manner of "pursuing inward holiness or a union of the soul with God" to be essentially humanistic and that it therefore is irreconcilable with "the continual sense of total dependence on God" and with "the true, genuine Christian humility arising from a sense of the love of God, reconciled to us in Christ Jesus." [21] The subjectivity of mysticism contradicts the essence of Christian experience. Now in some way or manner he became aware of this fact that mysticism is at bottom the ascent of man by his own effort to God, that it makes righteousness or holiness a human achievement preliminary to union or communion with God, that it succeeds in throwing an imaginary bridge across the infinite gulf between God and man, only by denying or ignoring the reality

[20] Journal, I, 468 f.
[21] Sermon 16.

of the distance between God and man. It knows not the sovereign significance of saving faith, which presupposes and recognizes the fact of man's sin and total dependence on the almighty grace of God. It knows not that "faith is the gift of God, a gift that presupposes nothing in us but sin and misery." [22]

Here we might conclude the study of Wesley's deep life-long opposition to the mystical version or perversion of Christianity. But the anti-rational and anti-social virus in mysticism attended by its unwholesome sentimentality in religion is one of the most important though unwelcome phases of this difficult subject. We must therefore go to the end of Wesley's radical critique.

The psychological affinity of the mystic writers for the sentimentality of the Song of Solomon presents a painful contrast to the mountain-like ruggedness, strength, and predilection of reformation thought for St. Paul's Epistle to the Romans. All of the early Reformers took deep counsel of St. Paul and steeped themselves in his religious understanding of the Gospel. But within the reformation there were important differences between the Central European type molded by Luther and the West-European type molded by Calvin. First of all, Justification has been taken quite often in Lutheran circles to be primarily, at any rate, far more, the quietistic enjoyment of divine grace, whereas in the Calvinistic branches it has always been understood more as a principle of strenuous activity. The subject of grace feels himself to be a chosen vessel of the Kingdom of God in human affairs. The ethic of grace in both branches is activistic, but the religious evaluation of activity in the world is in all the Calvinistic branches the highest. Likewise the estimate of God's power over the forces of our sin-bound human world is in the Calvinistic churches the maximum. Now Wesleyanism agrees in these points not with the Lutheran, but with the Calvinist conception of God's relation to human affairs. It is even a question whether Wesleyanism has not surpassed original Calvinism in the number and energy of the practical conclusions which distinguish the Wesleyan ethic of grace. Witness the extent to

[22] Journal, II, 256.

which the influence of the Wesleyan churches has been the chief propulsive force in the modern struggle against both African and Alcohol slavery. Wesley lived his life on the frontiers of practical Christianity. For him the problem of problems was to get the principles of Christianity put into practise. His amazing fertility and brilliant success as a pioneer in the field of practical Christianity have even obscured his high merit as a thinker and systematic expounder of the simple Gospel of salvation by faith.

Wesley detected and censored, soon after his acceptance of Luther's doctrine of saving faith, what he considered the taint of mysticism in the Reformer's teaching. Since Luther is the only authority beside the Scriptures, for his own doctrine of faith that Wesley ever acknowledged, his sharp criticism of Luther for mysticism is of the highest importance. He felt that Luther gave in some of his utterances altogether too much aid and comfort to the mystics. In fact he referred Moravian mysticism direct to Luther's teaching.[23] It was "the fury of Luther's Solifidianism" that had misled him to denounce St. James' as an epistle of straw. Wesley's objection to this judgment expresses more than the influence of the Canon of Scripture. It is rooted in a difference in the ethic of grace. It was Wesley's deepest conviction that "Christianity is essentially a social religion; and that to turn it into a solitary religion is to destroy it." "The social, open, active Christians" denote the Gospel at its greatest and best. Now it was Luther who first repudiated monasticism and created vocational idealism. But his vocational idealism is bounded by despair about God's power over the forces of our sin-bound human world. West-European Protestantism was more radical and thorough. It included the total transformation of our entire human world in the idea of the Kingdom of God. At least Wesley thought so. "Contemplation is only one way of worshipping God in spirit and in truth." Moreover, it is "not more excellent than the way of obedience." Love, Christlikeness, world-transforming obedience are essential to Christianity. "To glorify

[23] Journal, II, 467.

God with our bodies as well as with our spirits; to go through outward work with hearts lifted up to Him; to make our daily employment a sacrifice to God; to buy and sell, to eat and drink to His glory;—that is worshipping God in spirit and in truth, as much as praying to Him in a wilderness." "Nor is it any clog to a Christian" to play the part of a man in the world. There are many temples in which God can be worshipped, the choicest being our vocations in the world. This consummate activist ethic of divine grace completely superseded the ethic of a contemplative salvation in the Wesleyan understanding of the Gospel. The whole stuff of life, personal, social, all of it, must be shot through and transfigured by the white light of the Gospel. Here is foothold and foundation enough for any sound social Gospel. No human interest or activity can escape its comprehensiveness. It does not propose to shun the world in order to be a Christian. It does not propose to let our human world alone and content itself with a life unspotted by inevitable contact with the world to be a Christian. It proposes to transform our entire human world and to Christianize the social order. It is not necessary to assume that Wesley has thought out his social point of view and principle into all its concrete applications in order to recognize its presence and essential place in his doctrine of Christianity.

The second judgment upon Luther's work is found in the Journal for June 15, 1741. He read for the first time while riding in the chaise, his principal study, Luther on the Epistle to the Galatians. The criticism is extravagant. By it we sense how deep and earnest Wesley's reaction was against mysticism, the handmaid of monasticism. Even if too severe, over-reaching itself, it is scarcely less significant for our purposes. He now pronounced Luther's comment, in spite of "excellent sentences," not only on the whole a failure, much of it shallow, almost all of it muddy and confused, but he is "deeply tinctured with mysticism throughout, and hence often dangerously (Wesley in the first edition had said fundamentally) wrong. How does he (almost in the words of Tauler) decry reason, right or wrong, as an irreconcilable enemy to the Gospel of Christ. Whereas what is reason (the faculty so called) but the power of apprehending, judging and discoursing? Which power is no more to be condemned in the gross than seeing, hearing or feeling." [24]

Luther's bitter animus against reason in religion which was directed against scholastic notionalism rather than experiential thinking is well known. Wesley is of course right that reason is not the natural enemy of the Christian faith. But his strictures on Luther's anti-intellectualism argue on his part a lack of understanding for the great Reformer's fateful battles with the desolate and obnoxious theorizing Christianity of the scholastics. Scholastic theology, instead of confronting those about to enter Orders with the Word of God, buried it rather under infinite rubbish and made it next to impossible for any man, so Luther learned to his sorrow, to discover and experience the Word of God. Luther has referred to these costly soul-battles. Since he found in the answer of his heart to the study of God's Word what he failed utterly to find in scholastic theology, namely, the knowledge of a living and saving God, scholastic theology, which still had the upper hand in theological education, became Luther's pet aversion. He likened their rationalizing mania to an attempt to explain the Savior of Mankind by counting his bones. He even called them "swine-theologians." When therefore Luther pitches into reason in religion so unreasonably, we may be sure he had in mind the concrete example of a rationalizing theology given by the scholastics. Finally, action speaks louder than words. We have in Luther's own writings brilliant examples of Biblical and experiential reasoning in religion that at best is not easily surpassed. We may then well choose Wesley's guarded allowance to intellect in religion of its full rights rather than Luther's unbalanced denunciation of reason in general, but without so much injudicious disparagement of Luther. But when we look at the root of the matter we can only say of Wesley, What historical accuracy! What insight into the unique essence of religious experience! We know Luther drank

[24] Journal, II, 467.

pretty deep of Tauler's mysticism. Wesley knew his Tauler and instantly sensed in Luther's Galatians the spots of his influence on Luther's comment. Luther decries reason, Wesley acutely observes, "almost in Tauler's words."

But Wesley's criticism of Luther has two points, and in the second count he uses still more questionable terms: "How blasphemously (!) does he speak of good works and of the law of God—constantly coupling the law with sin, death, hell or the devil; and teaching that Christ delivers us from them all alike. Whereas it can no more be proved by Scripture that Christ delivers us from the law of God than that he delivers us from holiness or from heaven. Here (I apprehend) is the real spring of the grand error of the Moravians. They follow Luther for better, for worse. Hence their "No works; no law; no commandments." But who art thou that 'speakest evil of the law, and judgest the law.' " [25] Wesley preached next day at London on Gal., VI, 15. The Journal has this minute: "After reading Luther's miserable comment upon the text I thought it my bounden duty openly to warn the congregation against that dangerous treatise to retract whatever recommendations I might ignorantly have given it."

The second stricture on Luther is also not without a certain misunderstanding of Luther's position. For Luther would never have subscribed to the deductions being made by Moravian mystics. Then we may allow for the militancy of Wesley's opposition to mysticism and antinomianism. But with due allowance, Wesley never wrote anything more significant for his and for our understanding of the Gospel. It reveals his poise, balance and synthetic power at its best. He sensed in the fury of Luther's "faith-only" teaching a great peril to the ethical interpretation of the atonement. For Wesley was infinitely more concerned about salvation from the power of sin than about salvation from the guilt and penalty of it. He gave no quarter to any teaching that denied or endangered the boundless moral efficacy of the atonement. We must accordingly judge Luther by his God-given task and Wesley likewise by his, and not confuse them. But

[25] Journal, II, 467.

even on that premise the necessity of a corrective to Luther's doctrine of faith is not to be doubted. Harnack, master and utterly loyal interpreter of Luther's teaching, admitted that Luther's *religious* understanding of the Gospel neglected the *moral* problem, the "Be ye holy, for I am holy." Even with this necessity of a corrective in mind, Wesley did not here or any- where reject or deviate from Luther's religious understanding of the Gospel. Much rather after 1738 it became, as Wesley him- self said once and again, the central fire of his message. Of Luther's life-work as a whole and of Wesley's relation to it, it can with great propriety be said that Wesley was conscious of a mission not to destroy or deviate from it, but to renew it in full force, and then give it the necessary supplement. If only in his unguarded utterances Luther appeared to neglect or im- pugn the ethical interpretation of the atonement, it would ex- plain Wesley's instant reaction: We may not cast reason out of the Gospel, much less righteousness or actual holiness of heart and life; for these are the essence of the Gospel. In spite of Wesley's not unjust strictures on Luther's teaching, we may and must by right historical reasoning, always represent him as build- ing consciously, securely on foundations laid by the early Re- formers, and above all by Martin Luther. More adequately stated, we have in Wesley's doctrine a masterful synthesis of Luther's religious understanding of the Gospel with the evalua- tion of activity in the world which distinguishes the Calvinistic Ethic of Grace. Finally, we shall have to look beyond even these two major points of view in order to describe the full orbit of the Wesleyan system of Christian doctrine and to con- sider it as the embodiment of the wider interests of Christian thought, as a whole in the doctrine of holiness, and also of a much fuller measure of the institutional spirit of historic Chris- tianity.

If Wesley found that Martin Luther "is deeply tinctured with mysticism throughout and hence often dangerously wrong," he never reports having discovered such an element in John Calvin. It has often been, and justly, observed that in no other master

of early Protestantism and in no other great interpreter of the
Christian faith is there less, if indeed so little, of mysticism as
in the religion of John Calvin. Unlike most of his followers in
the Christian ministry, John Wesley knew his Calvin as well as
Luther by the careful reading of his writings.[26] While preserv-
ing complete independence of both and refusing to call either his
master, he knew that Protestantism must build on foundations
laid by Luther and Calvin and appraised them accordingly. He
calls Calvin's words: "Let Luther call me a hundred devils, I
will still reverence him as a messenger of God," "that glorious
saying of a great man." Now although there is much less humanity in Calvin's theology than in Wesley's idea of God and
although the tender, the mild, the emotional traits are far richer
in the Wesleyan theology, still the complete accord of Wesley
with Calvin in respect to mysticism must strike every observer
as very significant. He agreed with Calvin and Luther alike in
banishing philosophy and speculation and in reserving the interpretation of the Gospel to historical and experiential reasoning.
But Wesley stands closer to Calvin not only in his anti-mysticism,
but also in the vigor and clarity of his historical and experiential
exposition of the Christian faith, and in the boldness of his
practical deductions therefrom for the structure and conduct of
personal and social life.

The close vital affiliation of Wesleyanism with West-European
or Calvinistic Protestantism can be clearly traced along many
other lines, some of major importance. For Wesley shared in
full measure the lofty religious evaluation of profitable industry
and gainful activity in the world by which the Calvinistic has
been distinguished from all other branches of the Christian
Church. He concurred with Calvinism in the fundamental doubt
whether an idle man, bondholder or beggar—the ethical difference is superficial—could be in a state of grace. "We do not
suffer an idle man to remain in our Societies," so runs Wesley's
strong statement, "we drive him out as we would a thief and
a murderer." The corollary of this, that any person in distress

[26] Sermon 49; Letters, III, 246.

or want is entitled to work, was recognized by Wesley in his many ingenious expedients to provide work and wages rather than unearned charities for the unemployed. If then Wesley emphasized the witness of the Spirit much, he exalted the witness of Christian service more. In all this he was in the fullest sense a modern man.

A comparison of the Central and West-European branches of Protestantism in respect to fertility and efficiency in missionary enterprise throws a strong light upon the much closer affiliation of the Wesleyan and Calvinist churches. For by common consent these branches of Protestantism surpass all others in the energy and fruitfulness of their missionary spirit. Last but not least, and as a final word, among Wesley's great predecessors whose spirit was passed on to him either by their writings or by their successors, there is in Calvin's interpretation of the Gospel the minimum of mysticism. Among the masters of the Protestant understanding of the Gospel, Calvin is, with the exception alone of Wesley, the least mystical. In this particular Wesley is, if possible, even more radically anti-mystical. For in Wesley's doctrine of Christian experience God, the living and saving God, known as such only in the Gospel, is so transcendent that beside him the universe, in the language of Wesley, is nothing and so immanent that, also in the language of Wesley, he is the soul of the universe. If we considered Wesley's doctrine of transcendence alone, we might mistake him for a deist. If we considered his doctrine of immanence alone, we would conclude that he was an acosmic pantheist. It is in the first term that mysticism finds a corrective.

We moderns have doubtless lost much in the art of introspective mysticism. We shall scarcely ever again recapture the blissful beatitudes of monk and mystic. It would not be amiss to drop some natural tears over the loss. Even so, we can not return to this type of Christianity if we would, and we would not if we could. The world is all before us. Ours is the higher and more heroic task of finding out the personal and social implications and applications of the Gospel and of realizing the

Kingdom of God on earth. If it be demurred that even if God's Kingdom should ever become in its plenary meanings a reality in our human world, millions on millions of personal lives will have vanished long before the event and therefore the great concern must be not to wait and work for the Kingdom of God in human affairs, but to save the vanishing factors, it can well be answered that God's Kingdom is no little affair of this planet, but spans the universe, the whole gravitational field, and by building our lives securely into his Kingdom here, we not only come upon the choicest spiritual opportunities and acquire the highest religious values here, but we also, by so doing, discover and unlock the door into something better there. At any rate, John Wesley's unique synthesis of Luther's deep religious appreciation of the inner direct experience of divine grace with Calvin's unsurpassed religious evaluation of activity in the world offers a satisfactory formula or guide for Christian thought and action in the twentieth century.

CHAPTER VII

FROM 1738 TO THIS TIME

Two major events were indissolubly welded together in Wesley's personal religious experience and in his numerous accounts of the origin and progress of the Revival. They were the entrance of the "new doctrine" of salvation by faith into the content and the simultaneous advent of power in his preaching. Thrice Wesley has referred to this inner connection between a change in the doctrinal substance and the advent of power in his preaching; he wrote the first account at once after the event, the second in the twenty-seventh year, and the third in the forty-third year of his conversion-experience and of the Revival. "As soon as I saw the nature of saving faith clearly, namely, on Monday, March 6, 1738, I declared it without delay. And God then began to work by my ministry as he never had done before." [1] Moreover the new doctrine of salvation by faith not only found entrance for the first time in the Spring of 1738 into the subject-matter of his teaching and preaching; Wesley has asserted roundly that it also became from that time henceforth what it had not been before, namely, the standing topic and dominant theme of his message and ministry. "After we had wandered many years in the *new path* of salvation by *faith and works,* about two years ago it pleased God to show us the *old way* of salvation by *faith only.*" This was set down in the twenty-fifth month of the conversion-experience.

The doctrinal minutes for the Third Annual Conference which met in May, 1746, differentiated the Oxford and the Evangelical periods of Wesley's message and ministry as follows:

Q. 4. Wherein does our doctrine now differ from that we preached when at Oxford?

[1] *Short History of the People Called Methodists,* 1765, 1781.

A. Chiefly in two points: (1) We then knew nothing of that righteousness of faith, in justification; nor (2) of the nature of faith itself, as implying consciousness of pardon.

Conversation III also further defines and declares the new position and sovereign significance of saving faith for all Christian experience. Undoubtedly prior to 1738 the idea of the love of God as the one sole source and resource of all Christian holiness was central and controlling in Wesley's teaching and preaching. But a fundamental reconstruction has taken place in his entire doctrine of Christian experience. "Christian holiness in all its branches springs from Christian principles: (1) No true Christian holiness can exist without the love of God for its foundation; (2) the abiding love of God can not spring but from faith in a pardoning God." Thus saving faith has entirely superseded the love of God as the first principle of all Christian experience. For this cause the question, *Whence then is saving faith?* assumes absolute importance in Wesley's doctrine of Christian experience. Accordingly Wesley admitted that *"from 1738 to this time* we could hardly speak of anything else either in public or in private but the doctrine that we are saved through faith. *It shone upon our minds with so strong a light that it was our constant theme.* It was our daily subject both in verse and prose; and we vehemently defended it against all mankind. But in doing this we were assaulted and abused on every side. We were represented as mad dogs, and treated accordingly. We were stoned in the streets, and several times narrowly escaped with our lives. In sermons, newspapers, and pamphlets of every kind, we were painted as unheard-of monsters. But this moved us not." The conversion-experience in 1738 is here vividly represented as the sunrise of the Gospel in the hymnology and preaching of the Wesleyan movement.

The Short History of Methodism is the most objective by far among Wesley's accounts of the origins of the Revival. It makes but a small pamphlet of five pages and was done in 1764. It looks back over twenty-six years of the Revival. It was written to disarm popular misunderstandings and to fix attention on essentials. Wesley later expanded this short account—it was sixteen years later—into over a hundred pages and printed it as a part of Mosheim's *Ecclesiastical History* to bring the account of Church History down to the present. Moreover Wesley has not only translated the Latin text of Mosheim's *History* but he has also abridged it; and in doing so he edited and altered (!) the subject-matter with the greatest freedom. He as a rule abridged severely to save printer's ink and reader's time. But such abridgement of the text also afforded editorial freedom to revise and alter the subject-matter.

Although Mosheim's Church History (1755) at once took high rank, marks a great advance, and breathes the freer air of a more liberal spirit, although it began to displace the prejudices of dogmatic theology with the premises of historical science, still it continued to represent the Independents and the Sectarians, the so-called Schismatics and Heretics of Church history, in the darkest light. As far back at least as Athanasius, it had been the fixed tradition of the Church that "the devil alone could be the sower of the opinions and instigator of the practises" of all who would not submit to the hierarchy. Nowhere does Wesley appear in a more admirable light than in his editorial work on Mosheim's Church History. For to his everlasting credit, he began to wash this Satanic theory of heresy out of Church history and out of theology. He had a penchant for good opinions of heretics. "Heresy and schism, in the modern sense, are sins that the Scripture knows nothing of; but were invented merely to deprive mankind of the benefit of private judgment and liberty of conscience." [2] In fact Wesley was inclined to associate the true Church with the history of heresy. "God always reserved a seed for himself; a few that worshipped him in spirit and in truth. I have often doubted whether these were not the very persons whom the rich and honorable Christians, who will always have number as well as power on their side, did not stigmatize, from time to time, with the title of

[2] *Wesleyan New Testament*, 431.

heretics." [3]   He cited for this purpose the names of Montanus,
Pelagius, Luther, the leaders of Nonconformity in England and
finally the Methodists—a very interesting apostolic succession
of heretics indeed.   In the same spirit, after cleansing out of
Mosheim's portrait of Montanus the unamiable prejudices and
after actually representing him in a much more favorable light,
Wesley interpolated this final remark: "Such is the account
which is generally given of Montaus.   But I have been frequently
in doubt, whether he was not one of the wisest and holiest men
who was then (c. 150-170 A.D.) in the Christian Church.   And
whether his real fault was not the bearing a faithful testimony
of the general apostasy from Christian holiness." [4]

Now *The Short History of Methodism* refers the origin of the
Revival to the irruption on March 6th, 1738, into Wesley's
preaching, of the Early Reformation doctrine of salvation by
faith.   No reference whatever is made to the private and personal aspects of Wesley's conversion-experience.   On the contrary, "After we had wandered many years in the *new path* of
salvation by *faith and works,* about two years ago (this statement was made June 22, 1740) it pleased God to show us the
old way of salvation by *faith only.*" [5]   By this reckoning, which
we now propose to show was for Wesley a category of thought,
the origin of the Revival is referred to the year 1738.

The essential facts about the Revival were reviewed in the
year 1746, in two of Wesley's weightiest doctrinal letters—they
make 100 pages of print—to the Rev. Thomas Church of St.
Paul's.   In these epistles Wesley observes that his account of
Christian faith as at once experiential and God-given had drawn
down upon himself for "near these eight years past" the charge
of being an enthusiast, or in eighteenth century parlance, a religious madman.   Going back eight years from 1746 we are again
in the year 1738.   Inasmuch as Wesley for upwards of half a
century thought about it constantly, consistently in these terms,

[3] Sermon 68.
[4] *Concise Ecclesiastical History,* Vol. I, p. 114.
[5] Journal, II, 354.

it is necessary at least tentatively to accept 1738 as the epoch of the Wesleyan Revival. And we are now confronted with the task of defining in connection therewith the objective significance of Wesley's conversion-experience in conjunction with this revolution of religious principles and accession of power in his preaching.

We propose therefore to consider the increment of power in Wesley's preaching, due to his rediscovery and adoption in 1738 of the Luther-Calvin idea of the sovereign saving significance of a God-given faith in Christ as the clue and key to the objective significance and historical importance of his conversion-experience. For the objective significance of Wesley's conversion-experience, whether it is associated with March 4, 1738, when he was "clearly convinced of unbelief," or with April 23rd, when all doubt or dispute about the nature of saving faith was hushed into silence before the concurring evidence of the New Testament and the living witness, or with May 24th, when helped by an authoritative word straight from Luther, he himself first experienced the nature of saving faith, and felt the heart strangely warmed, must in any case be sought in the religious principles involved and not in any transitory gust of religious ecstasy or in any of the exceedingly variable psychological concomitants of the transition. We have the full warrant of Wesley's seasoned judgment for this method of interpretation. He never referred the origin of the Revival to the private and personal aspects of his Christian experience, however deeply involved they may have been. He always referred the origin of the Revival to the revolution of religious principles and the correlative increment of power in his preaching. He deduced the power of the Revival from a change in the content of his preaching, sealed and sanctioned of course by his own inner experience of its truth. He located the origin of the Wesleyan Reformation in the exercise of the prophetic office of the Church, namely, in the preaching of the Word of God and not in any phase of his personal experience as such. It belongs in the history of the Gospel.

Between Wesley's decision in the Spring of 1725 to enter the

Christian ministry as his life-work and his ordination in the Fall, September 19, 1725, by Bishop Potter of Oxford, he confided to his incomparable mother his first tentative thoughts on the principles of his vocation and on the nature of Christianity. Naturally these thoughts were immature and impressionistic. They do little more than echo the books he was reading. In the letters which passed in the interim between graduation and ordination from Oxford to Epworth, Wesley set down his thoughts very much in accord with the prevailing climate of opinion on the nature of faith. He called faith "a species of belief," proceeded to define belief as "assent upon rational grounds," and concluded with the remark that "faith is assent upon rational grounds and must necessarily be resolved into reason." To this statement of what he then supposed faith to be, he subjoined the astonishing explanation that Christian assurance comes down to an intuition of our own sincerity.[6]

All this has been identified as rank humanism, and that too of the intellectualist sort. It savors of religion within the limits of reason alone. Faith, belief, religious experience come down to the intellectual function of man's personal life and to the intellectual content of religion. The young collegian had not yet found out how much of chaff, how little of wheat, this desolate theorizing Christianity afforded. Wesley's religious ideas at this stage were scholastic, bookish, with just a tincture of experiential thinking in them. His first sophomoric experiment in gathering religious figs from intellectualist thistles soon came to grief. The most constructive word in the first stirrings of his mind on the highest themes of religion which had a relish of deep conviction in it, was his emphatic protest against Jeremy Taylor, one of the greatest preachers of his age (1613-1667), bishop and author of great eminence, who through his widely read *Liberty of Prophesying* (1647), *Holy Living and Dying* (1651) and other works was an oracle of religious thought and piety for half a century after his death. His was a name to conjure with on religious subjects. But he seemed to Wesley to

<hr/>

[6] *Letters*, I, 15-26.

condemn the subject of faith to perpetual "uncertainty of being in a state of salvation." "Whether God has forgiven us or no, we know not; therefore still *be sorrowful for ever* having sinned." Wesley recoiled against the cheerless gloom of this doctrine of Christian experience. It seemed to him also to collide head-on with the realities of Christian experience under the means of · grace. The great bishop had admitted that "The Holy Spirit confers on us the graces we pray for." But these realities of experience, so reasoned Wesley, "surely are not of so little force" as to be imperceptible. Of course the crux of the issue raised was whether the truth-values of the Gospel can be submitted to the sure trial of experience. The import of Wesley's critique is perfectly clear. "If Christ be in us and we in Christ" that must be a fact of experience. Already the novitiate in theology is not afraid, at the very outset of his ministry, to array the indications of Christian experience against the dogmatic theorem of a high authority and to assert a principle of doctrine that must bring every dogma to trial in the court of experience.

Needless to say, this early deposit of the spirit of empirical science in theology was for Wesley only a small beginning. But for all that it had in it the seed and promise of a great new departure in theology. It would of course be crediting Wesley in his Oxford days with far more than he had, to claim for him any foresight of a systematic theology of experience. But beyond question, the fundamental reconstruction of his idea of Christianity carried out in the period 1725-1738, changed the venue in the case of religious belief from the court of logic and speculation to the court of life, action and history. The highest test of truth-values in the Christian faith came to be, through his pioneer work, more and more the sure trial and verdict of experiential thinking, their adequacy to our deeper personal structure and biologic necessities and the fact that they work well in life. Great new departures in theology often break into reality unawares as tendencies of thought. Systems of theology have been more often the mausoleums than the nurseries of such creative tendencies.

But Wesley's earliest ideas about Christianty were still so rankly intellectualistic and radically humanistic as to leave small room for the religious element. His doctrine of experience as yet hardly took in more than the intellectual function. He did not tarry long in this misadventure of religious thought. Soon after ordination he confided again to his mother that he had made a discovery. He had by his own reflection discovered in his first thoughts about faith—they were only echoes anyway—a confusion of faith and science. Then too he had mistaken the intellectual function for the whole of man's response to the truth-values of the Christian faith. But the only alternative he then could find to an intellectualistic religion (*via rationis*) was to define saving faith as assent to what God has revealed because he has revealed it, and not because the truth of it may be evinced by reason. The quick reaction against a religion within the limits of reason alone, and against "a faith that must necessarily be resolved into reason" was followed by a brief trial of the *via auctoritatis* or implicit trust in the Scriptures. Whatever is plainly taught in the Scriptures must *ipso facto* be true. This second position also was soon abandoned.

The story of how Wesley finally cleared himself of this narrow choice between the *via rationis* and the *via auctoritatis* is the true account of his return to evangelical principles and of his adoption of a theological method which transcended this false antithesis of reason and authority, while doing justice to both. We may use for this purpose the weighty letters written in the twenty-first year of his ordination and the eighth of his conversion-experience to Thomas Church of St. Paul's, characterized by Wesley as "a gentleman, a scholar and a Christian," in answer to Church's criticism of the Wesleyan Revival under six heads:

1. Wesley's relations to the Moravians.
2. His views on justification by faith.
3. The point of Church communion.
4. The Methodists are enthusiasts.

5. It is implied they are miracles of grace.

6. Wesley's whole manner of speaking and writing about the Revival has too much Wesley and too much enthusiasm in it.

Church thought Wesley pretty free in referring his own experience, his activities, and the fruits thereof outright to "the work of God."

There are three facts in the Wesley letters to Church that are very useful in defining the epoch of maturity in Wesley's understanding of the Gospel and by implication the birth of the Wesleyan reformation. First, the letters state, "what our [Wesley and his associates] constant doctrines are whereby we are distinguished only from heathens and nominal Christians, not from any that worship God in spirit and in truth. Our main doctrines, which include all the rest, are three—that of Repentance, of Faith and of Holiness." Secondly, "concerning the gate of religion . . . which is *the true Christian saving faith,* we believe it implies *abundantly more* (!) than an assent to the truth of the Bible." [7] "It is for giving this account of Christian faith (in experiential terms) that I am these eight years past accused of enthusiasm." Evidently this "abundantly more" was the new element in Wesley's theological method in distinction from the *via rationis* and *via auctoritatis* which was all he knew in the first decade of his ministry. And this "abundantly more" was the reference to Christian experience which drew upon him the hostility of the hierarchy as well as the illuminist stigma of enthusiasm.

Finally what Wesley had to say concerning "the gate of religion" or the experiential apprehension of the true Christian, saving faith was offered as an elucidation of a revolution in his preaching, which was consummated between March 6th, when he "began preaching the new doctrine of salvation by faith alone" and May 24th when principally by the help of Luther, the richer meaning of the Christian revelation first flooded his own inner

[7] This "abundantly more" was strongly reaffirmed in the sermon "On Faith" preached in 1788.

consciousness, and the sovereign saving significance of a God-given faith in Christ received his final personal affirmation. The inner aspects of the experience: "I felt my heart strangely warmed," "I felt I did trust in Christ," and "what I now first felt in my heart," constituted for Wesley "the mystery of Christian experience." But the strange increment of power in his preaching, however difficult it might be to lay bare the realities of his own inner experience, was objectively attested by results. Wesley therefore submitted to Church and those for whom he spoke a concise account of this revolution of religious principles in his preaching as the best credential or proof that his account in the Journal of the singular power and amazing fruit of his preaching after 1738 could not fairly be considered as "mere boasting and vanity"; for had he not duly confessed that he had preached much, the first decade of his ministry, with little or no fruit; but had spent most of his time simply "beating the air"! The singular increment of power in 1738 could not therefore refer to anything purely personal, nor to anything in his talent or technique of preaching, but must refer to something objective, to something different in the content of his preaching, to a change of religious principles. He had found out after a long and arduous search, a reservoir of power in preaching that was not at all special to himself but accessible to all. This new reservoir of power was unlocked for Wesley by the Luther-Calvin idea of faith.

It may seem passing strange in the light of the clear, cogent, super-abundant evidence furnished by the original sources for the objective significance of Wesley's conversion-experience, that it has been of late widely doubted and heavily discounted. On humanist premises it would be only natural, inevitable, now as then, that the objective significance, not alone of instantaneous but also of any kind of conversion or communion with God should be doubted and denied. The shallowing effect of this rationalistic humanism upon the Christian faith and its total inability to discover or admit anything objective or significant in Wesley's conversion-experience has found of late at least an ally in the dissertation of Dr. Maximin Piette—*La Réaction Wes-léyenne dans l'Evolution Protestante,* 1925, submitted to the University of Louvain and accepted *ad gradum magistri.* Piette sees in the Wesleyan Revival a powerful movement away from early Protestantism [8] and he pares down the actual significance of Wesley's conversion-experience—"the Official Wesleyan Legend"—close to the vanishing point. Wesley himself, so far as he was able to make out, made little of it, almost never referred to it, was indeed consistently reticent about it. Presumably but for the accident of its recording in the Journal, it might well, as a transitory gust of religious feeling, have been early and entirely forgotten. Thus the "Official Wesleyan Legend" concerning Wesley's conversion would be little more than an invention after the facts and in total disregard of the facts to suit the exigencies of later Methodist orthodoxy in which everything reverts to the vital importance of conversion.

Piette's Dissertation submitted in 1925 to the scholarly world purports and claims to be, in respect to its main thesis, a strict induction from the cold facts *(des appreciations rassises faites).* It ought to be received and considered on no other grounds. Piette's inability or failure to discover the objective significance of Wesley's conversion-experience arises chiefly from two sources: First, he operates with a special definition of conversion that will not fit the case of Wesley. It is assumed that conversion can have a positive meaning alone on a personal background of lurid sinfulness. Secondly, his analysis of the original sources was far from adequate, so that the decisive considerations have been entirely overlooked.

Piette's annotation of the conversion-experience reads: "The rallying of John Wesley to the doctrine of faith as the School of Herrnhut or, more exactly, Peter Boehler, apprehended it (for the theology of Pietism had very little consistency in it), was not at all the finishing stroke *(le coup de grâce)* which Wesley-biography has in general emphatically designated as his

[8] Has this impression been taken from original or from present-day Methodism?

conversion proper. . . . This famous conversion that has been called upon to play such a huge rôle in the doctrinal life of nineteenth-century Methodism, *played a very modest part* in the life of the founder and in that of his companions. In reality whether it is considered in its preparation or examined either in itself or in its results, it amounts to little more than a simple experience (a gust of feeling) whose growing cold was but a matter of time. Had it not been made a matter of record in the first draught of the Journal, it is possible that Wesley might have entirely forgotten it. In any case a critical appraisal of the cold facts in the sequel reduces it to the very slight value of a rapturous outpour of feeling which first accompanied it."

"The Authors who have been so forward to speak of the Grand Conversion which came suddenly in May, 1738, and have made out the undergraduate before 1725 to have been the Grand Sinner so familiar to us in the picture, ought not, even so, to have overlooked the fact that there was not the slightest excuse left after Wesley's entrance into Holy Orders, for representing him as a grand sinner. Would they not have done much better to have placed, as M. Leger did,[9] his true [does true mean entire?] conversion fourteen years earlier than the position which the "Official Wesleyan Legend" has so far, as it were, arbitrarily bestowed upon it?"[10]

Now it is in general true, as Piette has acutely observed, that apart from the single entry and reference in the Journal, Wesley was for upwards of fifty years (1738-1791) decidedly reticent about the purely private and personal aspects of his conversion-experience. What he experienced in the Aldersgate Street Society meeting May 24, 1738, about a quarter before nine has been described in the Journal simply, accurately, completely, but *once for all*. The reference to the conversion-experience in this psychological sense is therefore in the light of later tradition about Wesley conspicuous in everything Wesley said or wrote of a public character solely on account of its absence. Neverthe-

---

[9] *La Jeunesse de Wesley*, Augustin Leger, Paris, 1910.
[10] *La Réaction Wesléyenne*, 2 ed., 1927, pp. 442 f.

less there is a most decidedly important reference to May 24, 1738, in the Secker-Wesley correspondence. Here for once May 24, 1738, is invested with a pivotal significance in the history of the Revival. True, reference is made in this case not to Wesley's subjective experience, but to the radical change in the content of his preaching and its effect upon the Church at large. But under that head Wesley has made a distinction of capital importance. A clear distinction is drawn between the two steps by which a radical deficiency in his experience and preaching of faith was overcome. The deficiency in his preaching was overcome on March 6th, when he first preached salvation by faith. The deficiency in his experience was overcome on May 24th, when he first let Luther's belief lay hold of him. So that after May 24th he not only preached but he also "knew (experientially) salvation by faith." This account of his conversion-experience is clear enough to satisfy the wariest critic. Nevertheless Wesley's habitual reticence about the conversion-experience as a personal affair still stands in painful contrast to the "Official Wesleyan Legend" about it, and it is undeniable that the traditional Methodist interpretation of the event is foreign to Wesley's own way of referring to it and the doctrinal use he made of it.

Admitting the fact of silence, it would be first of all rash inference that the conversion-experience was historically insignificant. It is on all hands agreed that next to, if not co-equal with, the inquiry into what the Scriptures, more precisely, the New Testament teaches, the systematic reference to experience outranks everything else in Wesley's method of teaching and preaching. Of course, Piette has also recognized what everybody knows and nobody denies. But he has done much more and done it well. He has stated in a manner that is at once sound and important not only the central and sovereign significance but also the far-reaching historical importance for Modern Christianity of the reference to experience as the essence of Wesley's theological method. Every interpretation of the conversion-experience of John Wesley therefore which is inconsistent with the supremacy of the appeal to experience in his theology is on the face of it at least suspect. The argument from silence is in general and in such a matter in particular notoriously problematic. Whether, for example, the quite analogous and equally noticeable reticence of Jesus about his Messianic call and consciousness argues its non-existence or insignificance raises a similar issue. Able scholars have so concluded. But Wesley rightly saw in the reserve of Jesus only a reflection of his methods.[11] Again how much specific reference to the Damascus road experience can be found in St. Paul's epistles to the churches? Are we therefore going to doubt its occurrence or its objective significance? The reticence of Wesley, *such as it was,* is obviously not the interpretation but the fact, not a solution, but the problem.

The Wesleyan reformation and the work of John Wesley as a master of essential Christianity is, as Piette rightly observes, more and more being recognized as unique and original in respect to the primacy accorded to religious experience, the consistency of its appeal to it, and the radical use made of the principle in theology. The time is at hand when Wesley will, in accord with the facts, be recognized as a principal and the primary founder in modern Christianity of *the theology of experience.* Too long has one man's work been little more than another man's reputation. We therefore warmly welcome Piette's concurrence with and his advocacy of a general view of Wesley's Theological Empiricism which has for a full quarter of a century been fundamental to our interpretation of his work on the issues of doctrinal and practical Christianity as a pioneer of the scientific spirit in Christian doctrine. Likewise Wesley's thoroughgoing reconstruction of theology upon experiential foundations has at length rightly been accorded its inevitable place in the history of Christian thought. Wesley's pioneer work toward a theology of experience has exerted not alone "an incontestable influence upon the theories of Protestant liberal theology from Friedrich Schleiermacher to William James," but what is far more im-

[11] *Wesleyan New Testament,* pp. 30, 59, 116.

portant, it carries within itself, by its sure grasp of early Reformation principles, *the necessary corrective* for the current drift of that theology toward an irreligious humanism.

"From a doctrinal point of view, John Wesley arrayed himself against *the anarchy of thought* which was turning English orthodoxy into a desert. It was the appeal to religious experience which manifested itself above all in the fact of justification concentrated in the crisis of the New Birth. . . . Finally we single out for description the way and manner in which the ideas of the Wesleyan reaction have undergone a considerable development and how *they have exerted an incontestable influence upon the theories of Protestant liberal theology from Friedrich Schleiermacher until William James.*"

"Meanwhile the intelligent appraisal of religious experience, so precious to the founder, still holds also for Methodism in the twentieth century. While some want to go back to the custom of looking to Wesley proper and to his messages which have been the rallying center, the others, more modern, perhaps more numerous, have rallied themselves to the conception of religious experience brought into repute by theoreticians, such as Schleiermacher, the father of liberal Protestantism, and William James, the prophet of religious pragmatism." [12]

It ought not to be too difficult in the light of certain ideas in these sound representations of Wesley's principles and of his pioneer relation to the New Protestantism, to find the door into a constructive appreciation of his own conversion-experience as a veritable crisis of faith. The primacy accorded to religious experience in Wesley's system of doctrinal and practical Christianity is at least consistent with a constructive view. The perception that Wesley's theology was above all a theology of crisis also points clearly to it. The religious experience to which Wesleyanism appealed, while not confined to it, was certainly focalized in the crisis of faith called the New Birth. [13] Piette has rightly chosen to follow William James who considered that

[12] *La Réaction*, 2 ed., 296, 650 (italics mine).
[13] Piette, *La Réaction*, p. 296.

Methodism (as a theology of crisis) surely follows . . . on the whole "the profounder spiritual instinct" of historic Christianity. [14]

This *accident of record* theory as to the special position accorded to conversion as the keystone of Methodist doctrine and to Wesley's own conversion as the paradigm of them all, is, we submit, at war not only *with the unbroken Wesleyan tradition*—this objection would not in itself be at all insuperable—but the theory is also at war *with the facts* and *with itself;* and these are the decisive considerations. There is in fact not an inch of ground for the thesis to stand on.

It would of course be quite as easy as the temptation is strong, in the face of the very great distance between the "Official Wesleyan Legend," which rates the conversion-experience and its implications of maximum importance, and the accident-of-record theory which concurs with rationalistic humanism in reducing the conversion-experience to a temporary gust of religious ecstasy (*à bien peu de valeur des épanchements enthousiastes*), soon chilled by time, to strike a judicial pose and to assert with a great show of wise impartiality that of course the truth must lie somewhere, probably about halfway, between these two extremes. That would indeed be a very discreet guess, if it were so. But what are the facts? What light do the records, the logic of events, the opinions alike of Wesley's foes and critics, then also of his disciples and colleagues as well as of Wesley himself, throw upon the so-called "miracle of an unimpeachable conversion"? Note in this definition of the problem the question-begging epithet "miracle," as if a perfectly natural conversion could not, precisely on that account, be of epoch-making importance. For as the historian Lecky, who has never been accused of any taste for the miracle, observes: "It is scarcely an exaggeration to say that the scene which took place at that humble meeting in Aldersgate Street forms an epoch in English history. The conviction which then flashed upon one of the most powerful and most active intellects in England is the true

[14] *Varieties of Religious Experience*, pp. 211, 227.

source of English Methodism"—and we would run no risk in adding, *of vastly more.*[15]

It will be of distinct advantage and serviceable to a deeper insight to divide the argument. Some of the weightier considerations have already been submitted in the comment on the "Last Oxford Sermon."[16] The reactions of the Anglican Bishops and Clergy to Wesley's preaching furnish a powerful argument that is alone sufficient to carry the conclusion with it. Here we submit further the fact that the *epoch-making importance* of Wesley's conversion-experience does not stand or fall with some of the admittedly impossible features of the earlier interpretations by the older school of Methodist orthodoxy of what the founder of Methodism acquired from the conversion-experience. What if they have painted Wesley prior to not only 1725 but also prior to 1738, in the language of Piette, "as a grand sinner," inventing for the conversion a lurid background of nobody knows what immoralities! What if Wesley and his disciples had set up—as a matter of fact Wesley never did set up—emotional states as indispensable tests of being a Christian. The truth is that Wesley, at his wits' end to avoid the necessity of it, walked out of the Fetter Lane Society, July 20, 1740, severed all relations with the parent society of the Revival of which he was an original and devoted member and the ablest leader, severed it in twain, rather than suffer the very psychological extravagances so often but erroneously laid to his charge. His exceedingly reluctant breach with Moravianism in the very beginning of his evangelical period was actuated by his refusal to adopt the very doctrine of Christian experience so habitually but falsely imputed to him.

What if he had now and then himself slipped into a fallacious emotionalism—once more, he never did—but what if he had? That could afford no inference adverse to the conviction that the return of John Wesley both in his public preaching and personal religious experience in the Spring of 1738 to the Luther-

---

[15] *England in the Eighteenth Century,* II, 558.
[16] Journal, III, 147.

Calvin doctrine of justification by faith was his Religious Rubicon. The Church historian, Friedrich Loofs, in a masterful
article on Methodism (1903), after a thorough investigation,
fixed upon the conversion-experience and the famous Oxford
Sermon June 11, 1738, on "Salvation by Faith," which was the
first manifesto of the Revival, as the decisive turning-point in
Wesley's career. Loof's representation of the facts and the significance of Wesley's conversion-experience is so weighty and informing that it is here submitted for the first time, I believe, in
English translation. After giving in German translation Wesley's
own terse account in the Journal, Loofs continues:

"This experience was John Wesley's 'conversion.' But it is
important with reference to the event itself and also for right
understanding of present Methodist thought about conversion,
to point out two facts which weaken the *solitary* significance of
the event. First of all, Wesley said of himself in the Fall and
Winter of 1738-1739, that he did not have the witness of the
spirit, but was waiting for it.[17] On the other hand, he interpolated in Part Two of the Extracts of his Journal, published
in 1740, over against the statement in Part One, 'I who went
to America to convert others, was never myself converted to
God,' the remark: 'I am not sure of this.' Then on the day (it
was several days) before May 24, 1738, he wrote the very severe
if not discourteous letter to William Law repudiating his teaching. So then Wesley's conversion to a Christianity sure in its
faith was not a momentary experience."

"But just as sure as John Wesley's high-church mystical
period in which he did not understand justification by faith was
different in principle (italics mine) from the period of his later
evangelical preaching, just as sure as his fiasco in America broke
the power of his old views and his commerce with Boehler in-
augurated the new, just so surely may we see the decisive turning point there where Wesley first experienced the truth of
Boehler's instructions, namely, a quarter before nine on the 24th
of May in 1738. Then on the nineteenth day of his conversion-

[17] Tyerman, I, 190-192.

experience he preached his celebrated sermon on Ephesians II, 8, which opens his Standard Sermons."[18]

This essentially sound representation could nevertheless be very much improved. First of all, it still tangles up, much too much, the objective significance of the conversion-experience with the variable psychological concomitants of the transition, with the question of instantaneity, something Wesley himself was very careful not to do. Secondly, Loofs was wholly in error that Wesley interpolated in the first edition of Part Two of the Journal, which is the important conversion document, the remark, "I am not sure of this." Probably the most important thing that could be said about that interpolated doubt is the fact that Wesley himself never allowed it to get into print at all nor is he responsible for its publication. Even if authentic, it had to wait full thirty years after his death before it first saw the light of day in print. Even if authentic, even if the words "I am not sure of this" were penned by Wesley himself, still the fact that they were not allowed to get into any one of the five or more editions of Parts One and Two made in the course of Wesley's life, strictly prohibits any doctrinal use of the interpolation at variance with Wesley's doctrinal positions. The fifth edition of the conversion document in 1775, and so in the thirty-sixth year of the Revival, is an exact reprint of the first edition. It does not have the so-called retraction in it. Wesley's refusal or failure to retract in print the views set forth in the original account of his conversion and consistently maintained in all of his writings, simply forbids by every principle of sound criticism any appeal to Jackson's interpolation to weaken the significance of the religious principles which for half a century held without variableness or shadow of turning the conspicuous position in his message, ministry, and entire doctrine of Christian experience. But strong as this argument may be we are not beholden to it: we have something better, something decisive. Thirteen years after Wesley penned and published the words,

---

[18] Loofs' Art. "Methodismus" in *Realencyklopädie für protestantische Theologie und Kirche*, Bd. 12, ss. 747-801.

"wrote in the anguish of my heart, when I was confessedly in a state of unbelief, namely, I went to America to convert Indians; but, oh, who shall convert me," Bishop Lavington tried to turn them much to Wesley's discredit. Did Wesley then retract his position? Not a whit! Did he then qualify his statement that "he was at that hour (1738) in a state of damnation?" Not a hair's breadth! On the contrary he reaffirmed and defended the Journal diagnosis of his spiritual state, i.e., the extremely depressed and embittered self-estimate in the light of the divine holiness and according to the standard of grace, as entirely accurate. Now this is conclusive evidence that the idea of retracting the self-estimate according to the standard of grace recorded in the first edition of the Journal never entered Wesley's mind during the period (1738-1763) in which he constructed and established the doctrinal standards of the Revival. The use, therefore, of the posthumous interpolation—"I am not sure of this"— be it authentic or no, to nullify or qualify Wesley's theological judgment in the epoch of his maturity must be pronounced illicit. Whether it can be defended on other grounds is beside the question. Our conclusion is simply that the credentials for that purpose are in any case not Wesleyan.

As the objective significance of Wesley's conversion-experience does not postulate a personal background of lurid sinfulness, so is it also a false scent which seeks for the objective significance in transitory gusts of religious feeling. This is the vitiating fallacy that reigned supreme, not to be sure in Wesley's doctrine of Christian experience, but only in that of the much later and lesser lights of the movement. But is it sound criticism to borrow this vitiating fallacy which perhaps reigned supreme in the older school of Methodist orthodoxy but demonstrably wants the sanction of Wesley, and then use it to discredit, as it was once used to glorify, the change through which Wesley passed in 1738? A method of reasoning that is wrong because it sets up improper tests is just as wrong for the purpose of refutation as it is for the demonstration of a thesis. This is in fact the proper inference to be made from Wesley's meticulous reticence in public statements about the purely private and personal elements in his conversion experience. The method is wrong. He does not refer to what is special to the subject of faith—that is not the key to its objective significance—but to the principles involved.

Moreover, we would go far astray if we inferred from Wesley's consistent objectivity in his public preaching and writing that he did not at any time unbosom his Christian experience in the intimate circle of his class meetings. He must have set an example of that *sharing of Christian experience*[19] which he inculcated in season and out of season upon all his followers and was the peculiar dynamic of early Methodism. To suppose that he stood outside and aloof from *the experience-sharing* into which he labored indefatigably to draw every member of the Methodist household of faith and that he remained a foreigner to a practise in which the Methodist Revival lived and moved and had its being would render the Wesleyan Reformation historically unintelligible. He who thinks Wesley an outsider and not rather the principal source of this practise simply has not read that wonderful stream of pastoral letters from his pen to some of the choice spirits among his disciples. They throb with all the vital elements of Christian experience. Or again let any one analyze Wesley's frequent use of the words "close" and "open" in reference to experience-sharing among Christians. Or again, what did he mean by taking "sweet counsel" with Whitefield, both reading to each other the records of their religious experiences? The problem really is not what Wesley's practise was, but what is wrong with our point of view and presuppositions that makes it so difficult to see things as they were and are. Last but not least, on this phase of the subject Wesley was himself a man of deep, strong, ardent religious feeling. It is true that his Journals are less subjective, more objective documents of Christian experience than, for example, *The Confessions of Augustine.* As a rule, he has left no written record, to borrow a term current in and characteristic of early Methodism, of his "melting times."

[19] See *Rules of the Band Societies,* drawn up December 25, 1738.

But, as above noted, he passed through them just the same. And we are grateful for even the rare moments when either Wesley himself or those with him have unveiled his inner personal responses to the truth-values in the Gospel. We may rest assured that his doctrine of Christian experience did not lack the seal and confirmation of his own experience, but was rather a simple transcript thereof.

But the burden of this chapter is to show that Wesley always read the objective significance of his conversion-experience in the Spring of 1738 not primarily in terms of his personal feelings, but in terms of the religious principles involved. And he has said, if once then literally a thousand times, that the essence of the great transition was wrapped up in the fact that he then first understood fully, accepted finally, and laid to heart Luther's doctrine of justification by faith, and that this whole-souled acceptance of Luther's religious understanding of the Gospel, when it occurred, made his heart beat perceptibly faster. A whole swarm of errors about this event, whether in his mind or in that of his disciples, would never be able to throw this one fact into eclipse. Exactly fifteen months after the conversion-experience Wesley himself said all that needs to be said, in fact all there is to say on this subject: "Indeed the report now current in Bristol was that I was a Papist, if not a Jesuit. Some added that I was born and bred at Rome, which many cordially believed." "Oh, ye fools, when will ye understand that *the preaching of justification by faith alone* (italics mine) . . . is overturning Popery from the foundation? When will ye understand that the most destructive of all those errors which Rome, the mother of abominations, hath brought forth (compared to which Transsubstantiation and a hundred more are 'trifles light as air'), is 'that we are justified by works'; or (to express the same a little more decently) by faith and works? Now, do I preach this? *I did for ten years; I was (fundamentally) a Papist and knew it not."* [20]   All this, and precisely this, is set forth in the

[20] Journal, II, 262.

first manifesto of the Revival preached at Oxford the nineteenth day of his conversion-experience.

We are now in a position to define the exact importance which Wesley himself, for all his meticulous reticence about the conversion-experience as a personal affair, did attach to it as a dynamic revival of Reformation principles in Christian preaching. He always divided his sixty-six years of preaching into two periods: *Before* and *after* he understood *justification by faith.* He has done this so often that we forbear to illustrate at large. But one note runs through them all: "As soon as I saw clearly the nature of saving faith and made it the standing topic of my preaching," "God then began to work by my ministry as he never had done before." Exactly what this meant is thus described more at large: "From the year 1725 to 1729 I preached much, but *saw no fruit of my labour.* Indeed, it could not be that I should; for I neither laid the foundation of repentance nor of believing the Gospel; taking it for granted that all to whom I preached were believers and that many of them 'needed no repentance.' From the year 1729 to 1734, laying a deeper foundation of repentance, *I saw a little fruit. But it was only a little;* and no wonder; for *I did not preach faith* in the blood of the covenant. From 1734 to 1738, speaking more of faith in Christ, *I saw more fruit of my preaching* and visiting from house to house than ever I had done before; though I know not if any of those who were outwardly reformed were *inwardly and thoroughly converted to God.* FROM 1738 TO THIS TIME—speaking continually of Jesus Christ; laying Him only for the foundation of the whole building, making Him all in all, the first and the last; preaching only on this plan, 'The kingdom of God is at hand; repent ye, and believe the Gospel,' *the 'word of God ran'* *as fire among the stubble;* it 'was glorified' more and more; multitudes crying out, 'What must we do to be saved?' and afterwards witnessing, 'By grace we are saved through faith.' " [21]

This is Wesley's own account, given in the twenty-first year of his ordination and the eighth of his conversion-experience. of

[21] Letters, Vol. II, p. 264. (Italics in quotation mine.)

the revolution wrought in the content and in the power of his preaching. Now we very much miss, in view of its traditional position, any reference in this account to the conversion-experience of 1738. For if the objective significance of the conversion-experience rests not in this revolution in the content and power of Wesley's preaching, it rests not anywhere. Now there is no clearer, more tenacious and important concept in Wesley's writings than his way of referring to and reasoning about what in his life went before and what came after "I preached or knew salvation by faith." Note that Wesley has two points of reference. First, before I *preached* salvation by faith, secondly, before I *knew* salvation by faith. The doctrine found entrance into his preaching on March 6, 1738, "I began preaching this new doctrine though my soul started back from the work." [22] But it did not become the center of gravity nor gain complete ascendency and control over his teaching and preaching until May 24, 1738. But their common objective significance for Wesley, who used both dates, was the change in the content and power of his preaching. The account of the revolution in the content and power of his preaching given in the letter to Church can be associated with either date or both together. The *Short History* gives Monday, March 6th, as the date when the new doctrine of salvation by faith first gained a foothold in Wesley's preaching. But the first and second of the Wesley letters to Bishop Secker, written six months before the Church letter, are positive and explicit that the words "Before I either preached or knew salvation by faith" refer to May 24, 1738. "From May 24, 1738, wherever I was desired to preach, salvation by faith was my only theme." There is an incisive reference to his conversion-experience, fixing the date, in a letter to his brother Samuel, October 1738. It was penned ten weeks after his personal conferences with the Moravian masters at Herrnhut and Professor Franke at Halle and excels all others in cogency and pertinency. "By a Christian I mean one who so believes in Christ as that sin hath no more do-

[22] Journal, I, 442.

minion over him; and in this obvious sense of the word *I was not a Christian till May the 24th last past.*"

Over against Wesley's consistent, constant definition of the objective significance of the conversion-experience as a revolution in the content and power of his preaching, stands the hierarchical-humanist disparagement of it and the traditional Methodist glorification of it on purely psychological grounds. The disparagement and the glorification are both tarred with the same fallacious pitch. They both set up the number and saltine quality of Wesley's tears as the proper test of the reality and objective significance of the conversion-experience. Turning from this source of fog and confusion to consider the revolution in the content and power of Wesley's preaching inseparable from Wesley's insight into the nature of saving faith, well may we ask, What is there in any man's life more worthy to be called a conversion-experience and that too in a transcendental sense? Let him find a better interpretation who can! Before this fact and its dynamic implications for Wesley and modern Christianity, all quibbling over fluctuating religious feeling, a commonplace in the psychology of religion, might well feel rebuked into silence.

It can not be much of a surprise to any one, in the light of these facts, though I believe it is here for the first time mentioned, that there is in Wesley's Journals, Letters and Sermons *a double system of chronology.* In addition to the common way of timing events *Anno Domini,* by the year, month, day, hour or even the minute, pursued in his writings, especially the Journal, there are scattered throughout the twenty-five volumes of his writings —references, not a *few cases* but *numbered by the score,* to his conversion-experience, *anno meae conversionis.* Here are two typical cases. He writes in May, 1765: "I think on Justification just as I have done any time these seven and twenty years, and just as Mr. Calvin does."[23] The following reference will carry an unusual weight of authority on this question: Thomas Rutherforth, 1712-71, Regius Professor of Divinity at Cambridge, and later Archdeacon of Essex, published, 1763, *Four Charges to the*

[23] Note that "twenty-seven years" refers to the year 1738.

Clergy of the Archdeaconry of Essex. The first three are against
the Methodists. The charges fell five years later into Wesley's
hands. The very day after, he began a formal reply, saying,
along with much more, in particular this: "You charge me likewise, and that more than once or twice, with maintaining contradictions. I answer: (1) If all my sentiments were compared together, from the years 1725 to 1768, there would be truth in the
charge; for during the latter part of this period I have relin-
quished several of my former sentiments. (2) During these last
thirty years I may have varied in some of my sentiments or expressions *without observing it.* (3) It is not strange if among
inaccurate expressions there are some seeming contradictions, especially considering I was answering so many different objec-
tors, frequently attacking me at once, and one pushing this way,
another that, with all the violence they were able. Nevertheless
(4) I believe there will be found few, if any real, contradictions
for near thirty years." In other words, Wesley has admitted the
fact of contradictions in what he taught and preached. But he
has referred them summarily to a radical change in his religious
principles and located the change definitely in the year 1738.

Thirty years ago indicates here that his acceptance in the year
1738 of the Luther-Calvin idea of faith fixed for him the period
of his theological maturity. "And this is the doctrine which I
have constantly believed and taught for near eight and twenty
years. This I published to all the world in the year 1738 and
ten or twelve times since." The highly important sermon on
"The Lord Our Righteousness," 1765, makes the conversion-experience and the epoch of the Revival one and inseparable. Again
writing John Erskine of the Old Greyfriars Church, Edinburgh,
in the year 1765, Wesley said simply: "As to my principles, in
the main point (justification by Faith) I have not wavered a
moment for these seven and twenty years." Finally Wesley
wrote in 1778: "Forty years ago I knew and preached every
Christian doctrine which I preach now." The virtual, if not total,
neglect by the hierarchical-humanist criticism of the conversion-
experience, of the indissoluble bond in Wesley's thinking, over a

period of fifty years, between the objective significance of the conversion-experience and the origin and progress of the Revival, does but attest how ill-informed much writing about Wesley still continues to be.

Now the great frequency and entire consistency of these references, over a period of fifty years, to his acceptance of "Salvation by Faith," as the turning point of his career ought in all reason to put the matter at rest. Wesley was at once clear in his own mind, as the documents abundantly demonstrate, that he had, in accepting Luther's religious understanding of the Gospel, crossed his Religious Rubicon; and he began soon after to interpret the new developments which flowed from his personal acceptance of Luther's doctrine of faith, as events of vastly more than personal importance, yea, of Church-wide importance. In fact the importance which he attached to these events rose at once to almost painful heights. It had been a powerful tradition in English Christianity, easy enough to understand in the light of its origins, to look largely to Protestantism in Europe for orientation and guidance. Wesley also thought that recourse to European sources to find out what Christianity is may have been advisable a while back "when the case was widely different," but now that he had recovered for himself the original impulse and dynamic principle of the early Reformation, he judged (see the revealing preface to Part Two of the Journal, dated London, Sept. 20, 1740) it to be no longer wise, rather those are *"unwise (to say no more) who run to inquire after God in Holland or Germany.* When I went (it was in the summer of 1738) the case was widely different. God had not then 'made bare his arm,' before us as He hath now done, in a manner, I will be bold to say, which had not been known either in Holland or Germany at that time, when He who ordereth all things wisely, according to 'the counsel of His own will,' was pleased by me to open the intercourse between the English and the Moravian Church." Here Wesley's sovereign assurance of himself as a chosen vessel of God flashes with blinding force through the lines. One has to go back to Calvin and Luther, to Francis, to St. Paul, to the

Prophets and then to the "figured flame which blends, transcends them all" for the models of this God-consciousness. He saw already in the beginnings of the Revival for which he bore the responsibility of leadership the history not only "of what God hath done and is still doing in our land," not only "such a work in many respects as neither we nor our fathers had known," but also a new point of departure and of orientation. The Revival had been in progress but seven years when Wesley boldly threw out the challenging question: "When hath religion, I will not say since the Reformation, but since the time of Constantine the Great, made so large a progress in any nation, within so small a space? I believe, hardly can either ancient or modern history supply us with a parallel instance." A bishop denounced this question as "vain boasting and enthusiasm." And Wesley in the fourteenth year of the Revival made answer: "I repeat the question, giving the glory to God." Ten years later he wrote Charles Wesley, "I do not at all think (to tell you a secret) that the work will ever be destroyed, Church or no Church."

We are confronted in these utterances with a vocational consciousness that simply refuses to be rationalized by ordinary standards. Wesley explored every channel of Christian thought, every stream of Christian tradition. He was in 1725 first seized of *the idea of the Holy*. Then he rediscovered in 1738 Luther's religious understanding of the Gospel. He felt that he had in so doing reestablished vital relations between English Christianity and European Protestantism. He thus entered into himself more deeply, laid deeper foundations in Scripture and experience for his doctrine of faith, emancipated his mind from every restraint of external authority and advanced into a full-orbed consciousness of his theological independence. The immediate and extraordinary significance which he has here attached to the new developments introduced into English Christianity by his personal recovery of the original impulse of the Reformation and by his fresh contacts with the Reformation churches seems hitherto to have escaped the attention of investigators.

There are excellent reasons for differentiating as the late Ernst

Troeltsch has done in his able monograph on *Protestant Christianity and the Church in the Modern Age* (1906), the Old from the New Protestantism, not to deny continuity, but to indicate radical developments and solid differences. What then would be the position of Wesley in this great Protestant Evolution? Does his return to early Reformation principles, which as to the fact is for us henceforth a closed question, preclude his parental relation to the New Protestantism? Hitherto the answer to this question has been sought solely from the standpoint of Wesley's contribution to practical Christianity, as if the history and development of Christian thought or theology were a thing apart, without root or fruit in the soil of practical Christianity. That has, indeed and alas! been the nature of much theology,—but not all! This divorce of theology from the stream of Christian experience is unsound. The prophet makes theology. The apologist writes it. The work of the apologist is for a generation, that of a prophet for the ages. It is a deep-seated prejudice of intellectualism that it would be useless to look to the early Wesleyan movement for any theologian who directly advanced the progress of Christian thought. This might be true only if the dynamic of Christian thought were but a matter of the books, of the monastic or the academic mind, and if theology lived, moved and had its being in the intellectual interest.

It would ill suit the genius of Wesley's work to credit him either in the formative period of his theology or in that of his maturity with a scholastic purpose or to say of him that he was primarily concerned with a reformation of theology. He had no such purpose clearly in mind, nor was it ever a conscious project. Nevertheless it certainly would be no more than was involved in his return to the faith of the first Reformers, in his recovery of the original Reformation impulse and in his far-flung plans and purposes, should we venture to see in all these things and the logic of events that issued from them, the necessary, at any rate far and away the best, bridge for thinking our way out of the Old into the New Protestantism. Wesley's understanding of the Gospel was saturated with New Testament thought and thoroughly rooted and grounded in historic Christianity. In fact so many major streams of tendency in historic Christianity are, as analysis shows, confluent in the Wesleyan movement as to suggest only a composite of incompatibles. But deeper analysis discovers not only a great and incommunicable individuality that presided over its beginnings and stamped its image indelibly on the movement but also a wealth and variety, a judicious correlation and balance of religious principles without parallel in Protestantism. The extent to which Wesley had in effect emancipated himself from the misplaced confidences of traditional Christianity, his wide knowledge and deep appreciation of the positive advantages and values in historic Christianity, his comprehensive catholicity and deep tolerance, his ability to unite great truths which have more often been fatally divorced, above all his ability to hold fast the truth of humanism while recovering the religious element of the Reformation and of joining them together, finally his open-minded and untrammelled experimentalism and essentially progressive spirit are among the high indications of exceptional worth in his work as a means of orientation in both doctrinal and practical Christianity, both within the Wesleyan Churches and still more in all churches that "desire a league offensive and defensive with every soldier of Jesus Christ."

Right now there are *compelling reasons for this rediscovery of John Wesley*. First of all, the successive attempts of liberal Protestantism, largely within the university circles of Central Europe, but also everywhere, to build such a bridge for the purposes of Christian thought, undertaken and carried out for the most part aloof from the vital work of the Church and from the issues of practical Christianity, have resulted in the judgment of both its friends and foes in relative failure. Out of these intellectual undertakings has come no dynamic revival of Christianity, no purposeful reformation of the Christian Church. The fact and the confession of a tragic deficit in the liberal reconstruction of the Christian faith has found in the first quarter of our century among the master-minds of liberal Christianity other equally significant and authoritative voices.

Over in Europe a critical reaction has set in against the in-dubitable and self-confessed practical religious failure of the liberal reconstructions of Christianity. This critical reaction arose in the midst of the travail of post-war privation, disturb- ance, insecurity. It has been intensified and darkened by the world-wide unrest and distress of the hour. It is not the first time in human history that suffering has caused the scales to fall from prosperity-blinded eyes. But in any event this critical reaction in the Church of today against the desolate theorizing and humanistic Christianity of an age that is going out was already long overdue, and is destined to make a difference in the Church of tomorrow. For the liberal reconstructions of the Christian faith have not so far come to the birth in any dynamic revival of religion or genuine reformation of the Church. They have never been able to represent the religious energies and to continue the vital work of the Protestant Reformation in any manner adequate to the needs of the Modern Church. The ex-perienced feebleness and futility of preaching on the basis of pronounced liberal principles, the clear perception that the mes-sage of the Church has not on those premises been with the dem-onstration of the spirit and power, the discovery that such preach-ing has brought forth a lean harvest of the saving faith which is the necessary and true effect of the Gospel, are driving many dis-quieted souls into a new search for spiritual power. "Having the form, and seeking the power" is again a fact to be reckoned with in the collective consciousness of the Christian churches.

This renewal of the search for power in Protestant preaching has again taken the direction primarily of a return to the early Reformers, if haply we may again feel in our own souls the creative impulse and principle of the Reformation, if only we may come into fresh, direct communion with the Word of God in Scripture and last, but not least, with the immediate voice of God in our own religious experience. It has taken the form and direction of a radical shift of the center of gravity in preaching from a man-made to a God-given faith; from the chronic and paralyzing reference of the truth-values of the Christian faith to the human subject to the quickening reference of these truth-values to the work and witness of the Holy Spirit; from a psychology of the Gospel to the divine initiative in the Gospel; from experience as merely an event in the soul of man to the objective principle of all Christian experience, namely, revelation. In all this we are actually planting our feet, it may be unconsciously, yet identically, in the footprints of John Wesley, who, after having for thirteen years drunk the cup of humanist religion to the dregs, went back to the experience and insight of the early Reformers, and above all to the Scriptures, and began with them once more to build an absolute trust upon the grace of God in Christ and upon saving faith as the voice of God in the heart proclaiming itself. This it was that had revolutionary consequences both in Wesley's own experience and in his preaching.

Over against this tried and true orientation and foundation of the Christian faith, and in the midst of the present crisis of the Christian faith, evident as it is that the Protestant churches have for a quarter of a century been, if not actually losing ground, then doing no more than mark time, it must in all candor be admitted that the modern mind, though magnificently productive along some lines, has, when left to itself and thrown back upon its own resources, proven itself to be in the procreation and birth of religious truth-values strangely impotent and barren. There is no sounder or stronger induction from the Christian centuries—an open book of instruction—than the basic truth that any new departure within the Christian movement or any reconstruction of the Christian faith which does not send its roots deep down into the soil of historic Christianity simply has no future. Right here modernism as religion is pathetically feeble. The liberal reconstructions of the Christian faith for all their militant boastfulness of superiority shine in religion by a borrowed light and warm their cold hands secretly by the fires of historic Christianity which on the whole, liberalism has done little to tend or replenish. Meanwhile the Christian Church, guardian of revelation and redemption, commissioned to continue the revealing and redeeming activities of Christ, secure in the inexhaustible resiliency of the Christian faith, unlocks the treasure-house of her riches and lavishes them on every beggar at her doors.

Verily, faith and freedom belong together. Science, free research, criticism applied without let or hindrance, without cavil or question, without external constraint or restraint to the entire subject matter of Scripture and dogma, the untrammelled right and the bounden duty to explore and think through all the truth-values of the Prophetic-Christian religion in terms of history and experience, finally to assess the results in their total bearing on our world-view, all these are indispensable necessities. But these alone are not enough. Once it was nature-miracles. Now it is natural science. But saving faith in God does not have its birth in either of them, neither does it live and grow primarily by them. The rock on which the Christian Church is built—the Christian faith will last as long as the Christian Church, but no longer—is primarily a religious appreciation and interpretation of Jesus as a perfect revelation of God and a complete atonement for sin. It lives and moves and has its being in the consciousness that Jesus Christ is the fountain-head of our religious strength and security. Our ultimate is the experienced fact that the religious energy of the person and work of Christ is still the great reality, the central fire, of all Christendom as a believing community and that saving faith as an individual experience arises only as a perception of the pulse-beats of his spirit and life still to be found and felt in all parts of Christendom. It is precisely because the essentials of our total problem were the essentials of John Wesley's problem, that we do exceeding well to avail ourselves once more of his example and counsel.

Thirty years ago the late Friedrich Loofs, professor of Church History in the University of Halle-Wittenberg, Germany, perhaps best known to American churches for his Haskel Lectures at Oberlin, Ohio, 1911, on *What is the Truth about Jesus Christ?* and one of the ablest spokesmen of liberal Christianity, brought his interpretative historical study [24] of Wesley and his work (1903) to a close with this heart-searching and significant confession: "We (of Protestant Germany) need to cultivate Church fellowship. The helplessness of our laymen in the presence of the forces of the age which threaten the very foundations of the faith, the ritualistic bondage and ceremonial pomp of our preaching, the want of contact between the churches and the charitable enterprises for which collections are made, all that indicates wherein church fellowship could really mean something. But what we have need of will not grow of itself, nor without offense to anxious politicians. (*How prophetic!*) *If the twentieth century brings a new, modern John Wesley—he will find the fields ripe for the harvest.*"

It must be left to the considerate judgment of the well-informed reader whether the present crisis in the state of the evangelical churches does not accentuate a thousandfold the truth of this wistful far-flung prophecy. It is almost pathetic today how theology wistfully watches for some crumb of comfort to fall from the tables of natural science or turns away from historic Christianity and the living stream of Christian experience to considerations of natural reason. If ever, then now do we supremely need, after the manner and in the measure of John Wesley, to seek and find the meaning of God in Christian Experience!

[24] There is no better in print.

CHAPTER VIII

SAINTS OF THE WORLD

The four sermons, three by John Wesley—"Salvation by Faith," June 11, 1738; "The Almost Christian," July 25, 1741; "Scriptural Christianity," August 24, 1744—and one by Charles Wesley—"Awake, thou that Sleepest," April 4, 1741—preached before the University of Oxford, occupy the conspicuous position in the first volume of Wesley's doctrinal discourses selected to give doctrinal guidance and coherence to the Revival. These discourses, twelve in number, expound the religious principles of the Wesleyan message which are summarized in the Preface as "the substance of Wesley's preaching" and "the essentials of true Religion." They develop the central idea of the Christian religion as experience and their common theme is the sovereign saving significance of a God-given faith in Christ. All the points in the Wesleyan doctrine of Christian experience are said by the Preface to be traversed in them. A second collection of discourses was made two years later to develop more strongly the doctrine of Christian perfection as the central idea of the Christian ethic of life and to study further the fundamental relation of a God-given faith to the progress of Christian experience (sanctification) in distinction from its relation to the beginnings (justification) on which the emphasis falls in the first series. Wesley placed another of his Oxford Sermons, "The Circumcision of the Heart," preached Jan. 1, 1733, at St. Mary's, at the head of this second series. It expounds the doctrine of holiness or Christian perfection, and it was written during his editorial work on *The Christian's Pattern*. It is the only pulpit utterance made before his return to Reformation principles which satisfied his mature judgment and it did not fully satisfy; for

195

he revised it to include and to agree with his final position in 1738. Its inclusion in the Standard Sermons attests that his doctrine of sanctification, historically considered, had other than Reformation sources and that his interest in it is older than his concurrence with the Luther-Calvin doctrine of faith.

Three reasons are given for the primacy accorded the Oxford Sermons. Friends had advised and requested their publication in that position. Then too his plan and purpose to print "the substance of what I have been preaching for between eight and nine years past" called for precisely these discourses. Finally they were the strongest refutation of the assertion frequently made that "we have changed our doctrine of late." The argument and the exposition rest here, as in all of Wesley's preaching, on two pillars: (1) "The Oracles of God" or the Word of God in the Scriptures, (2) "the sure testimony of experience." The sermons propound the general question *What is Christianity? What is it to be a Christian?* The answer given is that Christianity is the true, because it is "the Scriptural, experimental religion." Sometimes Wesley said it is the true, because it is the rational religion. But where he has once called it a rational religion he has a hundred times called it the experimentally true religion. These sermons describe "that great work of God among the children of men called Christianity, not as it implies a set of opinions, a system of doctrines, but as it refers to men's hearts and lives." [1] The whole approach then is experiential, vital, practical. It is concerned to know what Christianity is in the living present and not simply what it has been in former times. They herald Wesley's simple purpose to bring the Christian Church back to religion as experience in the face of a dead theology and a dead ceremony. And the standard of religion to which he summoned the whole Christian World was not a mutilated or desiccated Christianity but the Christian faith in the plenitude of its significance. To an age where compromise and carelessness in religion reigned supreme, the Wesleys and White-

[1] Sermon 4.

field proclaimed an uncompromising Christianity as the supreme practical concern of human existence.

"I avoid that bane of piety," so Wesley wrote his father in December, 1734, "the company of good sort of men, lukewarm Christians (as they are called), persons that have a *great concern for but no sense of religion*. . . . I never came from among these *Saints of the World* (as J. Valdesso calls them), faint, dissipated and shorn of all my strength, but I say, 'God deliver me from *an half-Christian*.'"[2]   Valdesso (1500-1540) was a son of Italy who labored indefatigably by tongue and pen for religious reform.   In his *Alfabeto Christiano*, the Christian Alphabet, he taught with deep conviction that the soul must choose between God and the World.   He was one of numerous pioneers of reformation throughout Christendom whose lights were blended and transcended in the figured flame of Martin Luther (1483-1546). Wesley's profound kinship of spirit with all these religious reformers is everywhere revealed by the most infallible tokens. But it is very remarkable that he found so many of them out and nurtured his own spirit by them.   He sought emancipation from a Christianity utterly conformed to this world and the power of victory over it chiefly by the renewal of his mind at these original springs of reformation.

The character drawn by Valdesso of the representatives of a Christianity "conformed to this world," namely, *Saints of the World*, struck fire with Wesley.   Wesley wrote this letter also while he was working away at his new edition of *The Christian's Pattern*.   The spirit of his uncompromising Christianity breaks forth in his use of Valdesso's *Saints of the World*.   It found further vigorous expression in the preface to his new translation of Thomas à Kempis' *Imitation of Christ*. "The Spiritual Pharisees" or "Saints of the World" are in the Wesley Preface warned to "expect no softening here; no mincing or palliating of evangelical truths.   Here is no countenance cruelly given to Half-Christians; no false hopes to those of a double heart; to the trimmers between God and the world, who love to

2 Letters, I, 169.

term religion, the *main* end of their lives, who say, they do make it their *chief* business, and are willing to allow God the larger *part* of their affections. Nay, but He hath told thee, O man, as by his Son, so by this his faithful follower, that it will nothing avail thee to be *almost*—unless thou goest on to be *altogether* a Christian! That He abhorreth faint hearts and feeble hands, and the sinner that goeth two ways! That thou must serve Him, if at all, with *all* thy strength; That is the *whole* of man! That thou hast *one, only one* end to regard on earth; that thou hast *one, only one* business to pursue! That since but *one* thing is needful, on that *alone* thou art to fix thy single eye, namely, to love the Lord thy God with *all* thy heart, and with *all* thy soul, and with *all* thy mind, and with *all* [3] thy strength. The good God be merciful unto me and thee, and give us so to run, that we may obtain the prize of our high calling!"

The discourse on "The Almost Christian" contains, as a commentary on "the sure testimony of experience," an open reference to Wesley's experiment "for many years" (1725-1738) with a moralistic, intellectualistic, mystical achievement of "the life of God in the soul of man." He has described (I, 13) the laborious self-salvation that diverted his mind from the objective reality of the Word of God and fixed his attention upon subjective experiences instead of upon the sole, full, final revelation in Jesus Christ of a living and saving God. It is to be noted that the differential of the almost and the altogether Christian is said to be *the experience of saving faith that has in it the power of God,* and this experience is referred to "Thus saith His Word," "Thus saith our Lord" and "the Oracles of God." Here again it is the objectivity of revelation and of Christian experience that is the great foundation.

The reference in this Oxford Sermon of 1741 to his own experimentation and progress from the *almost Christianity* of several varieties to the *altogether Christianity* of revelation links up the outcome of the experience indissolubly with his acceptance of Luther's doctrine of faith and the Word of God. It was this

[3] Italics by Wesley.

insight of his conversion-experience that shifted the center of gravity in his preaching, altered the whole course of his life and sent him forth upon those magnificent, life-long pilgrimages of Gospel passion that place him in the front rank of Apostolic evangelism.

Wesley's analytic judgment passed on his thirteen-year experiment in religion is as follows: "I did go thus far for many years, as many of this place can testify; using diligence to eschew all evil, and to have a conscience void of offence; redeeming the time; buying up every opportunity of doing all good to all men; constantly and carefully using all the public and all the private means of grace; endeavouring after a steady seriousness of behaviour, at all times, and in all places; and, God is my record, before whom I stand, doing all this in sincerity; have a real design to serve God; a hearty desire to do His will in all things; to please Him who called me to 'fight the good fight,' and to 'lay hold on eternal life.' Yet my own conscience beareth me witness in the Holy Ghost, that all this time I was but almost a Christian."

This retrospect of his religious experience as "Almost a Christian" is then completed by a positive statement of what it is to be a Christian in the plenary sense. There are but three particulars: (1) The love of God, (2) The love of our neighbor, (3) Faith—a sure trust and confidence which a man hath in God, that by the merits of Christ, his sins are forgiven and he is reconciled to the favour of God,—whereof doth follow a loving heart to obey His commandments. Now of the interrelation of these three, ultimately two, principles, Wesley observes that *Faith is the ground of all.* He then cited Scripture to illustrate that faith is, has, does all in Christian experience and life.

Since now Martin Luther is known to be, along with his own independent inquiries into the Word of God, the only authority other than Scripture, that Wesley ever acknowledged for his understanding of *Justification by Faith,* it seems long overdue that the pertinent section of Luther's preface to the *Epistle to the Romans*,[4] perpetual fountain of Reformation impulse, should be translated and introduced into English-speaking Methodism. For in listening to Luther in his preface to St. Paul's masterpiece, Wesley was confronted with the great, the infinite gulf between man's utmost effort and the grace of God. Man of himself can not achieve his own salvation. He can only in utter humility let God, the most high God, give it to him. Under the decisive influence, the great authority of Luther's voice, Wesley let this belief take hold and master him. It was a crucial decision, a crisis as of life and death. It went to the bottom of the heart. At last religion had got out of the intellect into the will and the feelings, and swept the whole personal life into the response to the Word of God. Fifteen centuries ago Augustine relates of his discerning mother that "she felt sure (Bishop Ambrose who Augustine said was "preaching salvation most soundly" gave her the assurance) he was to pass through a conflict of faith and doubt, from sickness to health, after the intervention of a great and growing peril, rising to a maximum which physicians call the crisis" (*quam criticam medici vocant*).[5] Harnack, historian of dogma, has affirmed that this Pauline-Augustinian version of the Gospel in terms of experience (this theology of crisis which has been the a b c of the Wesleyan Reformation) as the deliverance of the sin-sick enslaved spirit of man from the bondage of sin and doubt, as if the energy of a compressed spring were suddenly released, has formed and informed the major portion of the hymnology and devotional literature of the Christian Church and has with rare exceptions prevailed in Christian preaching and teaching in all ages. That is simply a fact that will be respected.

Here then is Luther's description of the *"change which God (not man) works in the heart through faith in Christ."* The Preface is dated 1522:

---

[4] It is thus linked up with Wesley's Conversion-Experience; Journal, I, 424.
[5] *Confessions*, Bk. VI, Ch. 1.

"This letter to the Romans is truly the main part of the New Testament. It is the very purest gospel and is of such dignity and value that a Christian man should not only know it by heart, word for word, but he should meditate on it every day as the soul's daily bread. For it can never be read or reflected upon too much or too well and the more it is delved into and discussed the more precious it becomes and the better we like it.

"For this cause I will do all I can to make it so and by God's help I offer this preface as a door of approach in order that this Epistle may be so much the better understood by all. For it has hitherto been badly veiled in darkness by commentaries and all kinds of theological twaddle, whereas it is in and of itself a bright light, almost enough to flood all scripture with illumination.

"We have got to get acquainted first of all with the language and find out what St. Paul means by such words as law, sin, grace, faith, righteousness, flesh, spirit and the like; otherwise there is no use in reading it."

After a terse explanation of the terms law, sin and grace, Luther continues with his description of saving faith in Jesus Christ:

"Faith is not what many suppose it to be, namely, something that man fetches up from his own imagination and puts over on himself, and so when 'tis seen that men do not live better lives nor do good works, though a lot can be heard and said among them about faith, it is falsely concluded that faith is not enough for the salvation and blessing of man; works are essential. And so it goes when they hear the Gospel, that they make up in the heart, relying upon themselves, a thought that says *I believe.* And then suppose that is genuine faith. But that which is feigned and is just a notion never goes to the bottom of the heart, and such a notional faith does nothing and nobody is any the better for it.

"But faith is God's work in us that changes us all over and makes us like new (John I, 13). It kills the past and reconstitutes us utterly different men in heart, disposition, spirit and in all the faculties and the Holy Spirit is implicitly, dynamically present in all of it. Oh! there is something vital, busy, active, powerful about this (experience of) faith that simply makes it impossible ever to let up in doing good works. The believer does not stop to ask whether good works are to be done, but is up and at it before the question is put. He who is not doing such works is simply an unbelieving man, poking and casting about for faith and good works in the dark, and does not know what either one is. All he does is to scrub and chatter away about faith and good works. Faith is a lively, reckless confidence in the grace of God, so sure of itself that the believer could die a thousand times for it. Such assurance and insight into the grace of God sets a man up, makes him buoyant, sure of himself, bold-hearted, joyful toward God and all creation. That is what the Holy Spirit does in (the experience of) faith. So it is that a man unforced acquires the will and feels the impulse to do good to everybody, serve everybody and suffer everything for the love and praise of God who has bestowed such grace upon him. It is therefore just as impossible to separate works from faith as it is to separate the blaze and the light from the fire. And so look out for your own false notions and for the idle theological chatterers about faith and good works who appear to be very clever but are in fact consummate fools. Pray rather to God that he work this faith in you (*in dir wirke*); otherwise you will never, never come by it, feign all you will or work all you can. Now righteousness is such faith and it is called the righteousness of God, etc."

These words give us as true a picture of Wesley's own experience as they are an honest report of Luther's. Note that men "relying on themselves" feign a notional faith that "never goes to the bottom of the heart." There is not the least power of moral goodness in it. The human side of faith sinks from sight. Then note that "faith is God's work in us"—thrice repeated. Note especially the ultimacy of the grace of God and Luther's heart-warming jubilant praise of it. Note that no man comes by saving faith of himself, but only by God's working it in his experience. All this, precisely this, Wesley laid to heart. On it henceforth he built, if not at once an absolute trust, at least an

increasingly victorious confidence. And he never wavered henceforth in his interpretation of the direct, immediate intuition of
God's saviorhood in Christ, which he acquired chiefly by the help
of Luther, as being itself the *gift and work of God*. "That great
truth that *we are saved by faith* will never be worn out; and that
sanctifying as well as justifying faith is *the free gift of God*."[6]
This was Wesley's: "Give me where to stand and I will move the
world"; and so he did.

The Moravians, to whom Wesley was deeply indebted, strongly
insisted that the personal intuition of the truth and absolute importance of "salvation by faith alone" need not be, and in the
light of Christian experience ought not to be, a long-drawn-out
and dreary affair of the soul, neither is the decision to throw
oneself utterly upon the mercy of God in Christ the Savior like a
loose pile of information, like so much sand, to be slowly picked
up and pieced together bit by bit, or fragment by fragment; but
it can and should be a great creative intuition of God's grace and
goodness to save, immediate, assuring, heart-warming, liberating,
regenerating, full of cleansing and uplifting power.

The Moravians who exactly a half century later exerted an influence upon Schleiermacher, were representatives of German
Pietism in which the original impulse and emphasis of the Reformation upon *saving faith as an experience* reasserted itself against
the relapse of Lutheranism into a formalistic Christianity. This
experimental and practical view of Christian faith that was the
creative principle of the early Reformation (*Cum experientia
testetur—Luther*) was reaffirmed in eighteenth century Pietism
with its radical emphasis on conversion. The point of view
is distinctly reflected in the following remarkable statement by
another mind that was also deeply influenced by this reawakened
Protestantism. It is Immanuel Kant's account of conversion in
relation to character and it is given here because it noticeably
omits from the account the objective reference in Christian experience to the grace of God, which was the peculiar dynamic of
Wesley's preaching. Kant recognized alone the human side of

[6] Letters, IV, 268.

conversion. He could not apprehend in humanistic terms the reality of communion with God and so could find no meaning of God in human experience. On this account he could honestly say, "He who has made progress in the good life ceases to pray: for candor is one of its first maxims." This is the voice of natural religion which robs man of prayer and is therefore not religion at all. For who among the master-minds of the Christian faith has not known that to be religious and to pray come to one and the same thing? If, as Wesley taught, "the continual sense of total dependence on God is the essence of religion," then prayer is its primordial, perfect and indispensable expression. But even if Kant's view of a *religion within the limits of reason alone* inevitably missed the unique essence or inner nature of religious experience, namely, the feeling of total dependence and its exercise in prayer, if his humanist spectacles hid from sight the meaning of God in Christian experience, still he has given a realistic description of conversion in the very terms of Christian experience even while eschewing its vital premises.

"The man who is conscious of character in his mode of thought and manner of life, has it not as a gift of nature, but must in every case have acquired it. It can also be taken for granted that its first foundation, being somewhat of the nature of regeneration, will, owing to a certain solemnity in the covenant vows which a man makes with himself, invest the experience itself and even the exact time when the great change came over him with an epoch-making and unforgettable significance."

"Education, example, instruction can not little by little bring forth this firmness and steadfastness in principle at all, but it arises more or less explosively in experience as an immediate reaction from inner loathing of the fluctuating state of the instincts and passions. Probably but few will have attempted this revolution before the age of 30 and still fewer are fully confirmed before their fortieth year."

"The will or resolve to become a better man a little bit at a time is a futile experiment. For one good impression grows faint and the impulse vanishes, while the piecemeal mender is working up another (good) impulse. But the basis of character is in general the absolute unity of the principle that underlies the whole course and conduct of life."

"In one word, truth, honesty, reality in the Holy of Holies, where the soul is its own confessional and likewise these same qualities in all behavior toward others is the one authentic proof of a man's consciousness that he has a character."

"Now since being a man of principles and of character is the very least to be expected of every rational being, and is also the maximum of intrinsic worth or human dignity, it is the prerogative of mind and will in the lowliest, the humblest to have principles, character and so surpass in intrinsic worth the greatest of talents." [7]

Righteousness then, or, in the language of religion, holiness of heart and life, is the greatest of values in the universe, besides which all the gifts of nature pale into trivialities. And the basis of character is not a broken, fragmentary, feeble will, but a resolute, integrated, victorious will. It is as if the philosopher had in these words echoed the words of the greatest teacher of Western Christianity: "The way into God's will and covenant we go not by ships or by chariots or by walking,—for not merely to be going but to reach the goal, calls for nothing but the will to go; but it has to be a resolute and an integrated will, not a half-wounded will, darting hither and thither, throwing itself about in a constant struggle between the part of it that is going up and the part that is going down." [8] The Christian teacher does what the philosopher has not done, perhaps had better not do. After giving virtually the same description of the experience, the Christian thinker sublimely ventures to ground it in divine agency. The philosopher and psychologist are wont to say that it has the same meaning whether we refer this mighty change in the human spirit, be it instant or gradual, either to natural law or to the divine will. That is true, very true and important, provided the Christian consciousness is not tricked and robbed of its

[7] Immanuel Kant; *Werke* (Akademie Ausgabe, 1907), Bd. VII, s. 294.
[8] Augustine's *Confessions*, Lib. VIII, Cap. viii.

right thereby to assume and trust what Christian experience indicates. The mode of God's activity in a human consciousness
which is freedom and the power of moral goodness can not be
assimilated by our intellect to the idea of natural law which we
acquire by observing and analyzing the transformations of energy beyond the realm of our personal life; unless indeed the
conclusion, toward which scientific thinking now seems to tend,
be true, that the whole realm of energy is honey-combed with
creative spontaneity—an idea that has always been an intuition
of the Christian consciousness, even if it has been crudely expressed in the doctrine of the miracle. For that doctrine at bottom stands for the ultimate kinship of all things in the universe
with the roots of our experience, and instead of levelling our
personal life in God down to the level of our ignorance of what
lies beyond our personal life, we may and must level all energy
and all life up to the clearest indications of our own personal
life. Our personal life in its entirety transcends the analysis of
what strikes upon us by the gateway of the senses and it is our
deepest organ of communication with the nature of things. The
Christian consciousness does and must insist either that the mode
of God's presence and power in our personal experience is unique,
sui generis, or else that it is the pattern of all his immanent activities. Wesley has been, from the philosophical standpoint,
ineptly disparaged for his keen, vivid sense of God's universal
presence and for his daring thoughts that the whole world of
nature is always plastic to the divine will and purpose. But the
primordial intuitions of the religious consciousness now seem
to tally far better than materialism with the logic of science and
with its ripest conclusions.

There are ideas that have no meaning beyond a free curiosity.
They start no action and cause no forebearance in the depths
of our being. Then again there are religious ideas meant to
be lived. They often cross the threshold of a human consciousness and startle us with surprise like a sudden but welcome visi-
tant; then as a sunrise fills the morning they impart an unspeakable glory and hope and power of saintliness. And if it be

in the life of one utterly "tired of devouring time and of being devoured by it," it may come as a miracle of release and freedom. Externally it may only seem that some one has just pulled himself together. But inwardly the awakened consciousness of sharing in an infinite spiritual existence, perfect in power and purity, has brought not only salvation by faith, but a new center of moral gravity. An inexhaustible resource of spiritual regeneration has been established.

Now it is very significant for understanding Wesley and his century that although Kant has represented the achievement of character as a radical conversion-experience, still he has done so in the terms of an atheistic humanism. Kant of course was no atheist but, as the high priest of critical rationalism, he did represent the drift of religious thought in the eighteenth century toward an atheistic humanism. The best that critical rationalism could do was to tolerate with distant coolness "a religion within the limits of reason alone." The Christian pulpit of the age, taking its cue from the latest fashion in philosophy, lost the courage to associate the thought of God with Christian experience. Only timidly did many preachers venture in the subject matter of the sermon, beyond the boundaries of a pure humanism. Wesley put the Word of God back into the sermon. The burden of these great Oxford Sermons was not the trifling cavil—how long should the conversion-experience, the experience of saving faith, normally last? His thesis was that saving faith, regardless of its tempo, in terms of experience, is first and foremost, last and always the gift and work of a living and saving God. This is the theme-note of the sermons on Salvation by Faith and of all that follow, as it is of Wesley's entire theology of Christian experience.

Wesley's Journal for July 25, 1741, records that he preached that day at St. Mary's, Oxford, before the University. "So numerous a congregation (from whatever motives they came) I have seldom seen at Oxford. My text was the confession of poor Agrippa." [9] St. Mary's was crowded to hear him. They did

[9] Journal, II, 478.

come from very mixed motives, but they at any rate knew this particular preacher was not a reed shaken with the wind of popularity, nor a man who lived softly, dressed smartly and said smooth things to the rich and powerful. He was not a man to make popularity nor even the approval of the pillar authorities in church and university the first principles of his preaching.

Every syllable of the sermon is an indictment, and of a very militant kind, of the low-level morality and the easy-going formalistic Christianity of his day and generation. He turned the powerful searchlight of the full prophetic Christian ideal and standards of life upon the half-heathen religion and morality of his generation. He forced the men of his time to look into the chasm between their nominal Christianity and the real Christianity of Jesus. The average Oxonian, typical of his time, was either wholly unconcerned or else complacent with a Christianity whose practical significance had been pared down close to the vanishing point. It was sufficient to explain Christianity. It was not necessary to live it. The average Oxonian, like the *Illuminati* of his century, had at his command two highly convenient dogmas, not so much hard-won, well-tested principles, but raw deposits of reactions against the fury of the wars of religion in the 16th and 17th centuries. His first dogma was: Historic Christianity is just about all priestcraft; and the second was like unto it:—The experience of religion is all fanaticism. He who appeals to priestcraft to prove anything is a knave. He who appeals to fanaticism is a fool. What is left? The appeal to pure reason in which there is neither fire nor frost. Here enter Hume and Kant: Reason in their hands, after confounding the dogmatist, turned upon itself to scrutinize its resources and returned from the quest, so far as practical religion is concerned, empty-handed. But the great spiritual instincts of human nature—the aching heart, the unappeased soul hunger, the empty void, the laws of spiritual gravitation—remained in full force after this reduction of Christianity to the lowest possible intellectual, ethical, experiential levels. At this stage and long before the intellectuals had finished their inquiry into the re-

sources of the intellect, there came upon the scene a man of
epoch-making energy who shook his age to its foundations with
the dynamic truism that the best argument for religion is religion. He spoke as one having original insight and not as one
who had learned it out of a book. It is absurd in arguing with a
blind man about sight to rule out all reference to the main fact—
sight itself. Wesley won. Relying on the concurrence of the
"Oracles of God" with the sure testimony of experience, he set
himself one man against a stone-walled city of irreligion and
prevailed against it.

But this sermon on "The Almost Christian" is not the one
which Wesley first intended to preach, and that is perhaps the
most important fact about it. He wrote on June 24, 1741, for the
purpose a sermon on *How Is the Faithful City Become a Harlot*
(Isa. I, 21). One can imagine what the militant Wesley would
have done to his Oxford audience with that text. We still have
this sermon, translated from the Latin by A. Clark. It assails
fiercely the doctrine and practise of the University. It pitches
into the authorities in Church and University, the pillars, and
paints a dark picture of their several apostasies. It argues that
the doctrine of the Church has been undermined by "these miserable corrupters of the gospel," whereas the practise of Christianity has fallen to even lower levels of corruption. Scarcely is the
mere form of godliness seen any more among us. As for the
power, the living witness, *"Who among us (let God witness with
our hearts) experimentally knows the force of inward holiness?"*
He characterized Oxford as a hive of nominal scholars among
whom the intellectual drones predominated.

Wesley's dark picture of Oxford life as he knew it in the
thirties was sustained by the judgment of the economist, Adam
Smith, who knew Oxford in the forties, and of the historian,
Edward Gibbon, who was at Oxford in the fifties. These three
fully agree. Smith pronounced Oxford life lazy and shiftless from
top to bottom. The professors made no pretense of teaching.
Discipline was contrived for the ease of the masters. The
under-graduates wasted their time in drinking and gambling.

The historian Gibbon says of his tutor, "He remembered that he had a salary to receive, but forgot that he had a duty to perform." "To my *Alma Mater* I acknowledge no obligation, and she will as cheerfully disown me for a son as I renounce her for a mother. The years I spent there were the most idle and unprofitable period of my life." It is a striking fact that these three distinguished sons of Oxford, who seem to have little else in common, were in sharp contrast to Oxford life alike paradigms, each in his own field, of intellectual industry. There were among the masters and men at Oxford rare exceptions like these who had a sense of vocation and a spirit of industry. And it was Wesley's industry far more than his piety that made him a sensation at Oxford. He believed in "plugging" as well as praying, and was *inexorably methodical in both.* And this fact got him a nickname that has become historic. The university which disowned the heart of Wesley later disowned the intellect of a Gibbon. On these premises we must understand Wesley when he denounced from the pulpit of St. Mary's idleness of every name and nature as the sin of sins, and declared productive industry of head, hand, and heart to be the first and last duty of religion. Small wonder Oxford circles entertained a doubt about his sanity. Lady Huntingdon, to whom the excoriating sermon was submitted, dissuaded Wesley from delivering it, not perhaps for what it said as for the way and manner it was done. Wesley wrote accordingly and delivered instead "The Almost Christian," which omitted some of the more aggressive statements and toned down the rest. But he was not to be wholly denied. For he returned three years later in his last Oxford sermon of 1744 and renewed the attack in full force.

It would be a mistake to look for a well-guarded and carefully stated doctrine of Christian experience in these reformatory sermons. They must be understood in the light of what they are, namely, Wesley's ultimatum to the decadent Christianity of the times. Overlooking his problem, ignoring what sort of axe he must lay to the root of this superficial, dead, do-nothing Christianity, critics have taken many exceptions to his well-nigh absolute distinctions between *the Almost* and *the Alto-gether Christian*. Wesley has made many solid improvements upon his earlier statements of the doctrine of Christian experience. He learned to appreciate better the irreducible varieties of Christian experience. On justification or conversion he said, in the forty-seventh year of the Revival, "there is an irreconcilable variability in the operations of the Holy Spirit on the souls of men, more especially in the manner of Justification." [10] A little later he said as much of sanctification: "There is great variety in the manner wherein God is pleased to lead those who are being saved from sin." [11] In the twenty-seventh year of the Revival he laid down a broad principle which, if sensibly applied, leaves no room for any of the wild extravagances and unwholesome tendencies which have infested the doctrine of conversion and sanctification in the history of Methodist piety and brought them into much disrepute. "It is all one how it began, so you do but walk in the light. Be this given in an instant or by degrees, hold it fast." [12]

Probably the most interesting and not the least important book written by the incomparable Augustine was his *Retractiones*. It is a catalogue of things no longer believed or of things better understood. He had on a number of important issues learned better and in his later years said so in writing. A catalogue of Wesley's retractions would be most interesting and instructive. The sermon "On Faith" preached in the fiftieth year of the Revival has in it one of his most important retractions. Looking back over his preaching, he said, "Indeed nearly fifty years ago, when the preachers, commonly called Methodists, began to preach that grand scriptural doctrine of justification by faith, they were not sufficiently apprized of the difference between a servant and a child of God." [13] But, let it be said once for all, this retraction touched no religious principle of the Revival, nor can it be used to abate one jot or tittle from the supreme importance of the conversion-experience in 1738. On the

[10] Letters, VII, 298.
[11] Letters, VIII, 110.
[12] Letters, IV, 308.
[13] Sermon 106.

contrary, the confessed exaggeration in the first preaching of justification by faith fifty years ago (1788 — 50 = 1738) only confirms in psychological terms both the time and the epoch-making importance of its entrance into Wesley's preaching. What the retraction has done is to forbid any such narrow conception of the conversion-experience which excludes anything and everything but the culminating act or stage, marked in Wesley's case by the acceptance of the Luther-Calvin idea of a God-given faith, precisely what Wesley's earliest statements seemed to do! The retraction simply widens the conception of conversion to include all the first steps and all the successive stages up to and including the master-insight into "the nature of saving faith." Moreover Wesley's ascending scale of spiritual values given in the sermon affords the truest comment. He grades all the varieties of faith, from the lowest sort of faith which is that of a materialist, to the highest in the evangelical sense, (1) Materialist, (2) Deist, (3) non-Christian, as the Mohammedan, (4) the Old Testament, (5) Roman Catholic, (6) Protestant. But he also identifies among all Christians cutting across historic divisions another distinction between what he calls the faith of a servant and that of a son.

There is nothing in this retraction that either directly or indirectly militates against the Luther-Calvin idea of the sovereign saving significance of a God-given faith. On the contrary, the crescendo of religious values implies it. It corrects and sets right the narrow evangelicalism that would so bound the idea of conversion, so hem and hedge it in, as to rule out all the first steps and intervening stages of Christian experience. What Wesley retracted then was not the maximum significance of his return to Luther-Calvin principles, in the doctrine of conversion. Rather this retraction so construed affords, I believe, the only permissible and positive meaning for the unpublished entries in Wesley's Journal, made no doubt shortly before his death and therefore coincident with the writing of the sermon (1788) "On Faith." The sixth Savannah Journal, in which his conversion before 1738 is denied, was brought to a close somewhat in the spirit of the maxim, *The good is the enemy of the best.* In this spirit Wesley drew an indictment of his entire religious experience prior to 1738, as if nearly everything good in it had been only a fatal barrier to the best, which was identified with Faith as it is expounded in Paul's Epistle to the Romans. He protested, "I am not mad" in confessing that "I who went to America to convert others was never myself converted." [14]

Now the *absolute importance* of what in January 1738 he consciously lacked and still had to be learned from the Gospel, degraded all that went before as if nothing worth. The comment fifty years later, "I am not sure of this," simply had the effect and force of widening the meaning of the conversion-experience so as to include a positive instead of a purely negative religious evaluation of his earlier religious experience. But the inference from Wesley's unpublished emendation, "I am not sure of this," that he had so far changed his doctrine of Christian experience as to renounce the radical significance for himself of the revolution in his message and ministry which occurred in the Spring of 1738, or that he intended to eliminate the understanding of saving faith from the doctrine of conversion, would be an absurd misrepresentation of Wesley's mind in the matter and still more of the realities of Christian experience. The fallacy which limits the conversion-experience to baptism or reception into Church membership or to man's first feeble effort to have God in his thinking is of the same sort, only worse than the fallacy which limits it to mature Christian experience. Worse; for the idea of saving faith ought to be associated with the heights and not merely with the lowest levels of Christian experience.

If we look past details to first principles it is plain to see that Wesley's approach to the religious question in this sermon is essentially that of Jesus and of all his great interpreters. Wesley, following the teaching of Jesus, herein proclaims the higher righteousness and the precept of love as the sum and substance of Christianity. This for him is the whole of the Gospel. This is the pure morality of holiness with faith in Christ for its main-

[14] Journal, I, 422.

spring and motivation. There is nothing higher nor more inclusive than this principle. This higher righteousness has indeed two branches, one personal and the other social, but they are one and inseparable in root and fruit. The sum of the law and the prophets is to love God and to love our neighbour as ourselves.

It may help to illuminate the substance of Wesley's teaching to recall here the fact that there are three distinct focalizations for all of Jesus' teaching: (1) the Kingdom of God and its coming, (2) God the Father and the fact that personal life is in all his creation the value of values, (3) the higher righteousness and precept of love, or the faultless life of perfect love toward God and man. Now a religion of the quietistic enjoyment of divine grace is properly deducible from neither of these three focalizations, but each one and all three supply a principle of activity to man's spiritual life. This being so, Jesus can not properly, but only in a very far-fetched sense, be classified as a mystic. It is when we look at the teaching of Jesus through this third focalization that we see most clearly the close affiliation of Wesley's doctrine of Christian experience with it and the derivation of Wesley's teaching from it. Wesley's predilection for the Pauline terminology need not obscure this deeper relation to Jesus' thoughts about the better righteousness and its attainment.

Another and most important fact about this sermon on "The Almost Christian" is its complete fidelity to the method and instruction of Jesus. For Jesus severed the connexion between two things: There is first religion and ethics as experience and life,— religion as an experience rich in and controlled by the pure feeling of total dependence on God, the Beatitudes, and an ever-growing intuition of his infinite grace, issuing forth in ethics as the appropriate conduct of a life, in Pauline phrase, "hid with Christ in God." There is secondly *religion and ethics objectified in external forms of worship and the technical observance of a code of morals.* The pursuit of good works on the first premise can and should be simple, sincere and unselfish. On the second it may and is liable to be designing and self-seeking. In the second place Jesus laid down the principle that the disposition and intention are of supreme importance in religion and morality. It is of the nature of the higher righteousness if, when the depths of the heart are proved, conduct is found firmly grounded in the will and the affections. A man's work must be judged by the inner spirit. This quality of conduct and life is so important that, in the language of Jesus, on the presence or absence of it hangs heaven or hell. In the third place, the one true, sufficient, all important motive is love. It takes complete possession of personal life and has its outlet in the service of all mankind. It cuts across every boundary and overleaps every barrier. Those who are far as well as near, foreigners no less than fellow citizens, enemies no less than friends, come within the empire of this Christian principle. Fourth and finally, love to God begins in humility, in poverty of spirit, in pure receptivity toward God, in the consciousness of inner need, in an abiding and growing hunger and thirst after righteousness—a righteousness that is the very nature of God. This pure feeling of total dependence on God and the rich intuition of the grace of God are expressed in the words—*God be merciful to me a sinner;* and *forgive us our trespasses as we forgive those that trespass against us.* But there is here a deep unity. The love of God that begins in humility and prays for God's grace and forgiveness is the same love that issues forth in the love of one's neighbor in service to all mankind, in peace-making and human helpfulness to the uttermost. We love God in the spirit of humility; we love man in the spirit of service.

Briefly then for Wesley, as for Jesus, Christianity lives first and foremost in the inner spirit. The outward forms are but instrumental. What counts most is the inner motivation and experential meaning. And here God's initial love is the motive. The answering love of man begins in humility before God and issues in service to all mankind. Thus we can see the teaching of Jesus and see it whole in his simple message concerning the higher righteousness and the new commandment of love. In precisely this manner Wesley has proclaimed the higher righteousness, the pure morality of holiness, and the precept of love to

be the sum of Christianity as an ethic of life and has severely
censored the nominal Christianity around him in the light of it.
Except your righteousness exceed what now obtains in our midst
you can not be reckoned genuine Christians.

The goal of this sermon as well as its chief accent regulative
for Wesley's understanding of the Gospel are found in the sentence: "May we all thus *experience* what it is to be not *almost*
only but *altogether* Christians." The whole practical application
is based on two parts. The first part delineates "the outside of
a Christian," which the Wesleys called *having the form of godliness*. There are three steps: The first described the great simple
moralities essential to the art of living together in any degree
of civilized society. The second described the ethics of the
golden rule in its negative form, the great "don'ts" of morality—
profanity and evil speaking, unchastity, intemperance, and adds
to this active charity and decent conformity to the established
religion. The third step probes deeper and allows a deeper ethical
motivation than a consideration of consequence—one that is
rooted in a sincere desire to do the will of God and serve him
alway. Well does the preacher pause at this point to ask, How
much farther than this can an altogether Christian go? What
then is lacking? Conscious of his radical break with current
Christianity, Wesley, as he believed on the concurrent authority
of Scripture and experience, denied the genuineness of current
Christianity and confessed that he had himself tried it out in vain
for many years and was driven at length, in his search for power,
to higher levels.

The delineation of *the Inside of a Christian, the altogether
Christian,* falls into two parts: (1) The love of God and of your
neighbor is the one all-inclusive rule of Christian perfection. (2)
Faith is the sole ground of being an altogether Christian. This
is the crucial point. Now this faith is not a notional faith but
a personal and dynamic experience. It is not simply the orthodoxy that holds stoutly to Holy Scripture and the Articles of
Faith. It is a sure trust built upon a flaming intuition of God's

grace in Christ. It is saving faith working by love—a truth that must be felt as well as thought to mean anything.

But, finally, where shall we find Christians satisfied with nothing less than the standard of Christian perfection, satisfied with nothing less than an experience of saving faith? Here Wesley made his message very personal! "Are not many of you conscious you do not meet even the tests of *the almost Christian?* You lack even the form, to say nothing of the power, of godliness, and you have not even heathen honesty. Hell is paved with good intentions. Nothing else counts but the actual experience of justification and reconciliation with God and the appropriate life. Awake from your stony indifference and seek it with tears." Wesley's Oxford auditors were annoyed and embarrassed and blushed to think so able a Fellow as John Wesley should exhibit such bad taste as to take God so seriously and that too publicly before an enlightened audience. And then what right had a young man to rant thus against his seniors?

CHAPTER IX

A RELIGION NOT MORE THAN HUMAN

Wesley's Oxford Sermon on "Salvation by Faith," which was the first manifesto of the Revival, was preached on the nineteenth day of his conversion-experience. Its doctrinal importance as a document of Wesley's theology can not be overestimated. Writing in the thirty-fourth year of his conversion, Wesley reminded a critic who accused him of being a chameleon in his theology, that he had "published in 1738 the Sermon on *Salvation by Faith, every sentence of which I subscribe to now.*" This statement by Wesley, often reiterated, never retracted, should put an end once for all to the opinion, sometimes entertained, that the Oxford Sermon on "Salvation by Faith" represents Wesley in the earlier and immature stage of his theology and was probably written in America. The fact is that it represents him in the epoch of his maturity. The preface of the first volume of Standard Sermons, 1746, states that the four Oxford Sermons were placed first "as the strongest answer to the assertion frequently made that we have changed our doctrine of late." The Journal statement for September 1, 1778, is very strong: "Forty years ago I knew and preached every Christian doctrine which I preach now." The general stability of Wesley's doctrinal ideas from his acceptance in 1738 of Luther's religious understanding of the Gospel is not open to question.

The first doctrinal manifesto of the Revival heralds Wesley's return to the principles of the early reformation. It is a bold challenge to the current Christianity which had degenerated into a "false religion (1) of opinions, (2) of forms, (3) of works, (4) of Atheism." To an age and in a climate of opinion that wanted "a kind of rational religion that has not only nothing of Christ,

218

but nothing of God in it," Wesley came preaching the truth about God—"God in Christ reconciling the world unto himself," "as the first and last point of religion." The sermon does not therefore clasp hands with prevalent modes of opinion by "extolling humanity to the skies, as the very essence of religion," by construing a religion which recognizes "no relation at all to God nor any dependence upon him," nor by "so interpreting the Gospel as to place the whole principle of salvation—moral goodness, holiness—in all things really within man, but not more than human!"[1]

Wesley has therefore referred already in his Oxford days the decay of religion to the fact that this age so interprets the Gospel as to place the whole principle of salvation in things really within man but not more than human. The true objectivity of saving faith in Christian experience had been eliminated from the humanized Christianity of the Enlightenment. The doctrine of the Holy Spirit stands for the true objectivity of Christian experience; Wesley therefore placed that doctrine at the center of his theology.

Instead of patronizing this Godless, Christless Christianity of the age, the sermon is a bold challenge, an ultimatum. It represents every man utterly dependent on God, and then too a sinner in dire need of a savior. Wesley's message humbles man and confronts him, prostrate in the dust and ashes of repentance, with the fact of a living and saving God. It recognizes the infinite gulf between man's sin and God's holiness over which man's utmost resources can not, only the almighty grace of God can, throw a bridge. The crucial points are the inclusion of all the cosmic activities of God under the principle of grace and the strict deduction of all moral goodness in man direct from divine agency. For "sinful man simply can not atone for any the least of his sins." He simply does not have it in him of himself to do anything good. Whatever of righteousness may be found in man, that is also, all of it, the gift and work of God. If indeed any of our works have the least salt of saving holiness in them,

[1] Sermons 37, 114, 141.

they can not be our own works, but God's work. "All our works, Thou, O God, hast wrought in us."

Thus the first manifesto of the Wesleyan Revival develops with the impetus of a personal rediscovery the central thesis of all the early reformers. Every benefit of redemption, including the crucial experience of saving faith, must be referred to divine agency. In the thought of salvation by faith, God is everything, man is nothing. Just so the primary relation of man to God in the Wesleyan doctrine of redemption is that of total dependence, trustful apprehension and grateful appreciation of the grace of God. This manifesto would have gladdened the heart of a Luther and of Calvin too, and of all the early reformers. It voices the profound reaction in the soul of Wesley against the current humanist, libertarian theology prevalent in the great bulk of Anglican and in much Nonconformist preaching. The Christian consciousness has once and again reacted and protested against a futile "laborious self-salvation." It was the precise nature of the reaction in Wesley's own conversion-experience.[2] But the "self-salvation" of natural religion against which this manifesto pointedly and powerfully protests was not at all "laborious"; it was morally lazy and religiously indifferent to the last degree. A religion of human freedom, self-help and moralistic salvation, and of natural moral goodness, was duly advertised in that age by its fruits, not at all as Christianity in earnest, but its antithesis. Into this climate of practical atheism came Wesley, confronting man with the fact of God and proclaiming with early Reformation accents that "a continual sense of our total dependence on God for every good thought, or word or work" is the very pulse and life-principle of the Christian consciousness.

Although the doctrine, "For by grace are ye saved through faith, and this not of yourselves: it is the gift of God," [3] was clearly, strongly taught in the Articles and Homilies of the Church of England, yet Wesley acquired his interest in that subject neither from the Anglican Articles and Homilies, nor from the

---

[2] Sermon 2, ¶¶ 1, 13.
[3] Wesley's translation of New Testament, p. 492.

prevalent Anglican preaching or Oxford University instruction, nor from parental instruction, but from another source. It was in the month of April 1738, after the crucial religious importance of the central idea of the Reformation had been discovered, after the faith of the first reformers had knocked loudly for and gained admission into the content of his preaching, and the crucial issue had assumed the form of deep, vital personal concern, he began to identify and appreciate the new doctrine as "the Words of our Church."[4] The fact that it was the teaching of the Anglican Church played, according to the Journal account, a very small, if indeed any, part in Wesley's conversion in comparison with the teaching of the New Testament, the authority of the living witness, and above all the decisive word from Martin Luther. Yet it is safe to assume that the sanction and support of it by the Articles and Homilies were factors in Wesley's further progress toward full and final satisfaction with "the faith of our first Reformers." But the way and manner Wesley came by his interest in the subject, was inducted into an understanding of the first principle of the Reformation, and the steps by which the truth of it was mediated to him, tended to bring the teaching and preaching office of the Anglican Church, as it did the reputation of William Law, into reproach and largely explains Wesley's boldness in pitching into the authorities even to the point of raising the issue of apostasy. Wesley turned, just ten days before the final act in his conversion-experience, upon his once-trusted mentor, William Law, and sternly upbraided him for his dismal failure to build his excellent teaching of Christian perfection upon the idea of the sovereign saving significance of a God-given faith in Christ. This criticism of Law was really Wesley's general indictment of current Anglican teaching and preaching as religiously bankrupt. Religious thought was in a state of anarchy. He demanded, of Law, Where have you urgently taught? Where does any one now teach? "Believe and thou shalt be saved. Believe in the Lord Jesus Christ with all thy heart and nothing shall be impossible to thee. This faith, in-

[4] Journal, I, 454.

deed, as well as the salvation it brings, is the free gift of God." [5]

Wesley came to Oxford in the victorious spirit of one who felt that the battle of faith had been fought and won in his own inner experience and that the central idea of his message was sustained by the solid teaching of the New Testament, of the Church of England, of the Moravian disciples of Luther, by the testimony of Luther himself, and finally that he himself had come to understand and had been given to experience saving faith as God's voice in the heart proclaiming itself. The bitter fact that it had taken thirteen precious years of his utmost effort to come at the ultimate secret of Christian experience, the decisive fact that after laboring indefatigably at himself he was forced to admit frustration in his personal experience and relative failure in his preaching, over all and above all the fact that the key to the mystery of Christian experience had been put in his hand, not by the teaching and preaching of his own Church, though he had sought therein diligently for it, but that it had to come direct from Martin Luther, mediated by the Moravians, amounted in his mind to a bill of indictment against his own Church. In the strength of all this, he arraigned the Church leaders of his age for rethinking Christianity downward until not only was the central idea of the Christian ethics of life—the doctrine of Christian perfection given up, but the Gospel of saving faith in Christ which alone had in it the power of God unto salvation, was left a thing of shreds and patches. All the shafts of the first manifesto of the Revival are aimed at this decadent Christianity. The Wesleyan Reformation began exactly as did the work of the Prophets, of Jesus and St. Paul, of Luther and Calvin, by an attack on religion.

The conflict between a thoroughgoing ethic of divine grace and the irreligious humanism of the Enlightenment reverberates through all of Wesley's writings. The Journal for July 3, 1776, which was the thirty-eighth year of his conversion-experience, has this entry: "In the evening I preached at York on the fashionable (!) religion, vulglarly called morality, and showed at large

[5] Letters, I, 238-244.

from the *accounts given of it by its ablest patrons, that it is neither better nor worse than atheism.*" Here was another of his searching dissections of the fashionable religion of the age which had reduced the religious consciousness of man to a humanistic ethic. The strategy was to show by the witness of its ablest expounders that humanist religion is "neither better nor worse than atheism," that is, none at all. Once more it is enough to refer to the net result of Hume's analysis of Natural Religion: "The whole of Natural Theology affords no inference that affects human life or can be the source of any action or forbearance." [6] It makes no practical difference for either a philosopher or a peasant. Why has Hume been so much despised for telling the truth? But Wesley also knew that experience does not any time, anywhere, speak for the idea of morality without religion; new active powers of mind and will are always given to the human consciousness in connection with ideas about God. There is no other unfailing spring of righteousness, moral goodness, or holiness in man to compare with the experience of faith in a living, saving God.

No bolder, more dynamic challenge was ever thrown down to public opinion on religious subjects than this Oxford Sermon on "Salvation by Faith." The doctrine of religion in full control of most pulpits in that critical period of Protestantism consisted in an easy ascent of human thought and conduct from man to God. The whole idea of Christianity, as in Butler's *Analogy* between nature and revelation, which appeared in 1736 and stood therefore in close proximity to Wesley's Oxford manifesto, had become radically naturalistic and humanistic. It sought and sunk the whole meaning of Christianity in two terms—nature and man. Butler's thesis was that "The law of Moses and the Gospel of Christ are authoritative republications of the religion of nature." This was Tindal's thesis too: "The Gospel is a republication of the Religion of Nature," no more, no less. "Natural religion is the foundation and principal part of Christianity" and fully anticipates its meaning so that the latter can do no more

[6] *Dialogues,* Hume's Works, Vol. II, p. 467. (Ed., Green & Grose.)

than purify the former of any corruption or add the element of authority. So then for the ablest exponents of humanism the Gospel of Jesus Christ and natural religion come to the same thing.

These selected and central thoughts, found alike in Tindal's *Christianity as Old as Creation* (1730), and in Butler's *Analogy of Natural and Revealed Religion* (1736), are a true index of the times and are therefore for our purposes of first-rate importance. For Butler's *Analogy* was almost anything but an effective, if indeed it was any, answer to Tindal's treatise which, for its popularity, has been called "the Bible of Deism." How could an apologist who shied away from the incomparable quality of religious, in particular of Christian, experience, its ultimate uniqueness, as Butler did, write a defence of the Christian faith? How could a thinker who surrendered the master-key to the one really decisive argument adequately represent the cause? How could a theologian who allowed himself to be manœuvered into an untenable position stand his ground? Is it wise in an issue of color to waive all reference to sight or the artistic sense? Is it sound in an issue of tone quality to rule out all reference to the musical sense or to agree not to appeal to the talented and well-trained discernment of the experienced? A theologian who surrenders his most powerful positions and weapons before the battle is joined can win no victories. The highest possible reason that can be given or the clearest possible exposition that can be made of the truths of the Christian faith, is precisely the personal experience of their reality. The principal difference between Tindal and Butler lay in the term "authoritative." But the reference to authority in the old conception of it, the direct argument from the doctrinal ideas of the Scriptures or the dogmatic decisions of the Visible Church, without any intervention of experience, had already been destroyed once for all by the higher criticism of Scripture and dogma. The *Analogy*, for all its solid, earnest intellectualism, was, when the argument is bolted to the bran, little more than a tenderized edition of the Bible of Deism.

Of this theory of religion, David Hume (1711-1776) showed

by a remorselessly objective criticism that it could not make a particle of difference in any man's experience and life, but came practically to the same thing as atheism. For the yeas and nays among the considerations of natural reason are too evenly matched. Butler recognized revelation from afar but took refuge, if not flight, from its mighty issues in considerations of natural reason and religion. Christian thought in that age put the issues of Christianity on the lowest experiential levels. Butler trusted all to the logical use of intellect. Experiential thinking is wholly outside his purview, as if he expected a blind man to be the judge of a Sistine Madonna or a deaf man to appreciate a Beethoven sonata. He planted his feet in respect to method in the footprints of Anslem, whose thinking on the atonement was confined to considerations of natural reason. Criticism has utterly destroyed also this misplaced confidence.

Wesley read his Tindal [7] and the other deistic writers who were for robbing the religious consciousness of any right to refer to Christ or even to God and for reducing the values of religion to self-salvation; and many of them sincerely thought it would be a great emancipation of the Christian faith to starve it to death on considerations of natural reason. In the midst of this climate of opinion where naturalistic humanism ran and prevailed, and just at the time that Tindall was setting down his thoughts on "the religion of nature and reason in which reason must be supreme," in a book that proved to be "The Bible of Deism," running through four editions in three years, 1730, the Vice Chancellor with Heads of Houses and Proctors at Oxford held a council and resolved upon a bold move to set up a thorough censorship and index to determine what youth might or might not read with religious safety, and to safeguard their faith. But the dean of Christ Church would not suffer it. He was not, as Wesley's early biographer, Moore, superficially assumed,[8] any "friend to infidelity." Morley, the dean, rightly believed that as a defence of the Christian faith and cure of infidelity, the sacrifice

[7] Letters, I, 91.
[8] Moore's *Wesley*, Vol. I, p. 132.

of academic freedom would be the weakest possible defence and a remedy worse than the disease. Wesley was then absent from Oxford, serving as curate at Wroote when this happened. But soon after Dr. Morley, Rector of his College, recalled him to Oxford, "since the interest of College and obligation to Statute require it." The reasons for this recall may have been only routine and circumstantial. Nevertheless, in the light of the Rector's wise refusal to shield the undergraduates from the rough wind and weather of academic freedom, the thrusting of a man of John Wesley's religious calibre into this situation gives the imagination wings.

Deistic rationalism in Wesley's century was driving Christian apologetic out of its lazy supernaturalism and its misplaced trust in an infallible Church or Bible, or even in an infallible reason, and finally forced it to face the question, "What is Christianity?" in a new and hitherto unknown method both of putting the question and of seeking the answer. Wesley's theological development (1721-1738) took place in the midst of this rising tide of infidelity and growing contempt of historic Christianity, as if a compound of *priestcraft* and *fanaticism* with a microscopic element of rationality in it. Although critical rationalism by undermining the general confidence in traditional Christianity drove Christian thought into new paths, still on its constructive side it was far less fruitful. In fact deistic rationalism carried dissolution in itself and was itself bound hand and foot by the ingrained prejudices of the traditional orthodoxy which it assailed. It too was no less barren of true insight into the essentially experiential and historical nature of the Christian faith. By its abhorrence of fanaticism in religion, Deism had for its concomitant effect the casting out of the discussion of religion all reference to the experience of religion itself. By its abhorrence of priestcraft it had for its concomitant effect the casting out of the discussion of religion all reference to the historical development of Christianity. The only fact in the history of religion which Deism could see that had any baring on the nature of religion was the recurrent, if not perpetual, apostasy of mankind from the religion of nature. According to "The Bible of Deism," the only possible contribution that Christianity ever could make was and is to recover mankind from this falling away from the religion of nature in which reason must be supreme and to re-establish them in it. "The special mission of Christianity was and is to bring men out of the Fall from reason back to the eternal religion of nature, which is as old as creation and as universal as mankind." [9] Now it was in the nature of the case simply impossible for any mind, so long as men tried to look at the nature of religion through this high-sounding but empty for-mula, to discern the unique experiential and revelational nature of the Christian faith or to discover that a law of development underlies the whole Christian movement in history.

The inquiring spirit of Wesley soon brought him face to face with the fundamental issues thus raised by this revolution in religious thought. But he approached the issue "What is Chris-tianity?" from the opposite pole to that of naturalistic human-ism, or that of Hume's philosophical criticism of Natural Re-ligion. He came at his subject more and more from the stand-point of historic Christianity and the realities of the Christian consciousness. His own terms were the traditional evidence (history) and the internal evidence (experience) of Christianity.[10] Approaching the questions What is Christianity? or What is the nature of religion from the standpoint of experiential as well as historical thinking? he reached exactly the same conclusion as Hume did about natural religion. He pronounced natural re-ligion, as distinct from historical religion, simply "no religion at all." Moreover, Hume and Wesley fully concurred that "there can be no such thing as philosophical religion." Yet all around the great philosophical critic and the great religious individuality of the eighteenth century, Christian apologetic feebly rested the whole case for Christianity on considerations of natural reason. Rarely did the pulpit of that age, which had a great fear of

[9] What is this "Fall from natural reason" but a pale copy of the Genesis myth?
[10] Letters, II, 383 f.

either fire or frost in religion, especially fire, have either a convincing or a converting message. The easy-going strategy of most preaching was to prove little as touching the truth, promise less as touching the power, and avoid all reference to the experience of religion itself. Butler, prince of eighteenth-century apologists, felt sure that "the many persons of that age" who were for throwing the case of Christianity out of the court of reason without even a hearing, would find out by reading his *Analogy* "that it is not so clear a case that there is nothing in Christianity." Did it not rest on solid considerations of natural reason? Small wonder Hume reasoned it out, first for himself, then for all, that a religious faith which could not get farther than the dubitative subjunctive, the doubt of a doubt, a conditional if, would not matter much to either a philosopher or a peasant. It had nothing in it that could "affect human life or be the source of any action or forbearance." But rationalizing religious circles of the age still clutched at the theory that Christianity is only the adjutant of natural religion and merely a source, not of insight, but only of certainty. This singular point of view which reduced revelation to an echo of natural religion found in Butler's *Analogy of Natural and Revealed Religion* its representative voice. Offered as a check to the raging infidelity of the age, it was in the last analysis a desperate attempt to gather apologetic figs from naturalistic thistles, religious grapes from humanistic thorns.

Two of Wesley's early early Oxford sermons, one on "The Circumcision of the Heart," which he preached January 1, 1733,[11] and another on "Grieving the Holy Spirit," submitted in writing while he was absent on the Georgia Mission, for Whitsunday, 1736,[12] mirror his own clear consciousness of and deep concern about the decay of religion in the nation. Bishop Butler informs us in his famous *Analogy*, 1736, and again in his charge to the clergy of Durham, 1751, that Christianity had ceased in many minds to be even a subject of serious inquiry, had been detected as a work of fiction, and was widely treated as a fit subject of

[11] Sermon 13.
[12] Sermon 138.

mirth and ridicule; "The general decay of religion is now observed by every one!" The distinguished author of the *Analogy* had himself failed to notice in the Wesleyan Reformation a cloud the size of a man's hand. Wesley drew a like dark picture. His comment on the decay of Christianity, due largely to the shallowing, desiccating effects of rationalism, is made more specific in his sermon on "The Holy Spirit" (1736). "I think this age has made it particularly necessary to be well-assured 'What Christ is to us.' " There are three fatal disjunctives in current Christianity. First, there are two schools of thought which agree in divorcing piety and learning, *faith* and *reason,* one representing an obscurantist faith, the other an irreligious enlightenment. There are, secondly, two schools of atonement thought that agree in divorcing the objective religious significance and the subjective ethical view of "the righteousness of God," derived from Christ. The former gives "a sense somewhat improper and figurative"; the latter yields "no more than a charter of pardon and a system of morality." "Finally, some so interpret the Gospel as to place the holiness they are to be saved by in something divine, but exterior to themselves"; there is nothing experiential in it. *"Others interpret the Gospel so as to place saving holiness in things really within themselves but not more than human."* In a sentence, saving holiness, the substance of the Gospel, is understood by some to be divine but not immanent, i.e., not experiential; by others to be immanent but not divine, i.e., "not more than human." It is either a purely objective or a strictly humanistic religion. Here clearly the importance of the four words *"not more than human,"* as Wesley's key to the prevalent Christianity of his age which he tried out and transcended, can not be overestimated.

The issue of issues then which Wesley raised for the current religion of the Anglican Church was, as he conceived it, the issue between humanistic religion and the Christian revelation. When bolted to the bran, the conventional Christianity around him was a subtle form of the worship of humanity. He returned to this diagnosis of the sickness of religion in his century again and again. Not quite threescore years after Tindal's attempted rationalization of Christianity, he quoted with high approval the lament of a dying saint: "Oh, sirs, I am afraid a kind of *rational* religion is more and more prevailing among us . . . that has not only nothing of Christ, but nothing of God in it!" And then he noted how generally this Christless, Godless Christianity prevailed even amongst those who call themselves Christians. And no wonder; for "almost all men of letters both in England, France and Germany, yea, and all the civilized countries of Europe, *extol humanity to the skies as the very essence of religion.*" It is "a religion independent of any revelation whatever, self-sufficient, having no relation at all to God nor any dependence upon him." "It is no wonder that this religion should grow fashionable and spread far and wide in the world. But call it *humanity, virtue, morality* or what you please; it is *neither better nor worse* than atheism." [13] Wesley evidently knew the temper of his times, knew the spirit of his age, knew its mind, or lack of it, for religion. And he has thus gathered up the spirit of the Enlightenment in the observation: "Men of letters throughout Christendom, specially in England, France and Germany, extol *humanity* to the skies, as *the very essence of religion.*" But he judged this religion of *humanity,* this religion *not more than human,* to be "neither better nor worse than atheism." The only historical comment which this accurate characterization of an epoch that is gone calls for is to submit the question: Is this a truer description of an eighteenth or of an early twentieth century climate of opinion? Early! For signs are not wanting that this too shall pass away.

Wesley's Oxford manifesto was a flaming protest against this humanized Christianity. As he had already angered churches, so now he shocked his university audience by his bold and total repudiation of natural religion. In flat opposition to the *Analogy* and to the age, his thesis was that every consideration of man as the cause of his own faith must be banished from the doctrine

[13] Sermon 114. This lament referred to conditions in the second quarter of the century.

of salvation. He then threw the net of God's free grace around everything good in the universe, referred it all back to divine agency and subsumed under the category of free grace the cosmic activities no less than the redemptive activities of God. With ruthless severity he branded natural religion as "the faith of ancient and modern heathens." He unmasked every purely philosophical reconstruction of Christianity as "the faith of a devil"—"a train of ideas in the head," and finally excluded the faith even of the first disciples from the category of saving faith because it lacked the atoning significance of Christ's death and the power of his resurrection. For "the proper objects of saving faith are God in Christ as our atonement and our life, *as given for us* and *living in us.*" Above all, man can be given no share in his own salvation by faith. It is roundly asserted that faith itself is "one instance of His grace," is "the gift of God," must be referred to "God that worketh in us." In the thought of salvation God is everything, man is nothing. All man has is his sin and that puts a gulf so vastly wide between God and man that even man's thought can not span it, much less his effort bridge it. There remains for man nothing whereof to glory. God's grace alone can span the endless gulf of sin. Man's best never can. God's love alone can throw a bridge across the fathomless expanse of qualitative difference between God's holiness and man's sin. This crossing was for Wesley the Christian atonement.

Before analyzing further Wesley's radical reaction against the humanized Christianity of the Enlightenment, it is necessary first to note his constructive appreciation of the possible contributions to be made by critical rationalism to the improvement of Christian thought. For he was by no means an outsider to the inner spirit of the Enlightenment. On the contrary, instead of throwing the appeal to reason out of religion, he sincerely cultivated it. He was also prompt and decisive in correcting any assistant of his who began to cry down the use of intellect in religion. A sentence from a sermon puts the matter straight: "Religion is designed not to extinguish but to perfect the reason or understanding which God has given man." Wesley's *Appeals to Men of Reason and Religion* in the early forties are a true index of his mind. A correspondent writing Wesley in the accusative spirit said, "You are for reason, I am for faith." But Wesley answered simply, "I am for both." And he always was; that was his genius. Undoubtedly it was a confession in the spirit of the Enlightenment when he affirmed: "It is a fundamental principle with us that to renounce reason is to renounce religion, that religion and reason go hand in hand and that all irrational religion is false religion." Then we have another of his choicest epigrams: "True religion is the highest reason." [14] Finally, "I would as soon put out my eyes to secure my faith as lay aside my reason." Wesley was then no obscurantist in religion, no admirer of ignorant piety, no condoner of faith and worship in the dark. He was strong for every fruitful use of intellect in religion. "Let there be light."

On the other hand, Wesley with all his genius for straightforward thinking was singularly free, in all his life-long exploration by experiential thinking, of every nook and corner in the Christian faith, from those emotional and other rationalizations which might be called the original sin of dogmatic theology. Emotional reactions, thrown into propositional forms, are easily substituted for sound inference. The fatal objection to much so-called rational theology is that it has so very little real reasoning in it. Much so-called reasoning in theology is but the slave of the religious feelings. At any rate, Wesley so sized up the situation in theology. The discovery that reason is just as likely, if not more so, to be the servant as the master of the impulsive side of human nature helped his early emancipation from false intellectualism. Already as resident Fellow at Oxford he reached the conclusion that it is not entirely ethical "to charge any man with those consequences of his doctrine which he disavows." "If it were so," he observed thirty years later, "what would I do with poor George Whitefield?" Wesley's early emancipation from false intellectualism not only had something to contribute to his

[14] Letters, IV, 118; V, 364.

advanced spirit of toleration, but also yielded other results. It was only after considerable effort that he admitted: "In spite of all my logic (he taught logic at Oxford) I can not so prove anything in philosophy or divinity as not to leave room for strong, equally strong, objections." The insight that the logical use of intellect remains in philosophy and divinity forever indecisive is the counterpart to his early and increasing trust in experiential thinking as the only sound principle of method in theology.

If those who undervalue reason or cry down the use of intellect in religion and even, as Wesley put it, "despise and vilify reason," may not of right appeal either to Wesley's principles or his example as a credential, much less may those do so who "extol reason to the skies," as "little less than divine," "very near if not quite infallible," "able by its native light to guide the children of men into all truth and lead them into all virtue." Among the despisers of reason, observes Wesley, we always find those "enthusiasts" who want the dreams of their imagination to be received as revelations of God. If you ask them any questions or if you stop to think it over, they say, "This is your carnal reason." But to these Wesley said simply that the unstilled hunger for knowledge and the power to think through are "planted in our souls for excellent ends." [15]   For reason is supremely important not solely in the affairs of common life, but also "in religion reason can do exceeding much." It is a veritable "candle of the Lord."

Turning to the overvaluers of reason who pretended that the intellect was, if not all-sufficient, at any rate the major resource of religion, Wesley remonstrated against this fictitious and thoroughly mischievous overestimate. He confessed that "many years ago" he too had his fling with intellectualism in religion, having for several years honestly, earnestly tried to appreciate and use reason as the principal author and architect of Christian faith. "I made the trial for many years"—in both the experiment and in the results, Wesley's name is legion—"and

[15] Sermon 70.

found by sad experience" that the farthest reason can go, the utmost it can do, in respect to faith is to produce, never the real, but only "painted fire." "Painted Fire!" What insight! Reason can indeed direct and regulate, but it can not originate faith. Let "reason do all that reason can, it is utterly incapable of giving either faith or hope or love." Man can not of his own strength acquire faith. It must be sought and received as *the gift of God*. "He alone can give saving faith." Wesley's "trial for many years" to build Christian faith on reasoning refers back to the thirteen yeasty years of his humanistic seeking and finding between his ordination and his conversion-experience. All active minds are sure, like Wesley, sometime, somewhere to get into this mischiveous overestimate of reasoning in the Christian faith. But unlike Wesley, some never get out.

This false intellectualism in religion, this misplaced confidence in reason, criticism, itself an act of reason, can and must destroy. And when the intellect has duly chastened itself by observing that the Yes and No of reason in religion are so evenly matched, and when, like the great Newton, we are duly conscious that around the little island of all our knowing there is poured the infinite expanse of things as yet unexplored, when the humbling insight comes that our consciousness of the unknown inevitably deepens, widens, lengthens very much faster, for all the marvelous progress of science, than the actual increase of our knowledge, these insights need not touch the integrity of the intellect nor abate its energy. But they may and should cleanse the human spirit of that false pride of intellect which is no less poison to the scientific mind than it is to the Christian consciousness. Whether it be science or religion, the deepest humility is the soil in which the spirit of truth, the seed of discovery, brings forth its hundredfold.

It can not be said too often, nor with too much emphasis, that by the spirit and letter of John Wesley's doctrine of faith, when a true balance is struck, to rationalize religion is to destroy religion as religion. He confessed that he could never detect a rational necessity in the truth-values of the Christian faith.

Mathematical reasoning is the province of rational necessity and he pronounced the mathematical method of reasoning incompatible with the nature of religion. He would believe nothing great or small without such kind of proof as the nature of the thing allows. But it is not in the province and resource of reasoning as such either to create or confirm the truth-values of the Christian faith. The highest reason we can ever give for the truth-value of religion is our experience of its reality. In that sense only he asserted that true religion is the highest reason. He insisted on right use of reason in religion, but he also and oftener warned "to beware of the Reasoning Devil." In religion, reason counts for something, experience more, revelation most. Were you to substitute the deductions of reason for the witness of the spirit, you never would be established. Very revealing is his sharp admonition, "You want a philosophical religion; there can be no such thing. So far as you add philosophy to religion, just so far you spoil it." No master of practical Christianity or teacher of the Church ever made a sharper distinction between "the theory of religion" and "the living experience of it," or set relatively so little store by the former and so much by the latter.[16]

These statements may forcibly remind us that while Wesley was no obscurantist, neither was he a rationalist, in religion. Wesley's answer: "Irrational religion is false religion," given to Rutherford's "Every Methodist must *renounce reason* to be received into that school," is not a pronouncement for a "religion within the limits of reason alone." The idea of irrationality refers here solely to "the gross untruth" about *renouncing all use of reason.* It affords no information at all about how much of a resource religion has in the use of reason. A collection of Wesley's lifelong renunciations of all claims and his warnings against all attempts to rationalize the truth-value of the Christian faith are more informing. For example, in the sermon on the Trinity he not only renounces but reprimands every attempt to rationalize the doctrine and pitches into "merciful John Cal-

16 Letters, VII, 47.

vin" for passively consenting to the burning of Servetus alive as a heretic instead of accepting, as Wesley believed he should have done, Servetus' doctrinal statement as sufficient. When therefore-fore we weigh his renunciations and add his judgment that reason in religion can produce only "painted fire" we can be sure he knew the difference between saying the truth-value of Christian faith is reasonable, and that it can be rationalized. How far Wesley kept away from all rationalization of religion, how close he kept to the unique essence of Christian experience can be reliably known from his basal thesis, that the Christian conscious-ness is rooted, grounded, radically summed up in a *continual sense of our total dependence on God*.[17] This is the experiential equivalent to the thesis of the Oxford manifesto: There can be no reference in the doctrine of salvation by faith to human, but solely to divine agency. All this accords with the fact that Wes-ley did not reason out this view of Christianity but acquired it from the Oracles of God and the sure testimony of experience.[18] It is a radically experiential insight. It is an original intuition of which no further account can be given. It is final trust in experience and its indications.

But this sharp-sighted observer had a quick and sure discern-ment of important and lasting contributions which critical ration-alism was destined to make to the progress of Christian thought and also indirectly to practical Christianity. In a supplement to his reply to Conyers Middleton's attack on miracle, wherein, after wasting his time defending the miracle, he has outlined the only apologetic suitable and sufficient for the New Protestantism, he remarked that criticism was an afflictive dispensation of God and a fiery furnace of testing for the traditionalistic mind, driv-ing traditional Christianity out of its misplaced confidences into a search for deeper and firmer foundations of Christian faith. Christian apologetic would thereby be driven to make experience its principle of method. Thus criticism was proving itself a blessing, to Christian faith, in disguise. For while false tradi-

[17] Sermons 16, 28.
[18] Sermon 11 and frequently.

tionalism was being ground to powder by criticism, the knowledge of historic Christianity, sustained by the appeal to the continuous verifiability of the Gospel in experience and life, remained for Wesley, as it remains for us, in undiminished authority. This, that and the other argument might well be imperfect or fail us. But one stream—the living, abiding, cumulative witness of experience—could never fail; "one thing I know, I was blind, but now I see." How seldom indeed did Wesley preach a sermon or write a monograph on the highest themes of the Christian faith that he did not appeal at the crucial point to the authority of experience! [19]

Wesley in his ripest years wrote a thoughtful discourse which undertakes to show the more excellent way between an extreme pessimism which damns the present age as "the dregs of time" and locates the golden age in remotest antiquity, and the extreme optimism which damns the past as only "an immense sea of errors," despairs of the present and locates the golden age just over the crest of the hill in the valleys of the great tomorrow. Wesley pays an honest tribute to the "Former Times," but takes his stand on the solid conviction [20] that human progress is not fiction but fact, not a dream but a reality. He instances several particulars in which he thinks his age truly excels all former times, notably its great advance in the knowledge of nature, which is a reference to the scientific movement, and the triumph in religion of the spirit of toleration, which is a reference to the special influence of the Enlightenment.

On the second subject Wesley saw in the toleration movement in religion the choice fruit of the Enlightenment. As to the

[19] Letters, II, 375-388.

[20] Posterity will scarcely be impressed but rather amused at our present fit of doubt about the possibility and reality of progress through man's deliberate, forethoughtful effort. Our entire civilization rests upon the ability of the human intellect to profit by experience. We have not exhausted; we have only gotten a fairly good start in this procedure. The despondency of the men in the fifth century who knuckled mentally to the "Fall of the Roman Empire" and the "Sack of Rome" commands our pity, not our respect. Our case of despondency is no better.

fact, he asks, "Is not persecution well-nigh vanished from the face of the earth? In what age did Christians of every denomination show such forbearance to each other?" He recognized in the toleration movement something new under the sun and very significant. In respect to the birth of toleration, "If it be said, 'why, this is the fruit of the general infidelity, the deism which has overspread all Europe,' I answer whatever be the cause we have great reasons to rejoice in the effect. . . . Indeed so far as we can judge, this was the most direct way, whereby *nominal* Christians could be prepared, first for tolerating, and afterwards for receiving, *real* Christianity. . . . Oh, the depth both of the wisdom and knowledge of God; *causing a total disregard for all religion, to pave the way for the revival of the only religion which was worthy of God!"* [21] I doubt if anything more penetrating and profound has ever been said on the contribution of the Enlightenment to human progress in general and to progress in religion in particular. The path of progress from false religion, a system of force, to true religion, a system of freedom, lies through the (temporary) negation of all traditional religion. The Enlightenment cancelled the idea of force out of religion, and left Christianity with no resource but its own intrinsic merit and attractiveness. But Wesley believed the reduction of Christianity, thanks to the Enlightenment, to an experience we may ourselves verify, enlarge, instruct and stimulate out of the general Christian experience, was the best thing that ever happened to the Christian propaganda. Freedom, not force, is the natural instrument of religion. At this point it is plain to see that Wesley belongs "head and heart" not to the old but to the new Protestantism.

But while Wesley was thus no stranger to, but with a quick sense of value was much rather deeply responsive to the thought currents of his age, still what he set himself to do in pursuit of his vocation, was not to accommodate his message to the humanized and desolate theorizing Christianity around him, but rather with prophetic originality to conquer an irreligious climate of

[21] Sermon on "The Former Times."

opinion by preaching the truth, diagnosing both the sickness of religion and the one source of vitality with unerring precision. Many commentators are puzzled that Wesley's evangelical doctrines should have excited so much antagonism. But this perplexity overlooks the fact that the instant reaction to Wesley's message was perfectly natural. For he assailed not only the philosophy but also the morality and then even more militantly the religion of his age. He characterized the church members of his age as mostly "baptized heathen." He said, "They believed no more of Christianity than the Devil and lived no more than heathen." What was the issue? Let Wesley define it: "The doctrine of salvation by faith is peculiarly intolerable to *religious* and *moral* men. All religious people have such a quantity of (acquired) righteousness which is their wealth both for this world and the next. All other schemes of religion flatter them (keynote of humanistic religion) that they are very rich. The doctrine of faith takes all this wealth away; it is a downright robber. It tells these religious and moral people they are as bad, if not worse, off than 'the herd of vicious wretches.' They are but the same needy, impotent, insignificant vessels of mercy. This is more shocking to reason than transubstantiation." Wesley was, right from the period of his conversion-experience and for the remainder of his life, an opponent of this humanized Christianity and of a very militant kind. He became, under the drive of deep conviction, a disturber of the Church's peace. He coined in the sermon on "The Straight Gate and Narrow Way," which he defined as saving faith and inward holiness, the epigram that became a proverb among his followers: "You must be singular or be damned." He wrote a friend in June 1739, "God forbid that you should ever be other than generally scandalous." [22] He did not mark time or play safe with the world. He put on the whole armor of God.

The nature of this conflict is well mirrored in the sharp exchange that took place mid-August 1739 between Wesley and Bishop Butler at Bristol, England. The encounter occurred less

[22] Journal, II, 218.

than two years after Wesley's Oxford manifesto against "natural religion." The learned apologist of a naturalistic and humanistic Christianity questioned closely in two conversations this self-appointed rector of the world about his doctrine of justification by faith. "Why, sir," said the Bishop, "faith itself is a good work." "But," Wesley answered, "it is the gift of God, and a gift that presupposes nothing in us but sin and misery." The crucial point of the two conversations came when the Bishop, confronted with the Wesley and Whitefield theocentric doctrine of Christian experience, told Wesley: "Pretending to extraordinary revelations and gifts of the Holy Ghost is a horrid thing —a very horrid thing!" Wesley freely struck out the issue-clouding term "extraordinary" and then he took all the rest of that high doctrine to himself. Finally the Bishop waved him out of the diocese, "You have no business here." But here the Oxford Fellowship proved to be Wesley's tower of strength. "Wherever," said Wesley, "I think I can do the most good there I must stay, so long as I think so. At present I think I can do most good here; therefore, here I stay." [23] A clash of two strong personalities would in itself, however interesting, be out of place here. But it touched first principles. The point of Wesley's boldness in his doctrine of faith was precisely the point of Butler's greatest timidity, namely, the objectivity of Christian experience. Revelation in a far distant and receding past was an idea difficult enough for that doubting age. At most the Word of God but added authority to the ideas that man had and could by his own effort acquire for himself. But to subsume Christian experience under the category of revelation, in a deistic climate of opinion, "that was a horrid thing—a very horrid thing!" But it was the soul of Wesleyanism.

The issue was therefore joined between a naturalistic and humanistic religion and a most energetic and thoroughgoing theocentric reinterpretation of salvation by faith. Wesley says he was the first Englishman to visit Herrnhut. He did not take back all he found there. But he did find there the inner spirit of Luther's mighty work come back to live again in the souls of humble men, and he took back with him fresh credentials that Luther's message of the sovereign, saving meaning of a God-given faith in Christ had in it the everlasting Gospel. He had preached the great Oxford manifesto with his plans all set to go at once, that duty done, to Herrnhut—"this place where the Christians lived." He was appraising the Moravians idealistically in the glare of the fact that they had mediated to him, while in the valleys of spiritual despair, Luther's distinctively religious understanding of the Gospel, the only external authority for his doctrine of saving faith other than Scripture that he ever acknowledged.

CHAPTER X

THE VERY EDGE OF CALVINISM

The distinguished author of the *Analogy* between natural and revealed religion considered himself an Arminian and took the position of Bishops Secker, Horne, and others, that those who understand the faith of the Anglican Church in the Arminian sense are its truest guides and teachers. Where then did Wesley stand? How does he fit into this picture? He appeared at Oxford in June 1738 with a corrective for the current interpretation of Christianity in which the tendency was to define its highest values as a human achievement, but not more than human. What now was Wesley's corrective for "a religion not more than human"? What did he propose to an age which had rethought its Christianity downward close to the worship of humanity? Did he propose as a remedy for this humanistic reduction of the Christian faith to the very edge of Atheism, to ascribe still less of the content and meaning of Christian experience to God, and still more of it to man? For Anglican Arminianism he had another corrective; it was to restore "the knowledge of God to be won only from the Gospel" to its rightful sovereignty in the message of the Church. If the diagnosis of St. Paul was right that the radical malady of the whole non-Christian world lay in the failure to have God in its experiential thinking, as he is known in the Christian Revelation, what other source of redemption can there be but the preaching of a Gospel which has in it the power of God unto salvation?

Having examined the attempt of the Enlightenment to reduce historic Christianity to a religion of humanity in the light of Wesley's idea of a God-given faith or the Christian revelation as fundamental to Christian experience, we must reverse the

point of view and examine Wesley's return to the faith of the
first Reformers from the standpoint of a "libertarian theology,"
in order to assess the place and part and power of this concept
in the Wesleyan doctrine of Christian experience. Is the idea of
human freedom a first principle in Wesley's doctrine of religious
experience? Is it a real rival of the idea of the grace of God,
setting a boundary to it and even prevailing over it? Does it
hold the same conspicuous position in the Wesleyan teaching
and preaching which the Luther-Calvin idea of the sovereign saving significance of a God-given faith in Christ occupied in the
teaching and preaching of the Early Reformation? Does the
Arminian corrective to ultra Calvinism occupy a position in
Wesleyanism to justify the thesis recently advanced that the
character and content of the Wesleyan teaching and preaching
lies in its deviation from the Luther-Calvin idea of faith, rather
than, at any rate, much more than, in its unity with the faith
of the first Reformers? Can an objective analysis of the content
of Wesley's teaching and preaching justify the claim that we
have in Methodism *for the first time* (!) in the history of the
Church a great religious revival based on a libertarian theology?
Is the idea of human freedom the chief source, indeed we venture
to ask any source, for the religious energy of the Wesleyan
Reformation? The imperial idea of the Christian message
throughout the Christian centuries, as attested in Song and Sermon, has been, so Harnack found in his *History of Dogma*, not
the idea of human freedom, but the idea of divine grace. Is
Methodism after all an exception to the rule?

A doctrinal Epistle written in the twenty-fifth year of Wesley's conversion-experience repeats an entry in the minutes of
the second Wesley Conference (1745): "The true Gospel touches
the very edge of Calvinism." The exact language of the minutes
was "lies very near, within a hair's breadth, comes to the very
edge of Calvinism." Now this minute refers not at all to the
doctrine of sin and of salvation by faith which Wesley consciously shared in full with Calvin as well as with Luther. It
refers to the one disputed point of predestination. The specific

meaning is then that the true Gospel touches the very edge of predestination. If this explication is right, it would afford a hint that in respect to what he always considered fundamental to Christian experience, Wesley was at heart, and what is more, openly, avowedly a Calvinist. The conspicuous position of the idea of justification in Lutheranism, of Jehovah's electing love in Calvinism and the idea of Christian perfection in Wesleyanism have too long and too often been pushed into the foreground of the exposition to the fatal concealment and neglect of the fundamental unity of these main branches of the Reformed faith. It is time to weigh the deeper unities. The question submitted is whether the dynamic of the Wesleyan Reformation came out of Wesley's deviation from or lay in his concurrence with the Luther-Calvin idea of a God-given faith in Christ. The movement away from the Luther-Calvin position had, before Wesley appeared, run itself out and reached the end of its tether. What direction then did Wesley's search for power in preaching take? Must the progress of Wesley's religious thought from 1725 to 1738 be defined in accord with the facts as a retrograde movement away from the religious idea of the Early Reformers in the direction of a humanist reconstruction of the Christian faith or as a movement in the reverse direction, away from humanism toward a more deeply religious understanding of the Gospel?

The early Reformers affirmed the exclusive divine causality or man's total dependence upon God in the redemptive process, not in the least as a speculative principle remote from life, but in a tragic sense as a gateway of escape from man's sinful bondage into the peace and power, and *the true freedom of justification and reconciliation with God*. This insight then proved to be in the sequel also an instrument of emancipation from an ecclesiastical tyranny as well as a great highway of individual freedom. The doctrine of man's total dependence on God for salvation cancelled all human control of salvation and derived the freedom of a Christian man direct and sole from the grace of God.

This doctrine of redemption is at once center and circumference of Wesley's preaching and teaching. The idea of the *free grace of God,* impartial, unstinted, love-prompted, holds the conspicuous position in his doctrine of faith. Now he pushed this doctrine of grace to the limit. In this respect he was not a whit behind the early Reformers, nor has he deviated a hair's breadth from the early Reformation doctrine of salvation. The whole and sole point to the first great manifesto of the Revival which proclaims the sovereign significance of saving faith is that man's salvation must in its totality be construed primarily as the gift and grace of God. "Of yourselves cometh neither your faith nor your salvation. The faith through which ye are saved as well as the salvation which he of his own good pleasure, his mere favour annexes thereto, are the free undeserved gifts of God. That ye believe is one instance of his grace, that believing ye are saved another." The crux here is the reference of saving or justifying faith to the divine causality. Here Wesley agreed unmistakably with the early Reformers. In fact, and utterly contrary to received opinion about Wesley's Arminianism, although he always accepted the Arminian corrective to extreme Calvinism, nevertheless the Arminian element and accent does not any time, anywhere hold the conspicuous position in Wesley's doctrine of faith. The religious evaluation of human freedom, the liberty of the moral agent, the spiritual nature and essential dignity of man do not any time, anywhere hold the conspicuous position in Wesley's preaching and teaching of Christianity. On the contrary, when the doctrinal gist and grist of his preaching is bolted to the bran, all reference to man's individual resource is conspicuous therein chiefly on account of its absence. There is no more certain item of modern church history than the fact that the dynamic impulse to the Wesleyan Reformation did not come out of any humanistic reconstruction of Christianity, nor out of anything akin to it or remotely affiliated with it. It admits of strict historical demonstration that the Wesleyan Reformation arose primarily as a powerful reaction against a naturalistic and humanistic reconstruction of Christianity. The crisis of religion in the eighteenth century was caused by the general humanization and secularization of religion. Wesleyanism was a profound reaction against it. The creative impulse of the Revival was given by a thoroughgoing theocentric doctrine of Christian experience which dared to subsume the total fact of Christian experience under the category of revelation.

In the language of historical theology, it has often been said that "Methodism is Arminianism on fire." Undoubtedly Wesley accepted at the outset of his ministry the Arminian modification of extreme Calvinism, included it steadfastly in his theology, and put a high, practical value upon it. The foundation of the *Arminian Magazine* in 1778, the fortieth year of the Revival, to keep clear of the Calvinistic abyss in expounding evangelical principles and to check the extravagances of ultra-Calvinism, is the principal monument to this interest. But the fierce controversies that arose and raged around Wesley's staunch advocacy of the Arminian corrective of extreme Calvinism created and fixed the impression that Wesley's doctrine of Christian experience is fundamentally anti-Calvinistic, so that the term Arminian has commonly been taken to describe the content of Wesley's preaching, at any rate a conspicuous, if not the most conspicuous, element in it. But this thesis will not stand the test; it falls to the ground before an objective analysis of the content of Wesley's preaching. He himself said flatly that the corrective to extreme Calvinism was the special interest and burden of less than one in a hundred of his pulpit utterances.[1] The other ninety-nine were concerned solely with the fundamentals of Christian experience which he always claimed to share with Calvinism.

It may be then that the formula "Methodism is Arminianism on fire," if intended as an objective description of the content of Wesley's preaching, of its regnant doctrinal ideas, is much more felicitous in the phrasing than accurate as to the facts. For the Arminianism never has been, never was for John Wesley, Francis Asbury, and their colleagues, is not now and never will be the source of the fire. It admits of full proof that the religious energy of Wesley's message lay in its unity with the faith of the first Reformers and not in any deviation from them. There need

[1] Letters, IV, 297.

be no doubt or uncertainty whatsoever that the principle of power and the supreme resource in the preaching alike of White-field and the Wesleys by which, all agree, a religious revolution was begun in England, was the Luther-Calvin idea of the sover-eign saving significance of a God-given faith in Christ as a perfect revelation of God and a complete atonement for sin. It is often, perhaps commonly, supposed that the theological differences be-tween Whitefield and the Wesleys were profound while their doctrinal agreements were superficial, at any rate far less impor-tant. But they certainly did not think so and Wesley roundly denounced that view as close to absurdity. Wesley is on record, not once but often and always, that the peculiar religious energy of the Wesleyan Revival came out of the unity of the Protestant faith, the very heart of it, and not out of its divergences. "It is the faith of our first Reformers which I by the grace of God preach." [2]

The first Oxford sermon after Wesley's conversion-experience builds the doctrine of salvation sole and single upon the principle of divine grace. Saving faith, which is the first foundation of all Christian experience, is referred, all of it, to the work and witness of the Spirit of God. So radical and strong was Wesley's reaction against the reference of saving faith to human activity or the description of it as the human side of salvation, that he confessed to a scruple at first to recognize faith—going at this point and at this time beyond both Luther and Calvin—as the condition of salvation. The whole interest, emphasis, deep, almost tragic undertone of earnestness in the sermon is to proclaim the objectivity of Christian experience. It expounds with the singular concentration of overmastering conviction that the Christian faith as experience must be referred to divine agency. For a man to be saved, and this salvation comprehends man's entire Christian experience, is God's work, no more, no less. "It is God alone who worketh in us." "It is God alone who worketh in me both to will and to do of his good pleasure." [3]   The exclusive

[2] Letters, II, 134.
[3] Letters, II, 23.

burden therefore of the Oxford Revival manifesto is not in the least an Arminian corrective to the Calvinistic formation of the Reformation doctrine of faith; but it is an unqualified reaffirmation of original Reformation principles.

Now it is a fact of first importance for our expository purposes that Wesley has included in this radically and thoroughly theocentric doctrine of Christian experience, not the negation but the steady, strong affirmation of human freedom. The God consciousness of Luther and Calvin, or shall we not rather say their experience of God, is used in Wesleyan theology to undergird the humanism of Erasmus that was naturally cherished in the universities of Holland and introduced there into theology by Arminius and likewise with the humanism of the Oxford Reformers and developed by their successors in the Church of England. The tradition of humanism in both centers reverts to the influence of Erasmus and of the Renaissance. The affiliation of John Wesley with Arminianism is well known. Indeed we have already found reason abundant for the question whether the anti-Calvinism of Wesley has not so preoccupied the attention of his expounders as to throw the most important fact about his message, if not into total eclipse, then into a very misleading perspective. Since now Wesley's strong, stern criticism of Calvinism in the one point of predestination is, among those who know his doctrines, the best remembered fact about his theology, I have not carried coals to Newcastle by again parading the details of his criticism before the reader. It will serve every demand of the most exacting objectivity to recall that he pronounced in his Bristol sermon on "Free Grace" predestination a doctrine full "of horrible blasphemies," "with a direct and manifest tendency to overthrow the whole Christian revelation." For it seemed to him to cancel the essential righteousness of God and so in effect represented the God and Father of our Lord Jesus Christ as if "an omnipresent, almighty tyrant." Wesley read the whole meaning of the Christian faith in the light of one all-inclusive truth, "God is love." He was so sure of this that he declared,

"No scripture can prove predestination"—better insight, perhaps than exegesis.

It must in justice to Wesley be said at once that while he continued adamant against the doctrine, this extreme view does not represent him in the full maturity of his mind. He took back a good deal of it. He and his brother reasoned in 1735 that it was a duty, since predestination is subversive of the very foundations of Christian experience, to oppose it with all their might. He retracted this view just thirty years later and declared himself to be otherwise minded. He now thought it not subversive of the very foundations of Christian experience and stigmatized his earlier position as bigotry.[4] But while his earlier dogmatism toned itself down into patience and he became consciously broader in his theological outlook, he continued adamant against the doctrine of predestination. He brought Arminianism back to evangelical principles and built a fire under it, but never broke with it. But while the Arminianism of Wesley is still very well known, his essential and deeper Calvinism in the doctrine of sin and salvation is not. Wesley's early conferences with his assistants were chiefly seminars on Christian doctrine. In the minutes of the Second Conference, 1745, we find Q. 22: Does not the *truth of the Gospel* lie very near both to Calvinism and Antinonianism? A. *Indeed it does, as it were within a hair's breadth,* so that it is altogether foolish and sinful, because we do not *quite agree* either with one or the other, to run from them as far as ever we can. Q. 23: Wherein may we come to *the very edge of Calvinism?* A. (1) In ascribing all good to free grace, (2) in denying all natural free will, and all power antecedent to grace, and (3) in excluding all merit from man even for what he has or does by the grace of God. Wesley evidently was not a man to run away from basic Gospel truth because Calvin taught it. For he too did ascribe *all good to the free grace of God;* he too did deny *all naural free will and all power antecedent to grace;* and he too did exclude all merit from man, even for what he has or does by the grace of God. And he knows no other

4 Letters, IV, 295.

power of moral goodness in man but the grace of God. Beginning with his radical reaction in 1738 against the prevalent libertarian theology and humanized Christianity of the age, he taught precisely these three doctrinal ideas with the greatest energy and utmost consistency throughout the fifty-three marvelous years of his conversion-experience. It is a necessary inference from this—as well as from Wesley's explicit statements—that he was conscious of standing in his theology, not at all in opposition to the essentials of historic Calvinism and by no means at a great distance from it. On the contrary, he was conscious of agreeing so much in fundamentals with historic Calvinism as to come to "the very edge of Calvinism," i.e., of current Calvinism. And the Conference minutes define that since the agreement covered "the truth of the Gospel" it is altogether foolish and sinful, because we do not "quite agree," because the one point of predestination is at issue, "to run from Calvinism as far as ever we can."

Here then we come upon a first-rate problem. How has the fact of Wesley's conscious and avowed concurrence with historic Calvinism in evangelical principles been obscured? How has his own striking definition of his early theological position as a qualified or guarded Calvinism—"within a hair's breadth"—been ignored by his "Arminian" interpreters? How has his theology been identified, at variance with the facts as well as with his own reiterated protests, by most of his later interpreters, by some in part, by others outright, either with semi-Pelagianism or even Pelagianism, imputing to him a doctrine of faith which he earnestly, indignantly repudiated; namely, that man is in moral matters by nature free, or that the feeling of freedom ever can be, for the Christian consciousness, a reality distinct from the grace of God? Wesley's whole relation to early Reformation principles has been clouded and forgotten under the influence of this serious misconception.

Moreover in the first conference of the Wesleyan Revival, and more than once thereafter, Wesley entered the opinion in the minutes that the first Methodists leaned *too much* (!) to Calvinism. And he said in 1771 that he had himself "all this time (1738-1746) leaned towards Calvinism." Here we have full proof that the theology of the Revival was in its original motivation, conception, and first formation a positive and powerful reaction against the current humanist libertarian theology of the age and that Wesley's first reaction carried him—as he later informs us—too far, so far that he even scrupled in this first stage of his conversion-experience to do what both Luther and Calvin always did,—call faith a *condition* of salvation. The Oxford manifesto noticeably makes no reference to faith as a condition,—a significant omission! But this fact demonstrates that his conversion-experience was a reaction against humanism toward Calvinism, and not in the reverse direction, so that he later found it necessary to qualify and to guard his doctrine of grace, although less against historic than against ultra-Calvinism. From that hour he began with his doctrine of divine grace as a basis to develop increasingly along with the objective, not at all the doctrine of human freedom, as is commonly supposed, but the ethical, holiness view of the atonement. "Repentance is the porch of religion, Faith is the door of religion and *Holiness is religion itself.*" When hard put to it later to rein in the extreme Calvinists of his day, he censured their ultra or extreme Calvinism as poison to the Gospel and "the bane of true religion." [5]

But while Wesley thus developed later on not the doctrine of free will, but the doctrine of holiness with vigor as a corrective to extreme Calvinism around him, he has not deviated from the conviction of both Luther and Calvin in his doctrine that man's power to co-operate with the divine will is itself moment by moment the pure gift of God. In summa the Wesleyan doctrine of freedom is never philosophical, never naturalistic, always religious, theological. He never once used it to refute or to compromise or to qualify the early Reformation doctrine of saving faith. The theology of Wesley moved therefore securely, entirely in Pauline, Augustinian and early Reformation paths. The con-

[5] Letters, VI, 169, 191, 201.

spicuous position in this type or system of Christian thought is occupied not by the doctrine of human freedom, but by the doctrine of divine grace and of man's "total dependence on God for every good thought, or word or work."

At the height and in the heat of the Calvinistic controversy while Fletcher, Wesley's penman and the Melanchthon of the Wesleyan Reformation, was writing his *Checks to Antinomianism,* Wesley read a monograph on predestinationism from which he acquired the erroneous opinion that "it was hatched by Augustine in spite to Pelagius, who probably held no other heresy than you (Fletcher) and I do now." [6] We know from the writings of Augustine that his doctrine of grace was mature before he knew there was such a man as Pelagius. His doctrine of grace was no accident of controversy. It had its roots in the teaching of the Western Church and, above all, in his own experience and reflection. It admittedly does not do justice to the doctrine of holiness. And this omission justified a corrective and explains Wesley's active sympathy with the objectives of Pelagius' teaching.

It is an easy inference from such anti-Calvinist utterances, and it has often been made, that John Wesley as the disciple and expounder of the Arminian corrective to Calvinism broke away from the Pauline-Augustinian and early Reformation doctrine of saving faith as man's consciousness of his absolute emptiness of any good, and of his absolute dependence on God for everything good in his entire personal life. But Wesley's rejection of the extreme Calvinism of later and lesser minds is no clue to his own doctrine of Christian experience. That must be sought in the content of his preaching. And it thus appears that he stoutly maintained first, last and always with the early Reformers that God is the sole agent in our experience of redemption. All of Christian experience has faith as its first principle and what Wesley taught of one aspect of Christian experience, *Justification,* he taught of all Christian experience. Since Wesley thought he had leaned too much at first toward Calvinism, refer-

[6] Letters, VI, 174.

ences will here be confined to statements of his position made while the necessity of correcting current Calvinism was very much of a burden on his mind. "We" (he was writing Fletcher) "both continually maintain that the *means* of sanctification and the *fruit* of those means spring *solely* and *wholly* from *the almighty grace of God which alone worketh all in all and by them all*."[7]

Here Wesley affirms complete unity of principle in his doctrine of justification and sanctification. He is thus at great pains to free his doctrine of Christian experience from the least taint of humanism. He builds a logical fence around the idea of the grace of God and locks the very gates against any reference in our salvation but to the grace of God. There is an obvious intent to make the reference inclusive. The accent is cumulative. There is no principle of energy in man's salvation but the almighty grace of God. Faith and its moral energies spring *solely, wholly* from God's grace. God *alone* worketh *all in all* and *by them all*. Not a trace of humanism can be found in Wesley's doctrine of Christian experience. He taught the total depravity of man. He affirmed the exclusive divine causality in redemption. He recognized in the feeling of total dependence the unique essence of all religious experience. He denied that man is in respect to moral goodness in any degree independent of God. "I always did for between these thirty and forty years clearly assert the total fall of man and his utter inability to do any good of himself; the absolute necessity of the grace and spirit of God to raise even a good thought or desire in our hearts. Who is there in England that has asserted these things more strongly and steadily than I have done?"

Wesley preached in the twenty-fifth year of his conversion-experience a second sermon on the text of the great Oxford manifesto. It is one of his greatest expositions of the Gospel. Why did he preach it? The first manifesto banished humanism from *the doctrine of justification*. But "it has been roundly and vehemently affirmed for these five and twenty years that we be-

[7] Letters, V, 7.

lieve and teach that we are *sanctified by our works.*" "I hold," said Wesley, "just the contrary. We are sanctified by faith only; Faith is the only condition." The whole and sole point of these two sermons alike is that saving faith is the sole principle of Christian experience underlying its progress (sanctification) no less than its beginnings (justification). Thus Wesley laid another specter of the mind and banished all humanism from his doctrine of sanctification.

There is complete agreement among commentators that the sermon on "The Scripture Way of Salvation," written in the year 1763, is as simple, accurate and complete a statement of Wesley's doctrine of Christian experience as he ever made. In this sermon also the accent falls, as to methodology, on the joint witness of Scripture and experience. Then as to content, "These two little words, faith and salvation, are said to include the substance of all the Bible, the marrow, as it were, of the whole Scripture." Further, the salvation spoken of in Eph. II, 8, is a *present reality,* has its *one source* in the free grace of God, and "might be extended to *the entire work of God* from the first dawning of grace in the soul till it is consummated in glory." It includes *preventing grace,* somewhat ineptly called *natural conscience,* in three particulars: All the drawings of the Father and the desires after God; all the natural enlightenment of every human spirit by the Son of God; all the fruits which the Spirit of God works in every child of man. This might, in the language of Origen, be called Wesley's doctrine of the divine and the diviner immanence.

Turning to the diviner immanence in the beginnings and progress of Christian experience, in its two aspects of justification and sanctification, Wesley states: "I have constantly declared and continually testified in private and in public for these five and twenty years that we are sanctified as well as justified by faith, that exactly as we are justified by faith, so are we sanctified by faith." Verily this is, as to the meaning of faith, once more the voice of Luther: *Faith is, has and does all in the whole realm of Christian experience.* And there is never room in the

Christian consciousness for any self-righteousness, any trust in man and taint of pride or self-will. The more advanced we are in Christian experience, the more true it is that we are *after justification* "more ashamed of our best duties than formerly of our worst sins." [8] It is true not only of the entire work of God, but above all of Christian experience from first to last that it is permeated by "a conviction of our helplessness, of our utter inability to think one good thought or to form one good action, but through God's free, almighty grace, first preventing us and then accompanying us every moment." For Wesley then all the truth-values of religion, be it "natural religion" or revealed religion, or under any other name, are forever wrapped up in the feeling of total dependence on God.

The feeling of total dependence on God is thus not only the unique essence of all religious experience, but it is for Wesley the consummate truth of Christian experience at every stage. All Christian experience, not simply the first or any particular stage, but in every stage is rooted and grounded "in *a continual sense of thy total dependence on Him* for every good thought, and word and work, and of thy utter inability to all good unless He 'water thee every moment.' " [9] It is "the true nature and end of prayer" to exercise and deepen *the consciousness of our continual and total dependence on God*.[10] But while Wesley has occasionally described the unique essence of Christian experience as a subjective state of the soul—that of the feeling of total dependence—his usual habit of thought is to identify the unique essence of Christian experience with the objective reference in it. The idea that only the Word of God or revelation can produce Christian experience, that all saving faith is "the gift and the work of God," "an operation of the Holy Spirit," is his great focalizing thought. For every case therefore where Wesley has referred Christian experience to the human subject and has identified the unique essence of Christian experience with the feeling of total dependence, there are a thousand cases where he

[8] Sermon 50.   [10] Sermon 21.
[9] Sermons 16, 28.

has referred Christian experience to a God-given saving faith and has identified its unique essence with revelation or the work and witness of the Holy Spirit. The continual reference of Christian experience to the human subject and the reduction or reference of the unique essence of religion to the feeling of utter dependence may have a fateful tendency to cancel the objective reference out of Christian experience and to dissipate the idea of revelation altogether. But the spring of energy in Christian preaching always has been, history and experience bearing witness, in its sure foundation in the principle of revelation, not confined to well-attested events in the storied past, but given as the inner urge and quickening impulse of the whole Christian message in the living present.

Wesley was conscious of being even more strictly *monergistic* in his pure *ethic of grace* than some of the later Calvinists, and said so more than once. Certain English Calvinists, notably the Westminster divines, had relaxed their monergism enough to assert for every man a measure of natural free will. Wesley flatly rejected the idea. "I do not carry free-will so far." He simply would not admit any "natural free-will." He asserted "only a measure of free-will supernaturally restored to every man" and insisted that all of man's power of concurrence with God is itself "from God." "We allow it is the work of God alone to justify, to sanctify and to glorify; which three comprehend the whole of salvation." We must conclude then that Wesley's doctrine of freedom is completely religious, theological. Christian faith in its comprehensive and sovereign significance can be experienced only by a power equivalent to that which created the world and raised the dead.[11] "The Spirit of God is the immediate cause of all holiness in us." [12]

We know exactly in what sense Wesley was an exponent of the Arminian corrective of Calvinism. That corrective was not the motivation nor the main interest, if indeed it was any practical religious interest at all, of the Oxford manifesto on Justification

[11] Letters, IV, 12.
[12] Letters, III, 9.

or Salvation by Faith, or of the revival message as a whole. The sole and supreme interest of this pronouncement and of the Wesleyan message is the objectivity of Christian experience. That objectivity is summed up in the one word—God. Monergism means there is no energy of moral goodness in man outside our total dependence on God.

The theory recently propounded that Wesley anticipated Schleiermacher and even William James in respect to the primacy accorded to religious experience is true and important. But even so, the deeper element in Wesley's doctrine of Christian experience was his return to and reaffirmation of Reformation principles. The religion which had invaded the Anglican and other pulpits had virtually banished God from the sermon. The burden of Wesley's preaching, as of all great preaching, was how God has revealed himself in Christ concerning sin and salvation, and what he has done and is doing for our redemption. The last and deepest word of profoundly religious minds never has been human freedom, always has been the grace of God operative in Christ and in the actual Christian community for the salvation and blessing of sinful men and women called to Christian perfection. At this point Wesley stood exactly where the early Reformers stood, exactly where Francis, Augustine, Paul stood. The religious consciousness at its greatest and best flings itself at the foot of the Cross in utter trust upon the grace of God. The preeminence of this doctrine of redemption in preaching has been the strength, its neglect has been the feebleness, of the Christian pulpit. The interpreters of Wesley have too often, indeed have commonly, arrayed the Wesleyan type of Christian preaching at all points against Calvinism which shares this doctrine of redemption. Yet this is a grand mistake against which Wesley himself again and again warned. "I think on justification just as I have done any time these seven and twenty years and just as Mr. Calvin does. In this respect I do not differ from him an hair's breadth." [13]

The sharp admonitions from Wesley's own pen not to con-

[13] Letters, IV, 298.

strue his doctrine of faith too much as if in anything essentially
different from Calvin's doctrine and in ignorance of his essential
concurrence, carries with it the conclusion, since this essential
agreement in the doctrine of saving faith represents Wesley in
the epoch of his maturity and at the summit of his career, that
the religious energy of the Wesleyan Revival did not reside in
Wesley's Arminian deviation from Calvinism, but in the religious principles which Wesley in accord with Arminius consciously and consistently shared with historical Calvinism, and
therefore with all of the early Reformers.

Attention has been directed to Wesley's self-confessed active
scruple in the first years of his conversion-experience against construing faith as even a condition of salvation. There could be
no more infallible proof that the great transition in the Spring
of 1738 was of the nature (1) of a strong, almost violent reaction
against the Anglican Arminianism in which he was brought up,
confirmed at Oxford and kept beating the air for about thirteen
years, and (2) of a wholehearted reaffirmation of the Luther-
Calvin idea of a God-given faith. Wesley's sharp eyes detected
later that he had out-Calvined Calvin in this active scruple of
his earlier years against construing faith even as a condition of
salvation. "It is true," he wrote to "A gentleman at Bristol,"
"that repentance and faith are privileges and free gifts of God.
But this does not hinder their being conditions too. And neither
Mr. Calvin himself, nor any of our Reformers, made any scruple
of calling them so." This current Calvinist scruple which even
exceeded Calvin's position and wanted his sanction, was overcome by Wesley by his substitution for the notional dilemma
"either God's gift or man's work," of the experiential synthesis
"both God's gift and man's work." "You speak truly," says
Wesley to a Calvinist, "when you say, 'the free grace of God
applies to sinners the benefits of Christ's atonement and righteousness, by *working in them repentance and faith.*' You are
right when you say that 'the benefits of salvation are not an-
nexed to faith and repentance *as works of man; they are the
gift of God.*' You are wrong alone in ruling them out as con-

ditions. For they are no less terms or conditions, although *God works them in us.* And again, the Scripture has promised us the assurance of faith, to be *wrought in us by the operation of God.*" [14]

There can be no mistake about Wesley's position. He has defined it with the utmost simplicity and lucidity. Saving faith, even allowing, as he was careful to affirm, that man is not entirely passive in the business of salvation, and that his receptivity must be a significant act of self-determination, is even so, in its totality, the *gift, work, operation of God.* Wesley's analogy is the beggar who puts out his hand to receive a dole. All this and precisely this is affirmed in the sermon on "The Scripture Way of Salvation," in the most unequivocal manner. The sole point of distinction between the two sermons on Eph. II, 8, preached one in the first and the other in the twenty-fifth years of the Revival is that the idea of faith as a condition of justification, which is conspicuous in the first Oxford manifesto solely by reason of its absence, is distinctly taught in the second sermon but with this further addition, that the same faith is at once the divine principle and the human condition of all Christian experience. The postulate and regnant conviction of both sermons as of Wesley's entire doctrine of Christian experience is "a conviction of our helplessness, of our utter inability to think one good thought, or to form one good desire, and much more to speak one word aright or to perform one good action, but through His free, almighty grace, first preventing us and then accompanying us every moment." [15] It is obvious that Calvin himself could not have said more; for there is nothing more to be said. And for those versed in historical theology it need not be said that the root-thought in Schleiermacher's system is here completely apprehended.

Undoubtedly the doctrine of man's freedom in God, i.e., in a definitely and genuinely religious sense, underlies inferentially Wesley's entire doctrine of faith. But while Wesley flatly

[14] Letters III, 244-250.
[15] Sermon 50.

rejected the natural freedom of the philosophers [16] and affirmed that man is by nature an exile from the Kingdom of God and that the exile, as such, is in a state of utter bondage from which there is no egress into freedom but by the grace of God, nevertheless even freedom in this specific religious sense is not a conspicuous doctrinal idea in Wesley's theology. For this deeply religious understanding of freedom is not so much as once even mentioned in the Standard Sermons, while the natural freedom of the philosophers is referred to but once only to renounce it as a doctrine of irreligion. Wesley observed that it was customary in the philosophical approach to and reconstruction of Christianity to extol the freedom of man, the resources of human nature and the intrinsic ability of man to live in respect to moral goodness "off of his own stock." But this, he allowed, is the doctrine of irreligion. The Christian consciousness is the radical antithesis of this naturalistic faith. The faith that has any relish of salvation in it has its origin and abiding principle in "a continual sense of our total dependence on God, for every good thought or word or work, of our utter inability to all good, 'unless' He water us every moment." [17]

The second stage of the Calvinian controversy which was the longest and most bitter in Wesley's career, broke out simultaneously with the death of Whitefield after the publication of the doctrinal minutes of the 1770 conference. The storm-center was the doctrine of holiness or Christian perfection which Wesley insisted was the moral meaning of the atonement. He was ready and determined to veto any doctrine which separated the religious interpretation of Christianity from the ethical. God had joined them together; let no man put them asunder. It is more important to break the power of "cancelled sin" than to cancel the guilt of it. Indeed without the former the latter would be a futile gesture, unworthy of God. Wesley spent much time and hard work in the second and third decades of the Revival on doctrinal standards and guidance. He continued writ-

[16] Sermon 9.
[17] Sermon 16.

ing and printing sermons and monographs on the Christian faith.
Then in 1763 he began to revise his numerous works already in
print, making ready for the great thirty-two volume edition of
his works which began to come out in 1771. "All the leisure
hours while in London" were for several years spent "reading
over our works with the preachers," i.e., in seminars on Christian doctrine which took up "practically every subject of importance either in practical or controversial divinity." [18]

The doctrinal minutes of 1770 have as their background this
decade of solid and responsible work in theology. The Ten
Theses on theology recorded in the Conference minutes were designed as a corrective to that seductive species of extreme current Calvinism which insinuated into the popular mind and
seemed to sanction in principle a total divorce in the justified
between religion and righteousness. The minutes therefore stress
the activist ethical side of Christianity. Now Wesley's synthetic
and well-balanced understanding of both the religious or grace
side and the activistic holiness side of the Christian faith, as one
and inseparable, caused extremists alike among the Moravians
and later among the Calvinists to accuse him in all sincerity of
being a *legalist*, a preacher of salvation by good works, therefore a Papist and an apostate from Reformation principles. On ·
this premise alone may we rightly understand the protest lodged
a year later by the Calvinist wing of the Revival against the
Ten Theses of the 1770 doctrinal minutes, all of which loudly
accented the ethical side of the Christian faith. The Calvinistic
branch of the Revival protested their own "warm interest in the
revival of *spiritual* religion and the doctrines of the Reformation" and they professed a deep concern, yes, alarm, lest "a
veteran in the cause of the Gospel (Wesley was in his 68th year),
and one of the chiefs in the late Reformation," should by teaching *salvation by works* be going back on "what is eminently
called by us the doctrine of free grace" and so betray the cause. [19]
Wesley was in their eyes and so far forth no longer, as they put

[18] Journal, V, 41.
[19] Journal, V, 41.

it, a "real protestant." We would however do these extremists
an injustice, if we imagined their move to induce Wesley to re-
cant was only an impertinence and so failed to perceive how
profoundly sincere and serious they were about it.

Now in the light of these facts and of the subject matter of
the Ten Theses, did Wesley retract any of the teaching of the
first great manifesto of the Revival? Not at all. He simply took
the necessary measures to keep the fatal leaven of current Antinomian Calvinism out of the Revival. Wesley and those with
him refer often at this time to the havoc which it wrought in
the Methodist household of faith. The storm-center of this controversy was the question, Is the ethical interpretation of the
atonement essential to the Gospel? Can saving faith that is not
an active principle of holiness be called saving faith? The fact
is that Wesley denied once and again throughout this stormy
period any, even the slightest, change in his doctrine of faith.
He did instruct his helpers as a corrective to preach holiness
more than ever. But on the two main points of his message
wherein he, always, fully agreed with Calvinism he denied any
change. "I always did for between these thirty and forty years
clearly assert *the total fall of man and his utter inability to do
any good of himself; the absolute necessity of the grace and
spirit of God* to raise even a good thought or desire in our hearts."
And he asked, "Who in England has done so more strongly and
steadily than I have?" So in the very moment when Wesley
struck out from the shoulder against current Calvinism and insisted that Christian behaviorism is of the deepest importance
and essential to saving faith, he was more emphatic than ever
that the Ten Theses did not at all qualify his earlier and constant
teaching on justification by faith wherein he still thought and
taught exactly as John Calvin did. "Man is not entirely passive
in the business of salvation." But man's dependence on God is
the fountain of all his activity in moral goodness. It is highly important to note that the sermon on "The Lord our Righteousness,"
written 1765 as a corrective to current Calvinism and a sermon
frequently preached in contrast to that on "Free Grace," written

1739, which was very seldom preached, twice appeals to historic Calvinism against current Calvinism. "Neither Mr. Calvin himself nor any of our Reformers made any scruple of calling faith a condition of salvation" as well as the free gift of God. But they were right that the faith which the Scripture has promised is "wrought in us by the operation of God." "I entirely agree that justifying faith is the gift of the Holy Spirit." As for the current doctrine of the imputed merits or righteousness of Christ, that, said Wesley, "is blasphemous Antinomianism such as Mr. Calvin would have abhorred." [20]

Wesley was clearly conscious then that in his doctrine of faith and freedom, his quarrel was not as much with historic Calvinism as with a degenerate species. The epigones, the later and lesser lights, were not equal to the master-mind.

Likewise when Wesley's well-balanced doctrine of Christian experience is compared with early nineteenth century Methodist teaching and preaching, we are confronted on some subjects with almost a caricature of his doctrine. The high intellectual and spiritual altitudes of the master were again too much for the later and lesser lights. Reasonable discipline in the history of thought soon discovers the fact that second generations of great movements very often, indeed commonly, get the perspective wrong, so that, wanting original documents, the founder must often be seen through the mists of very imperfect and one-sided representations and interpretations. But of both the progress and the stability of Wesley's doctrinal ideas we have a superabundance of records. Moreover this shift of position in the transition from the master-mind to his disciples is not always due solely to inferiority. The controversies that were started by the work of the founder and raged around his personality may cause disciples to go off on a tangent and mislead them, if not to shunt it out of their message, at any rate to allow that to fall into the background which was first in the message and foremost in the emphasis of the master.

The history of preaching in the Wesleyan Churches lies en-

[20] Letters, III, 244-250.

tirely outside the scope of this inquiry into Wesley's principles,
but the relation of Wesley's message to the early Reformation
doctrine of faith is vital to it. Now Wesley never allowed the
Calvinistic controversies to change either the subject-matter or
the distribution of emphasis in his preaching. He did not allow
this controversy to mould or modify his doctrinal ideas. He
wrote just two discourses on the Calvinistic specialty; one in
1739 on "Free Grace," the other in 1773 on "Predestination."
Certain writers outside the Wesleyan connection have rated the
sermon on "Free Grace" one of Wesley's greatest sermons. And
Tyerman places it in the forefront of Wesley's most significant
utterances. This judgment still prevails in much, if not most
secondary writing about Wesley. The reader must form his own
opinion of this estimate in the light of the fact that Wesley
never relished preaching the sermon on "Free Grace" and seldom did.[21] Further, he deliberately barred it from the Doctrinal Standards which he set up for the Revival. Finally he
asserted roundly that even at the height of the Calvinistic controversy, though he preached all of eight hundred sermons a year,
yet he actually preached less than one in a hundred "over a
period of twenty years" that dealt with the peculiar tenets of
Calvinism. The ninety-nine sermons dealt with Christian doctrines which Calvinists shared fully with all other Evangelicals.
How has this one sermon been made the master-key of Wesley's
message and ministry as if less than one sermon in a hundred, on
the theological specialty of Calvinism, outweighed in importance
the ninety and nine other sermons on the essentials of Christian
faith and experience in which all the main branches of Protestantism share alike, as if important enough to dislocate Wesley in
the Protestant evolution and to place him outside the main stream
of Protestant religious thought!

It is possible from these facts and reflections to form an accurate idea of how small a place the specifically anti-Calvinistic
element actually occupied in the Wesleyan doctrine of Chris-

---

[21] The text is not listed in Wesley's Sermon Register for the fifteen years from
January 1747 to December 1761.

tian experience. The facts point securely to the conclusion that the Wesleyan theology apprehended historically was (1) not at all a reaction against Calvinism in the direction of a libertarian theology but was (2) a positive powerful reaction against the humanist libertarian theology which then reigned supreme in Anglican teaching and preaching and (3) a conscious return to and reorientation in the faith of the first Reformers. All the facts about Wesley's doctrine of Christian experience are intelligible alone on the historical premise that the original purpose, the deeper meaning, and inner genius of the Wesleyan Movement was to redeem the current religion of the Church of England from humanism, to recall Anglican Arminianism to evangelical principles, and to restore the faith of the first Reformers to its rightful but lost ascendency in Christian teaching and preaching. The Wesleyan Movement was therefore essentially an evangelical reaction against humanism in religion and a genuine revival of the first Reformer's theocentric faith. There emerged then in the progress of the Revival as its secondary and subsidiary phase the deliberate refusal of Wesley to scuttle the Arminianism which he undertook to recall to evangelical principles and his strong measures taken to safeguard the Revival of the Protestant idea of faith from running off again into ultra-Calvinism. And so it seems that Wesley's anti-Calvinism must be radically subordinated to his anti-humanism in order to obtain a historically accurate view of his message and ministry.

But this leaves the way open to do justice to Wesley's Arminianism. It belonged to Wesley's genius, some will say to his superficial eclectic thinking, but we believe to his deep, clear synthetic thought, to join together the faith of the first Reformers with the valuable element in humanism as represented by Erasmus and Arminius in Holland and by Erasmus and the Oxford Reformers with their successors, the great Anglican divines. How often did he say of the alternative views on the major issues of the Christian faith, "God has joined these together, and it is not for man to put them asunder"? [22]   He ob-

[22] Sermon 107.

served once, verging on paradox, that a good Methodist would be a happy mixture of the Mystic and the Pharisee. A list of the instances where on a major question of Christian doctrine Wesley has joined together what dogmatic theology has chronically put asunder would throw a strong light upon a most remarkable quality of his mind. Even if it involved no more than a superficial eclecticism in Wesley's theology, the results would still be most remarkable. But only a superficial acquaintance with Wesley's work can be satisfied with that theory. Substituting experiential thinking for logical or notional thinking in theology he was enabled not only to revive and stand by early Reformation principles in their integrity, but also to do justice to the important truth of humanism. It was not Wesley but his disciples who were unequal to this masterful synthesis, who were thrown off their balance by the Calvinist controversies and were pushed by them into a gradual subordination once more of the creative religious ideas of the Wesleyan Reformation to the humanist libertarian accent in theology, until the distinctively religious accent in Wesley's message has been lost.

The fact to be examined from every point of view is that the irreligious climate of opinion around him with which, and not with the Calvinist preachers, Wesley had his main battle,—how oft did he say so!—was dominated by a libertarian theology. We have seen that Wesley himself thought the Christianity of his age was a religiously anaemic humanism and said so. His sermon on "The Spirit of Bondage and Adoption," which reminds much of Luther's immortal tract on "The Freedom of a Christian Man," refers to the humanist Arminianism of his age. The watchword of this bankrupt religion was: "I will lift up mine eyes to the dignity and resources of human nature, from whence cometh plenty of help. For they are sufficient to every exigency of man's religious and moral life!" Wesley acutely observed concerning exponents of natural religion that they "talk at large of man's rational faculties, of the freedom of his will, and the absolute necessity of such freedom in order to constitute man a moral agent." "They," that is, "those who are termed men of learning," rely on a philosophical approach to and reconstruction of religion; they "read and argue and prove to a demonstration that every man may do as he will." Then Wesley roundly denounced this philosophical approach to religion with its libertarian theology, as "a double veil of blindness" which "the god of this world spreads over the heart lest by any means the light of the glorious gospel of Christ should shine upon it." When Wesley preached his first Revival sermon at Oxford, June 11, 1738, this Arminian theology of natural freedom and natural religion was everywhere in the ascendent. Before Wesley's time few, if any, theologians in England knew how to qualify ultra-Calvinism without landing in Pelagianism. That was largely due to the fact that they made *logical or notional inconsistency* rather than *experience and its indications* their principle of method. They mistook notional contradictions for experiential contradictions. Wesley's theology moved much more in experiential paths and with far more success.[23]

The inference from the "Free Grace of God" to human freedom, as the primal fact and prelude of redemption, has often been made, as in the case of Bishop Butler, to avert the inference that God would be a tyrannical being, if of his free grace "without any goodness of man preceding," he justifies some and does not justify all. For if the justification rests not on some preliminary moral goodness, why are not all justified? Butler's dilemma was that either justification rests on some primordial moral goodness in man or else God is a tyrant. But Wesley flatly rejected the whole dilemma. He was as strong to deny that justification depended on any power or merit, that is,

---

[23] The term Arminianism may be used to denote (1) exactly the position of Arminius who introduced a corrective of Calvinism on the point of predestination, or (2) the position of later Arminian theologians who remembered the corrective and forgot the theology to be corrected, as if nothing worth. So Calvinism may denote the teachings of John Calvin himself who pronounced the scholastic denial of human freedom a blasphemy; or it may denote the position of some of his later disciples who made a theological hobby-horse of predestinationism and forgot all the rest of Calvinism. See especially Wesley's illuminating letter to John Bennett, Letters, II, 23.

on any originality or actuality of moral goodness in man, as he was to affirm that there is nothing at all of partiality or arbitrariness in the grace or love of God. Human wit and wisdom may never be able fitly to frame these two affirmations together in the structure of reality. To Butler's demand, if there can be in justification no reference to moral qualification in the recipient but solely to the free grace of God, to know why then saving faith has not been given to all, Wesley answered, *"They resist his Spirit* and they can not be *saved* because they *will not believe."* Thus Wesley has here as elsewhere invested the human "will to believe" or the power of response or resistance in man's total personal life with such relative finality of decision and responsibility for the outcome of the atonement as any freedomist would care to assert.

But to begin or to stop with this affirmation of human freedom, as if a limit notion, would totally misrepresent Wesley. His first and last word never was freedom, always was the grace of God. To Bishop Butler's question, "What do ye mean by faith?" Wesley replied: "By justifying faith I mean a conviction wrought in man by the Holy Spirit." "Why then have not all men this faith?" "We answer (on the Scripture hypothesis) *it* (i.e., saving faith) *is the gift of God. No man is able to work it in himself."* Now Wesley had heard in connection with his conversion-experience Martin Luther say so exactly: "Faith is not something we fetch up from our imagination and put over on ourselves. Faith comes over us in the mighty impact of God's revelation of Himself to us. It is God's own work in us. The Holy Spirit is at once implicit and actively present in it all. Pray God this faith may be wrought in you by the Gospel or it will never be yours, fancy what you will or do what you can!" Just so Calvin too called this faith "the principal work of the Holy Spirit" and believed it to arise from and bear a perpetual relation to the Word of God.

Precisely in this meaning Wesley also taught that Faith can not be man's work. It is the work of Omnipotence. It requires no less power thus to quicken a dead soul than to raise a body that lies in the grave. It is a new creation and none can create a soul anew but He who at first created the heaven and earth.

The analogy here drawn between the power of creation and of the resurrection and that of a God-given faith was characteristic and fundamental in the early Reformation doctrine of saving faith. Whether or no Wesley's unmistakably monergistic doctrine of salvation can be kept clear of "notional contradictions," he is at any rate entitled to be understood on his premises. What are these premises to which his thinking unfailingly recurs? (1) "We answer, *on the Scripture hypothesis*, that saving faith is the gift of God"; (2) "May not *your own experience* teach you that saving faith is not in your power at all but that *God freely gives Faith*. The final trust of Wesley's theology is therefore built on the experiential confirmations of the Word of God and not on any notional consistencies or inconsistencies. From this monergistic view of salvation he does not deviate. From his thesis that *free grace is all in all* he never strays.

If any doubt remains, if there is any hesitation to accept the conclusion which these typical though far from exhaustive data clearly carry with them, it should be swept away by the simple reading of Wesley's very strong, in fact one of his most radical anti-Predestinarian utterances from the Christian pulpit. We refer to the seldom-preached sermon on "Free Grace," which was written as a corrective to extreme current Calvinism and preached in 1739 at Bristol, England. Surely this sermon must be an obstacle to our thesis. No, not at all! Once more, the main thesis, exactly as in the Oxford manifesto, was that "in the doctrine of salvation, God is everything, man is nothing." But we ask, Is this thesis anywhere contradicted or qualified either inferentially or directly by the sermon on "Free Grace"? The sermon has for its theme "Free grace is all in all." But what means this "all in all"? Wesley divided the subject into two parts: "The grace or love of God, whence cometh our salvation, is *free in all* and *free for all*." In the first point "free in all" Wesley was always, as he is here, a radical Calvinist. In the second he is a radical Arminian. The second thesis that God's grace is *free for all* cancels of course, and this is the point of the sermon, "the decree of predestination." But Wesley's interpreters have for the most part overlooked his division of the subject. They have confused what he has distinguished under the two heads and have drawn certain conclusions concerning man's part in salvation from the distinct and definite rejection of predestination, which Wesley himself always openly, consistently disavowed.

The fact is that no more radically monergistic statement of the doctrine of justification by faith ever came from Wesley's tongue or pen, or, for that matter, from any Reformer's tongue or pen, than the statement made in this corrective of the current Calvinism. "God's love or grace whence cometh our salvation is *free in all*." "It does not depend on any power or merit in man; no, not in any degree, neither in whole nor in part. It does not in any wise depend either on the good works or righteousness of the receiver, not on anything he has done, or anything he is. It does not depend on his endeavors. It does not depend on his good tempers or good desires, or good purposes and intentions. For *all these flow from the free grace of God;* they are the streams only, not the fountain. They are the fruits of free grace and not the root. They are not the cause, but the effects of it. *Whatsoever good is in man or is done by man, God is the author and doer of it. Thus is his grace free in all.*"

If then in the most radically anti-Calvinistic discourse Wesley ever wrote, wherein he pitched into the doctrine of absolute predestination as a doctrine "full of blasphemy," as a doctrine which cancels the first principle of the Christian revelation, namely, the essential righteousness of God, he has taken the precaution and been at particular pains to reaffirm in the most complete and unequivocal manner· a monergistic and in the same manner to deny a synergistic view of faith and repentance, of justification and of sanctification, it would seem an end of all argument about, not the soundness of Wesley's doctrine, but what his position actually was. For us Wesley's thesis, which he taught consistently for full fifty years, that "whatsoever good is in man or is done by man, God is the author and doer of it," and the further fact that he has crowded into this category every particular of Christian experience, carries the conclusion with it and is final.

Having traced the central thesis of Wesley's teaching and preaching, argued, amplified, expounded in season and out of season, set forth and sustained without variableness or shadow of turning for over fifty years, we turn back to the outset of his Evangelical ministry when he embraced justification by faith and renounced apostolic succession, for one more clear and, for our purposes, concluding statement of his position: "The author of faith and salvation is God alone. It is he that works in us both to will and to do. He is the sole Giver of every good gift, and the sole Author of every good work. There is no more of power than of merit in man; but as all merit is in the Son of God, in what he has done and suffered for us, so all power is in the Spirit of God. And therefore every man, in order to believe unto salvation, must receive the Holy Spirit. We do not know how the Spirit of God works on the soul; but it is certain all true faith, and the whole work of salvation, every good thought, word, and work, is altogether by the operation of the Spirit of God."

The Wesleyan doctrine of saving faith as set forth in the first manifesto of the Wesleyan Reformation, and no less clearly in all his expositions of Christian doctrine, is therefore a complete renewal of the Luther-Calvin thesis that in the thought of salvation God is everything, man is nothing. The vigorous development in early Methodism of the Arminian qualifications of extreme Calvinism, the gradual loss of Wesley's original perspective of the truth-values of the Christian faith, the absorption of interest in controversial subjects and the recession of emphasis on the first principles of the Revival gave concern already to Wesley and still more to his earliest biographers, lest Methodist preaching should relapse again from evangelical into humanist principles. The bitter controversy then fastened upon early Methodist theology, after Wesley's departure, a bias without pattern or warrant in Wesley's own work in the creative period of the Revival. This bias, deviating radically from Wesley's first principles as set forth in the doctrinal standards which he set up, is the parent of the opinion that "the Wesleyan Reformation is the first great religious revival based on a libertarian theology." While it is easy to trace the origin of this theory of the Revival to sources other than Wesley's preaching, there is in fact not an inch of ground for it to stand on. The facts are all against it. Wesley's preaching in the creative period of the Revival (1738-1770), instead of magnifying, as this theory assumes, the human resource as an element of saving faith, is in fact singularly barren of any reference to anything even remotely suggestive of man's originality in the experience of saving faith. The structural and total emphasis of his preaching is altogether in the opposite direction. The fact that he developed with the utmost energy in season and out of season the Augustinian doctrine of original sin and total human depravity would alone be a sufficient refutation. But wholly apart from this decisive consideration, an inductive examination of his preaching yields no other conclusion but that the idea of the religious and moral significance of human freedom was conspicuous in his preaching solely on account of its total absence. He wasted no time with such a doctrine on factory hands, coal miners, keelmen, tinners, on the contrary he told them exactly what he told academic audiences, namely, the same unpleasant truth: man can not by his own resources in the least degree help himself into a redeemed life of moral goodness. There is in him to that end outside the grace of God not an infinitesimal resource of saving faith. The spring of religious energy in the Revival lay in Wesley's essential concurrence with the Luther-Calvin doctrine of salvation by faith; it lay in the Luther-Calvin doctrine how that faith is given and on the Luther-Calvin thesis that a God-given faith is the sole and abiding principle of all Christian experience; it is witnessed in the revolution wrought in Wesley's preaching by his abandonment of the libertarian theology and his adoption of the Luther-Calvin position. The nature of that revolution was the radical shift of the center of gravity in preaching from a humanistic doctrine of faith to the meaning of God in Christian experience.

CHAPTER XI

THE INFINITE DISTANCE OF SIN

The Wesleyan doctrine of Sin presents the severest test for every attempt to build an interpretative bridge from the Wesleyan Reformation to the vital work of the Christian Church in the twentieth century. A climate of opinion whether in the eighteenth or in the twentieth century which has reduced Christianity to a religion in Wesley's words, "not more than human," "extolled humanity to the skies, as the very essence of religion," wanted "a kind of rational religion that has not only nothing of Christ but also nothing of God in it," and represented man as morally, religiously "able to live on his own stock and little inferior to God himself,"[1] in short, a religion either of pure atheism or pure immanence can never come to terms with the Wesleyan doctrine of sin and grace. The humanist trend of recent religious thought and the inevitable clash between Wesleyanism and the prevalent humanistic drift in religion is indirectly indicated in the tendency of late to deny that "total depravity is an essentially Methodist doctrine." Recent religious thought in the United States has been stricken with radical doubt about the reality not only of original sin, but of any kind of sin. We are in fact just now emerging from an era of prevalent humanism and prosperity blindness—who can read plain print through a gold-eagle—wherein the consciousness of man's sin and need of redemption was, if not conspicuously absent, at most but a faint and indifferent factor in the message of the Church. Even within evangelical Protestantism some were beginning to entertain a question whether the doctrine of sin could have in the prevailing climate of opinion any practical religious value. In conformity

[1] Sermons 37, 114, 138.

273

with the spirit of this age that is going out, a disciple of John Wesley could do one of two things: He could in effect nullify Wesley's principles by accommodations and reinterpretations to suit the spirit of the age, or he could gradually disregard and forget the essentials of Wesley's message until even his triumphant confidence in the appeal to religious experience had been lost. The latter course has commonly been pursued. There is need just now supremely to reconsider this course with all its gains and losses.

The Wesleyan picture of man as the subject of redemption is very black. It could not be blacker. Of course, the blackness has no meaning but in the light of the Christian consciousness of salvation by faith and of the unbounded efficacy of God's entire work of grace for us in Christ, in us by the Holy Spirit. Now Wesley taught from first to last, and with all energy, the doctrine of original sin and total depravity. And he pushed this doctrine to the limit. He did not temporize and tone it down. He did not qualify it. He did not evade it. He did not shrink back from its unmitigated offense to natural reason, nor yield an inch to the humanist principles of the Enlightenment. He taught the doctrine of sin harshly. He not only assumed the possibility; he also asserted the fact of our being damned souls. Able churchmen, good men too, were deeply offended in him for it. One of the foremost churchmen in his time admonished him: "Do not so profusely fling about everlasting fire." There is in Wesley's answer a touch of grim humor: "You put me in mind of an eminent man, who preaching at St. James said, 'If you do not repent, you will go to a place which I will not name *before this audience.*'" How much preaching and praying begins and ends "before this audience" and "to this audience"? Wesley changed all that. He put God back into the preaching and the praying. Communion with God became again real and significant. "I desire to have both heaven and hell ever in my eye while I stand on this isthmus of life between these two boundless oceans." [2] It is only in the presence of God and in the light of

2 Moore's *Wesley*, II, 464.

the eternal that the dark tragedy of sin in this transient life of ours is first unmasked in its hideous reality and true proportion. And who is this God in whose presence the fear and favor of man sink into nothingness? "The almighty, all-wise God is the Holy One, inhabiting eternity, *infinitely distant from every touch of evil.*" [3] This intense feeling, this final intuition of the infinite difference between the Eternal Holiness of God and the transient sinfulness of man is at the bottom of Wesley's radical doctrine of sin. Irreligious minds simply need not, ought not to try to understand it.

We ought therefore not to be too easily repelled on the very threshold of our subject by this Wesleyan doctrine of original sin and total depravity. It is indeed not all true, certainly not in all the details and devices, but it has truth in it. And the truth-values in it are inseparable from and essential to the Gospel. We therefore owe it to ourselves as truth-hunters in the highest concerns of human existence and destiny to come at so difficult a subject at least with the open mind. We need above all to be forewarned. For the doctrine of sin imbedded in the Prophetic-Christian view of life and the world, and interwoven into every vital variation of historic Christianity, is precisely the point where the inevitable clash between genuine Christianity and human nature reaches its climax of intensity.

The doctrine of sin as developed by Wesley—and here he is entirely faithful to historic Christianity, planting his feet identically in footprints made by St. Paul, Augustine, Luther, Calvin—brings every man to his knees in the dust and ashes of repentance. It is a most humbling doctrine. It crucifies all self-pride. "The doctrine of faith is a downright robber." [4] Nothing like it ever was or will be found among considerations of natural reason. We simply need not look for it in that way of thinking. There is nothing in the progress of religious thought to gainsay the Pauline instruction: The natural man receiveth not the things of God. The truth about the reality and ravages of sin is an

[3] Sermon 114.
[4] Journal, I, 462.

unmistakable intuition of the Christian consciousness of which no further account can be given. Being an ultimate of the Christian consciousness, we can simply take it or leave it. But the choice we make will have consequences which point far beyond the horizons of our present system of human experience. St. Paul knew all genuine Christian experience has a cross in it. A veritable crucifixion of human pride is the alphabet of Christian experience.

And so it is that all the great teachers of the Church, all the master-minds of the Christian faith, have anticipated and shared for substance of doctrine Wesley's tragic view of man as a subject of redemption. Accordingly too much Christian experience has flowed in that channel to ignore, much less to make light of it. The late Adolph Harnack, first among masters of historical theology, bore witness out of his thorough life-long discipline in the history of ideas that the great preaching and hymn-writing of the Christian centuries has virtually all been rooted and grounded in the Church-form of Christianity, in the thought of man as lost and undone in the bondage and doom of sin, in the thought of redemption as altogether God's work in the sense of a radical regeneration of human nature. There is pronounced consciousness of sin, total renunciation of all self-salvation, absolute trust in the grace of God, the personal God, apprehended in the humility of Christ as the compassionate one. This God who is our creator has redeemed us through Jesus Christ and filled us with his spirit. The type is one; the variations are many. But in one and all the general sinfulness of man is the presupposition of religion. By common consent Augustine is the paradigm of this understanding of the Christian religion. Now although the Wesleyan doctrine of sin and grace has beyond question an individuality of its own and has modified the Augustinian type in most important particulars, yet with Augustine well in mind it is instantly clear when we turn to Wesley that he felt essentially as Augustine felt, thought as he thought, spoke as he spoke. For the Wesleyan Exposition of the Gospel links the essentials of the Christian system closely with the doctrine of original sin. It is the general ground of the whole doctrine of justification.[5] The doctrine of salvation by faith in all its branches hangs on it.[6] That is equally true of the doctrine of the sole efficacy of divine grace.[7] The doctrine also defines the point where "Christianity leaves all pagan religion behind" and it underlies the doctrine of sanctification or growth in grace.[8] "Original Sin, Justification by Faith, Holiness of Heart and Life are the three cardinal doctrines of Christianity." [9] Any interpretation of the Gospel that does not reckon with the total usurpation and perpetual tyranny of sin, but for the grace of God, is building on sand.[10]

All of Wesley's sermons presuppose this doctrine of sin and are built upon it. Many of them revert to it. Some state it in all its repellent realism. The concluding lines of the Sermon,[11] on "Justification by Faith," preached June 8, 1742, from his father's tombstone at Epworth,[12] less than a twelvemonth after Jonathan Edwards preached the sermon at Enfield, Connecticut, on "Sinners in the Hands of an Angry God," July 1741, may explain why among Wesley's auditors, as among Edwards' hearers, some were convulsed in tears of agony and distress and fell down as if struck by lightning. "Thou ungodly one who hearest or readest these words! Thou vile, helpless, miserable sinner! I charge thee before God, the judge of all, go straight unto Him with all thy ungodliness. . . . Go as altogether ungodly, guilty, lost, destroyed, deserving and dropping into hell. . . . As such thou shalt be brought unto the *blood of sprinkling,* as an undone, helpless, damned sinner. . . ." There were plenty of polite, respectable people in Wesley's day who felt a horror at such preaching which always stirred the emotions, sometimes violently. Yet these same cultured critics felt no shame, rather felt proud of themselves for crying their eyes out at the play over the sad fate of the poor innocent victim of the plot. Wesley failed to per-

[5] Sermon 5.
[6] Sermon 38.
[7] Sermon 14 and everywhere.
[8] Sermons 16, 36.
[9] Letters, IV, 146, 237.
[10] Letters, I, 279; II, 335, etc.
[11] Sermon 5.
[12] Journal, III, 20.

ceive the consistency and continued to use such resources as he had—he felt they were God-given—to rescue sin-cursed thousands from the pit of destruction in time and eternity. We expect surgeons to be not too fastidious to cut, but to be accurate and get results. Wesley meets that test.

On these historic premises and practical principles alone can we do justice to Wesley's startling thesis that the doctrine of "the entire depravation of the whole human nature, of every man born into the world, in every faculty of his soul, not so much by those particular vices which reign in particular persons, as by the general flood of Atheism and idolatry, of pride, self-will, and love of the world, is *the first grand distinguishing point between Heathenism and Christianity.* Here is the *shibboleth:* Is man by nature filled with all manner of evil? Is he void of all good? Is he wholly fallen? Is his soul totally corrupted? Allow this, and you are so far a Christian. Deny it and you are but an Heathen still." [13] This demarkation is in no sense racial or geographical or conterminous with Christendom, but a purely religio-ethical perception of the facts by the Christian consciousness that is no less valid within than without geographical Christendom. This doctrine of sin is the major premise of Wesley's entire doctrine of Christian experience. And it represents his mature theological judgment and deepest conviction.

Commenting on the powerful attack which Taylor of Norwich, one of the ablest expounders of a humanistic Christianity in Wesley's time, had made on this doctrine, Wesley insisted with high courtesy but with the utmost deliberation and gravity, taking five full years to mature his reply,[14][15] that the attack was the greatest "wound to Christianity since Mahomet," that "Taylor's books, chiefly that upon Original Sin, have poisoned so many of the clergy and even the fountains themselves—the Universities in England, Scotland, Holland and Germany" (note the sweep of Wesley's observation) [16]—and finally that the issue was no less than "the whole of Christianity." For Wesley believed that Tay-

[13] Sermon 37.
[14] Journal, III, 520.
[15] Letters, III, 180.
[16] Letters, IV, 48, 66.

lor's doctrine of Original Sin, if true, simply cancelled "the whole difference between Christianity and Heathenism." It subverted "the doctrine of Redemption or Justification and that of the New Birth, the beginning of sanctification." We would miss the whole force of Wesley's conception of the issue, if we should take the term heathenism in a grovelling sense. It must be taken in the highest and best sense. It denotes not the lowest levels but the loftiest heights of the religious consciousness without the Christian revelation. Witness Wesley's decisive putting of the question: "Has the religion of St. Paul any pre-eminence over that of Socrates or Epictetus?"[17] And so Wesley pressed home the point that it is not "a personal controversy" but rather the fact that "the whole of Christianity from the beginning to the end" and "all the things that concern our eternal peace" are at stake. And this fact indicates the length and breadth, the depth and height of this great argument. Whatever opinion we might form of the merits of the argument, one can not but be deeply impressed with Wesley's moral earnestness about the gravity and greatness of the issue.

Wesley's long and labored reply to Taylor's treatise on the subject of Original Sin ran into 262 pages. He hoped and waited for others with far more free time, and perhaps more talent, to enter the lists. His work as preacher, pastor, superintendent of the Revival already far outran his time. Then too he sincerely detested controversy. But a champion of "the very foundation of all revealed religion" did not appear. The tide of opinion seemed to be against Wesley. He noted[18] that Taylor's influence had spread "to the Alps also." It now appeared to him to be his inescapable duty to enter the lists against this humanized Christianity. For it was "old Deism in a new dress." In the strength of it "persons of quality" were saying, "I can not see that we have much need of Jesus Christ." Humanistic religion then as now rendered historic Christianity superfluous.[19]

Wesley submitted as his authorities *Scripture, reason and ex-*

[17] Letters, IV, 48, 66.
[18] Journal, IV, 200.
[19] Preface to Wesley's *Treatise.*

perience. Judged as to pertinency and logic, much of the argument is neither interesting nor convincing. The extensive use of material from the Book of Genesis is a veritable millstone around the neck of his cause. Some of the material used by both writers comes pretty close to rubbish. But there are in Wesley's reply elements of great power and pertinency. One of these is his vivid and thoroughly objective description of the reality and ravages of sin in human history. Wesley's sermons and utterances, like his lengthy treatise on the subject of original sin, fall into two parts. The first concerns itself with the facts about "the real state of mankind." The second part undertakes to give an account or explanation of these, i.e., to rationalize them in terms of the Genesis story of the Fall of Man. In the nature of the case these two parts are entirely distinct and may be of very unequal value.

Now any religious judgment of the facts about the real state of mankind, which involves the Christian conception of sin, can never arise as a consideration of natural reason—but only in the light of Christian revelation. It can have no other basis than a Christian experience which is itself identified with *the believing fellowship,* produced by Christ's redemption and in turn continues, communicates, diffuses the revealing and redeeming activity of the Savior. In brief the doctrines of sin and redemption are so strictly correlative—this is bed-rock truth in Wesley's exposition—that either is meaningless without the other. Since the experience of redemption, *the benefits of Christ,* can be given to the individual only through the mediation of the Church as the community of saving faith in Christ, the idea of sin that corresponds to redemption, which is the idea of sin in the Christian sense, always arises in, rests back upon and must be deduced from *the common consciousness* which marks "the fellowship" of Christ's redemption. It has no other scientific objectivity whatsoever.

Moreover, the idea of sin in the Christian sense can never be deduced as a consideration of natural reason from the idea of the miserable in the natural course of events. The inference to the

idea of sin in the Christian sense is always given in the presence
and power of that which is holy and refers to it. It is the
prophet awe-stricken, sin-stricken by a fresh revelation of the
Holy One of Israel crying, "Woe is me for I am a man of unclean lips and dwell in the midst of a people of unclean lips."
It is the Apostle Peter shrinking back in the presence of the
ineffable moral goodness of Jesus: "I am a sinful man." It is
the Apostle Paul prostrating himself at the foot of the Cross
before the endless vistas of moral goodness opened up to sinful
man. It is St. Paul in the person and work of Christ rating all
self-righteousness as abhorrent, "vile refuse, dross, dregs, ex-
crements, base offal," [20] after having heard, heeded, surrendered
to God's voice calling to him out of the life and death of Christ,
calling him into a triumphant, victorious progressive experience
of the ineffable moral goodness of Christ—the righteous which
is from God by faith. We know not sin but as we are seized of
both the divine holiness and the boundless moral efficacy of the
atonement. Full insight into the Christian doctrine of sin
marks the summit, not the base of Christian experience. It is in
the living conscience of the saints, not in the dead conscience of
the reprobate, that the meaning of sin, the feeling of total dependence on God and consummate trust in his grace reaches its
climax.

It has been well said and truly that the doctrine of total depravity and cognate thoughts about "the past and present state
of mankind" constitute one of "the blackest strokes in the Augustinian picture of humanity" and "an extravagant slander against
the race which ought never to have been perpetrated." But true
as this may be, there are nevertheless truth-values in that representation which we are bound in obedience to the Christian
consciousness to disengage and defend. At any rate, the Wesleyan representation, which goes the limit with Augustine, must
never be divorced from his doctrine of prevenient grace called
"natural conscience," and his sure, unfailing grasp of the idea of
the divine immanence. He, too, well knew that this principle is

[20] *Wesleyan New Testament,* 511.

of vital importance for the entire doctrine of Christian experience. Although "man's present state is death; a death from God," that is, destitute of real communion with him, which is the unique essence of Christian experience, still "it is true while we have a being, *in him* we must live, and move and have our being." But a man can simply "exist in him" on the same spiritual level with "even the meanest creatures." "It is one thing to receive from God an ability to walk and speak, eat and digest, to be supported by his hand as a part of this earthly creation and upon the same terms with it, for further trial or vengeance; and another to receive from God a life which is his own likeness; to have within us something which is not of this creation and which is nourished by his own immediate word and power." [21]

There is in Wesley's doctrine of Christian experience or its presuppositions not the least taint of the philosophy of deism. Nature was for him but the garment of the living God. If Augustine's view of nature was, as Harnack informs us, an acosmic pantheism, Wesley's view of nature was, if possible, even more pantheistic. Nature was for him nothing but God at work. His oft repeated and favorite terms for the religious consciousness of man was "the life of God in the soul of man." If Wesley regarded conversion as an intervention of God in this soul-life of ours—and he did—it was only and always in the sense that one mode of the divine immanence is properly distinguishable from another mode. No other teacher of the Church since Origen has had a surer, steadier apprehension of the difference between the divine, the diviner and the divinest immanence. Wesley's doctrine of Christian experience, masterful in its comprehensiveness and its coherency, is in every particular the antipode of the deistic naturalism which infested the religious thinking of his century. It is the warmest possible type of Christian theism, and will endure the severest scrutiny. Natural conscience and all it implies was for him God's voice and presence in us; but even so, it is not identical with Christian experience wherein a man is "raised above himself into God," i.e., into real communion

[21] Sermon 141.

with God. The most common and recurrent idea in Wesley's preaching, teaching and total interpretation of the Gospel is this: Christian experience is "the life of God completed in us." "Christ is not only God above us, which may keep us in awe, but can not save; but he is Immanuel, God with us and in us." As this was the first principle of his earliest preaching, as it was also the regnant idea of his maturest understanding of the Gospel, so was it the last golden utterance to fall from his prophetic lips.

It was a man thus steadfastly minded about God and all his dealings with us who taught in all its repellent realism the doctrine of total depravity. Now the heightened contrast between God's grace and man's sin drawn by Christian preaching and teaching in all ages to magnify and exalt the grace of God is a purely religious idea and it runs easily into hyperbole. For this reasonable allowance is needful. On the other hand it would be worse than hyperbole to ignore or deny the evil strain in human experience or to make believe in the presence of the appalling fact and force of sin that it does not exist, or even where admitted, to belittle it. The "total depravity" of traditional theology is for all its hyperbole much nearer the facts than is the easy-going, superficial optimism of much modern religious thought which can not perceive nor appreciate the terrible strength of the evil forces that must be met and mastered alike by the individual who has chosen progress in Christlikeness as the supreme business of life, and by all those groups who seek to lift humanity to higher levels of well-being, of culture and above all of spirituality. One need not look very long at the facts of history to feel the terrible repulsion of the evil as well as the redeeming attraction of the good. And our human scales to weigh these facts against each other and to strike a balance are utterly unequal to the task.

The loss of the original Wesleyan perspective of truth-values in the Gospel and the radical dislocation of emphasis due to the Calvinistic controversies, the reception into Methodist theology within the last fifty years of the historical and higher criticism of Scripture and Dogma, and the radical shift from evangelical to humanist principles in much recent Methodist religious thought

have given rise to such humanist accommodations as that total
depravity is not an essentially Methodist doctrine, or that
Methodism is the first great religious revival based on a libertarian theology. These humanist accommodations do indeed
represent the temper of much present-day Methodist theology,
but if imputed to John Wesley, they are pure fiction. It has
been demonstrated in these researches that Methodism as represented by John Wesley was at heart really Calvinistic. By
which I mean simply this, no more, no less: The conspicuous
position in Wesley's message and in his entire doctrine of Christian experience is occupied not by the ideas of an ethical humanism but by the purely religious concept of redemption. Wesley
himself pronounced the evangelical principles, the theocentric
doctrine of Christian experience, and the idea of a God-given
faith wherein he consciously and confessedly concurred with
Calvinism a thousand times more important than the points
about predestination wherein he dissented from Calvinism. And
he affirmed point blank that his doctrine of sin was exactly that
of Calvinism. So also was he at one with Calvinism in his
view of justification by faith.

Wesley's tract on *What is an Arminian by a Lover of Free
Grace*, 1770, would seem as good a source of information as any
of his writings. Wesley, as an Arminian, was often accused of
doing precisely what many, perhaps most, of his theological successors and expounders have done, namely, of denying the doctrine of original sin and justification by faith. To the two
charges that he, as an Arminian, denied the doctrine of original
sin and justification by faith, Wesley replied, "Not guilty."
"The charges," he said, "are entirely false. No man that ever
lived, not John Calvin himself, ever asserted either original sin
or justification by faith in more strong, more clear and express
terms than Arminius has done. In these two points both parties
agree; in this respect there is not a hair's breadth difference
between Mr. Wesley and Mr. Whitefield." [22]

Wesley became actively interested in the third decade of the

[22] Wesley's Works, London, 11 ed., Vol. 10, p. 345.

Revival in the forming of a more perfect union of all clergymen "who preach those fundamental truths, Original Sin and Justification by Faith, producing inward and outward holiness." But he confessed that although he had long desired "an open, avowed union," all his endeavors so far had been frustrated.[23][24] He had sent out a letter (1764) with proposals for a closer union of Church of England men upon evangelical principles. He read a paper five years later at the Leeds Conference (1769) in which he said: "Out of fifty or sixty to whom I wrote, only three vouchsafed me an answer." Whatever the merit of Wesley's proposals in the abstract, whatever the difficulties to be overcome in the concrete, the circular appeal for a closer union upon evangelical principles of Anglican clergymen certainly defined Wesley's conception of the dogmatic basis of such union. Any clergyman should be eligible who agreed in these essentials: (1) Original Sin, (2) Justification by Faith, (3) Holiness of Heart and Life. These are the essential doctrines. Predestination and Perfection were also listed in the circular letter as optional opinions, not essentials. The distinction between regular, half-regular, irregular in the attitude toward Church order was also listed as optional. And so of many other theological differences which touch not essential evangelical principles.

Now Wesley always understood the doctrine of Original Sin in the sense of total depravity. And he has said, if once, then a thousand times over a half century of consistent teaching and preaching, exactly what he submitted in this proposal for an evangelical alliance of Anglican ministers. The doctrine of original sin, the doctrine of total depravity is essential, fundamental to the Gospel. It is a necessary inference from perfectly typical facts that original sin or total depravity is an essentially Methodist doctrine, if that formula is intended to describe the actual teaching of Wesley and the founders and not the departures of present-day Methodist theologians from it. We claim the right and admit the duty to depart from the historic

[23] Journal, V, 47.
[24] Letters, IV, 235, 239.

Wesleyan doctrines any time the truth, as God gives us to see the truth, clearly points the way; but we deny the right to impute these departures from the founders to the founders themselves, in particular to the master-mind of the Revival himself. The expounder of John Wesley in the present state of opinion who is actively interested to speak in the name of John Wesley, to bank on his authority and to capitalize his rising reputation is liable at best to substitute personal predilections for Wesleyan affirmations, and where the exposition is made without adequate historical information, the confusion of past and present is a fatal certainty. The only remedy for this is *back to the sources!* And then to tarry at the Jerusalem of critical research until the facts are ferreted out in their true relations.

When it comes to the reality of sin and to its ravages and ruin in human life and history, Wesley, in drawing his black picture of "total depravity," has done his work and done it well. He summons us to consider the brute forces of animalism which engulf again and again man's higher life; to mark the exasperatingly slow progress made in subordinating the brute side of our nature to the human. He summons us further to reflect upon the thick, murky stream of vindictive wickedness that runs through the history and experience of mankind. He piles heaps upon heaps of evidence exhibiting the endless cruelties, injustices, irrationalities that make up a large, if not the larger, part of human life. He refers us to the infinite superstitions of mankind, to the idolatry, bigotry and corruption rampant in religion itself.

Turning to his own immediate environment, he bewails the lack of business integrity among the body of English merchants who, in case of conflict between the man and the pound, not only consider profit first, but also last and only. He denounces justice in the courts as little else than ferocity and brands it as corrupt and purely mercenary. The trade-world is essentially dishonest. To be honest and righteous in buying and selling is to be one in a thousand. The English peasants, the natives of Ireland, the mass of humanity are represented as grossly, stupidly, brutishly ignorant and living lives little above the scale of the beasts of the field.

Finally, the whole earth since the first man-killing has been turned into a slaughter-house. Man is to man every kind of beast. Wesley points us to the awful scourge of war with its innumerable cruelties and immeasurable evils, how from the dawn of history every nation has played the wolf and the tiger to every other. "Whence comes that complication of all the miseries incident to human nature,—war?" "So long as there is such a thing as war in the world" all declamations about the dignity of human nature are stark staring nonsense. The warship is "a floating hell." War is a horrid reproach to Christianity, reason, humanity. The fact of war is the strongest proof that the very foundations of things, civil and religious, are utterly out of kilter. It is indeed hard to believe it until we have looked into Wesley's *Treatise* that the simple recitation of human iniquities and wickedness of every name and nature could be piled so high. And when we turn from the mighty flood of human wickedness to the trickling stream of human goodness, we are instantly thrown into consternation by the appalling percentage of the myriad millions of our race whose feet have trod this foot-stool without attaining in their total experience of life to any considerable fruition in the things of the mind and the spirit. If the positive and the negative views do not prove the truth of Wesley's view, if we decline a catastrophic view of man's origin and place in the world, if we choose, as most of us do, though not in any blatant know-it-all assurance about it, to take an evolutionary view, then the facts do prove the exasperating slowness of the ascent of man and the infinite patience of God.

Wesley came at all religious subjects in full reliance upon the guidance of Scripture and experience. On this basis he has given, in obedience to the deepest intuitions of the Christian consciousness and to the authority of Biblical teaching, a clear, strong statement of the Christian doctrine of sin. But he has by no means confined himself strictly to Biblical thought. Even if we heeded not the conditions imposed on our thinking by the scientific account of man and his place in the universe, still Wesley's extravagant and fanciful representation of man as having been created not in a state of untried innocence, but in a state of moral perfection, not as a candidate for humanity, but a being in the full maturity and power of sinless perfection, not simply as a being with the undeveloped potentialities of the highest experience in the things of the mind and the spirit, but as a finished paradigm of the divine perfection, "holy, merciful, perfect, pure as God is holy, merciful, perfect, pure," [25] is at best a flight of ideas that is as unbiblical as it is unscientific. This romantic picture of a primitive perfection has its fit companion piece in Wesley's idealization, before he had seen them, of the American Indians. They were such innocent, simple, sincere people, unspoiled by civilization, just ripe and ready for the pure Gospel. The facts made short work of this romance,[26] just as pick and shovel leave no doubt how primitive man lived and what sort of being he was. It belonged exclusively to the eighteenth century imagination to rave over primitive and savage peoples, uncorrupted by civilization as if in a state of perfection. Rousseau gave to this turn of thought in the eighteenth century its classic expression.

In addition to doubtful features of this character derived not from Scripture, but borrowed from his age, Wesley has developed his doctrine of sin along truly traditional lines. He assumed the strict objectivity of the narratives in the Book of Genesis. His use of these materials is precritical. The inescapable conditions imposed upon our thinking by the results of modern science, and by the historical and higher criticism of Scripture, simply forbid us to follow Wesley in freely mingling primitive "science" with the simple gospel of salvation by faith. The Christian faith is deeply indebted, far more than we yet know, to the modern criticism of Scripture for setting Christian thought free from many misplaced confidences. It has gone a

[25] Sermon 5.
[26] Journal, I, 407.

long way toward redeeming theology from the precritical practise of trying to gather religious figs from mythical thistles.   It
has cleared out of the Christian message much useless theological speculation.   It has sent us back to a freer, deeper study
of the revolution wrought in religious thought by the prophetic
Christian movement whereby the religious consciousness of man
has been emancipated in principle from bondage to cosmology,
whether the ancient primitive sort or the modern philosophical
sort.   It is not necessary to solve the universe, explain all creation, or give a metaphysic of the existence of evil before we can
learn to put our trust in God, experience saving faith in Jesus
Christ and enjoy the blessings of salvation.   There is a very
large element in Wesley's doctrine of sin that instead of being,
as he supposed, essential to the Gospel, has as little foundation
and warrant in the higher ranges of Hebrew and Christian thinking as it has in the work of modern science.

The second part of Wesley's doctrine of sin, that part which
is derived from primitive thought, has to do with the question
as to the first origin of evil in our experience-world.   It is the
part of his doctrine which thrusts upon us the inescapable necessity of subjecting it to a critical scrutiny.   It is supremely important to bear ever in mind as the regulative idea for all reflection
on this perplexing subject, that the truth-values of the Christian
message and the unique revelational and experiential nature of
the Christian faith do not stand or fall with our ability or inability to give a theory of the presence of evil in our human
experience-world that may claim the universal assent and homage
of the Christian consciousness.   Christian teaching and preaching
at its best throughout the Christian centuries has never recognized any obligation to give an account of the first source of evil
as essential to the Christian faith beyond the one fact that its
existence must be referred to Man, and not to God.   Beyond
this conviction, it has followed the example and method of Jesus
who renounced all speculation on the first source of evil and has
disdained to follow the example of the second century Gnostics
in whose theology the question "unde malum?" or "Whence then

is evil?" occupied the conspicuous position. It is the judgment
of sound theology that all the theories as to the origin of sin could
be put out of sight without any loss to the Christian faith.

Wesley first came to grips with this perplexing subject as a
graduate student at Oxford. He read in 1729 "a sort of essay on
the Origin of Evil" by one named Ditton. Exactly a year later
he had "at last procured the celebrated treatise of Archbishop
King, *De Origine Mali*" (1702). It appears from letters which
passed between Epworth and Oxford that his father, then rector
of Epworth, had thrust this tormenting problem upon the attention of his gifted son. For Wesley began to read, he says, "in
the hope of sending you a full and satisfactory solution of your
great question." It did not take long for young Wesley to find
out, too, that as he wrote his father, *"unde malum* has been a
mighty question." [27] It clearly appears from Wesley's comment
on these and other writers that they had all developed theories of
the Origin of Evil which led inescapably to an abridgment either
of God's power or of his moral perfection or of both. "God himself could not have prevented natural evils." "All natural evils
are owing not to God's want of will, but want of power to redress
them as necessarily flowing from the nature of matter." The
drag of materiality on the mind and will of God is propounded
as the root of natural evils. "King," said Wesley, "takes his
theory to be entirely new," and then he dryly remarks: "If I do
not much mistake, the reference of the existence of evil to the
nature of matter is at least two thousand years old." The most
original element in King's theory was, as Wesley perceived, his
imagination that it was new. It will be convenient, and quite
sufficient for our purposes, to compare Wesley's entirely accurate
historical judgment with an observation by a contemporary of
his, David Hume, the most original and conspicuous expounder
in modern philosophy of the doctrine of a finite God. Hume
showed with icy objectivity that every straight thinking and
sincerely cosmological religion must abridge either God's power
or his good will or both, and credited Epicurus (340-270 B.C.)

[27] Letters, I, 44, 64.

with a certain originality in putting the question: "Epicurus' old questions are yet unanswered. Is God willing to prevent evil, but not able? then is he impotent. Is he able but not willing? then is he malevolent. Is he both able and willing? whence then is evil?" [28]

These two individualities, Wesley and Hume, were poles apart in their published writings in respect to active religious principles; yet Wesley entirely concurred with Hume's conclusion that a religion, sunk in cosmology and thereby driven, if the logic is good, into the doctrine of a finite God, is for practical religious purposes simply good for nothing. The great critic and the great Christian reached this conclusion by entirely different routes, the former by a remorselessly objective analysis of the premises and logic of natural religion, the latter by a profound historical understanding and a warm sympathetic and experential interpretation of the Christian faith plus his own transcendent genius for godliness. Hume wrote his *Dialogues on Natural Religion* and Wesley wrote his *Sermon and Treatise on Original Sin* at the height of their powers. Natural theology to which the doctrine of a finite God belongs is not historical and experimental Christianty from which that doctrine receives no sanction. To heighten the interest and significance of the comparison, it may be useful to recall that exactly at the time David Hume at Ninewells, near Berwick, March 10, 1751,[29] was bolting natural religion to the bran and subjecting natural theology to the criterion of natural science, John Wesley formed his resolution April 10, 1751,[30] "If God should give me a few years' life, publicly to answer Taylor's new gospel," wherein Christian faith is set back to the poverty-stricken levels of naturalistic humanism. Taylor's standpoint was frankly Pelagian, whose doctrine, if Harnack's historical judgment may be trusted, terminates in irreligion. It is at bottom naturalistic humanism which, if it does not make void, certainly makes little of the grace of God. Pelagius fifteen centuries ago reasoned that

[28] Hume, *Dialogues concerning Natural Religion,* p. 440.
[29] Burton's *Hume,* I, 331.
[30] Journal, III, 520.

at worst man needs no more than instruction. He is quite able to achieve righteousness. Now all this fits exactly into the picture of a serenely self-satisfied Christianity. Well does Wesley say of such a natural religion, of a religion confined to considerations of natural reason, without any root or resource in historical Christianity, untouched by the unique revelational and experiential nature of the Christian faith, that it simply is "no religion at all." [31]

Wesley's spiritual insight told him that any theory as to the origin of evil which terminates in the doctrine of a finite God is irreconciliable with the Christian faith, and he reacted accordingly. Two of his utterances, one as a theological student at Oxford, the other at the summit of his maturity, must do duty for all. His discipline in historical theology enabled him at the outset to identify this inference from the existence of evil to a limit on God's power, as a recrudescence of the Manichaean error. The Manichaeans assumed two first principles in the universe, the one good, the other evil, to rationalize the strange mixture of good and evil in our experience-world. Wesley called it "a monstrous scheme." He could never brook any idea about the evil in the world which either impugned the supremacy of God or impeached his essential righteousness. He reacted against it as an impiety. Writing in the forty-fourth year of his conversion-experience, he deplored any thought of God which carried any of these implications in it. "God is not to blame, says a bold man who personates and passes for a Christian, for either natural or moral evils that are in the world; seeing evil must exist in the very nature of things." But "Let every sensible infidel be ashamed of such miserable *excuses* for his Creator. He needs none to make *apologies* either for him or for his creation." [32] Numerous, weighty and sound are the considerations to sustain us in following Wesley's example in rejecting any inference from the problem of evil that could cloud or corrupt the prophetic-Christian thought of God. In that conception three elements

[31] Sermon 44.
[32] Sermon 56.

stand out clearly: absolute supremacy, distinct personality and intensity of ethical life. In the doctrine of God unfolded in the higher, not in the lower ranges of Hebrew and Christian thinking, God's power is subject only to his righteousness. That is the only limit on God's power, if limit it be, which the Christian consciousness ever has recognized or sanctioned. It may be serviceable for guidance and insight to conclude this brief comment on the bearing of the doctrine of sin on the thought of God with a reference to the judicious Sheldon's *Essentials of Christianity*. He says: "With substantial unanimity through the Christian ages, and in emphatic terms the absolute supremacy of God has been affirmed. But strangely enough in our time a few writers have shown a fondness for the conception of a limited God. . . . It is quite certain that in the long run religion must be damaged rather than helped by such a way of thinking." [33]

But if we are thus well advised not to wander amid considerations of natural reason, seeking in vain there for a solution of the problem of evil, how fares it with Wesley's free use of materials derived from the Story of Creation and the Fall of Man for the same purpose—to answer the question *unde malum?* If to sink Christianity in cosmology takes the heart out of the Christian faith and cancels revelation, when it is done by modern philosophy, how can the Christian faith be thrust back into bondage to primitive cosmology without even a worse injury? The Christian Church never has surrendered to any philosophy of any name or nature, ancient or modern, its confidence that it possesses in the person and work of Christ and in his ability to regulate in exhaustive fashion all our human trust in God, the incomparable guide to right thinking about God and the gateway to real communion with him. That confidence has weathered a thousand storms. The fears about the future of the Christian faith and so of the Christian Church are mostly specters of the mind. There is not today the whole world round a real rival to our Christian faith.

It is unnecessary, even if space permitted, to traverse all the

[33] Sheldon, Henry C., *Essentials of Christianity*, 1922, p. 136 f.

weighty considerations that sustain this position. It is enough to know that it is securely grounded in the higher range of Hebrew and Christian thinking, that it adopts the same premises and pursues the same method, and above all, that it represents, with fidelity and fulness, the prophetic Christian teaching respecting God. First of all, we know that the entire priestly element of the Old Testament, whether we consider its precepts or practises, found little if any recognition or approval in the teaching of Jesus. We know further that Jesus subjected the entire legalistic element of the Old Testament to a searching criticism, completing the higher criticism of the law begun by the prophets, reaffirming in the law whatever is consistent with the higher righteousness and principle of love, rejecting all else. He rejected radically the materialism, narrow race-nationalism, and the appeal to force which were at least ingredients, if not prevalent elements in the current ideas about the Kingdom of God. But with the higher range of Hebrew thinking as represented by the prophets, Jesus was conscious of being in full accord, supported it with the full weight of his influence, and took up into his own teaching all of its truth-values. If Jesus was conscious that he had set aside much in the Old Testament, the system of rites and ceremonies, the vindictive spirit in its ethic and piety (*lex talionis, imprecatory Psalms*), he was much more conscious of the wider, deeper agreement and so defined the total significance of his work as that of fulfillment. Whatever therefore is clearly rooted and grounded in the higher range of Hebrew and Christian thinking, in the teaching of the Prophets and of Jesus, possesses for us the highest religious significance.

Now it is a fact of major importance for all our thinking on the doctrine of sin that nowhere in the higher range of Hebrew and Christian thinking, represented by the prophets and Jesus, is there a single clear reference to the Fall of Man and his expulsion from paradise. There are but two apparent exceptions, Hosea VI, 7; Job XXXI, 33; and these are not. For the reference to Adam in both cases is quite obscure, if not improbable, and their solitariness in the Old Testament completes the uncertainty. With respect to the Creation Story and Fall of Man, the prophets are silent. The New Testament preserves a nearly equal silence. There are a few references, mostly for illustrative purposes. If St. Paul's reference in Romans V, 12-19, is more than illustration, it came like his inference from Gen. XXII, 18 (cf. Gal. III, 16), out of his courses in Rabbinic theology and Rabbinic exegesis before he accepted Christ. But if St. Paul was nearly free, Jesus was utterly free, from Rabbinic exegesis. For in the written record of Christ's teaching the name of Adam is not so much as mentioned nor is there a single distinct reference to any item associated with paradise or with the fall of the first parents. In contrast to the desolate theorizing religion of the scribes, Jesus spoke out of the authority of his own experience and insight. Jesus then unfolded his matchless thoughts about the Kingdom of God and its coming, God the Father and the infinite value of the human soul, about the higher righteousness and precept of love, about poverty of spirit, personal humility and total trust in the grace of God quite independent of current thinking and of traditional thinking on these subjects. Above all the teaching of Jesus is entirely clear of entangling alliances with cosmology. His teaching is not encumbered with any theory as to the Origin of Evil. In one instance only, the Gospel of John credits Jesus, not with a theory, but with a summary refusal to entertain a question on the origin of sin. On this refusal Wesley observes that "it was not the method of Jesus to answer useless questions or gratify idle curiosity."[34] Enough! We know in the light of these facts that the nature and condition of man as the subject of God's Kingdom, as the subject of redemption, can be clearly described and the doctrine of sin can be fully, cogently stated without reference to the Book of Genesis, without recourse to cosmology, without entanglement with transient philosophies. For it has been done in the most authoritative manner possible for us in the religious teachings of the Prophets and above all in that of Christ. In so far as John Wesley's doctrine of Christian

[34] *Wesleyan New Testament*, 240.

experience has reproduced the prophetic-Christian teaching concerning God and concerning man as the subject of redemption—and he has done so thoroughly—it affords us the securest possible foundation and guide for preaching and teaching in the twentieth century.

CHAPTER XII

THE BURNING FOCUS OF FAITH

There is among the voluminous writings of John Wesley no special sermon nor any treatise on the subject of the atonement. There are references aplenty to the subject; but there is no formal treatise or sermon such as he wrote and preached on the doctrines of original sin, justification by faith and Christian perfection. The thought of atonement was for him too comprehensive of the whole meaning of the Gospel to lend itself to a special treatise. Being for Wesley the whole of Christianity, he has not expounded it as if but a part. His preaching and teaching was all of it radically, thoroughly evangelical and the atonement is felt to be in his message the very pulse of the Gospel. "*The gospel,* that is, good news for guilty, helpless sinners, means comprehensively, the whole revelation made to men by Jesus Christ and the whole account of what he did and suffered." "The sum and substance of the whole scripture is in two little words: faith and salvation." "The substance of all is Jesus Christ come into the world to save sinners." [1] Thus all of Wesley's preaching and teaching revolved in a steady orbit around his own inexhaustible intuition of the free redeeming grace of God in Christ working in and through the actual believing community of the great redemption, while his Christian ethic, a thoroughgoing ethic of grace, took shape in his indefatigable and pioneer efforts to extend and realize the Kingdom of God among men.

It is not difficult to trace this supreme focalization of the Christian faith at every turn in Wesley's message and ministry. It shines out everywhere. Perhaps the best commentary on the thesis: "The sum and substance of the whole scripture is in two

[1] Sermons 7, 44.

little words: faith and salvation," is furnished by Wesley's two letters written to the mystic William Law in the month of May 1738 just before he crossed his religious Rubicon. If a fraction of the attention bestowed on the etiquette of these two letters for their supposed petulancy and blindly charging into Law for his failure to teach Salvation by Faith had been given to the real issue and its relation to Wesley's mature doctrine of Christian experience, they could be very informative. The facts fully confirm, as Wesley duly and more than once frankly acknowledged, that he felt himself to be deeply and personally indebted to William Law. But the influence of Law was demonstrably not comprehensive of the whole field of Christian thought but had its hot-point in the transcendent importance of inward holiness or Christian perfection as Christlikeness, for the exposition of Christian faith and morals. But one of the flimsiest pieces of reasoning to be found in the secondary sources about Wesley is the argument which identifies the origin of the Revival with Wesley's personal indebtedness to William Law and at the same time acknowledges that the evangelical principles of John Wesley were not the religious principles of William Law, but that Law was quite at variance with the evangelical teaching of Wesley. It would follow that the content of Wesley's preaching after 1738 had nothing to do with the power thereof and so nothing to do with the origin of the Revival. Let him believe it that can!

The most important fact to be learned from these terribly earnest Wesley letters is that in breaking with Law's mysticism in 1736 and in going back to the faith of the first Reformers in 1738, Wesley realized that he was no longer building either exclusively or primarily on Law's foundations. He knew that the growing insight into the nature of saving faith which attended and defined his progress out of a humanistic into a theocentric doctrine of Christian experience had come to him from the early Reformers by the help of the Moravians, and since he now attached an importance to it transcending all other doctrinal considerations, he turned on Law in bitter disappointment that the teacher once taken as an oracle had left him to wander thirteen years in the humanistic wilderness. Had he not met with others to point him to the wicket gate of saving faith in Christ he would still be wallowing in the Slough of Despond. He drew the conclusion that he had not met Mr. Evangelist in Law's mystical doctrines, precisely because Law had never experientially explored and understood the richest element of Christian experience, namely, that "this faith indeed as well as the salvation it brings is the free gift of God." The crucial point here is not in the thesis that salvation is the gift of God, but rather that saving faith in its totality is the gift of God.

Wesley began in the Spring of 1738 consciously to plant his feet in the footprints of Luther when he began to understand that the *donatio fidei* is the radical meaning of *justificatio* and that likewise regeneration, renovation, sanctification are religious concepts before they are ethical concepts. And in this equation of the *donatio fidei* with *justificatio,* as well as with all the other stages and steps of Christian experience, Wesley began to read the true objectivity alike of the atonement and of all Christian experience. Practical Christianity was henceforth understood as just these experiencible and only through experience attainable roots in religious faith, that is, a God-given faith. But Wesley found in William Law no such equivalent, nothing approximating this definitely, dynamically religious understanding of Christianity. Not from Law then but from other sources did Wesley discover and recover the practical self-estimate of believers according to the standard of grace that underlay the Reformation activity of all the early Reformers.

It is a well-known fact that the early Reformation teaching was more than ever before in the Church very much in earnest about the objectivity of the Atonement. And this fact is capable of a positive and constructive appreciation without subscribing to all their explications of this idea. But, be that as it may, this energetic emphasis of early Reformation teaching on the Atonement reemerges in Wesley's general remark on Law's mystical Christianity. Law's defense against Wesley's criticism was that he had sent Wesley to the best sources of insight into the

Gospel, namely, the *Theologia Germanica* and the other standard mystical writings. Wesley replied: "I searched them diligently and found therein something of Christ our Pattern (the doctrine of Christian Perfection), but nothing express of Christ our Atonement (the idea of the sovereign saving significance of a God-given faith in Christ)." And Wesley's distinction from Law lay henceforth not in a choice between the idea of Christian Perfection and the idea of saving faith, as if two disjunctive and disparate teachings, but in a magnificent synthesis of both points of view. But after 1738, not before, the Cross of Christ became the *burning focus* of John Wesley's entire message and the center of the Gospel alike for an age of doubt and for a world of sin.

In this sense and on these premises it is to be affirmed that the doctrine of the atonement in all its rich and varied, in something of its infinite meaning, is set forth vividly, definitely in the Wesleyan songs and sermons. It is fundamental, implicit, regnant in all of them. It is the life principle of the Wesleyan doctrine of Christian experience. Wesley's well-known major theme was salvation by faith. "By grace are ye saved through faith and this not of yourselves: It is God's gift." Now while Wesley firmly taught that man is not wholly passive in the business of salvation, still it can not be said too often that he expurgated from the thought of salvation without variation or shadow of turning every trace of humanism, every reference to the human subject as a primary source of saving faith. Grace is both the beginning and the end. "Not of yourselves" covered for him every meaning of the assertion "ye are saved through faith!" "We are his workmanship" proves both that salvation is by faith and that faith is the gift of God. Any reference to human agency is out of place. This teaching "lays the axe to the very root of spiritual pride and all glorying in ourselves." [2] Wesley regarded any qualification or limitation of the idea of divine grace by a reference to the human subject as so much poison to the Christian consciousness. It is the Wesleyan doc-

[2] *Wesleyan New Testament*, 492 f.

trine that man is by nature absolutely void of all spiritual life [3] and that "an operation of the Spirit of God by a power equivalent to that which raises the dead is indispensably necessary to the lowest degree of Christian faith." [4]

The crises of the Christian faith are all marked historically by a deeper apprehension of the thought of God and the recovery of the Pauline emphasis upon the all-sufficient grace of God in Christ. Wesley exactly as he understood St. Paul has confronted man, sunk in the bondage of sin, with the fact of a living and saving God whose dynamic and redeeming presence is the fountain of all good in man, including the experience of saving faith. While therefore Wesley has given a full, clear exposition of the atonement as the actual experience of reconciliation with God, of saving faith and all its moral energies, nevertheless, as we are bound to expect from the way and manner in which over against the atheistic drift of eighteenth-century humanism he has pushed the thought of God into the foreground of his message, he was concerned first and foremost to expound the atonement as altogether God's work before he expounded it as altogether man's benefit. And thus his exalted religious appreciation of Christ as revealer and redeemer has transfigured his radical doctrine of the human need of revelation and redemption. He too saw the nature of Christianity and the necessity of the atonement arise out of the structure of man's personal life, his creaturely dependence on the creator, his possession of the image of God and his position as crown of creation, a fact never entirely effaced, a position never all lost under even the worst ravages of sin and never incapable of restoration by the almighty grace of God. He confessed in the maturity of his experience that it was very hard for him, in the light of his understanding of the Gospel, ever to despair of any man. He uses dialectic and resorts to paradox in order to give expression to his confidence in the boundless efficacy and utmost significance of the atonement. He reasons earnestly that humanity is not the loser but infinitely the gainer by the

[3] *Ibid.*, 491.
[4] Letters, II, 71.

catastrophe of the Fall. He has censored the outcry against "our first parents" as inept. He has satirized in the Sermon on "God's Love to Fallen Man" those who refer sin and pain in the world to the nature of matter which God is not able to alter: "It is very kind of this sweet-tongued orator to make an excuse for God." He needs no defense. Turning from this miserable apologetic, Wesley deduced the universal necessity of revelation and redemption from the risk and ruin latent in the vast experiment of man's personal life, proceeding not from any inscrutable necessity in God, but from His immaculate goodness, perfect justice, absolute power. Unclouded foresight of every implication and consequence is the major premise for the possibility and reality of all sin, and for all the evil, natural and moral, in the world. The great experiment, the whole venture of man's personal life is God's will with full foresight of all its implications and all its consequences.

Why, asks Wesley, do so many stumble and fall in their thinking about these facts, these dark facts, in our experience world? "Thousands even of those that are called Christians have questioned the mercy, if not the justice of God; others again have referred sin, evil and suffering back to the nature of matter which God is not able to alter." What makes them do it? What is lacking in all such thinking which perpetually stumbles and falls into a misconception of God's mercy or justice or power in the presence of the tormenting problem of evil? Why do men question God in the presence of the facts which suggest in man "the image of the devil" and "the image of the brute" rather than "the image of God"? The root cause of all these misconceptions, Wesley tells us, is the failure to perceive the true, full significance of the Christian revelation and atonement, the failure to consider that "not as the offence so also is the free gift," the failure to discern the infinitely greater advantages for time and eternity that spring from God's revealing and redeeming activities. Stripped of all references to the Fall of Man, it is simply our lack of faith in a living and saving God, the knowledge of whom can be won only from the Gospel, that lets the picture of the evil, the sinful, the suffering in this world get us down and lead us astray.

We must then have ever in mind Wesley's appraisal of the Christian revelation and atonement, while we consider his very dark view of man as the subject of redemption. All criticism, even the most friendly, agrees that the Wesleyan picture of human nature in terms of original sin and total depravity is extremely dark. The most sympathetic and appreciative interpreter will have to understand and appraise it in the light of its purely religious purpose. Its one sole purpose is to make away with a godless humanistic religion and to destroy root and branch the proud pretension of human reason to be the self-sufficient architect of all righteousness, all moral goodness in man. Its master aim is to magnify the grace of God and to bring every man, a sinner in need of a saviour, in utter humility to the foot of the cross of Christ. Viewed objectively without reference to its origin in and dependence upon the Christian consciousness, the Wesleyan representation of human nature would certainly be one-sided.

Wesley was well aware of this and said so. He well knew the other half of the better story of Man's personal life. It is covered in his doctrine of "prevenient grace," of which he had a firm grasp in all the stages of his ministry. It is given in his profound insight into the divine, the diviner and the divinest immanence. Briefly he taught that no human being ever escapes the beneficent presence of the living God. Not only are all the human springs of moral goodness in God, but human life at its worst is never without a positive principle of goodness in it. And then at its best, religion is "the life of God in the soul of man." So then his black picture of humanity need not be misleading, unless, as usually happens, it is dissevered from his all-embracing doctrine of the divine immanence, and divorced from its distinctly religious motivation and meaning. Then of course it becomes at once absurd and repulsive. But this understanding of Wesley is without excuse. Viewing as he did all nature as a system of forces utterly plastic and freely administered to moral ends, he lived and moved and had his being consciously in the presence of God. Every sunrise, every sunset and all between are acts of God to further the ends of his kingdom. His view of nature was decidedly pantheistic. "God is in all things." "To look on anything as separate from God is indeed a kind of practical atheism." "God pervades and actuates the whole created frame and is, in a true sense, the soul of the universe." "He is the only agent in the material world and he is the spring of action in every creature visible and invisible." The bursting bud of spring-time, the fluttering leaf of the Fall are with all other events in the natural world the direct acts of God. "General providence is stark staring nonsense." His providence is always and only particular and special and spans the universe from the atoms to the stars. "God is the soul of the universe"; this thesis comes not out of the deistic climate of opinion against which Wesley set himself to change it. It is more nearly the "acosmic pantheism" that emerges in any man's mind who takes the Christian faith seriously. The light of God's presence does not break into our lives through the narrow windows of miracle, but our human experience world is all of it wide open to his creative, sustaining will. "A continual sense of total dependence on God" is basic to the Christian consciousness.

Wesley was further very well aware that the doctrine of the divine immanence set a boundary to the doctrine of "original sin" and "total depravity" and that the latter, when divorced from its major premise, is misleading and true. The Conference Minute, 1745, on this subject denies the inference very often made from this doctrine of sin that "the works of him who feareth God and from that principle does the best he can," that is, the works of one who has had no experience of saving faith in the Christian meaning, are only "sin and as such an abomination unto the Lord." The truth is that the idea of the "natural man" is at best but an approximation to the facts. Wesley himself thought so. For "there is no man that is in a state of mere nature. No man is wholly void of the grace of God. No man living is entirely destitute of what is vulgarly called natural conscience." Only

Wesley insisted that this active principle of moral goodness in man is "not natural," but is "preventing grace." For he held there is nothing good in the universe outside the grace of God. The world view of Wesley was rooted and grounded in religion and in the thought of God.

It was not in fascinating vistas of speculative thought but amid the grim realities of experience and life and in the total bankruptcy of a semi-humanistic version of Christianity that Wesley sought the nature of Christianity and found decisive incentives to accept Luther's doctrine and description of saving faith. On these premises and in a climate of opinion where under the violent attacks of criticism the old apologetic was tottering to its fall, Wesley was driven to build on the rocks of a deeper confidence and to construct his own theocentric doctrine of Christian experience. He divided saving faith, which is as wide and deep of meaning as man's total response to the knowledge of a living and a saving God, revealed in the Gospel, into two organic parts: The finished and the unfinished work of Christ. The finished work of Christ refers to all that God in Christ [5] is believed to have actually, genuinely, thoroughly done for the salvation and blessing of sinful men. The unfinished work of Christ refers to all that God continues to do in the collective experience of the Christian Church and in the individual experience of its believing members. It is one and the same historical revelation of God's purpose of grace in the person and work of Christ and in the work and witness of the Holy Spirit. God was in Christ reconciling the world to himself and has appointed the believing community, "called to be saints," to be the bearer to all mankind of this "reconciling ministry." A living and saving God speaks to us in the person and work of Christ, also in the living witness of the Christian Church, last but not least in the realities of our own Christian experience. This in outline is Wesley's Atonement theology—all of it God's work, all of it man's benefit.

One school of atonement thought has amid all variations tended strongly to limit the atonement to the first point, namely, the

[5] II Cor. V, 19.

finished work of Christ and that too construed quite objectively. The satisfaction of Christ and the effect of his death have been referred in the main, sometimes exclusively, to God. This has been the prevailing interest of much traditional atonement thought. Another school of atonement thought which has had its most energetic development in modern times within the liberal reconstruction of Christianity, in order to transmute a religion of revelation into a religion of culture, limits atonement to its effect on man or the actual work of saving sinful men. This view of atonement is affiliated in principle with the traditional doctrine of the work and witness of the Holy Spirit, although it must be admitted that in most versions of the moral view of atonement the salt of this doctrine has lost its savor. The modernistic conceptions of atonement are remote from the theocentric views of early and historic Christianity. Wesley's wider, richer thought is unmistakably synthetic. For he refused to divorce what the common faith and general conscience of the first Christians and the great body of Christians in all ages have joined and held together: God's work for us in Christ and in us by the Holy Spirit. But the historical distinction between the work which Christ began and its continuation in the Church ought never to be confounded with the question as to the objective meaning of the atonement. Wesley saw an objective element no less in God's hand in the actual experience of saving faith than in the person and work of Christ. As for all the great Prophets, notably Jeremiah, there was an objective reference in their experience of God, so we find this God-consciousness in Jesus in transcendent measures. Likewise St. Paul's faith came down to the fact that *"it pleased God to reveal his Son in me;"* so for Wesley there is an objective reference in all Christian experience. His doctrine of faith rests on the unity of a thoroughly theocentric view of the whole prophetic Christian movement in history and a radically theocentric doctrine of Christian experience. God is no less dynamically present, sovereignly active in all Christian experience and in the actual work of saving sinful men than he was in the person and work of the historical redeemer. In very truth Christian experience is the seal and confirmation that God was in Christ reconciling the world unto himself. Therefore in our own Christian experience we are confronted with the fact of God. The revealing and redeeming activity of God is for Wesley always, everywhere primary and fundamental. Moreover, the mode of God's activity as creator is for Wesley utterly transcended in the mode of His activity as redeemer, so that the inner unity and relation of God's several immanent activities are hidden from human insight. The frequency and dignity with which Wesley gave expression to his devout agnosticism in such matters is worthy of thoughtful attention and all acceptance. He believed the goodness of God to be no less clearly manifest in what is withheld from us than in what is revealed to us.

In this vast sense Wesley was a radical and thorough-going atonement preacher. He did not sink the truth about God in the thought of man and his natural development. He did not cancel God out of the interpretation of the Gospel. He did not leave God in the dim shadowy background of his message. He put God back into the sermon, into human thinking, into Christian experience, into human affairs, into history, into the whole realm of nature. God is center and circumference of his doctrine of Christian faith. Here the thought of redemption as the pure act of divine grace dominates all. The features of this well-known type of Christian teaching—for there is no merit of originality in the main points of Wesley's message, he would instantly have spurned the suggestion—are: A pronounced consciousness of sin in the searchlight of God's holiness; all trust in one's own strength and all recourse to one's own effort is given up and foresworn; an absolute trust is built sole and single on the grace of God, the personal God, who is revealed and understood in the humility of Christ as the Compassionate One. Salvation is, all of it, God's work. Even saving faith, often assigned to man's effort, since it has its birth and life-principle in the means of Grace, is also for the Christian consciousness the gift of God and to the last drop the work of the Holy Spirit.

This general thought of redemption as a divine work of con-

descending grace for the salvation and blessing of men, does not
have any boundary in our system of experience but encircles the
cosmic activities of the creator no less than the redeeming activities of the Heavenly Father.   The rich records of Christian
thought, of songs and sermon, of prayer and piety in all ages furnish plentiful evidence that this way of *receiving* the Gospel—
"God be merciful to me a sinner"—of *experiencing* it—"the spirit
bears witness within the Christian consciousness"—and *living* it—
"I can do all things through Christ who gives me strength"—has
always been the imperial mood of historic Christianity.   This is
the light of the Christian faith, hope and love that never was on
sea and land, but under the impact of the Gospel upon us shines
out like a beacon light alone upon the summits of our inner life.
This is the knowledge of God, sought everywhere else in vain,
revealed only in the Gospel.   It has flamed up again and again
in the master-minds of the Christian centuries.   Moreover, this
light can be seen, this voice can be heard, only in so far as the
Gospel has enabled us to perceive and recognize the voice of the
universe in our own experience.   "Faith is the voice of God in the
heart proclaiming itself."   All our Christian experience, in particular the experience of saving faith, is, according to Wesley,
the work and witness of a living and saving God.   It is simply
comprehensively "the life of God in the soul of man."

Thinkers of the abstract tendency who are zealots in reducing
experience to notions and trust the pure logic of ideas as the
one source and test of all truth will be quick to light upon a
"contradiction in terms" between Wesley's Calvinistic doctrine
of grace, which affirms man's total dependence on God, and his
Arminian doctrine of human freedom which makes man a subject
of action and moral obligation.   For total dependence can only
mean an exclusive divine causality which in turn cancels human
activity and thus swallows up all human responsibility.   So it
seems, but it is not so; in religion and elsewhere, experience and
reality come to the same thing.   Now if notions were the sole
stuff of experience, a contradiction of notions would be one in
reality.   Such is not the case.   Life, experience is infinitely larger,

richer than logic. The logical intellect is always divorcing what is married in experience. The analytic mind is forever putting asunder what in experience is joined together. Dependence and freedom may be a notional contradiction but not an experiential contradiction. It is never safe to infer a contradiction in experience from a contradiction in terms. The logical intellect is forever barking dialectic contradictions at the subject of faith and Christian experience. But criticism holds the logical intellect in leash and sends it back to its kennel. We have actual experience of both dependence and freedom, of things done to us and things done by us. We live and move and have our being in an immense system of power and we discover in and through experience a little pinch of reality in ourselves. Since for a knowledge of reality experience is the supreme court, there can be no appeal from its decisions to the inferior court of notionalism. For all we know, our total dependence on God may well be the birthplace of personal freedom, as history and experience abundantly indicate and not at all its graveyard as notionalism presumes. This paradox which so stumps the rationalist, namely, that the pure logic of ideas can not tell us all about reality, does indeed tell us very little; but that all our knowledge of reality comes down to some important intuition—experience and its indications—of which no further (logical) account can be given, is abundantly verified by the historical-experiential solution in contrast to the abstract solution of the religious problem of dependence and freedom. The consciousness and continual sense of total dependence on God may logically annihilate human energy and initiative. But history and experience prove incontrovertibly that the feeling of dependence on God has been the rich native soil, producing a plentiful harvest, of stalwart individualism in religion whence it has overflowed into all other departments of human interest and activity. In a very profound sense, man's religious reliance on God at its heights has been revealed and demonstrated by experience to be the *ne plus ultra* of self-reliance. Here alone in the highest consciousness of God does the spirit of inner freedom and power in man stand tiptoe on the mountain top of fulness and resourcefulness. The ultimate thoughts about man's personal life and his relation to God according to the teaching of the Christian faith are found in such Biblical Dicta: "All my springs are in God"; "When I have Thee, Lord, what is there else beside?" "With God all things are possible"; "I can do all things through Christ which strengthens me." "Work out your own salvation with fear and trembling, for it is God that worketh in you according to His good pleasure, both to will, and to do." [6]   Thus the atonement as the discovery of God's actual presence and experience of His power is the burning focus of our religion.   And the entire practical religious significance of the atonement stands or falls with its secure or insecure foundation in the thought of God.

[6] *Wesleyan New Testament,* p. 509.

CHAPTER XIII

RELIGION WITHIN THE LIMITS OF REASON ALONE

The focalization of the Gospel and of all Christian thought in the subject of the atonement, always characteristic of Western or Latin Christianity, still more so of the early Reformation doctrine of faith, appears to be even more characteristic of the Wesleyan doctrine of faith. The doctrine of sin and salvation holds the conspicuous position in Wesley's understanding of Christianity exactly as it did in that of St. Paul and Augustine, in that of Luther and Calvin. Now the Church form of Christianity has its first source, its life principle and its abiding strength in the fact of Christ and in the idea of the *free redeeming grace of God in Christ operating through the actual historical church*. The conception of "the actual historical Church" as the necessary organ of all the revealing and redeeming activities of God that enter into the Christian system of redemption was modified by the early Reformation by substituting "the actual believing community" for the visible Church, with no intention however of striking the idea of the Church out of the doctrine of salvation, but for the sole purpose of purifying the thought of the Church and of making it a more perfect organ of the divine ministry of reconciliation which was begun in the person and work of Christ and then committed to the Church. For Wesley, whose appreciation of historic Christianity was unclouded by the bitter conflicts which embarrassed the early Reformation doctrine of Christian experience, at any rate it was much less so, also considered the believing community and that, too, in a deeper, richer, fuller sense to be the organ of redemption and the parent of all Christian experience. The Reformation idea of the church is inextricably interwoven with and it is one and inseparable from Wesley's doctrine of Christian experience of which the atonement as God's purpose of grace and its fulfilment in Christ and the Church as a believing community is the life principle. We can not therefore even begin, much less complete the exposition of his atonement theology until its relation to his religious evaluation of the Church and means of grace is clearly apprehended. For his atonement theology is a positive development of an idea that is the great essential of the church form of Christianity. We can accept or reject his view in whole or in part, but we can not in a faithful exposition divorce his idea of atonement from his attitude toward historic Christianity, in particular toward the church and its redemptive function as a believing community. This is the key to his superlative simplification of admission into the Christian fellowship as in the New Testament by the one door of faith, saving faith, in the Lord Jesus Christ and his sovereign rule again following the New Testament that the one entering by that door shall simply lead a life suitable to his profession of faith in Christ and "walk worthy of the Gospel."

The atonement idea must then be investigated first and foremost as the life-principle of the Church form of Christianity. But this idea has undergone profoundly important developments in the experience of the Christian Church. For our exposition purposes we need to recall that it was Anselm (1033-1109), a devout rationalist, who for the first time in his well-known monograph, *cur deus homo,* made the attempt to hang every truth in the teaching of Scripture and in that of the Church, on the reasoned necessity of an atonement. By no means the least part of this audacious venture of thought by Bishop Anselm was the attempt, apparently in the utmost simplicity of faith in its practicability, to drive home the truth of his atonement theology, in Anselm's words "by the mere force of reason," "as if nothing were known of Christ," that is without any appeal to or argument from the facts of Christian experience. The foundation on which he argued the truth of the atonement is the assumption—he must be taken seriously though it is not easy—that the reasoned necessity of the atonement can be made so clear and cogent that any intellect, though untouched by historic Christianity and without any consciousness of sin and the need of a redeemer, must be fully convinced of its truth and persuaded to accept Christianity. He assumed *a priori* that while *fides praecedit intellectum,* still revelation and reason are in perfect accord and are co-extensive. They are perfectly matched and mated so that while reason must always follow, it can never come short of revelation. But when he tried to convert this idea into experience, he was besieged by disquieting doubt. He even forgot his meals, lay awake nights, lost sleep and was pursued even during the most solemn moments of worship by the haunting whisper of the unappeased intellect that after all many, indeed the most precious, intuitions of the Christian faith utterly transcend the resources of rational demonstration. The incontrovertible argument so ardently sought seemed to flee from him like a mirage in the desert and he was driven to refer the active intellect within him to the suggestions of Satan and sought deliverance from it. But in vain. At last he succeeded in throwing into propositional and logical forms the faith which he already had. Success in doing so—it came one night with the impetus of a great discovery —brought with it the peaceful assurance that the profoundest intuitions of Christian experience which could be acquired under the total impact of historical Christianity, under the power of the Gospel and under the personal use of the means of grace, had received an objective confirmation by this performance of the logical intellect upon them.

The objective confirmation of the Christian faith which the mediaeval mind, working in a lonely cell, and so more or less in a moral and social vacuum, sought in such formal rationalizations is much more likely to be sought by the modern Christian mind in the great and inexhaustible laboratory of personal experience and of applied Christianity. But Anselm represents the dawn of intellectualism in religion seven centuries before criticism exposed "the weakness of the speculative reason when it comes under experience and its indications." Anselm's attempt to focalize all the truth of the Christian system in the doctrine of the atonement was natural enough to any disciple of Western Christianity which has always given first place in the Gospel to the doctrine of sin and grace. There is in this respect not much merit of originality in Anselm's treatise. But this innocent unbounded confidence in the natural resources of the human intellect to discover the necessity and to demonstrate the truth of the atonement is not indigenous to any branch of Christianity. The whole movement of thought in Anselm's classic monograph on the atonement is confined to considerations of natural reason. He insists that *fides praecedit intellectum,* but he also assumes with a serenity of assurance utterly mystifying to the sons of criticism, that the mind of man is able to see every intuition of faith shot through with the white light of intellect and to go to the bottom of the mystery of "God in Christ."

Although Wesley made a free and affirmative use of Anselmic thoughts in his doctrine of atonement, yet he has categorically rejected the one element of originality in Anselm's atonement theology: namely, the sufficiency of an atonement whose meaning is hemmed and hedged within the limits of reason alone. Writing in the twenty-sixth year of his conversion-experience, and at the close of the decade during which he was impelled to formulate his own views and to fortify and safeguard his societies and preachers against the extremely one-sided subjectivity of Law's mysticism and the equally one-sided objectivity of Hervey's extreme Calvinism, Wesley, in keeping with his own anti-intellectualistic, *experiential theology,* made this candid confession to his brother Charles: "I am like Simonides. The more I think, the less able I am to answer the king's question; to prove the necessity, expediency, or propriety of an atonement to an unconvinced sinner." And a month later he added in a letter to his brother, "I do not yet find anything on the atonement fit for (i.e., to convince) a Deist." He thus has confessed himself unable to meet the challenge to rationalize the doctrine. He has made the supremely important discovery that the doctrine of the atonement does not make the Christian consciousness but presupposes it and appeals to it. What Anselm, voicing an emergent rationalism, proposed to do—try the doctrine of atonement by the non-Christian mind and make the reasoned necessity of the atonement the parent of faith—Wesley, son of criticism, conscious of the misplaced confidences of Christian apologetic and pioneer of experiential thinking in religion, frankly pronounced futile and inept.

Wesley weighed long and carefully the religious significance of the intellect. The findings are set forth in his sermon on "The Case of Reason Impartially Considered." He undertakes to guide Christian faith between the opposite perils of Gnosticism and of Agnosticism, i.e., between too much and too little intellect in religion. Nevertheless he shared unmistakably the anti-intellectualistic groundtone of modern religious thought in contrast to the mischievous overestimation of reason in religion which was the legacy of Greek thought to early Christian theology and reigned supreme for fifteen centuries until the rise of criticism set the mind free "to perceive both in the Real and the Ideal what makes both more than all reason." Over against the dogma of the exclusive originality of reason in religion Wesley rated the originality of reason low. "Reason can not produce faith." Since "hope can only spring from Christian faith" and since "love can flow from faith alone," it is clear, if the premise be granted, that reason can not produce either Faith, Hope or Love in terms of Christian experience. "Reason then however cultivated and improved can not produce that faith," which is the first principle of all Christian experience. "It may present us with fair ideas; it can draw a fine picture of love; but this is only a *painted fire*. And farther than this reason can not go. I made the trial for many years. I collected the finest hymns, prayers and meditations which I could find in any language; and I said, sung or read them over and over, with all possible seriousness and attention." The experiment failed; wherefore, "Let reason do all that reason can; employ it as far as it will go. But at the same time, acknowledge it is utterly incapable, as experience confirms, of giving either faith, hope or love. . . . Seek and receive these, not as your own acquisition; but as the gift of God. He alone can give saving faith." [1]

The originality of Anselm lay then very little in his representation of the atonement as the ransom or release of man from an infinite indebtedness (the guilt of sin) on terms honorable for God and sufficient for man, but very much in the bold attempt to rationalize the idea and to coerce the non-Christian mind into the acceptance of it, by a reasoned necessity. He would have intellectualized the atonement. Whatever his merit as exponent of a dawning intellectualism in religion may be, he bequeathed, as father of scholasticism, fashioner of the rational proofs of God's being, founder of an atonement theology, pathfinder for rationalizing theologians after him, a heavy burden of rationalism to Christian teaching and preaching. The empire of this intellectualism in religion lasted all of seven centuries until the negative criticism of Hume and Kant destroyed it and the contemporaneous positive Wesleyan theology of experience began to supersede it in principle and in practise. For since the rise of criticism has exposed to Christian apologetic its misplaced confidences and has confronted the Christian messenger with the fact that there is no infallible bridle of any kind to guide the Christian faith upon its venturesome course, neither in the form of a visible church, nor of a printed Bible, nor least of all in the form of pure reason, the Christian doctrine of faith has moved— this is the pioneer and epoch-making theological importance of the Wesleyan doctrine of Christian faith—increasingly in experiential paths.

It is this theological empiricism that makes it so easy to throw a bridge across from Wesley's way of asking and answering the question, "What is Christianity?" to the work of modern science. The Wesleyan point of view and rule of faith: "try me and know my nature, let experience decide," is the counterpart and equivalent in religion to the principle and procedure of the modern

[1] Sermon 70.

scientific movement. The analogy goes still deeper. As the scientific mind has reached its maturity, it has been increasingly aware of a mysterious beyond to the work of science, and the master-minds of science have been divorced from the dogmas of materialism and have joined their work at its best together with the reverence of religion—its natural concomitant. So St. Paul, after his utmost to explore the unsearchable riches of Christ, finally rested his thought, assured that the frontier of human reasoning is not the limit of experience, in the "mystery of God, of Christ, of the gospel." Wesley too after doing his utmost to discover and realize experientially the meanings of God's revelation in Christ, has translated the Pauline formula into "the mystery of Christian experience."

The atonement in Anselm's monograph carries no reference to the work and witness of the Holy Spirit in the collective experience of the church or in the individual experience of its believing members. There are references to the Holy Spirit, but never with experiential connotations. The fact is the atonement has not been defined in terms of Christian experience. The actual work of saving men is quite sunk out of sight in the exclusive investigation of man's colossal burden of sinful debt and the method of its satisfactory liquidation as the sole objective meaning of the atonement. Anselm has defined the atonement so objectively, with such a pure and strenuous objectivity, with such an exclusive interest in how God could bring himself to allow it and provide it, that the actual results of it, the holiness of heart and life, that is the final cause of it in the mind of God, appears to be only an accessory after the fact. We can not even admit that Anselm, for all the great depth of his piety and nobility of thought, has portrayed the objective form of the atonement in such a manner as to make it the great dynamic of Christian faith and life, and pour all its incentives into the fulfilment of the high command: "Be ye holy, for I am holy." His theory appears very ineptly to place the infinite grace of God upon a bargain counter. Christian experience is neither the major premise nor the middle term in his proof and exposition of the atonement. Imputed righteousness is everything; implanted righteousness is hardly more than an afterthought of atonement theory.

Soon after the saintly Anselm, with his *fides praecedit intellectum*, undertook to reduce atonement to its objective meanings and then to rationalize it—it was about a half century later—Abélard (1079-1142), also a pioneer master-mind and the intellectual brilliant of mediaeval theology who was in every vital particular of Christian thought, save one, the antithesis of Anselm, appeared with a new type of atonement teaching. His ideas were doubtless developed largely as a reaction against Anselm's extremely objective theories. Abélard described the saving significance of the Redeemer's death so beautifully, so impressively, yet withal so exclusively in terms of its moral effects and experiential fruits as to insinuate and nourish a perpetual doubt whether after all is said and done God himself had any need of it or any necessary part in it. Abélard's view of the atonement retains the idea of revelation but concentrates the whole meaning of it in the one idea: God is love. It is true that Christian thought since the Reformation has striven more and more to comprehend, as Jesus did, all the moral attributes of God in his love. It is also an axiom of the Christian consciousness that every attribute of God must be subject to the meaning of his ethical love. But Wesley sensed a danger in this rationalization. If he taught that Christianity is all in the sentence: God is love, he also warned that all of God's holiness and essential hatred of sin is liable to be confounded and swallowed up all at once in that unwieldy idea of mercy.[2] But with this quick sense of a liability to mutilate rather than complete, impoverish rather than enrich the thought of God, Wesley himself endeavored to comprehend all of God's attributes, the cosmic and moral attributes alike, in his ethical love.

Wesley accordingly fully concurred in the central thesis of Abélard that our belief that God is love with all its boundless benefits finds its highest conceivable motivation in the life and death of the Redeemer. It may be a supreme leap of thought, but

[2] Sermon 9.

"Let all the world fall down and know
That none but God such love can show."

So Wesley, too, was never done saying the Gospel is all in the sentence, "We love him because he first loved us." And Paul has it, "If God be for us," for which fact, the gift and death of his own Son is a credential beyond which we are not able to ask or think anything further, then what need we more? When I have thee, Lord, what is there else beside? This perception of the love of God revealed in the life and death of the Redeemer with all of its quickening impulses and practical consequences was for Abélard the totality of the atonement. If the atonement had an important Godward bearing for Abélard, which it doubtless had, still it is evaded and hidden by the exclusive consideration of the experiential and moral effects in man. But if for the moment we forget what he omits or denies, then Abélard's affirmations have indisputably the idiom and savor of New Testament thought in them. And it is a painfully impressive fact that the atonement thinking of the devout Anselm moved entirely amid considerations of natural reason and even made the insight of the non-Christian mind the touchstone of truth and worth in the atonement, whereas the view of Abélard is much closer to the ideas of the New Testament and to the moral realities of Christian experience. Anselm seems to lead us away from the New Testament sphere of thought and fails utterly to ground his view in Christian experience. Abélard, on the contrary, seems to lead straight back to the New Testament and to dip deep into the moral meanings and actual experience of atonement, so that if this were all, and choice had to be made, the choice would not be difficult.

But investigation of Abélard's omissions reveals an impoverishment of the doctrine of Christian faith. Any reference of Christ's satisfaction to God, any reference to a revelation of God's wrath against all unrighteousness, any reference to a moral recoil in God's being, nature or experience against the fact of sin, as having been made perceptible in the life and death of the Redeemer is at any rate passed over, if not ruled out. Corresponding to man's profoundest experience of the moral recoil against the fact of sin, there is left in Abélard's picture of the divine life and experience only a dead blank and the conclusion is inescapable that God is condemned by the theory to a certain moral inferiority. For if the voice of the universe ever has been or can be heard within the precincts of the human spirit, then we can know with a maximum of subjective certainty—a certainty measured by our confidence in the analogical inference from the forces and standards that shine out upon the summits of our inner life as our highest good—that if God is not capable of moral recoil against the fact of sin and all unrighteousness, *He ought to be.* This inference from what is highest and most trustworthy in man to what must be true of God can be stated more simply, directly. God must hate iniquity to love righteousness. Obviously "wrath" and "love" are human passions and these concepts, since derived from human experience, can both the one and the other be ascribed to God only in an analogical sense (*Wesleyan New Testament* on Romans V, 9, "saved from wrath"). But as Wesley acutely observes, the analogy holds as stoutly in the inference to God's wrath as in the inference to his love. If we choose to think God is most nearly like the best we can experience, know or think of—and we must do so if we are to think of Him with any peace of mind and any power of moral goodness at all—then we can not cancel out of the thought of God that something equivalent to our own moral recoil against the fact of sin and our own desire of holiness without concluding to his total ethical indifference. This inference would cancel his essential righteousness or ethical love. With this conclusion would go the foundations of all faith in a living and saving God, would go all strength of soul to fling across the starry spaces and the whole history of creation as the deepest concern of the universe, the idea of moral goodness as a life-principle of the spirit, would go finally any and all trust that the soul of man has an eternal value which distinguishes it from all else.

Moreover, a crucial inescapable question lurks in any view

of atonement which throws the believing mind in suspense about its objective necessity. Can the objectivity of revelation be retained when the objectivity of atonement is denied? Critics who reject any necessity in God of an atonement and defend the moral view of it generally insist that the idea of atonement must be assimilated and reduced to that of revelation. Let us at once try this out: Admit there is in God no necessity of any name or nature for an atonement. Agree that the essential meaning of atonement and revelation is one and the same. What then must we think of revelation? Is God in any sound sense obligated? Apparently not. Thus the cancellation of the objective element out of the atonement thrusts into the heart of the Christian faith a cancer of doubt whether there is anything objective in it at all. We would thus be driven back upon the desperate conclusion— the natural outcome of a thoroughgoing humanist reconstruction of Christianity—that the whole Christian revelation is, as Socinius said, of "The whole of our redemption, only a metaphor." A theocentric doctrine of Christian experience puts our atonement thought upon a truer path. Expounders of the moral view of atonement assume and assert an objective element in the Christian revelation. Let us avail ourselves of this resource: There is an objective element in the Christian revelation. But it is agreed that atonement and revelation have the same meaning. There must be then an objective element in the atonement and we are committed by this insight not to a denial of the objective form but to a resolute search for a better definition of the objective meaning of the atonement.

Even the judgment that God has been reconciled to the world, which Wesley has used affirmatively in several instances, and it seems without any consciousness of its grave inherent difficulties, apparently unaware that this language is not Biblical, and can be understood in a sense utterly repugnant to the Gospel, can from our point of view be given a meaning that is perfectly consonant with the Gospel. It would be so, if it can mean that God satisfies his own ethical nature by measures adequate to their object and overcomes the moral recoil in himself against all sin and unrighteousness in man by overcoming and removing the cause of it in humanity. He is thus as much reconciled to sinful humanity as man in sin is reconciled to God. If sin in man is a barrier to real communion with God, then its removal must mean something real in the fulfilment of God's purpose of grace alike to God who is obligated to redemption and to man who can only gratefully receive it.

So then perhaps Abélard and all his modern followers from afar may be entirely right in the demand that the atonement must have only moral meanings. Any other meaning has got to be cleansed out of atonement thought. Augustine pointed all this out long ago, and why not admit he did so once for all; [3] God's purpose of grace can not be deduced from the atonement, when it is done, but is itself the original fact and first source of the atonement. The nature and will of God are revealed and realized in the atonement. It is Augustine's logic that there is a living and saving God not because there is atonement. But there is atonement because there is a living and saving God. And the whole Trinity is equally implicated in the atonement. The sunrise of all we ever can know about the atonement is in the sentence, "First we have had to be persuaded how much God loved us." [4]

Now even if this persuasion of a living and saving God, even if this human response to God's love revealed, were the whole meaning of atonement, even on that premise, the divine initiative still has the preeminence over every other fact. Thus the experiential view of the atonement (commonly called the moral view) really gets its significance from an objective view of revelation. So, then, Anselm's view, derived from the church's tenacious belief in the objective meaning of the atonement, might well be built upon the solid rock of truth, even if his definitions of the objective meanings have failed partly or wholly to satisfy the reason and conscience and, what is more serious, to warm the heart of the worshipper. Abélard's view which has so strong a

[3] *De Trinitate*, Eng. Tr., Bk. XIII, Ch. 10-16.
[4] *Ibid.*, 4, 1, 2.

pulse of Christian experience in it may still be otherwise wrong precisely in limiting the necessity of an atonement to mankind. His reduction of the whole meaning of Christ's saviorhood to its subjective influence upon the mind of the sinner has left Christian faith wide open to the tormenting suspicion that the whole problem of sin, and therewith of moral goodness as a life-principle of the spirit, is only a triviality of this planet and no proper concern of the universe. Strike out of atonement thought the original and abiding conviction of the church that it is a necessity in God's own life and how long will it have any practical religious significance in man's life? The moment atonement theology has ceased to be primarily theology, to be rooted and grounded in the thought of God, the Christian faith has been delivered up in principle to a pure humanism. Over that door is written, "I will lift up mine eyes unto nature from whence cometh my help. My help cometh from the plenary religious and moral resources of human nature wherein is no necessity of a power higher and better than humanity to enter in, possess and redeem it."

But wide apart as these founders of the two historic schools of atonement interpretation appear to be, antithetic as they were in their premises and doctrinal positions, they unwittingly concurred in the spirit of an incipient rationalism in respect to one fateful particular. They clasped hands in rationalizing the objective meaning and necessity of the atonement in the divine life, and the factual necessity of it arising out of man's dependence and "sinful depravity," apart into a hopeless disjunctive. They jointly bequeathed and imposed this unholy divorce, entirely unknown to the New Testament and to early church thought, including the incomparable Augustine, as a heavy liability upon Christian teaching and preaching. Intellectualism in religion is long since detected as the principal fountain of these dialectic contradictions. The slogan of early Christianity, "Believe on the Lord Jesus Christ and thou shalt be saved," probably had, as it came again to have in the Wesleyan Reformation, a thoroughly experiential meaning. The scientific search for

truth is not alien to the Christian faith or the original genius of
Christianity, but is the essence of it. It clamors for the test of
experience. "Try me and know my nature," is the challenge
of Christianity. "Let experience decide!" It was a long journey
before the religious consciousness discovered in reason "a bridle
to guide its course steadily, surely and truly." And then after
another long journey the Christian consciousness had to learn
that "the bridle can not originate the motion which it should
guide." The rise of criticism and the return to the theology of
experience, which is on its negative side associated with the work
of Hume and Kant, and is on its positive side superbly exemplified in the pioneer work of Wesley, put an end in principle
to this "mischievous overestimation of reason" in religion and,
as previously observed, set the Christian doctrine of faith again
upon truer paths. Christian experience as the response of man's
total personal life to the Gospel is itself a veritable apocalypse
of God and remains the unsealed and forever open book of discovery and interpretation.

CHAPTER XIV

LOVE'S CATEGORICAL IMPERATIVE

In full accord with the theology of the great teachers, especially of the Western church, Augustine and his successors, including the Reformers for whom the doctrine of sin and grace and of salvation by faith holds the conspicuous position, the idea of the atonement is the heart of Wesley's evangel. Whatever the motive and merit of Wesley's representation of Christ's saviorhood, he has in his doctrine of Christian experience overcome and transcended the divisive and harmful antithesis between the objective and subjective views of salvation which Anselm and Abélard bequeathed to the church. Since Wesley opposed the purely subjective and moral view of atonement by the mystic William Law,[1] likewise the purely objective, substitutional and satisfaction theory of the extreme Calvinist, James Hervey,[2] and since the criticism which he directed against these extremists who made the Christian doctrine of salvation a house divided against itself shows every evidence of prolonged and earnest thought, we must conclude that his synthesis of, or, if we choose, his refusal to disjoin the reference of Christ's satisfaction to God (Anselm-Hervey) from the definition of the atonement in moral and experiential terms (Abélard-Law) was not a mere thoughtless reproduction of Christian tradition but the result of full deliberation and deep conviction. Incidentally, Wesley leaves us in no manner of doubt that he considered it much easier to modify the objective view of extreme Calvinism so as to reconcile it with all the truth-values given in the New Testament and Christian experience than to reconcile Law's humanist reduction of the

[1] Letters, III, 332-370.
[2] Ibid., 371-388.

atonement with an objective view of the Christian revelation. His positive exposition of the idea of atonement together with his correctives to these one-sided and unsound thoeries will be found fully developed in his doctrinal discourses.[3]   The sermon on "The Lord our Righteousness" was a reply to Hervey and a corrective to his extreme Calvinism.   But being a controversial sermon, it could not be a Standard Sermon.

It is a just observation of the sharp-sighted Tyerman that the real issue between Wesley and the (extreme, not the moderate) Calvinists, was not the doctrine of predestination but that of the atonement.   The idea that a believer could bank on the active righteousness of Christ and so continuing indifferently in sin, could commute with God—many drew this devastating conclusion to Christian morality, though Calvinist teachers always scorned it—was subversive of Wesley's doctrine of holiness, i.e., the experiential view of the atonement.   Wesley as shepherd of souls and disciplinarian set himself therefore resolutely to uproot this antinomian teaching.   His unexampled tolerance stopped short at any teaching which left men self-satisfied, content in wrong-doing, failed to inspire and spur them to pursue Christian perfection, lamed or diminished the moral energy of saving faith.   He really thought the blessing of salvation consisted in freedom from sin, an earnest pressing on and real progress in Christlikeness, not in any divine complacency with our unrighteousness.   If God punishes, it is to make us better.   If he forgives, it is to make us better.   Holiness is the sole and final cause of atonement.

For Wesley the true beginning of all theology, all right thinking about God and about our relation to him must rest securely in ethical considerations and never deviate from them.   How firm his grasp of this principle was may be noted in his thesis, that we know *a priori* that the Scriptures simply can not teach predestinarian views which impeach the essential righteousness of God.   That could obviously be unsafe exegesis, but it certainly is sound theology.   Here we come upon one of the deepest and

[3] Sermons 5, 6, 7, 9, 16.

most significant of the constructive insights to be found in Wesley's voluminous writings. It is his daring deduction of revelation, atonement, all the benefits of the Gospel, as the simple, ethical obligation of an infinitely resourceful God. All of God's work for us in Christ, all his work in us by the Holy Spirit, is his ethical nature in action. It is meet, right and our bounden duty to trust in God as the most deeply obligated being in the universe. "When God pardons a mourning, broken-hearted sinner, *His mercy* obliges him to another act—to witness to his spirit that He has pardoned him." What boldness! God is obligated! Not indeed for aught we can do, but for an infinitely deeper and more significant consideration. Out of the depths of his own nature, his infinite resourcefulness and ethical love as its everlasting categorical imperative, springs forth "the whole benefit of God through Christ for the salvation of a sinner." [4]

Now it is not the subject matter of this reasoning, namely, the truth-value in Wesley's doctrine of the Witness of the Spirit—though that is of maximum importance—but the nature of the inference and the method of reasoning itself to which attention is here specially directed.

"God's eternal, essential righteousness includes both justice and mercy." [5] Righteousness is therefore the systematic idea of Wesley's theology. And so we may say in our human way, never forgetting that humility alone is proper to man, "His mercy obliges him to act thus and thus. A month later Wesley returned to this subject and gave to his thesis that the beginnings of theology lie in ethical considerations, a fresh and more far-reaching application: "I see no reason either to retract or soften (evidently strictures from Calvinist sources had been made upon it) the expression: 'God's mercy in some cases obliges Him to act thus and thus.' Certainly as His own nature obliges Him (in a very clear and sound sense) to act according to truth and justice in all things, so in some sense His love obliged Him to give His only Son that whosoever believeth in Him might not perish." [6]

[4] [5] *Wesleyan New Testament*, 362 f.
[6] Letters, III, 138, 161.

Here Wesley, instead of reducing "the whole of our redemption to a metaphor," as expounders of the moral view are all too prone to do, has defined it as an ultimate obligation, a categorical imperative of God's ethical love. Here we come upon a great idea, beyond which human thought can not go, that affords, under a proper use of it, a truer definition of the objective meaning of the atonement. Whence comes the confidence that enables a man, prostrate in the dust and ashes of repentance, to lift his face Godward, but out of the assurance that God is inwardly bound always to do what is right and that his righteousness is encircled by the light of eternal love? This insight set St. Paul upon his feet, made Luther conscious of himself as reborn, started Wesley upon those pilgrimages of Gospel passion that changed the face of Modern Christianity. Of course such knowledge of God can be won only from the Gospel. "Righteousness (He that hath seen me, hath seen the Father), wholly unknown to nature, is revealed by the gospel." [7] "God out of Christ is a consuming fire" (Luther). The face of nature is a sphinx, waving aside the distinction of good and evil with calm indifference. Only after we know God as Christ knew him, can we confess: He out of pure boundless grace, unstinted love, bestows sunrise and rainfall exactly alike on the righteous and the unrighteous. It is in the Gospel that God comes and finds me. My highest good is to accept Him: For "all my works, my righteousness, my prayers (!) need an atonement for themselves. So that my mouth is stopped. I have nothing to plead. God is holy, I am unholy. God is a consuming fire; I am altogether a sinner, meet to be consumed." [8] Wesley converted thirteen years before he made this confession! Oh, no! That kind of conversion, while not worthless, is still not the healing of iniquity or the help of redemption. It is only the Gospel of the grace of God, not the gospel of self-help and self-trust, that abases every man, a sinful being called to perfection, in the dust only to admit and exalt him in a new and hitherto unknown consciousness of communion with God.

[7] *Wesleyan New Testament*, 363.
[8] Journal, I, 464 f.

The church-form of Christianity has always pushed the objective meaning of the atonement as the basis for its subjective benefits into the foreground of its message, worship, piety. Now it is very significant that the powerful criticism of the church-form of Christianity, developed in modern liberal theology in the hands of Law and Coleridge in England, Schleiermacher and Ritschl in Germany, has seized upon the most questionable element in the traditional doctrine of salvation and has always assumed and often asserted that the definition of an objective atonement as the appeasement of a wrathful God and the conversion of a vindictive deity into the Merciful and Compassionate One is the only possible objective meaning which the Christian atonement could have. *Some basal alteration in the will-attitude of the Creator toward his dependent but sinful creatures* is thus propounded as the only possible objective meaning which the Christian atonement could have. On this premise manifestly the negative criticism and formal refutation of the so-called older objective theories—ransom, satisfaction, substitution theories—have been made extremely easy—we submit, suspiciously easy! Moreover this reductive definition of the objective meaning of the Christian atonement manifestly sins against the inviolate principle that no doctrine is overthrown until overthrown, not in its worst and weakest form, even if that be the essence of tradition, which it is not, but only in the clearest and strongest statement of its meaning of which it is capable. Now amid the wide variety and to some extent the very conflicting traditional representations of the objective meaning of the Christian atonement, amid the diverse, sometimes grotesque, illustrations, e.g., "The Cross was a mouse-trap set for the Devil," an illustration used by Augustine for his illiterate Africans, all the types of Christian teaching about the great redemption meet and unite in *the one point of tenacious belief, ineradicable from the church-form of Christianity, in the objective meaning of the atonement.* Climates of thought, social structures, attitudes, ideals change from age to age and the representations of the atonement partake largely of these climatic changes; Anselm's perplexity over God's honor is feudalistic. But the invincible belief in the objective significance of the atonement, though the strength of it has had its incessant ebb and flow, nevertheless abides in its oceanic fullness across all changes. The grace of God in Christ—"God was in Christ reconciling the world unto himself"—and the continuation of the whole Christian ministry of reconciliation in the revealing and redeeming activities of the Christian Church, is not just a figure of speech, not just a metaphor, but it is the great reality of our Christian experience just as it is of New Testament teaching, just as it is the spring of the Church's abiding significance.

We must therefore with all energy of conviction press home the question why, in deference to Christ's satisfaction and oblation for the sin of the whole world, some inner change in God's whole attitude from the will to punish (wrath) to the will to forgive (love), from a vindictive to a pardoning God, should be considered a better, indeed the exclusive signature of the objective view of the atonement? Whence shall we take the proof that the objective meaning of the atonement must be limited to this one simple idea and that it admits of no other definition? The critic of the objective views of the atonement can hardly plead that this has been very much the traditional definition of the objective meaning; for he does not admit the finality of tradition. Truth alone is final. "I love Calvin a little, Luther more; the Moravians, Mr. Law, Mr. Whitefield more than either. . . . But I love truth more than all." [9] "Heresy and schism, in the modern sense of the words, are sins that the Scripture knows nothing of; but were invented merely to deprive mankind of the benefit of private judgment and liberty of conscience." [10] The plea of modern liberal thought is right. Faith and freedom belong together, are one and inseparable. There is just as much genuineness in our faith as there is freedom of the mind. Truth alone is our final trust. But this pledge to find and follow the truth at all costs does not commit us against traditional Christian

[9] Letters, II, 25.
[10] Wesleyan New Testament, 431.

teaching, may indeed lead us back to it under an injunction to disengage its abiding truth-value from the purely transitory elements. Above all, the *a priori* impoverishment of the whole conception of the problem of the Christian atonement and its interpretation, which has held modern liberal thought as in a vise, must be overcome.

A more inferior definition of objectivity in the atonement, it may be freely granted, than a reference of Christ's satisfaction to the wrath of God and the deduction of God's will to save and bless men, his entire work of condescending grace, from an infinite punishment of the historical Redeemer is indeed inconceivable. The radical censorship of this picture of God by liberal theology in such harsh terms as "oriental despot," "almighty Shylock" or even in violent reaction against the terroristic picture of "sinners in the hands of an angry God," as a "gorilla God," is perhaps too emotional but it is in its essential point well taken. Our reaction against the whole criticism of the traditional doctrines of the atonement developed in modern liberal theology is that it has contented itself too often and too much with borrowing the worst methods and imitating the worst features of traditional theology. If but a fraction of the moral energy and intellectual skill that has gone into the violent and just criticism of the traditional teaching of the Church had gone into a sympathetic understanding and a constructive appreciation of the rich elements of undying merit, let us say, the indispensable truth-values in the church-form of Christianity, it stands to reason that much more substantial contributions could have been made with far less friction to the progress of Christian thought.

The incomparable Augustine, who was never satisfied until his thinking touched first principles, pointed out long ago that any conception of the attitude of God, when we think of him as the Father, which is different from the attitude of God revealed in the person and work of Christ, as if now a wrathful being needing to be appeased and then a loving creator eager always to work a reconciliation in sinful men, simply divides the Trinity and cancels the divine unity. We ought, he remonstrates, not to think God the Father was still so far wroth with us that except and until his Son died for us He would not be appeased. Nor ought we to think he was appeased by the death of his Son. Much rather, as the Scripture teaches, God's love in not sparing but giving his own Son for us demonstrates that in God the will to forgive, save, bless men is the cause and not the consequence of the atonement. "For together both the Father and the Son, and the Spirit of both, work all things equally and harmoniously." To think wisely and well, to think soundly and savingly about God, we must then, with Augustine, simply let the knowledge of God to be won only from the Gospel regulate and control utterly all our thinking about God. But on this premise, that all of God's attributes must be comprehended in his grace, Augustine knew how to put a positive value upon and to give a positive meaning to "God's wrath against all unrighteousness." We submit that our preaching of the Gospel in the twentieth century will be not richer but poorer in truth-values for our inability, if such is the case, with deep conviction to think so too. All our thinking about God is analogical [11] and, as Wesley rightly observed, there is no more difficulty but an equal necessity for using the empirical concept of wrath as the symbol of God's moral recoil against sin and the empirical concept of love—both concepts must be used in theology critically— as the symbol of a divine work of condescending grace for the salvation and blessing of men.

But if the definition of the objectivity of the atonement as a radical change in the Creator of the Universe from a punitive to a pardoning mind and will concerning mankind is utterly inadmissable, so is the deduction of the entire work of God for the salvation and blessing of men direct from his essential righteousness, as the obligation of an infinitely resourceful Creator to his dependent creatures, as "Love's Categorical Imperative," the highest definition of an objective atonement of which the mind of man is capable. Here we can do no better than follow

[11] *Wesleyan New Testament*, Comment on Romans, Chapter 3.

Wesley's sublime thought, implicit in all our trust in God, that "in a very clear and sound sense, God's love, His mercy, His own nature obliged Him to give His only Son that whosoever believeth in Him might not perish, but have eternal life." Farther than this human thought can not go. The assurance of the essential righteousness of God is the *ne plus ultra* of the teaching of the Hebrew Prophets (Genesis xviii, 25 f.), of the insight of Jesus (Mark XIV, 32-36), of the piety of St. Paul (Romans VIII, 31-39; 12, 1, 2). This and this alone enables any man to say with Luther:

> A mighty fortress is our God
> His Kingdom can not fail us.

Only be it never forgotten, forever remembered as the masterminds of the Christian faith admonish, that only a man prostrate in the dust and ashes of repentance, stricken with deep humility, has any right to plead the essential righteousness of God and then only for the healing of his iniquity and help of his redemption. Whether at the gates of Sodom and Gomorrah, man who is but dust and ashes builds an absolute trust on the righteousness of God, whether it is in the Garden of Gethsemane, the Son of man conquers the Cross by his assurance that the Will of an infinitely resourceful God is always good, acceptable, perfect, whether it is the great apostle on his endless pilgrimages of Gospel passion, invincibly sure nothing can separate from the love of God which is in Jesus Christ our Lord, we may with them all build our absolute trust on the all-powerful Creator of the Universe always doing only what is right, may say with the Christ of Gethsemane and of Calvary, "Not my will but Thy will be done." The will of God, infinitely resourceful in power, is always, only good, acceptable, perfect in its essential righteousness. The righteousness of a transcendent God, is no provincialism of this planet, no fickle accident of the human evolution, but holds from everlasting to everlasting the universe in the hollow of its hand. On this rock the house of our faith is built.

Wesley, for whom all of God's attributes are comprehended in his grace and all of his activities are subsumed under his righteousness, divided these for convenience into prevenient, justifying, sanctifying grace.[12] He has given three specifications under his general thought that everything God is doing for his dependent creatures must be referred to his essential righteousness. First God acts in all things according to truth and justice. Secondly, God's work for us in Christ is an obligation of his mercy. Finally his work in us by the Holy Spirit is likewise an obligation of his mercy. Thus whether we think of God as the creative energy of the universe, or think of the Christian revelation, the atonement and the work and witness of the Spirit, we come down with Wesley to the essential righteousness of God as the limit notion or first principle of theology. Christ our atonement may be referred directly to the love of God as its simple categorical imperative. His love obliged him to the gift of his only Son for the salvation and blessing of men. This is the objective significance of the atonement and affords a meaning at once positive and profound.

The right to read the character of an infinitely resourceful God —"Abba, Father, all things are possible to Thee" [13]—in his essential righteousness as given to us in Jesus' trustful acceptance of the Cross, is the objectivity of the atonement. This construction passes by every hint of a change of disposition in God; for as the Gospel of John teaches and Luther again reminded us, all our trust is in a Christlike God. It therefore gives to revelation and atonement identical meanings. But in doing so it does not level revelation down to a subjective view of atonement, but lifts the entire thought of the atonement up to an objective view of revelation. The deduction as Wesley has done, of God's work for us in Christ and his work in us by the Holy Spirit, all of it from the essential righteousness of God as the categorical imperative of His ethical love, makes it more than metaphor, rather ultimately truth, to say that "God reconciles himself

[12] Sermons 44, 12, etc.
[13] Mark XIV, 36.

through Christ" to sinful men in the actual work of their reconciliation to himself. By his work for us in Christ, the finished
work of Christ, and by his work in us by the Holy Spirit, the
unfinished work of Christ, and together the first principle of
saving faith and Christian holiness, God overcomes in himself the
moral recoil between his holiness, "infinitely distant from every
touch of evil" [14] and our human sinfulness, and we may reverently
think that he derives from this atonement an infinite satisfaction to Himself. Our New Testament has planted this principle
in the bosom of God. "Thus joy shall be in heaven over one
sinner that repenteth." Oh, but the universe is too big an affair
to tolerate such a flight of ideas! But the Christian faith is not
intimidated by the size of the universe! Hear Wesley! "In
recovering a lost soul, God as it were labours." And God himself so readily forgives and receives the exiles from his Kingdom
that "he may be represented as having part in the joy." [15] We
can not then be making any mistake in building our trust upon
the objectivity of the Christian Revelation. It is also an issue
of life and death that we apprehend the atonement in the same
way. It is all of it God's work for us in Christ. It is all of it
his work in us by the Holy Spirit. What we tragically need
is to understand both revelation and atonement as all of it utterly
objective.

When the Christian Church forgets this, it will pass away and
cease to be. It never has forgotten it unless for a season, and
we may rest assured never will. And if all the imperfections and
crude expedients and even the grosser elements that encumber
traditional Christian thinking about the meaning of salvation
through faith in Christ could be cleansed out of it and forgotten,
would there not remain this all-inclusive truth, towering like a
sunlit mountain above the mists and clouds of every difficulty and
of every obscurity, as the heart of the Church's tenacity in its
teaching, as Wesley also taught, that God and man alike are reconciled in Jesus Christ? Let faith in Christ, which is the voice

[14] Sermon 114.
[15] *Wesleyan New Testament,* 182.

of God in the heart proclaiming itself, give the answer. No other answer is competent.

In the strength of this conclusion, which in the last analysis is but a simple intuition of the perpetual truth-values in the church-form of Christianity, that may be for a time forgotten, pushed aside, neglected, but will again and again return to supremacy in the Christian consciousness, and come to us clothed with the authority of a Wesley's insight and the lofty credential of the actual results of his evangel, we may go forward to consider a little further Wesley's interpretation of the atonement in its manward as well as its Godward bearing and meaning.

CHAPTER XV

THE ENTIRE WORK OF GOD

Wesley's doctrine of Christian Experience is built solidly upon the objective form of the atonement. He accepted and developed the doctrine of atonement for purposes of preaching and practical theology along traditional lines, although he can hardly be said to have confined his atonement thoughts strictly to the traditional teaching of the Church. His explanation of revelation, atonement, justification, sanctification, the Witness of the Spirit, all of them as a divine work of grace, and his bold definition of the entire work of grace as a supreme and ultimate obligation laid upon God by his ethical nature and infinite resources, might have been taken from St. Paul's deduction of man's salvation or "the whole benefit of God through Christ for the salvation of a sinner," from the essential righteousness of God revealed in the Gospel, still it appears to be less a rigid following of tradition than a departure from it. Certainly this conception of salvation, though implicit, is far from conspicuous, in the traditional teaching of the Church. What he appears most concerned about was not the conformity or nonconformity of his ideas with the teaching tradition of the Church, though he had the greatest respect for it, but rather to apprehend to the utmost by experiential thinking the riches of divine grace. He sensed in the atonement an ocean of meaning. Our utmost thought of the grace of God in Christ may be likened to the arm of the ocean. It is only an inlet or bay or gulf, and always too small for the great sea. It may have in it the true quality and rhythmic movement of the wider ocean, but it tells us chiefly of a boundless more. If Wesley had found other thoughts of atonement than those he had, at all in keeping with the great redemption, he would, I think, have seized them eagerly and used them freely, exactly as he did make use of every atonement thought he could find in traditional theology. He seems never to have experienced the distress of rationalizing specialists over the fact that the many and varied appreciations and illustrations of Christ's saviorhood are not all cut precisely by the same intellectual pattern. Shall man by the little footrule of his own mind measure the grace of God? "My thoughts are not your thoughts, my ways your ways." It must be admitted that the amazing wealth and variety of Wesley's atonement thoughts are more in keeping with the infinite bounty of the grace of God than any reductive rationalization. His capacious mind simply could not brook or bear the narrow quarters of a single theory. He put into practice the thesis of the Church's oldest homily: "We must not be small-minded or think meanly about our salvation, rather we must think greatly, as of God, so also of Jesus Christ." [1]

But the great wealth of Wesley's atonement thought is subjected to certain simple, masterful convictions. He was immovable in the belief that an objective atonement is the life principle of the Christian message and the all-inclusive differential of genuine Christianity. "There is nothing in the Christian system of greater consequence than atonement. It is the all-inclusive issue between Deism (we would say naturalistic humanism) and Christianity." As the correlate of this fundamental belief, he was relentlessly careful to safeguard the doctrine of redemption from its liability to abuse in the popular mind. For when the Grace of God is seen only in the light of a transaction within the relation of God and Christ and not equally as a principle of holiness in the justified, such apprehension of the atonement has in the popular mind often fatally dulled the edge of conscience, dimmed the eye of the soul to the majesty of the moral law, weakened the moral will, covered the highest spark of divinity in man, namely, the moral recoil against all sin and unrighteousness, with the dead ashes of indifference. It is the function of the Gospel to fan this ethical spark, this first principle of moral

[1] *Apostolic Fathers*, II Clement, Ch. 1.

goodness in man, into a purifying flame. But the doctrine of grace can be, for it often has been, apprehended and preached so as to be not a creative fountain of new active powers of mind and will in a regenerate life, not the active spring of holiness in heart and life which is "the innermost kernel of Christianity," not a perpetual urge to progress in Christlikeness, but rather an ethical relaxation and release from the higher righteousness and the pursuit of Christian perfection. It is the peril of a purely objective view of the atonement that it may be much less an ethical tonic to human behavior than chloroform to the conscience.

The most notorious of cases perhaps goes back to the visible effects of Augustine's classical portraiture of how his own wayward, wicked, sin-bound life was redeemed and renovated by the pure grace of God. The accent on total human depravity and absolute grace in his *Confessions* and other writings failed from the standpoint of practical theology to connect properly with the mandate "Be ye holy for I am holy." It was the visible effects on the popular mind of Augustine's *Confessions,* one of the matchless pearls in the literature of Christian piety, that provoked Pelagius, a returned missionary, to push the doctrine of holiness of heart and life, a manful righteousness, into the forefront of the Christian message as a first principle of the Christian system. Unfortunately in doing so, he appeared to divorce the doctrine of holiness, the moral question, from the religious principle of divine grace which thus ceased to be the primary source, and became only the crutch of man's crippled freedom. His doctrine of Christian faith appeared therefore to terminate in a naturalistic humanism. Pelagius seems to have blamed the mortal wound given by Augustine's *Confessions* to Christian ethic upon Augustine's theological deduction of human freedom. We perceive the practical religious error in this disjunctive, either God's grace or man's freedom. Wesley warned one of his preachers: "You are in great danger of running from one extreme to the other, from Calvinism to Pelagianism. For no power but that which made the world can give me to experience saving faith, the love of God, the Witness of the Spirit. It is God alone who worketh in me both to will and to do of his good pleasure." [2]

All the more remarkable, in view of Wesley's theocentric doctrine of salvation, his thorough-going theological deduction of man's freedom, and his radical ethic of divine grace, is his decidedly favorable judgment of Pelagius. Always the master, never the slave of traditional opinions, Wesley broke radically with the traditional estimate of Pelagius as a heretic. Wesley had a penchant for good opinions of many heretics, especially those that had good words for the doctrine of holiness. At any rate he gave Pelagius right and censured Augustine harshly [3] for his failure to discern the relative truth and radical importance of the Pelagian doctrine of holiness—the moral problem. "By all I can pick up from ancient authors, Pelagius was a wise and holy man," [4] and also sound in the main point of his doctrine.[5] Wesley met in his own work the Pelagian problem firsthand. He found too many in his societies who were quite "satisfied without any holiness at all," but in the manner of sharp practice used the doctrine of grace as a dispensation from righteousness, a compensation for the lack of it and a city of refuge from the guilt and penalty of evil-doing. The doctrine of Christ's active righteousness as a substitute for "man's actual progress in vital holiness," observed Wesley, "has done immense hurt." [6] This was the point where Wesleyanism really clashed with extreme Calvinism. But while Wesley had the problem of Pelagius, namely, antinomian inferences from the doctrine of Grace, thrust upon him in his pastorate, he never adopted or countenanced the Pelagian solution. There is no clearer mark of merit in Wesley's doctrine of Christian experience than his skillful union of the continual sense of total dependence on God as the essence of religion with an activist type of Christian ethic as the necessary fruit of saving faith.

There could be no conflict over the doctrine of justification by

[2] Letters, II, 23.
[3] Sermon 68.
[4] Letters, IV, 158.

[5] Sermon 68.
[6] Letters, III, 372.

faith and its presupposition. For the doctrines of man's sinful depravity and moral bondage were shared equally by Luther and his acknowledged disciple Calvin. And Wesley set himself to a renewal in its fullness of the early Reformation doctrine of justification by faith and its presupposition. Through him the full force of Luther's distinctively religious understanding of the Gospel was first felt, at any rate, made itself again felt, in English Christianity. Luther reduced practical Christianity to the doctrine of salvation in a religious sense, and thus restored to Christianity its definitely religious character and energy. In this fact lies its intrinsic superiority to every moralistic, intellectualistic and mystical understanding of religion. The central fire of early Reformation teaching and preaching lay in the formula: *Justificatio* and *donatio fidei* have one and the same meaning. "The sense and persuasion of God's love, particularly applied, we term faith," is Wesley's exact equivalent. Thus Wesley recaptured for himself and others the central fire of early Protestantism.

But he joined this insight into the sovereign significance of the grace of God, for which he is wholly dependent on the early Reformers, together with an equally urgent emphasis on saving faith as an active principle of holiness—holiness of heart and life, in which particular, we may venture to think, he has transcended the principles of the Reformers, at any rate, has corrected a recognized limitation. There was present in the work of the early reformers in unsurpassable measure the insight that we as persons are sinful beings, morally bankrupt and absolutely dependent upon the grace of a living and saving God. But this thesis, that we as persons are sinful beings wholly dependent on the grace of God, lacks something that is the very kernel of Christianity and final cause of the atonement. For we are sinful beings *called to perfection in this life*. The Reformation conflict cost both sides dearly. It caused good men on both sides, as fierce conflicts are bound to do, to put asunder what in the nature of Christianity belongs together, namely, the doctrine of justification by faith central to Christianity as religion and the doctrine of holiness, central to Christianity as an ethic of life. Early Protestant thought was thrown by this conflict off its balance respecting the doctrine of holiness exactly as Catholic thought veered away from justification. Now we find these two central ideas joined together again in Wesleyanism in a well-balanced synthesis—a synthesis of no small importance for both the interpretation and practical application of the Gospel. Moreover we have in this synthesis the key alike to concurrence and conflict between Wesleyanism and Calvinism.

Wesley well knew the deadly peril of morality without religion, a religion reduced to naturalistic humanism. He had both seen and suffered it. It is for religion like a rainless desert. It was this godless climate of opinion that he met and mastered. He also knew the equal dangers of religion without morality, unloosed from right reason. It is like an undrained, untilled marsh. What this peril is appears in one of Wesley's specific warnings: "I have found that even the precious doctrine of *Salvation by Faith* has need to be guarded with the utmost care or those who hear it will slight both inward and outward holiness." Accordingly he warns that "it is impossible for any sinner to commute with God." [7] The religious enormity of second-century Gnosticism lay in the fact—this is Wesley's penetrating yet sound diagnosis, "that it taught not *sinless,* but *sinful* perfection." That is like his profound remark that it is the nature of the Gospel "to save men not *in sin* but *from sinning.*" The Gnostics and their disciples, ancient and modern, have wrapped the principle of sin, as if an unbreakable band of steel, around not only the will of man, but also the being of God. This was for Wesley a complete renunciation of faith in a living and saving God and cancelled both first principles of his atonement theology, namely, the almighty grace of God and the power of sinless perfection in the atonement.

Wesley was therefore adamant that the doctrine of the atonement must be preached only so as to be the first principle of holiness and never a compensation for the lack of it. He con-

[7] Sermon 17.

strued the desire of forgiveness without the aspiration after ethical goodness or holiness as the maximum of spiritual perversity. The atonement can have, must have, only moral meanings. Here he hits the nail on the head. All fiction, all unreality, all evasion must be cleared out of the doctrine. "God can on no consideration think me good when I am evil," sinful in my impulses and practises. Nothing of fiction or unreality can enter into the moral judgment of God. Wesley, like St. Paul, construed all the truth about the atonement, the truth of the Gospel, in terms of righteousness—which term gathers up into itself as into a head, God's ethical nature, his cosmic and redeeming activities, all his ways unto men and the holiness imparted to and implanted in the justified. In particular the righteousness of God covers in its meaning "the whole benefit of God through Christ for the salvation of a sinner." [8] "Least of all does justification imply that God is deceived in those whom he justifies, that he thinks them to be what in fact they are not." Moreover "God whose judgment never can be contrary to the real nature of things, never can think me innocent or righteous or holy because another is so. He can no more, in this manner, confound me with Christ than with David or Abraham." These are golden words and of infinite moment in all atonement thoughts! There is no system of spiritual bookkeeping in God's world by which the moral goodness of one, even if it be the Christ, can be placed to the credit of another. Every element of truth and worth in the experiential (moral) view of the atonement is implicit in this statement of it. Beyond it we can not readily go. The atonement, whatever else it can mean, must mean the actual work of saving sinful men unto righteousness. [9]

But this statement of the meaning of forgiveness or justification by faith, according to the moral judgment of God in which there can never be anything fictitious, but only matter of fact, does not deny the creative significance of genuine faith. What all saving faith in the evangelical sense can mean has never been

[8] *Wesleyan New Testament*, Romans I, 17.
[9] Sermon 5.

said better than Harnack has said it in his critical comments on mysticism. Although mysticism was originative, fruitful, rich in valuable elements, still it never dawned on the mystics that we can become in the spiritual life only what in faith we already are. Thus mysticism did not have the key to the ultimate secret of Christian experience. Although the Christian is always in the making and progress, ceaseless progress, is the first law of the Christian life, still all progress in the spiritual life can and should have its fixed unfailing foundation and resource in a sure trust in the grace of God. This is the sovereign unique significance of Christ for all Christian experience. It blends joyous possession with the eternal quest.

We now know how to take the objective form of the atonement as shaped in Wesley's hands. His views follow frankly, avowedly and energetically the lines of the substitution, satisfaction, ransom, and other objective theories. It may not be, indeed it is not, possible to bring his doctrinal ideas at all points into a full consistency with his own principles or to render them altogether satisfactory to right reasoning about the Christian faith. And right reasoning there must be, if intellect is to have its full right in the Gospel. For there are particulars in Wesley's utterances that overstep the boundaries of his own principles. The critic must therefore face the duty of a critical revision, of pruning, qualifying, modifying somewhat his atonement theology, not so much with a view to a purely logical consistency, but rather with a view to the practical religious efficacy and the ethical propriety of his atonement thoughts. He has sometimes used, as was only natural, the language of the Anglican creed which inverted the Pauline thesis that "God was in Christ reconciling the world to himself." But regardless of creeds, the thesis that God has been reconciled to man is genuinely Wesleyan. "If God had never been angry, he could never have been reconciled. I do not term God a wrathful being—a wrong idea, yet I firmly believe . . . he was reconciled to mankind by the death of his Son." "That God is reconciled is the very root of

the atonement." [10]   The Wesleys wove the idea of a blood atonement into song and sermon. It is so much in the very woof and
warp of their message that any attempt to tear it out must leave
the garment of their Christian thought a thing of shreds and
patches. But why should we want to tear it out? We submit
that this idea of atonement can without constraint be given a
moral meaning consistent with the Gospel. Still this language
may be less useful today as it is certainly liable to misconstruc-
tion. But Wesley was never inconsistent with himself and never
wavered in the conviction that whatever the atonement means,
it can have only moral meanings alike for God and man. Saving faith does not find moral goodness in us as its basis. But
with the grace of God as its basis, it must bring moral goodness
in us as its fruits. The atonement does not vacate the law of
holy love, does not commute with God for the lack of holy love
toward him and our neighbor. It creates and verifies Holy Love
in sinful humanity and so admits and fits them into the Kingdom
of God, the society of the believing, the fellowship of the redeemed, the communion of saints or the Christlike.

The doctrinal discourses [11] on the moral law and religion were
prepared and preached to give a better mind to those who were
prone to rule the sovereign claims of righteousness out of the pure
doctrine of redemption. They were designed to help those who
had difficulty in thinking that doctrine through, consistent with
the idea of the holy as the deepest element in theology. "Religion," he said, "is the spirit of a sound mind. Faith does not
cancel but fulfils the higher righteousness of holy love." For
we learn from daily experience as well as Holy Scripture that saving faith (not the alternative) is the true dynamic of all Christian perfection, of all progress in Christlikeness. "By faith we
go swiftly on in the way of holiness." It is the active principle of
all progress in holiness or Christlikeness. It is the most direct
and effectual means of promoting all righteousness and true
holiness. Why then is this so? And how can these things be?

[10] Letters, VI, 298.
[11] Sermons 29 to 31.

"There is no motive which so powerfully inclines us to love God as the sense of the love of God in Christ." Nothing else enables us to give our hearts to him who was given for us like a piercing conviction of the love of God in Christ." "This principle of grateful love to God" (this is Wesley's own happy phrase) is the fountain of all other principles in Christianity. Here we come upon the seraphic refrain in all of Wesley's preaching. The whole Gospel is in the sentence: "We love him because he first loved us."

If then we consider Wesley's representation of the benefits of Christ's saviorhood, what the atonement means for man, it must be said that he has gathered up into his thought everything of value in the experiential view. But he has more, very much more than the moral view. He has not contracted the Gospel to a humanistic interpretation of the atonement. He has all of that, but the theology of the atonement is for him the foundation of its human significance. The unwearied reiteration of the moral, or still better, the experiential view of the atonement throughout Wesley's oral and written exposition of the Gospel forbids us to multiply references. All we need further is the explanatory note that "the sense and persuasion of God's love to man in Christ Jesus, particularly applied, we term faith." What means this "particularly applied"? Is this to be understood as man's own distinctive contribution? By no means. The objectivity of Christian experience forbids it. The sum total of the responses in the entire personal life of any one who hears and heeds the Gospel, to the righteousness of God revealed in the Gospel, is completely comprehended in saving faith. But these complex human responses, all this saving faith, must never in the Wesleyan doctrine be construed humanistically. Wesley's *ne plus ultra* about saving faith, his first and last word about it, is the will and work of God. He invariably gathers up the human response into the principle of divine grace. For Wesley, man's faith is never ultimate; the grace of God always is.

If then Wesley has defended and exploited, for practical re-

ligious ends, the objective form of the atonement in a very energetic way, if every important point of view in traditional atonement theory is affirmatively recognized in his preaching, all this
must be taken and accepted in the light of the fact that, as a
principal founder and first conspicuous exemplar of a theology
of experience, all his thinking on the atonement and therewith
on a living and saving God, moved increasingly in experiential
paths, everywhere strives after and is satisfied with nothing but
moral meanings. But the transcendent importance of this observation will only be perceptible after we have learned to recognize in Wesley's doctrine of holiness or Christian perfection
precisely the total ethical significance of the atonement for man.
As a descriptive formula for the actual work of saving men
from sin unto righteousness, the ethical and experiential meaning of the atonement is exactly what Wesley always meant by
holiness of heart and life, by evangelical or Christian perfection.
But if this be true, if the Wesleyan doctrine of holiness or Christian perfection does simply describe the utmost possible ethical
significance of the atonement, it follows of necessity that the
Wesleyan doctrine of holiness or evangelical perfection is not,
from the general point of view of historic Christianity, a provincialism of the Wesleyan Reformation and its actual sphere of influence, but must rather be understood and appreciated in the
widest perspective of the whole prophetic-Christian movement.
It points securely to a conclusion, of the very greatest importance for our understanding and appreciation of the Wesleyan
doctrine of Christian faith. Moreover the truth of this thesis
can in the light of the facts be clearly seen and deeply felt.

The Wesleyan reconstruction of the Christian ethic of life is
an original and unique synthesis of the Protestant ethic of grace
with the Catholic ethic of holiness. The special interest in and
tremendous emphasis of early Protestantism upon the doctrine
of justification by faith, what Harnack calls Luther's distinctively religious understanding of the Gospel, was reunited, as in
the New Testament, with the special interest of Catholic thought
and piety in the ideal of holiness or evangelical perfection. It

may be assumed that the idea or the ideal of the higher righteousness, of holiness or moral goodness, of evangelical or Christian perfection is the central, sovereign idea of New Testament
ethic. This needs only to be stated to see the truth of it. The
place and power of the imitation of Christ as the admonitory
refrain of all New Testament thought and piety—"Follow me,"
"He is our example," "Christ formed in us," "Till we all come to
the measure of the stature of the fulness of Christ,"—just this,
no more, no less, is testimony enough to place and keep this jew-
eled doctrine of holiness or evangelical perfection forever out-
stretched on the forefinger of the Christian message. It indicates that the idea of the Holy is the heart of Christianity. It
cannot be expected that the human mind will ever create, much
less realize, an ideal beyond the transfiguring radiance of moral
goodness which is the reflected light of Jesus Christ in the Gos-
pels and Epistles of the New Testament. Much less may we
expect to find that the Church has been constant in keeping the
idea of evangelical perfection ever in the ascendant in its message and always regnant in the thought and piety of the justified. But this central sun of the Christian ethic of grace has
never been long, if at all, in total eclipse and has blazed forth
again and again with fresh revealing light and warmth.

Next after the New Testament, confining these references to
the conspicuous and convincing instances, we learn from the pen
of Sabatier that "homesickness for holiness," the consciousness
of the tragic emptiness of a life held fast in the chains of gainful
activity and material possessions, the consuming desire after
the freedom of utter sanctification, which he, Sabatier, calls "the
innermost kernel of Christianity," burst out, as it were, like
sacred fire in the soul of St. Francis, burned away not only the
consciousness of sin but also melted the chains of sinful bondage, and placed upon his brow the kingly resolve to consecrate
every moment and faculty of his being to the pursuit of evangelical perfection, to be in a clear, sound and profound sense himself a Christ even to the print of the nails in hands and feet.
This is the sum and substance, this is the soul and body of the

Franciscan understanding of the Gospel, of his mode of life and example of Christian service, and of his far-flung attempt to realize the Kingdom of God in the midst of a torn and tortured race. It can be said of St. Francis in some measure what is true only of Christ in full measure, that he who has once felt the pulse and quality of his life can never again be the same man he was before nor ever thereafter escape the empire of his influence. The fact of St. Francis alone would be more than enough to fall in love with the Wesleyan doctrine of holiness and evangelical perfection.

Christlikeness, no more, no less, is the nature of the Christian perfection, is the essence of the doctrine of holiness, which Wesley taught. It can truly be said of the Wesleyan doctrine of faith and pattern of life, as it has been said of the Franciscan ethic of the Gospel: "How high does it rise above the miracle-working, magical Christianity of certain Catholics or the desolate, utterly barren theorizing Christianity of certain Protestants?" Once it was miracle, now it is science. But neither miracle nor science ever held the key to holiness of heart and life. We are not saved by what we know, but by what we love. Whether we think of the truth and fitness of the utterance, whether we consider the idiom and flavor of it in the life of either of these two sceptered sovereigns of practical Christianity, who could tell solely from the words themselves whether a Francis or a Wesley had said it: "O, Brother Leo, may it please God that the Brothers Minor *all over the world may give a great example of holiness and edification.*" Francis too looked on all the world as his parish. He had his Leo and Brothers Minor just as Wesley had his Fletcher and "the people called Methodists." Otherwise it is all one. What else denotes them alike so truly: "God had raised up leader and people, 'the covenant of the humble' as it were, to spread scriptural holiness or practical Christianity over all lands." Not amiss has Francis been called the Wesley of the Mediaeval Church and Wesley the Francis of the Modern Church. And "homesickness for holiness," the imperious aspiration after, as well as the profound consciousness of alienation from, *that which is Holy* was the mainspring of the religious life, as of Francis, so of Wesley. Each in his own way consecrated every moment and faculty of his being to the search after the innermost kernel of the Gospel and to the ardent pursuit of evangelical perfection. Each wrestled with the angel of divine righteousness. Each engaged with agonizing earnestness in the search for spiritual power to realize in himself the image of Christ. And they alike sacrificed everything under "the sign of the Cross" to share his secret with humanity.

These hints or demonstrations that the doctrine of holiness is the innermost kernel of Christianity as an ethic of life are further confirmed in monumental fashion by the fact that holiness, which was in St. Paul's thinking the supreme differential of the body of Christ, witness the salutations in his epistles, was historically the first attribute of the Christian Church recognized in the collective consciousness of Christians. The early Christians, we know for sure, when they came together to hear God's Word, read and preached, to unite in the worship of God, in the Sacramental remembrance of him who lived and died for us, and in the common witness of saving faith, began to confess very early, "I believe in the Holy Church." Now they made this confession for a long, long time before they began to say, "I believe in the Holy Catholic Church." The consciousness of holiness as the essential attribute of the people called Christian is therefore much older, and, I believe, also much more dynamic, than the consciousness of Catholicity. The first touches the Christian ethic of life, the second dogma and outward things. The latter is truly important, but it refers manifestly much more to the outward agreements, much less to the inward spirit of the Christian fellowship than does the New Testament idea of holiness. Holiness is then first in time, first in importance, first in universality of recognition among the historical attributes of the Christian Church.

Whether we approve or applaud, whether we condemn or deplore, the way and manner in which the most idealistic sons and daughters of Christian parentage were drawn as by the power of moral gravitation into taking the monastic vow and veil, yet in the presence of the ideal that beckoned them and the soul-hunger for moral goodness that impelled them, we can only stand in awe and reverence before this phenomenon—this burning bush of Christian faith and piety. When Luther likewise at the age of twenty-two resolved to change a Master's robe for a Monk's cowl and came kneeling for reception into the order of Augustine, he heard these words of the ritual: "Lord Jesus Christ, our Leader and our strength, we humbly pray Thee to separate Thy Servants . . . from carnal conversation and from the uncleanness of earthly actions by holiness infused in them from on high, and pour forth into them the grace by which they persevere in Thee." He sought with consummate ardor and in all sincerity the shortest and surest way to Christian perfection and the power thereof. We on our part believe our several vocations in the world to be a far better laboratory than the monastery for the birth and trial of our faith and for our perfection therein by the things we experience. But we would not dare to do so unless we also believed that our life and labor can be a divine vocation and that over it may be the perpetual sign of the Cross. We are assured that the hope of it and the constant attainment of Christian perfection may shine upon us as a pillar of cloud by day and of fire by night.

Shortly before the appearance of Wesley upon the scene of action, a revival of Protestantism in the late seventeenth and early eighteenth centuries out of which came the whole Modern Missionary movement, had begun a reemphasis of the personal experience of saving faith and upon *the attainment of holiness of heart and life* as the two great essentials of Christianity. Here the effort after personal sanctity once more took its place beside or even above the objective form of the atonement. One citation must serve; it is a voice out of German Protestantism: "In all the text books *Christ for us* (the objective form of the atonement) *is everything!* Why so little or simply nothing of *Christ in us* (the experiential or moral form of the atonement)? Forgiveness of sin for Christ's sake is preached but not liberation from sin by the quickening Spirit of Christ." Now the fact that this particular appeal for a more ethical, experiential view of the atonement came out of the School of Bengel, the foremost New Testament Scholar in eighteenth-century Protestantism, on whose work the Wesleyan New Testament is based outright, is doubly important for our purposes. For in these circles too the doctrine of holiness is the moral view of the atonement.

These choice facts, only the more salient few out of many more like them, representing the principal phases and branches of the whole Prophetic-Christian Movement, are abundant to indicate and demonstrate how universal, vital, central the doctrine of holiness or Christian perfection ever has been and must be in it. They indicate that the doctrine of holiness or sanctification as the total experiential fruit of the atonement must be viewed not as a theological provincialism of the Wesleyan Reformation, but as the central idea of the Christian ethic of life. It would however be accurate to recognize on these premises and subject to them a certain individuality of the Wesleyan Reformation in the conspicuous position given to and the practical religious emphasis put upon the idea of holiness or Christian perfection.

Wesley conceived his mission to be a reformation of faith and morals which he pictured as the spread of scriptural holiness over the land. Only in contrast to early Protestant teaching can Wesley's doctrine of holiness or entire sanctification be defined as a departure. But this system is much more accurately defined as the recovery of the lost accents of historic Christianity upon a doctrine which had in early Protestantism, owing to strife, fallen into the background of interest.

But the impressive dignity of the doctrine of holiness and its universal presence, actual or inferential, in the Christian faith may finally be discerned from the part of the Christian revelation of God called the Holy Spirit. Three interests have been in the history of Christian thought one and inseparable: They are the doctrine of the Church, of Christian experience, and of the Holy Spirit. It was Augustine who began to explore with new zeal the revelation of the Spirit, and to interpret afresh saving faith as the voice of God in the heart proclaiming itself, as the work and witness of the Holy Spirit. Wesley's theocentric doctrine of Christian experience is first, last, always a doctrine of the Holy Spirit. Holiness is the primary attribute of the Christian Church. Holiness is the essential quality of Christian experience. Holiness is the third term of the Trinitarian revelation of God. This is the highest conceivable position for the doctrine of holiness in the Christian faith and its interpretation. One of Wesley's earliest Oxford Sermons notes that "the title Holy applied to the Spirit of God does not only denote that he is holy in his own nature, but that he makes us so; that he is the great fountain of holiness to his Church. The Holy Spirit is the principle of the conversion and the entire sanctification of our hearts and lives." Wesleyan theology, as both song and sermon in early Methodism abundantly attest, was preeminently a doctrine of the Holy Spirit. The experiential witness of a spirit of holiness as the necessary companion of Christian faith may even be called a special interest of Wesleyanism. It has in this respect a certain individuality of tone. But this is no afterthought or separate thought of the Christian revelation; it is the essence of it.

In further support of this guarded thesis, a few clear accents from Wesley's tongue and pen must suffice. Late in life—it was in the twenty-seventh year of his conversion-experience—he sharply reminded some of his critics that his consuming interest in the doctrine of Christian perfection and his ardent personal seeking after holiness did not arise out of his acceptance of Luther's view on justification by faith, but preceded it. We know exactly when and how he came by it. He entered in connection with his vocational awakening and choice of the Christian ministry for a life-work more deeply into himself and sought to clarify and profound his Christian thought and experience. For this cause he read and laid to heart and sought to put into practice,[12] *The Rules of Holy Living* by Bishop Tay-

[12] See *A Review of Life* in his Journal.

lor, *The Christian's Pattern* by Thomas à Kempis, and William Law's *Christian Perfection* and *Serious Call*. At this time he was seized of an idea that never after that let him go. The idea of a life rising to "the measure of the full stature of Christ" [13] took full possession of his Christian and vocational consciousness. Then it was he "began to aim at and pray for inward holiness." Accordingly he consecrated every moment and every faculty of his being to experimental research into "how to pursue holiness or a union of the soul with God." Note here and always that holiness and Christian perfection are synonyms, subjectively taken, for *communion with God*. "Without holiness no man shall see God. Communion with God whose name and nature is holiness, righteousness and ethical love is the privilege of "the pure in heart." Holiness is therefore the key to the meaning of God in Christian experience. It is the gateway to communion with God. Wesley did not invent this idea. He took it from others.

Here then were three able men: One a Monk of the fourteenth century, who set down the heart's promptings, then a liberal Anglican divine, one of the ablest of the seventeenth century, whose style in preaching equalled Milton's finest prose, and lastly a great High Church mystic of Wesley's own time. All of them had before Wesley made the doctrine of holiness the central idea of Christian ethic. Wesley then did not originate but simply acquired from good sources his special interest in the doctrine of holiness. In one of his weightiest doctrinal epistles to John Newton, May 14, 1765, he shows how he acquired from the writings of these men not only his lifelong idea of holiness or Christian perfection, but how he acquired from them also his lifelong interest in the subject. Then first it was that "I longed to *give God all my heart*. This is just what I mean by Perfection now (1765). I sought after it from that hour." He then shows how this new-born, overmastering and durable interest in the doctrine led to his preaching in 1733, as Oxford Fellow, "the sermon on 'Circumcision of the Heart' which contains all that I

[13] Letters, V, 198.

now teach concerning salvation from *all sin* and loving God with an *undivided heart.*" "The giving of the *whole heart* and *the whole life to God* was then as it is now my idea of perfection, though I should have started at *the word.*" (Italics all Wesley's.) Those who still startle and stumble at *the word,* whose eyes are not strong enough to look at the moral majesty of the Christian view of life and require to have the fact dimmed, may be content with the fact of a creative idealism in all of us that forever outruns and laughs to scorn every resource of human nature. Elsewhere Wesley observes that this sermon described "The Model of Religion from which the Methodists (at Oxford) set out." [14]   And this is the key to one of the most conspicuous ideas in the collective consciousness of the Wesleyan Reformation. The disciples of that Reformation are "a company of people having the form and seeking the power of Godliness." The originality of Wesley lay then not in the recognition that the innermost kernel of Christianity is in the desire, pursuit and attainment of holiness, but rather in the search for power and in the synthesis of the idea of holiness with the idea of the remission of sin, as equally essential to the atonement.

It is also a notable fact that among the many sermons that he wrote and preached from his ordination, 1725, until his conversion-experience, 1738—thirteen years—one only, this Oxford sermon on the doctrine of holiness or Christian perfection, was a successful candidate for admission into the Doctrinal Standards. And this sermon confessedly develops an idea acquired from Thomas à Kempis, Taylor, Law and other expounders of the Christian Pattern. But there was something dynamic, something radically important still lacking in Wesley's preconversion views on holiness or evangelical perfection. He had not yet discovered the greatest incentive, the source of power, for all progress in Christlikeness. And so when he prepared in 1748 the second volume of the Standard Sermons, he thrust the hand of Luther's doctrine of faith bodily into the text of this early Oxford Sermon. Thus the sermon was conformed to the perfect

[14] Letters, IV, 30.

doctrinal synthesis, characteristic of Wesley's mature preaching, between the dynamic of the Christian Faith—the revelation of Christ, of a living and saving God, in our hearts—and the ideal of the Christian life—going on to Christian perfection—which two, the new active powers of mind and will begotten of saving faith and the supernal radiance of the Christian objective, constitute exactly "the difference of the Spirit of Christ from the Spirit of the World."

There is at first sight no more mystifying phenomenon in the history of the Christian Church than the fact that John Wesley, a militant Protestant to whom many doctrines and practises of the Roman Catholic Church "were abhorrent," who in his Oxford Manifesto of 1738 commended salvation by faith to Faculties, Fellows and the undergraduates not only as *the strong rock and foundation of the Christian religion* but as the doctrine that first drove popery out of these kingdoms, the only one that can keep it out and the one effectual barrier then and always to the spread of "the Romish delusion," who then and there insisted that salvation by faith strikes at the root of all the errors of that church and that all of them fall at once before the power of that truth—can a greater paradox be imagined, I say, than the fact that John Wesley was in the very teeth of these utterances often denounced as a "Papist"?

The intended stigma had two sources: Wesley had incurred the ill-will of many of the lesser ministers and magistrates in England. Complicity with Romanism made a man, in view of the jumpy nerves of England at that time, peculiarly odious. Thus the temptation to fasten this odium on Wesley was in those circles too strong to resist. The stigma was used with telling effect to arouse turbulent passions against Wesley and his humble followers. This part of the charge has therefore value only as a mirror of ill-will and mass psychology. But there were not a few Anglican and other ministers intelligent and sincere, ardently Protestant along Calvinistic lines who honestly thought certain essentials of Wesley's doctrine of faith were affiliated far more closely with Catholic than with Protestant teaching. The judgment of Wesley, emanating from this source, has not received hitherto anything like the attention which its importance merits.

What gave rise to this arresting impression of Wesley's message? Was the conviction of intelligent Calvinists that Wesley was in some of his positions closer to Catholic than to Protestant Christianity pure fiction, mere prejudice, or was it well founded? Of course one of the major functions of the Methodist class meetings was about as near the Roman confessional as anything could be. But leave that out of the reckoning. Have we got to reckon at this point with another of those magnificent doctrinal syntheses which abound in Wesley's doctrine of faith, and, taken collectively, define its individuality? I think so. Nor does it lie in those features of his work which give a certain plausibility to the thesis that he remained a High Churchman after 1738 as he was before. All the prevailing trends of his thought and action after 1738 are overwhelmingly against that view of him. The man, his message, his method simply will not fit, after he put Luther's doctrine of faith at the center of things, any longer in that category. The proofs of this are so copious and cogent that it is a waste of time even to argue the point. His comprehensiveness did include so much of true, deep churchly feeling that it is easy to be deceived at this point. But the reaction of High Churchmen to his methods and message should count for something and his letters to the Bishop of Oxford are alone enough to put this notion of him at rest. And then we have his brother's clear judgment: "All the difference between my brother and me," we learn from Charles Wesley, "was that my brother's first object was the Methodists and then the Church: Mine was first the Church and then the Methodists." [15] For John Wesley then his vocational consciousness and purpose of reformation always came first. Moreover it is confusing to tag a man a High Churchman who believed himself without election or appointment as real a Christian Bishop—a Scriptural Episcopos— as the Archbishop of Canterbury and took it on himself to make Coke a bishop. And did he not call Apostolic Succession a

[15] Letters, VIII, 267.

fable! [16]   And he wonders that High Churchmen are so silent about "the late ordination of Bishops by a Presbyter." [17]

Wesley's sheer ecclesiastical pragmatism is the easiest thesis to demonstrate about him. The master-key to his churchmanship is found in the words: "Methinks I would go deeper. I would inquire what is the end of all ecclesiastical order? Is it not to bring souls from the power of Satan to God, and to build them up in his fear and love? Order then is so far valuable as it answers these ends; and if it answers them not, it is nothing worth." The Christian Church then, all of it, is never an end, but always and only an instrument. Wesley's leadership of the Revival is one continuous commentary on this rationalizing pragmatism. Piette is partly wrong and partly right in his judgment that Wesley's first principles were at once a reaction against both Luther and Calvin, and the anticipation of the philosophy of William James. The experiential and pragmatic tests are supreme in Wesley's doctrine of faith and pastoral procedures.

We must in Wesley's own words "go deeper than ecclesiastical order" in order to discover, if any, the principle of his agreement with Catholic Christianity. Good suggestions may be found in Wesley's insight into the corporate life of saving faith. The Christian experience of one can no more represent living religious experience than a bucket of water can give any idea of a running stream. Reference may here be made to Wesley's strong and unmistakable sympathy with the predominant position of the idea of love in Catholic thought and piety. In many other respects, Wesley embodied vital characteristics of historical Catholicism in his work. But far the most important for our purposes is the fact, noted by Harnack,[18] that Lutheranism in its purely religious understanding of the Gospel went to such an extreme in its reaction against Catholicism, that it neglected far too much *the moral problem*—the "Be ye holy, for

[16] Letters, VII, 262-284.
[17] Letters, VIII, 301.
[18] *History of Dogma*, Vol. VII, p. 267.

I am holy." Right here Wesley rises to mountain heights. He restored the neglected doctrine of holiness to its merited position in the Protestant understanding of Christianity,—a defect frequently attacked by Catholic critics and too much ignored by early Protestant apologists. John Newton of Calvinist principles objected strongly to Wesley's teaching on evangelical perfection, and quoted another very able Calvinist, Hervey, as saying that Wesley was for his doctrine of holiness "half a Papist." In Wesley's answer we find this: "What if he had *proved* it too? What if he had proved that I was a whole Papist? . . . Is Thomas à Kempis, Mr. DeRenty, Gregory Lopez gone to hell? Believe it who can. Yet still of such (though Papists) the same is my brother and sister and mother." The inference of course is that in the language of Jesus, Wesley sensed in these exponents of Catholic piety "doers of the will of my Father," and believed that no Christian should despise another man in whom he could find anything of Christ. But there is much more than Wesley's nonpareil tolerance in his conscious kinship of spirit with men like these. They and many more came into his life in Oxford days. There were two facts about them: (1) They taught thoroughgoing, uncompromising Christianity. (2) The aspiration after holiness of heart and life and the doctrine of evangelical perfection was a very strong element, the central fact in their portrait of the Christian life. They had already seen what Wesley by their help came to see, namely, in the aspiration after holiness of heart and life the innermost kernel of the Christian ethic of life. Wesley's view of Christianity had two foci: (1) "We love him because he first loved us." (2) "Be ye holy, for I am holy." Here then we come upon another of those magnificent syntheses which mark Wesley's Christianity.

The most important fact therefore about the Wesleyan understanding of the Gospel in relation to the Christian ethic of life is that the early Protestant doctrine of justification by faith and the Catholic appreciation of the idea of holiness or Christian perfection—two principles that had been fatally put asunder in the great Church conflicts of the sixteenth century—reappeared in the comprehensive spirit of Wesley's teaching fitly framed together in a well-balanced synthesis. Moreover Wesley was himself not at all innocent, but clearly conscious of the fact that the principal character of his understanding of the Christian faith lay first and foremost in its Christian comprehensiveness, or, as he conceived the term, in the wideness and the wealth of its "Catholic Spirit." In one of the noblest sermons he ever preached, Sermon Thirty-four on "Catholic Spirit," he unfolds and expounds the spirit of Christian comprehensiveness which underlay the Wesleyan movement. Bishop Lavington of Exeter, whose attacks on Wesley were in the unanimous opinion of all writers, whether apologists or critics of Wesleyan principles and practises, wholly unworthy and ignominious, said of Wesley in the year 1751, "we may see in Mr. Wesley's writings that he was once a strict Churchman, but gradually put on a more catholic spirit, tending at length to Roman Catholic." Wesley was justly indignant at the dishonesty of the intended stigma and made answer in a nobility of spirit that converted an intended defamation into a badge of true tolerance: "This is half true (which is uncommon with you) and only half false. It is true that for thirty years last past (1721-1751) I have 'gradually put on a more catholic spirit,' finding more and more tenderness for those who differed from me either in opinions or in modes of worship." [19] Then at the sunset of his career, after his conversion-experience, when first he clasped hands with the early Reformers, never again to break with them, he boldly claimed for himself and the people called Methodists a measure of fundamental Christian comprehensiveness that is "utterly a new thing, unheard of in any other Christian community. . . . Nothing like it since the age of the Apostle! Here is our glorying; and a glorying peculiar to us." [20] For seventeen centuries churchmen and sectarians of every name had incessantly boasted of a superiority in dogma. But here was a profoundly religious man, a true son of the Christian Church, immaculate in his loyalty, boasting of

[19] Letters, III, 326. What a debt and tribute to Oxford!
[20] Journal, VII, 389.

immunity from bondage to dogma as the true basis of Christian unity. He built his career on the principle that Christians can "think and let think" and still be one in Christ. That was, as he well knew, something different, something new.

But Wesley showed his Christian comprehensiveness in other ways than simply his personal, life-long progress in "a more catholic spirit" and in his epochal exemplification of "liberty of conscience in church matters," although these alone are sufficient to seat him among the immortals in the story of human progress. It is revealed in his positive appreciation of and synthetic power over tendencies in historic Christianity which lesser minds have felt to be irreconcilable and have radically, often ruthlessly, put asunder. About the same time he gave in the sermon on "Now abideth faith, hope, love: these three" the short account of Methodism, particularly expounding the Christian comprehensiveness underlying it, to which reference has just been made, he wrote, May 18, 1788, a discourse on "God's Vineyard" which contains a remarkable retrospect of his progressive understanding and life-long major concern with the doctrine of sanctification. In this retrospect he has clearly revealed his consciousness that his teaching was a necessary synthesis of the Protestant ethic of grace with the Catholic ethic of holiness. "Who has wrote more ably than Martin Luther on justification alone? And who was more ignorant of the doctrine of sanctification or more confused in his conceptions of it? As proof, let any one examine his comment on the Epistle to the Galatians. On the other hand how many writers of the Romish Church (as Francis Sales and Juan de Castaniza, in particular) have wrote strongly and scripturally on sanctification;—who nevertheless were entirely unacquainted with the nature of justification. As proof let any one examine the doctrinal guidance for teaching the people by every parish priest, ordained by the whole body of their divines at the Council of Trent." Objection may well be made that Luther and Calvin too were not "totally ignorant with regard to sanctification" and that Catholic teaching was not "entirely unacquainted with the nature of justification." These are perhaps overstate-

ments. But the error is in the overstatement and not in the historic fact that Protestant and Catholic teaching had begun a
fatal divorce between the idea of grace and the idea of the holy
in the doctrine of Christian experience, leaving it more and more
a house divided against itself. Nor can the overstatement of the
facts in the least obscure Wesley's intended synthesis of these
two ideas in his doctrine of Christian experience. For it is the
genius of the Wesleyan teaching neither to confound nor divorce
but to discern justification and sanctification in their true nature
and join them together "laying equal stress on one and the
other." Wesleyanism insists, "with equal zeal and diligence,
alike upon the doctrine of free, full, present justification (the
special interest of Protestantism) and that of entire sanctification both of heart and life (the special interest of Catholic piety);
being as tenacious of inward holiness as any mystic; and of outward, as any Pharisee." [21] In this synthesis we may find the cause
of Piette's strong liking for Wesley and his very important
half-truth about him that he is not a simple copy of Luther-
Calvin but exhibits a strong affinity with Catholic faith and piety.
It is also the key to the very evident and sincere dislike of Wesley's teaching by some of his Calvinistic contemporaries. They
sensed a leaning to the Catholic side. It is reflected in Wesley's
laconic remark that "the real issue between me and extreme
Calvinism is in the doctrine of holiness or Christian Perfection."
Thus from this standpoint fresh light falls on the essential differences between Wesleyanism and the Luther-Calvin understanding of the Gospel. He has "not deviated a hair's breadth"
from the Luther-Calvin doctrine of sin and salvation by faith.
But he has joined with this, substituting it for the predestinationism of Luther and Calvin, the Catholic appreciation of the progressive imitation of Christ as the concrete meaning of Christian
Perfection. The Wesleyan synthesis indicates therefore a juster
appreciation of the whole human response to and realization of
the truth-values of the Christian faith.

[21] Sermon 107.
[22] Letters, IV, 295, 298.

CHAPTER XVI

THE DECAY OF RELIGION

— I —

The Journal of John Wesley for October 12, 1760, has this entry: "On the three following days I spoke severally to the members of the Bristol Society. As many of them increase in worldly goods, their grand danger, I apprehend, will be their relapsing into the spirit of the world, and then their religion is but a dream." The text used for this purpose was, "Can I not do as I please with what belongs to me?" Matthew XX, 15. The text really calls for an affirmative answer. God is free in his gracious work for the salvation and blessing of men, and not bound by fixed relations between work done and wages received. But while the Master of the Kingdom is not bound by precise calculations of merit in the bestowment of his benefits, it does not follow that even he is or can be irresponsible in the use of his power over his subjects. On the contrary, Wesley asserts [1] that God is under obligation to do the very best he can by every soul. If now irresponsibility is outlawed even for God, how much more so for man? Irresponsibility, let it be noted, in the use of power among and over men is the same wherever it appears, whether expressed in the brazen words of a Constantius at Milan in 355 A.D., "Let my will be church law," or in the notorious claim of a Louis XIV, "I am the state," or in the defiance of a modern capitalist, "Society may have something to say how I get my power (make money), but as to how I use it, that is none of its —— business." Contrary to the apparent meaning of his text, Wesley inferred a moral mandate against the exclusive economic motivation and complete absorption of human effort in gainful pursuits, and the hedonistic spirit and

[1] *Notes on New Testament*, p. 67.

mode of life which arise from such motivation and absorption. Observing with growing concern the "danger of relapsing into the spirit of the world and of turning religion into a dream," Wesley began to develop energetically his well-known doctrine of Christian stewardship and of social service, comprehending all of human life and human activity.

Wesley's sharp-sighted observations and searching analysis of the spiritual peril of riches and the inevitable conflict between secularism and the Gospel went much deeper. The Journal for September 18, 1763, reads: "I gave our brethren at Bristol a solemn caution not to love the world, neither the things of the world. This will be their grand danger. As they are industrious and frugal, they must needs increase in goods. This appears already. In London, Bristol, and most other trading towns, those who are in business have increased in substance sevenfold, some of them thirty, yea, an hundredfold." Another entry for July 11, 1764, reads: "I gave all our brethren at Manchester, England, a solemn warning not to love the world or the things of the world. This is one way whereby Satan will surely endeavor to overthrow the present work of God. Riches swiftly increase on many Methodists, so-called."

These observations on the rapid rise in the economic status of the early Methodists coupled with the perception that Christianity of necessity produces certain economic effects adverse to the spirit of Christianity, first appear in the Journal for the third decade of the great Revival. Although Wesley was always fundamentally a Franciscan in his religious evaluation of poverty, he gradually developed his militant criticism of economic individualism with its train of consequences as a check upon the manifestations of "worldliness" among the Methodists. Beginning with frank personal conferences with his people at Bristol, England, he proceeded to give "solemn cautions and warnings" publicly in the societies and thereafter frequently, as Tyerman puts it, "lashed wealthy Methodists and others with terrific power." These utterances, oral and written, extending over his long and eventful career, reveal a *crescendo* of anxiety about the reaction of accumulated wealth upon religion. The early Journal entries not only record the interesting fact that "riches swiftly increase on many Methodists, so-called," but they also give a hint that the secularization of the Revival, due to the reflex influence of wealth upon spiritual temper, was inevitable. Apparently the business, or economic virtues engendered and fostered by Christianity must lead to riches and these in turn to the ruin of religion. Believing, therefore, that the influence of religion and riches respectively upon the spirit and ethical conduct of life was by nature contrary and incompatible, Wesley watched the rapid rise in the economic status of his adherents, not with complacency, still less with satisfaction, as we of this age might expect, but rather with deep distrust, yea, with undisguised consternation. He evidently considered the material prosperity of the Methodists was tantamount to the internal corruption of the great Revival. Only heroic measures could immunize the Revival against "the poisonous influence of riches." So he believed and so he preached for half a century. Even so he had to admit that all the remedies he had been able to propose had in the end proven quite ineffectual: "I have seen within these last fifty years a thousand melancholy proofs of the deceitfulness of riches. Of all temptations, none so struck at the whole work of God as did the deceitfulness of riches."

Wesley's dominant interest in this fateful conflict between "secularism" and the Gospel, his deep concern about the deadly peril of riches, appears already in his *Appeal to Men of Reason and Religion,* 1743, which was intended to be a "plain account of Methodist principles and actions," of their message and manner of life as well as a description of the moral state of the nation. These "Appeals," made at the very outset of the Revival, are among the ablest products of Wesley's fertile pen, and afford us excellent views of his convictions. In the midst of a nation utterly careless of religion and terribly fallen in its moral state came Methodism proclaiming the enduring truth of Christianity and making of religion, as the pursuit of eternal values, the great business of life. And the upshot of those remarkable "Appeals" is that the novelty of Methodism does not lie in its message, but in the militant moral energy it brings to bear on men to submit religion to the whole experiment of life and to make it the business, the great practical concern of life. It was just *Christianity in earnest*. Wesley pictured the great chasm between the principles of the Church of England, with which he had no quarrel, and the general practices of its membership and ministry. "How under God," he cries, "can we get these good principles put into practice?" Then he examined the principles of the Nonconformists or the Independents, "who are at the smallest distance from the Methodists," and also of the Quakers, who stand at "a still wider distance" from us. But Methodists, Presbyterians, Quakers are all agreed upon the essentials, and especially on the supreme importance of translating Christian principles into action. In all Christian communities, therefore, the problem of problems is how to get the principles of Christianity put into practice. To contribute to this great all-inclusive end, Wesley believed, Methodism was born, and was making its way in the world, being simply a company of men standing by historic Christianity and seeking to possess and utilize more fully its latent power.

For the enforcement and illustration of his theme, Wesley commented freely upon the Quaker movement. For the original principles and ideals of the Quaker communities, he had unfeigned admiration and praise. But in the light of their "present practices" he sternly indicted them for apostasy. "You were once what you know in your hearts you are not now." The radical change referred to was, in Wesley's opinion, the inner corruption and decay of the original Quaker spirit caused by the accumulated wealth of the Quaker communities. Having pictured their apostasy, Wesley turned to his own adherents. "Lay this to heart, ye who are now a poor, despised, afflicted people. Hitherto ye are not able to relieve your own poor. But if ever your substance be increased, see that ye be not straitened in your own sympathies, that ye fall not into the same snare of the devil." The allusion is to the multiplied signs of affluence in the Quaker mode of life due to Quaker prosperity based on their proverbial industry and frugality. "Before any of you lay up treasures on earth" (that is, accumulate property and indulge unnecessary expense of any kind as the Quakers, recreant to their first ideals, are doing), "I pray the Lord God to scatter you to the corners of the earth and blot out your name from under heaven." [2] From this attitude of relentless opposition, Wesley never deviated. He saw in the accumulation of wealth and the secularizing influence of property, likewise in the aesthetic and culturistic outlook upon life to which the possession of wealth always gives rise, the greatest foe of all religion. Christianity is thereby necessarily involved in a process of perpetual decay from which it can escape only by a process of incessant revival.

In weighing Wesley's observations and teachings on the interaction of religion and property, allowance must be made for the *circumstances of his ministry.* The outstanding fact of his ministry was the ready hearing accorded him by the common people, and the supreme contempt poured upon him by the rich and powerful. The wealthy, ruling, educated classes evinced for the Revival, as Wesley once described their attitude, "either an utter contempt of it or an enmity to it." The Bishop of London, taking a leaf out of the pagan attack on the early Christians, stated in his charge to the clergy that the Methodists and Moravians were drawing over to themselves "the lowest and most ignorant of the people." The bishop, who intended this as an indictment, really paid a high compliment to Wesley and his coworkers. And the truth of his statement is amply confirmed by Wesley himself in tract and sermon. Naturally marked success in reaching the masses, and corresponding failure to reach the "higher orders," reacted upon Wesley's ardent popular sympathies.

The Calvinistic Whitefield, as is well known, found a somewhat easier entrance to the homes and hearing of wealthy and titled families. His doctrine of election, suggestive at least of an aristocracy or a privileged class, may have been a little more

[2] Wesley, *Appeal to Men of Reason and Religion,* Part II.

palatable than Wesley's outrageously democratic doctrine that all men are absolutely equal before God. Wesley noted this leveling tendency in evangelicalism right early. "The doctrine of faith," he once said, "is a downright robber. It cancels all human differences, distinctions, and merit in the presence of God. It makes of those who pride themselves on these things the same needy impotent vessels of mercy with the others." Evangelicalism stressed the absolute spiritual destitution of all men alike, the equal dependence of all on the unmerited grace of God, the wide open door of salvation to all alike; in short, it proclaimed an absolute democracy of all men in point of spiritual need, opportunity, and outlook as they stand at the door of the kingdom of God. This point of view and these principles, above all the Christian valuation of personality, inspired Wesley's notable attack on human slavery, which he denounced as "the execrable sum of all villainies." It inspired his arraignment of the men engaged in the manufacture and sale of alcoholic liquors as "poisoners general" who "murder his Majesty's subjects by wholesale and drive them to hell like sheep," so that vast numbers of those who bear the image of God are, on account of strong drink, "lost to reason and humanity, as well as religion." It was the impetus given by the Methodist Revival to social reform and betterment which led the historian John Richard Green to say, "The Methodists themselves were the least result of the Revival," and to list among its numerous consequences "a new philanthropy which reformed our prisons, infused clemency and wisdom into our penal laws, abolished the slave trade and gave the first impulses to popular education."

Nevertheless, although a powerful spirit of philanthropy, reform, and social uplift attended and followed the Great Revival, Wesley's personal views on social and political questions (in this he resembled the great Luther before him) remained for the most part unaffected by the vigorous leaven of social democracy implicit in the movement. He was always a Tory in politics, so much a Tory that the significance of the American Revolution for the liberties of Englishmen as well as for Americans, to say nothing of its world-wide significance, wholly escaped him. He could see in it at first only the folly of indiscreet political coercion and later, when his opinions shifted, the folly of willful political rebellion. Like his great contemporary Edmund Burke, he considered it inexpedient or impolitic to coerce America into obedience, even though the laws were, in his opinion, entirely equitable. He was not a believer in democracy in any kind of government, whether in church or state. Jefferson's dictum, placed in the forefront of the Declaration of Independence, that "all governments derive their just powers from the consent of the governed," and Washington's no less radical doctrine that all sound government must be built upon "the right of the people to make and to alter their constitutions of government," were thoroughly repugnant to Wesley. He thought with Burke, the great exponent of political conservatism. "As long as I live," he wrote John Mason, January 13, 1790, "the people shall have no share in choosing either stewards or leaders among the Methodists. We have not and never had any such custom. *We are no Republicans and never intend to be.* It would be better for those that are so minded to go quietly away." The Republicans were the "Reds" of that revolutionary epoch.

The "Spirit of Seventy-six" and the mighty social transformation which dawned on Europe in 1789, the storming of the Bastile, the key to which Lafayette later presented to Washington, the exultation of liberal spirits in America and Europe over the advent to power of the rising middle class, only filled the mind of Wesley as it did that of Burke with a feeling of horror. "We are no Republicans and never intend to be" was his reaction to the American and French Revolutions. The conservative "higher orders" of the revolutionary age felt the same horror over the prospect of a business men's or middle class government which the conservative and powerful middle classes feel today toward the advent to power of the rising working classes. Now this revolutionary atmosphere of the eighteenth century was irreligious to the point of open hostility toward organized Christianity. The situation then bore a striking resemblance to conditions now, and for the same reasons. Organized Christianity in England and France had long been in league with political oppression and tyranny. As then, so now! Let this be said once for all. The great prison fortress in Petrograd, which stood for ages as the grim symbol of malignant oppression—this terrible dungeon of liberty—bore the lofty Christian names, "Saint Peter and Saint Paul." This gloomy fortress, this sinister dungeon in which the prophets and apostles of human liberty went with fatal precision to their doom, was named after the two chief apostles of Christ—Peter and Paul. This is an epitome of the degradation of the Church in France in the eighteenth and Russia in the nineteenth century. The Church had become in the public and popular mind the synonym of oppression and the tomb of liberty. No wonder Jean Valjean shook his huge fist at the door of the cathedral! No wonder the Russian revolutionaries have hated religion—or rather an ecclesiastical system prostituted to an autocracy which was the enemy of a vast people, at once its subjects and its victims!

In any event, the Revolutionists of the eighteenth century, first in America, still more so in France, were often skeptics to the point of irreligion as currently understood. "Tom" Paine's *Age of Reason,* index of eighteenth century atmosphere, is still a bugbear to the pious. And the Constitution of the United States is noticeably cool and distant in its attitude toward organized religion. Like the Soviet constitution of today, it contains a definite grant of freedom of worship, presupposing, of course, that there is no taint of treason in the worshiper. But as for positive recognition or active interest in Christianity of any type or description, it gives no aid or comfort to any of them. The fact has often been deplored, and the force of it parried with the argument that after all the true fathers of the nation are not to be found so much among the makers of the Constitution as among the founders of the colonies. They at least were actively religious and strong churchmen desiring state support of churches. The transition from the seventeenth to the eighteenth century carries us far along the great highway of modern liberalism whose goal was recorded in the mature judgment of Gladstone, that even atheism can not be held to be a legal disqualification from public office. Naturally the French Republicans, being more keenly conscious of the identity of the Church in France with political tyranny, were more resentful toward religious communions, and went much farther along the road toward a militant atheism. Considerations of this character prompted John Wesley to say in substance, if not in so many words, that the path of progress from false religion to true religion seems to lie through the negation of all religion. Thus it can readily be understood that Wesley thought and felt in this supreme issue of his century with the conservatives in spite of his ardent popular sympathies and the powerful leaven of social democracy implicit in his message.

But the sharp-sighted eyes of the ruling classes discerned much better than Wesley himself the democratic implications of his message and the potential social significance of the great religious awakening going on among the masses. The number of those tempted by the slight morsel of particular election were extremely few. With virtual unanimity those whose self-esteem turned on property, high position, and hereditary privilege spurned the Methodist preachers all alike. "I thank your ladyship," wrote the haughty Duchess of Buckingham to Lady Selina, Countess of Huntingdon, "for the information concerning the Methodist preachers. Their doctrines are most repulsive and strongly tinctured with impertinence toward their superiors, in perpetually endeavoring to level all ranks and do away with all distinctions. It is monstrous to be told you have a heart as sinful as the common wretches that crawl the earth. This is highly offensive and insulting and I can not but wonder that your ladyship should relish any sentiments so much at variance with high rank and good breeding." This scornful attitude toward the Methodist preachers and their message repeats the first impression of Wesley's preaching. At the outset of his ministry he was promptly notified after his first sermon in several of the large and influential churches that it would also be his last. His doctrines that all alike are sinners, equally in need of a Savior and as subjects of divine grace without merit or distinction, all that was too much for fastidious aristocratic ears. Therefore, from first to last evangelicalism as a message and as a mass movement stood self-condemned in the eyes of the "higher orders" inasmuch as it overleaped class barriers and disregarded the fixed spheres of life.   Moreover, it indirectly caused the "common wretches that crawl the earth" to revalue themselves in the light of God's redemptive purpose, and thus to think of themselves, as redeemed subjects of God, more highly than they ought to think according to the requisites of an aristocratic class consciousness.

The exclusive attitude and intense class consciousness of the "higher orders" left Wesley no outlook but the common people. Very early he had a clear perception that the future of the Revival lay with them. Methodists might become rich, but rich men would never become Methodists. "There was not one rich man among them when the Methodists were first joined together." In 1745 he wrote, "You have neither power, nor riches, nor learning. You are a low insignificant people"—a statement which reads like Paul's description of the Christians at Corinth, "You are poor almost to a man, having no more than the plain necessaries of life. Most even of your teachers are quite unlearned and (in things other than religion) ignorant men." [3] The early Methodists were social nobodies, poor, unlettered, the lowliest folks. It is but natural, therefore, to find in Wesley's record for the twenty-eighth year of the Revival that "the societies in the North Riding were increasing, that is, among the poor. For the rich, generally speaking, care for none of those things." And he wrote Freeborn Garrettson, 1786, that "most of those in England who have riches love money, even the Methodists, at least those who are called so. *The poor are the Christians.*" And elsewhere he betrays an animus against riches. "How unspeakable the advantage in point of common sense, which middling people have over the rich." It has been said

[3] *Advice to People called Methodists.*

that early Christianity was a middle-class movement. With equal truth it could be said that Methodism was a middle-class movement. Such, however, was not the case. For early Methodism, like early Christianity, was not so much a middle-class movement as it was a producer of middle classes. It evinced a singular efficacy to elevate the economic status and mode of living for whole communities.

The various references in Wesley's tracts and sermons to "rich Methodists so-called," as if such a combination were a contradiction in terms, indicates that Wesley's ideas concerning wealth and property went much deeper than the circumstances of his ministry. They rather were inspired by a sovereign ideal and sustained by masterful convictions. For no sooner had certain of the Methodists accumulated wealth than he at once pitched into them, hammer and tongs, for doing so. It is, indeed, to be wondered at that men of affairs suffered him to denounce in the strongest language at his command all surplus wealth as incompatible with Christianity. With every resource at his command, he inveighed against the accumulation of property and endeavored to convince his adherents that the will to accumulate was the natural enemy of religion, sending men down the broad road to destruction, and fostering in them every temper alien to Christianity. Those who have the "conveniences of life and something over," "walk on slippery ground," "continually tread on snares and deaths, are every moment on the verge of hell." [4] He who makes accumulation an aim "denies the faith, and is worse than an infidel; and if he is successful, he will have gained riches—and hell fire!" Those who deliberately set out to become rich "do, whether successful or not, infallibly lose their own souls." True, "other causes may concur, but in all ages wealth has been the principal cause of *the decay of true religion,* in every Christian community. Riches have in all ages been the bane of genuine Christianity." [5] Evidently St. Francis had not lived in vain.

[4] Sermon 23.
[5] Sermon 17.

In his ruthless exposure of the perils of riches and his stern denuncations of the will to accumulate property, Wesley points out that there are certain "reasonable purposes" for which wealth may be acquired, but beyond which it may not with spiritual safety be retained. What are these "reasonable purposes"? The answers given to this question varied not a little. In several instances he draws the line at the "plain necessaries of life." Frequently he includes in his conception of the goods of life, lawful for a Christian to have, in addition to the "plain necessaries," also the "conveniences of life." But these are always to be judged by a sternly Puritan standard which frowns on all needless expenditure as sinful. In one or two instances, he specifies as worthy objects of gainful pursuits:

1. To be honest and owe no man anything.

2. To provide the necessaries of life for self and family and dependents.

3. To establish these also in a position whereby they may with, not without, their diligent labor provide for themselves when he is gone hence.

4. To obtain what is needful to carry on the business itself, to be strictly limited to the achievement of an income sufficient for the foregoing objects.

These are the sound and reasonable purposes which must control and regulate and limit all gainful activity. He who goes farther and attempts to create a surplus is guilty of "entering into a covenant with death and hell."

I am not going to dwell upon the obvious difficulties which confront the practice of such ideas, nor the manifest deficiencies in Wesley's definition of the sound objects of economic activity. The conceptions of necessaries, conveniences, and luxuries which prevail in any community are in process of constant development. The luxuries of yesterday are the conveniences of today and the necessities of tomorrow. This observation is so obviously true that it would be carrying coals to Newcastle to multiply illustrations. Tacitus tells us in his *Germania* that the richest men of Northern Europe were distinguished by the wearing of underclothes. The modern working girl can afford better perfumes than ancient queens. It would require millions of slaves to maintain without machine power the standards of comfort and convenience enjoyed by the vast majority of American people. There is not and can not, in the light of the advancing scientific control of natural forces, be any fixed definitions of "necessaries, conveniences, or luxuries." Again Wesley stipulated that legacies and bequests must never exempt the beneficiaries from the duty of diligent labor. But what parent can foresee in relation to a fluctuating economic system the line between too little and too much for such a purpose? It will readily be granted that it is ethically superior to put an individual in a position to earn a living as against the mere possession and use of power without productive service of any kind. But under an individualistic political economy, where the means of living, the modes of production and the distribution of property are subject to incessant change, no human intellect could execute Wesley's advices. Wesley admitted as much and praised the celibate life over the parental estate because it did not encounter these difficult and insoluble problems. Still less does he know of a proper socialization, inspired by ideas of social justice and the one alternative to his impossible system of charity, of natural resources, of the means of production and of the fruits thereof, although some of his expedients hit upon as a remedy of unemployment certainly point in that direction.

But the *naïveté* of Wesley's economic ideas and the remedies proposed is most clearly apparent in the fact that he never thinks of increasing surplus and enlarging business with the avowed object and deliberate intent to provide more men with well-paid work and thus elevating the economic status of the workers. He knows nothing of the scientific and systematic organization of free labor as a vocation or business, nor the ownership of capital which such an organization presupposes.

What influence, we may ask, did preaching like this which dealt so frankly with principles touching the most delicate matters of business exert upon men of affairs among the Methodists in particular? Tyerman, in his well-known biography of Wesley, thought the "terrific power with which he lashed wealthy Methodists and others must have made them wince and tremble." But Wesley himself informs us quite to the contrary. It appears that he was listened to with complete respect and then just as completely ignored. He admitted that his injunction, enforced in every possible way, to turn all surplus at once into the channels of charity required something contrary to "nature, custom, and worldly prudence." Men, he said, had listened a hundred times to the scriptural mandate, "Lay not up for yourselves treasures on earth." This means simply, "Do not accumulate property." "And yet in what Christian city do you find one man in five hundred who makes the least scruple of increasing his goods just as much as he is able." "For above fifty years I have been a servant to you and your fathers. I have never wavered in my message (concerning the incompatibility of riches and religion). But who has believed our report? I fear not many rich." [6] Again he declared, "Who can convince a rich man that he sets his heart upon riches? For considerably above half a century I have spoken on this head with all the plainness that was in my power. But with how little effect? I doubt whether in all that time I have convinced fifty misers (that is, fifty having more than they need) of covetousness." This negative result did not suggest to Wesley the impracticability of his principles. No, the refusal or failure of men to obey the Gospel and not accumulate property was "just the most amazing instance of spiritual infatuation in the world."

Out of his observations and reflections there emerged for Wesley a great question. If the will to accumulate property can not be broken, and if religion is responsible for the economic virtues which lead to property, while the possession of riches is subversive of religion itself, does not the fact demonstrate an irrepressible conflict, a perpetual struggle between the spirit of Christ and the spirit of the world, between true Christianity and property, between the Gospel and secularism? And upon these

[6] Sermon 87.

premises does not the fateful conflict between riches and religion portend the ultimate decay of pure religion or the final failure of Christianity? Wesley's investigation and reflections upon the "decay of religion" (the phrase is his coinage), and his location of the causes in certain economic or wealth-producing virtues which are the essential product of religion, open up the greatest of all questions. What is Christianity? Is it to be realized by pouring its energies into the channels of secular activity, or is "the Gospel in the last resort and in the most important thing which it enjoins strictly a world-shunning and ascetic creed"? Anthony in the fourth century, Francis in the thirteenth, and Tolstoi in the nineteenth emphasized the ascetic and world-shunning spirit and features of the Gospel and made this law-giving for the conduct of life. The massive influence of asceticism upon Wesley's understanding of the Gospel, upon his presentation of its distinctive message and mode of life is sunclear. And yet he never wavered in the conviction enunciated at the beginning of his ministry, that "Christianity is essentially a social religion; to turn it into a solitary one is to destroy it." The supreme spiritual opportunities of life are to be found not in the desert but in the city, not in solitude but in society. The social, open, active Christians are the best representatives of that religion. Combined with this emphasis, we find in Wesley a religious evaluation of activity in the world unsurpassed by any former representative of the Christian Church. What has happened to the Western Church and its traditional interpretation of the Gospel to make this singular combination of asceticism with the highest religious evaluation of activity in the world possible?

It is true that Wesley's analysis of the total bearing of the Gospel on such fundamental problems as the Gospel and the World, Work and Wages, Poverty and Property, etc., was very casual and wholly inadequate. It is equally true that his ideas quite fail to point to solutions of these problems. Nevertheless, his observations and reflections on these subjects are of great value. The very fact that he did some radical thinking and

plain speaking is itself significant. A Bishop of London in the
seventeenth century informed his clergy that "Christianity does
not make the slightest alteration in civil property." It is but
natural that men who think and act upon such premises should
speedily give over or more accurately never begin the search for
the social terms in which Christianity can be defined and the
structure and conduct of life, individual and social, suitable to
its genius and spirit. We can not imagine an attitude more
distant from Wesley's epoch-making reaffirmation of Luther's
position. The Christian man is in virtue of his faith in God
most free lord of all things and subject to none. And by that
same faith he is bound over to service to express the whole of
life in the definite forms of Christian service. The bearing of
Christian principles upon a system of property which leaves men
who are in possession of enormous power also irresponsible in
the use of it, demands radical thought and investigation.

— II —

John Wesley discovered the problem of *"the continual decay
of pure religion"* not while pursuing sociological studies in the
history of the Christian Church, but in the course of his pastoral
oversight of the Methodist societies. The Great Revival, the
most important event, according to the judgment of the historian
Lecky,[7] in the history of modern Christianity, had spread over
England and across the Atlantic to the New World, where it
appeared simultaneously with the achievement of nationhood.

Wesley himself boldly advanced this opinion of the Revival in
1781.[8] The movement had been organized by a mind "having
a genius for government not inferior to that of Richelieu." It
had half a century of experience, of progress, and inspiring suc-
cesses behind it. It had set up a spiritual empire of souls unique
in the annals of the Modern Church. On this basis of great suc-

[7] *England in the Eighteenth Century,* Vol. II, p. 631.
[8] *Short History,* 91.

cess and of apparently still greater promise for the future its master-mind prepared his tract called *Thoughts upon Methodism* (1786). It gave a brief survey of the origins and a short statement of the principles of Methodism. These features are introductory to the main motive of the tract, namely, the searching question about the spiritual future of Methodism. The greatly altered economic status of his adherents appearing in the third decade of the Revival had been increasingly thrust upon his attention, while the unyielding tenacity of the gainful spirit which had laid hold of his people planted a doubt in his mind, not about the continued existence, but about the spiritual future of Methodism. The Revival was being rapidly secularized, at least in many of the societies. And this process appeared to him to be at once the fruit of religion and the cause of its decay. A community brought fully under the dominion of religious forces directed as Wesley directed them will of necessity rise rapidly in its economic status. That had happened to the Methodists as once also to the Quakers. Then the changed economic status had begotten in its subjects a more congenial outlook upon life. And this change seemed to Wesley to be subversive of true religion. He reasoned that religion which imparts to its subjects certain wealth-producing qualities is fated in turn to be devoured by its offspring, the wealth produced. Is there no way out of this dilemma? Or is Methodism doomed to go the secular way of all previous revivals, losing in spiritual dynamics all that it gains in social respectability? Wesley was not quite prepared to admit so much. He appears to offer a solution, although it is stated conditionally. His analysis of this problem is so fundamental for our discussion that we quote the pertinent section entire:

"Methodism is only plain scriptural religion, guarded by a few prudential regulations. The essence of it is holiness of heart and life. The circumstantials all point to this. And as long as they are joined together in the people called Methodists, no weapon formed against them shall prosper. But even the circumstantials are despised; the essentials will soon be lost. And then what remains will be only refuse.

"It nearly concerns us to understand how the case stands with us at present. I *fear wherever riches have increased* (exceeding few are the exceptions) *the essence of religion, the mind that was in Christ, has decreased in the same proportion.* Therefore I do not see how it is possible in the nature of things for any revival of true religion to continue long. For religion must necessarily produce both industry and frugality; and these can not but produce riches. But as riches increase, so will pride, anger, and love of the world in all its branches.

"How then is it possible that Methodism, that is, the religion of the heart, though it flourishes now as a green bay tree, should continue in this state? For the Methodists in every place grow diligent and frugal. Consequently they increase in goods. Hence they proportionably increase in pride, in anger, in the desire of the eyes and the pride of life. So although *the form of religion remains, the spirit is swiftly vanishing away.*   .

"Is there no way to prevent this? This continual declension of pure religion? We ought not to forbid people to be diligent and frugal. We must exhort all Christians to gain all they can and to save all they can; that is, in effect grow rich. What way then (I ask again) can we take, that our money may not sink us to the nethermost hell? There is one way, and there is no other under heaven. If those who 'gain all they can' and 'save all they can' will likewise 'give all they can,' then the more they gain, the more they will grow in grace and the more treasure they will lay up in heaven." [9]

We may pass lightly over the solution here offered for one of the most difficult problems of modern civilization, namely, the inequitable distribution of the fruits of labor. Wesley's solution may be stated thus: All surplus values beyond the plain necessaries, or at most a sternly Puritan view of the conveniences of life, plus the maintenance of the business, must be poured at once into the channels of a bountiful charity. Hoard nothing! Do not accumulate property! Extract the poison from riches by

[9] *Thoughts upon Methodism.*

giving them away! Capitalistic accumulation would be eternal death to the projector. "I do not say, Be a good Jew, giving a tenth of all you possess. I do not say, Be a good Pharisee, giving a fifth of your substance. I dare not advise you to give half of what you have, no, nor three-quarters, but all!"[10]

It is amazing how much confidence Wesley reposed in his little principle of charity as quite sufficient to bridge the chasm between monstrous opulence and monstrous misery. In a social order where the enjoyments of leisure go to a very few, while all the privations go to the rest, we cannot but wonder that Wesley, who otherwise evinced a firm grasp on the realities of life, should have seriously proposed charity as a remedy for the pernicious inequalities in the modern distribution of wealth. Then the deep moral injury which the practice of charity inflicts on both parties is entirely overlooked. But we are not primarily concerned with the merits of Wesley's suggested solution of a great problem. We are concerned mainly with his observation that religion, certain economic virtues such as industry and frugality, and their economic effect, riches, are related as root, tree and fruit; and that the type of religion described as "holiness of heart and life," which is productive of these results, is essentially ascetic. It is not an asceticism like that exemplified by the monastics of early and mediaeval Christianity, who fled from the world or hid themselves in it, but rather an aggressive militant asceticism carried into all the secular activities of life. It is an asceticism which offers the highest premiums to strenuous vocational activity. It is such a type of Christianity that engenders in men certain economic virtues which bear fruit in the production and accumulation of surplus values. And it is through the medium of these qualities that religion itself is involved in a process of perpetual decay.

This phenomenon, described as the "continual decay of pure religion," is nothing distinctive of the last great Revival of Protestant Christianity. Every great revival of Christianity has been arrested and transformed by such a process of seculariza-

[10] Sermon 126.

tion. Christianity itself, if we may somewhat arbitrarily call merely the first epoch of our religion by that name, was involved soon after its origin and the awakening in the followers of Jesus of a definitely Christian consciousness, in such a process of adaptation to its Graeco-Roman environment. The first intense flame of the Gospel called men out of the world, made of them a peculiar people, having their own community life, avoiding army service, law courts, and separating themselves to the utmost from all secular contacts.

The ardent hope for Christ's immediate second coming shared by the early Christians certainly intensified if it did not produce this sharp cleavage. At any rate, Saint Paul based the whole ethical conduct of life upon this outlook. We find these mandates in his Epistles: Let the secular order alone. Start no new enterprise of any kind. Don't make any changes in your business. Let those who mix in the world be indifferent to it. In particular, do not get married. Avoid all entangling alliances with this world's affairs. Let every man and woman remain in the state, position, occupation, etc., in which God's call found him. *For the time is short!*

But this outlook upon life typical of the early Pauline churches, these high-strung advent ethics, gave place in the course of about fifty years to a very different attitude toward secular contacts. The insurgent spirit which called the Christian not to do his part in the world's work, a world unspeakably wicked, but rather to the greatest degree of separation from secular contact, gave place to a more accommodating attitude. "I pray not that thou shouldest take them out of the world, but that thou shouldest keep them from the evil in the world." At this juncture conduct was no longer controlled by the belief that "the time is short." The lurid advent ideas of the Book of Revelation had been displaced by the philosophic calm of the fourth Gospel. We stand on the threshold of a new era, the second century, with its acute secularization of Christianity, when Christianity began to take out naturalization papers in the Roman Empire. In response to the challenge of Gnosticism, the Christian consciousness was slowly but surely developed into the Catholic consciousness. This process ended relatively with the union of the Christian Church and Roman State under Constantine the Great, who inasmuch as the army had been for a century the seat of power and source of political decisions, put the sign of a cross on a flag and unfurled it for his legions, announcing by this act that Christianity was to be the state religion. This act led logically to state support for the Church and state-paid salaries for the clergy. At this stage the ancient mandate, "Be not conformed to this world," had lost its arresting potency. Henceforth this ideal will survive chiefly among Nonconformists.

Long before this process was ended, long before the main body of Christians ceased to be different from non-Christians in their modes of thought and conduct, the invincible Protestantism of the Christian consciousness began to find potent voice. The Protestant spirit gained considerable momentum already in the second century. It can be detected outside the Church in Marcion and Montanus, inside the Church in the Puritan Tertullian and the pacific Irenaeus. But in the late third and early fourth centuries there arose a mighty reaction, an epoch-making outburst of the pent-up spirit of ascetic Christianity, in the monastic movement. These hidden energies of the new religion were destined to flame up again and again in the successive mediaeval revivals of Christianity, last but not least in the great sixteenth and eighteenth century revivals.   •

Monasticism in the moment of its birth and in the successive waves of its influence which flooded the old channels of church life and thought, "seemed like a veritable stampede away from the Catholic Church as though that creation of Christian energy were no better than the evil world itself from which escape was sought." The Church had become so fully implicated and identified with the secular order that the moral energy of Christianity, its native imperious impulse to translate itself into action and express itself in some worthy ethical conduct of life, was "cribbed, cramped, confined." The distinctly Christian conduct of life was confronted by insurmountable barriers. "Wherefore men fled from human society as a prison to revel in human solitude as a paradise." The Christian spirit got away from the heavy hand of tradition and conventionality, and threw off the fixed restraints of a social order which remained far more the servant of animal instinct and passion than of spiritual vision and purpose. The spirit of Christianity sought freedom of action where the ethical conduct of life might be worked out according to the deeper, richer thought of life as a vocation.

Protestant Christianity did not, as is often, perhaps commonly, assumed, repudiate this spirit of asceticism. Monasticism found its opposite not in Protestantism, but in the Renaissance. The former was a new and powerful formation of the monastic ideals. Where else but in the successive revivals of ascetic Christianity and the community life created by each revival are we able to trace the deep and growing thought of life as a vocation? Under what influences did men learn to think about all of life as a divine vocation? The monastic movement was a veritable ark of the covenant in which vocational idealism, perhaps the finest contribution of Christianity to the life and thought of the western world, was created and enriched, leavening whole communities. It is true that before Luther only the life work of priest and monk was considered a divine vocation. But the idea of a life in fulfillment of a divine vocation was there and in power, as every fresh revival bears witness. It burst forth in Luther's thought, took on increased intensity in Calvin's theocracy, and was reindued with great power by the Wesleyan Revival. Accordingly we cannot say that the reformers either created or repudiated this dynamic thought of life as a vocation. They rather seized upon the pent-up energies of this vocational idealism as it had gathered momentum in the special service of the Church and of the monastic community, and poured it into all the channels of secular activity. Henceforth for religion at its best every man's life must be regarded as a plan of God, at least by divine purpose, whatever the human fact may be. The greatness of Luther stands out imposing as the mountain in the way he universalized the priestly function, finding for it in saving faith a simple and a sufficient basis; likewise in the way he universalized the ideal of holiness, making it a mark of saving faith, detaching it from the traditional forms of the monastic life, defining it not in terms of abstinence but in terms of achievement; finally in the way he universalized the idea of the Christian ministry, investing every form of productive service with the loftiest attributes once monopolized by the special service of the altar. The universal priesthood of all believers, the universal sainthood of all believers, the universal ministry of all believers—these ideas demonstrate that in Luther's mind all the secular activities of men must be transfigured by the wondrous thought of life as a vocation. Henceforth the shortest and surest way either to Christian assurance or to Christian perfection was not to enter the cloistered walls of the monastery or to serve at the altars of the Church. Rather, the surest sign that a man is in a state of grace or is going on to perfection and possesses the ideal spirit toward the Creator of heaven and earth is to be found in his vocational activities, and the highest fruits of Christian faith are plucked along the paths of Christian service. This understanding of the Gospel transforms all productive service into a vocation wherein, as in the temple, God is most fitly worshiped. Finally, this transformation of vocational idealism, intensifying its quality and broadening immensely the scope of its application, this pouring of the energies of religion into the ethical conduct of the secular life, heralds the most significant events and movements of modern Christianity.

The evangelical reaction in the eighteenth century against a secularized church and a political religion may be viewed as a fresh outburst of this ascetic spirit, the last great revival of ascetic Christianity. It is not customary to think of it quite that way, but it is the only view which opens up the true and full significance of the Revival. The full proof of this thesis is supplied by the genuinely Puritan spirit, outlook, and character of Wesley's ethical teaching and writing. In his ethical ideals Wesley was a Puritan all over. He repudiated no doubt the characteristic emphasis of Calvin's theology upon the doctrine

of predestination, though he was at times no less radical in his
definition of man's salvation exclusively in terms of the divine
causality—God's work for man through Christ, in man by the
Holy Spirit. But the conspicuous position in Wesley's theology
is given not to Jehovah's electing love, the mark of Calvinism,
but to the article on justification, the mark of Lutheranism; at
the same time, Wesley took over Calvin's religious evaluation
of the ethical conduct of life and of activity in the world as the
highest conceivable expression of true faith. In this fundamental
he followed Calvin rather than Luther, of whom he once remarked that he was led by "the fury of his solifidianism" (the
term is Wesley's coinage) into a disparaging attitude toward the
practical side of religion, excluding human activity and achievement from the essence of religion. Luther's bitter animus against
"good works" that were really not ethically good embarrassed
him when he came to develop the vocational idealism which entered into the warp and woof of his understanding of the Gospel.
Wesley did not follow him at this crucial point. On the contrary,
he combined Luther's epoch-making religious understanding of
the Gospel with Calvin's religious evaluation of activity in the
world. This is a unique synthesis and is a distinguishing feature
of his work judged as a historic whole.

Luther's understanding of the Gospel came to Wesley through
the Moravians. Calvin's religious evaluation of activity in the
world came to Wesley through his Nonconformist antecedents.
It is therefore a mistake to see in the evangelical reaction simply
a reaffirmation of Luther's ideas or in Luther's influence the
sufficient historical basis of Wesley's work. For, like Calvinism,
the major emphasis of Methodism was not on dogma but on discipline, not on orthodoxy but on the ethical conduct of life. The
Nonconformist mother of the Wesleys gave to the greatest of
her sons the slogan of his life. "Happy you are if you from this
time forth make religion the business of life." The Puritan spirit
of Wesley manifested itself in the way he made war on pleasure,
in his diatribes against fashion in dress, in his praise of Quaker
austerity and simplicity, in his fierce denunciations of luxury

and waste, in his stern moral censorship of any needless expenditure on the externals of life, even expenditures for artistic, aesthetic, or culturistic purposes, in his utilitarian attitude, and his religious evaluation of industry and frugality, etc.—all these features stamp him the genuine Puritan. Indeed, Wesley was so essentially and thoroughly Puritan in his whole ethical outlook upon life that only theological controversy could have concealed or long delayed appreciation of the fact. He, too, considered Christianity as an ascetic spirit issuing forth in the ethical discipline of an active life in the world.

This conception of religion is the underlying thought of Wesley's sermon on the "Causes of the Inefficacy of Christianity," preached at Dublin in 1789. The same line of thought is developed in the sermon on the "Danger of Riches," printed 1781, and in the tract called *Thoughts on Methodism*, dated London, 1786. The Dublin sermon on the failure of Christianity is designed as a solemn warning to his adherents who were increasing in wealth and respectability. Wesley, in some ways a modern Franciscan, observed in his constituency a radical change very much like the fate which overtook the Franciscan movement in the thirteenth century. The Franciscan order, which was built upon the absolute repudiation, not only of private but of all property, passed through a crisis during the short life of its founder. Wesley's alarums about the secularizing influence of wealth, therefore, take us back to the last days of Saint Francis, who, brokenhearted, pensively faced the setting sun of his career, brooding anxiously over the first signs of apostasy from the ideals which had been the sum and substance of his life. He, too, had thoughts about "inefficacy." Since the time of Christ, Lady Poverty had been too much despised. He had taken her for a bride, and in a rapture of love went from city to city, from cottage to cottage, from castle to castle, preaching and practicing absolute poverty. But his contagious enthusiasm and unbounded idealism soon found their most serious obstacles in the very success of the movement. A few choice spirits were like himself exalted by the mystic flame of his love, while the power of his life was deeply felt by multitudes. But the practice of poverty as he visualized it soon broke on the rocks of success. Men gave themselves to the movement and all they had. Moreover, the founder of the Order of Brothers Minor not only made poverty, to own nothing, the religious ideal of all Franciscians, not only bound every member of the order to be utterly simple and frugal in his mode of life, but he coupled this powerful check on expenditure with the mandate for every member of the order to be required to labor, to work as a religious duty. Did Francis of Assisi ever face the question how a community which had gifts of property thrust upon it, and what is far more important, also how a community filled with the spirit of industry, mental and manual, and also an equal spirit of frugality could help creating and accumulating surplus values? Out of this inevitable conflict between the fundamentals of the order and the economic fruits speedily forthcoming there emerged a crisis:

"If we had possessions we should have to have weapons with which to defend them. For from property comes strife with our neighbors and relatives, so that charity to God and to men suffers many a scar, and in order to preserve love whole and unimpaired it is our firm resolve to own nothing in this world."

In his last Testament we read: "I worked with my hands and wish to work, and all the brothers I strongly wish that they may work at labor which is of honest nature." The inevitable happened as it had before to the Benedictines and the Cistercians. The Franciscans grew rich, and riches put to flight the creative ideals of the order. "How, then," Francis might have asked, "can pure religion endure?"

We cannot say that Francis detected this latent antagonism between religion as he understood and lived it and the reflex influence of certain economic virtues upon religion. But in Wesley the antithesis is clearly perceived and sharply defined. Wesley reasoned thus: Why is Christianity so ineffectual in the world? It is not simply that five-sixths of mankind do not know it all. For of those who are called Christians, the greater part are ignorant of it or unaffected by it. And where it is known, why is it ineffective? Why, in particular, is Christianity so ineffectual among Methodists? They have the plain old truths of Christianity, and for them discipline, "the spirit and discipline which make a Christian," has been added. Why so little success? Where is that active ascetic spirit, that spirit of strenuous self-denial, vanished? Why is so exceedingly little of it to be found even in the oldest and largest societies?

"The more I observe and consider things, the more clearly it appears what is the cause of this in London, in Bristol, in Birmingham, in Manchester, in Leeds, in Dublin, in Cork. The Methodists grow more and more self-indulgent, because they grow rich. Although many of them are still deplorably poor (Tell it not in Gath; publish it not in the streets of Askelon!), yet many others in the space of twenty, thirty or forty years, are twenty, thirty, yea, a hundred times richer than they were   . when they first entered the society. And it is an observation which admits of few exceptions, that nine in ten of these decreased in grace in the same proportion as they increased in wealth. Indeed, according to *the natural tendency of riches,* we can not expect it to be otherwise."

We may interrupt this quotation with a question and an explanation. If riches are poison to religion, nullifying the virtue of Christianity, why then is poverty "deplorable"? Why say that many Methodists are still "deplorably poor"? Francis of Assisi was more naïve, unsophisticated. He could praise poverty as something good. Wesley can not. Again by "self-indulgence" Wesley does not mean anything like a coarse gratification of the senses. He alludes rather to the growing ability and inclination to beautify all the externals of life. He observed a marked relaxation in the ascetic spirit which at first governed his most ardent adherents. Their early Puritan spirit, with its extreme negation of all pleasure and culture, so characteristic of ascetic Christianity, was, as they advanced in property, not only being softened in its asperities, but was being gradually displaced by a more artistic, aesthetic and culturistic spirit and ideal. Now in Wesley's mind this change spelled danger, if not disaster, to the Revival. "I am distressed" (so runs his comment on the fact), "I know not what to do. I see what I might have done. But alas! The time is past now. And what I can do now, I can not tell." And again he says:

"How astonishing a thing this is. How can we understand it? Does it not seem (and yet this cannot be) that true Christianity has a tendency in process of time to undermine and destroy itself. For wherever true Christianity spreads, *it must cause diligence and frugality which in the natural course of things must beget riches, and riches naturally beget every temper that is destructive of Christianity.* Now, if there is no way to prevent this, Christianity is inconsistent with itself, and of consequence cannot stand, cannot continue long among any people. Since wherever it generally prevails, it saps its own foundation." [11]

I pass over the solution proposed, namely, a species of charity drastic enough to exhaust or consume at once all surplus values. Perhaps with a change of name, this would amount to a social economy something like this:

"Inasmuch as most good things are produced by labor, it follows that all such things of right belong to those whose labor has produced them. But it has happened, in all ages of the world, that some have labored, and others have without labor enjoyed a large proportion of the fruits. This is wrong, and should not continue. To secure to each laborer the whole product of his labor, or as nearly as possible, is a worthy object of any good government and requisite to any sound social order."

But in his clear perception that certain sociological or economic effects flow directly or indirectly from the operation of religious forces, and in his sharp formulation of the apparently insoluble antinomy between the wealth-producing virtues of religion and the secularizing influence of riches upon religion—that is to say, between the power of religion to create riches and

[11] Sermon 116.

the power of riches to destroy religion—we are confronted with one of the most important phenomena and one of the greatest problems in the history of religion and civilization. How far is Wesley's insight from the conclusion that the economic superiority of Christian over non-Christian peoples is due in part at least to the operation of religious forces? That the economic superiority of Protestant over Catholic constituencies, and of the Calvinistic branches of Protestantism over all other branches, has its basis in the more energetic and definite influence of ascetic Christianity upon the ethical conduct and secular program of life among its subjects? The ascetic spirit as created and fostered in men by Christianity has in turn generated in men those practical virtues or business qualities which are vital to economic efficiency and essential to success in the modern world.

What these business or industrial virtues and qualities are and how far their development in men is due to the religious tillage of human soil is a subject by itself. Here we call attention to the fact that Wesley's insight into the causal relation between the operation of religious forces in human life and the rise in the economic status of individuals and communities is all the more remarkable and dependable since he regarded the growth of riches among Christians not as an unmitigated blessing, but rather as a great spiritual peril, perhaps a necessary evil. It can be gathered from his magazines, letters, journals, tracts, sermons, that he fully believed the growing riches of the Methodists was one of their greatest dangers. His last words to the Methodists, especially the fourteen sermons written in the early nineties, are full of this intense anxiety about the ruinous effects of property upon religion. All the more trustworthy, therefore, is his derivation of the wealth-producing and wealth-accumulating qualities of the Methodist constituencies from the influence of religion upon the ethical conduct of life.

It need not be observed that the orientation of this thesis has been made in this article with a minimum of historical illustration, and has therefore an appearance of deductive rather than of inductive reasoning. But "Christianity in history" furnishes abundant illustration and confirmation of the power of religion to produce varied sociological effects. It makes no vital difference whether we hold that religion has given rise to these economic virtues, originating them, or simply has fostered and enforced them. In either case the causality of religion in history is recognized and it is recognized at a vital point for economic theory, namely, in relation to the production and accumulation of wealth. Of course, the conclusion which Wesley drew from these phenomena was the acute secularization or the constant decay of Christianity. But it would be equally scientific to examine the same phenomena from the economic standpoint, and equally conclusive to infer therefrom the singular and significant efficacy of Christianity in its most ascetic formations.

— III —

The observations of John Wesley upon the direct and indirect interaction of religious and economic forces were quite casual and fragmentary. They furnish, however, a good point of departure and a sufficient basis for a closer analysis of this intricate relationship. Wesley discovered that religious forces could exert a positive influence upon men in their capacity as economic agents, just as it has been increasingly clear since Buckle and Marx that economic factors and material conditions exert a profound influence upon the *homo religiosus*. The distinct influence of religion upon the *homo politicus* and the *homo economicus* is one of the most important relations in the history of civilization. "The two great forming agencies in the world's history," as Marshall, the economist, has said, "are the religious and the economic." What else tells more of ages past than the tools with which a man works and the altars beside which he worships? By their tools we know the successive types of civilization as the stone, bronze, and iron ages, and more recently as the age of industrial machinery, of coal, oil and electricity.

The high intrinsic importance of the subject is further enhanced by a strong tendency of the *economic school of history,* following Buckle and Marx, to limit scientific history to the economic view. An exaggeration of the economic factor in history was acknowledged at an early date by those who adopted the Marxian theses, and recent writers show commendable critical caution and reserve at this point. But the economic school of history still tends strongly either to invalidate all other points of view or else arbitrarily to subordinate them to the economic—arbitrarily; for the *a priori* subordination of all other factors in history to the economic has its basis purely in the option of the observer and not in the nature of the object. To consider modes of material production as the basis of all social life, and therefore of all real history, or to assume that all historical reasoning to be scientific must accept economic factors—modes of production, labor processes, economic forms of society—as if original data, as if these factors could not be further analyzed, and then proceed to treat all else as derived therefrom, is to impose a highly artificial and purely theoretical restriction upon the scientific outlook of the historian. Such a limitation of method is dogmatic and is refuted by facts. Modes of production and economic formations of society, being themselves evolutionary products and, like all other historical phenomena, subject to the law of development, are necessarily not historical postulates, but problems.

The labor process supplies an excellent *locus standi* for the observer who wishes to investigate the bearing of economic formations and factors on the social, political, and spiritual processes of life. But the conclusions reached will inevitably betray just this economic point of reference. An economic interpretation of history which either excludes or subordinates all other points of view to itself is about as scientific as a geocentric astronomy. The astronomer knows that the footstool of his observations is very much in motion and extricates himself from his geocentric limitations by availing himself of every possible point of view. The outcome is the insight that all our conceptions of space, time and motion are largely relative to the position and outlook of the observer. Thus a revolution of thought in physical sciences is accomplished identical for substance of doctrine with a quite similar revolution of philosophic thought achieved at an earlier date. Physical space and time are found to be closely bound up with the observer. The "absolute space and time" becomes an "inane fiction" of the mind, as a great thinker has named it. Rather space, time, all motion are relative. So, too, the laws of Nature cease to be "absolutes" and become "only more or less convenient formulas."

The great forward movement in the world of physical science should be an object lesson to the scientific historian. "Einstein had," in the words of one of his best interpreters, "become tired of assumptions." The economic view of history is objectionable not because it is scientific, but because and in so far as it is not scientific enough. The theological and materialistic interpretations of history are equally in bondage to an assumption which prevents the advance of science. The exclusive concentration of attention upon the economic activities of men obscures the significance of other powerful human interests, in particular their power to produce economic effects. In order to escape the artificial limitation imposed upon historical investigation by the restrictive tendency of the economic school of history, it is necessary to reverse the procedure, to investigate, where sources of information permit, the genesis of the successive economic formations of human societies, and to utilize the *operation of religious forces* as a *locus standi* for investigating their bearing upon men in their political and economic relations. Such a view of history possesses exactly the same relativity to the position of the observer as the economic approach. Not, therefore, with any idea of refuting the economic approach to the study of history—its great value is beyond cavil or question—but to escape from the element of dogmatic assumption in that theory which obscures significant facts and relations, I propose to consider, within a very limited field of phenomena, *the way and manner in which religious forces have exerted a positive influence upon their subjects in their capacity as economic agents.*

Of course, the interest of John Wesley as an observer, like the Puritan divines in whose paths he trod, lay first and always in religion. He never valued religion for its economic consequences, plain as they were to see. An exclusively utilitarian appreciation of religion would have impressed him as the essence of irreligion. The utilitarian approach would in his view rob the salt of its saltness. Religion as he conceived it had to do first, last and always with the eternal values—values so great as to dwarf all temporal values into nothingness. The religion, sufficient to regulate in exhaustive fashion the ethical conduct and economic activities of men, was oriented, not on the here and now, but on the life eternal. In this view, all early Protestantism down to and including Wesley might, on account of its essential other-worldliness, its desire, like Bunyan's Pilgrim, to flee the wrath to come, be considered the arch foe of the capitalistic mind. For the spirit of capitalism appears to be altogether concentrated in the accumulation of treasures on earth. So it might seem on the surface. A closer scrutiny, however, of the deposit made by Protestantism, especially the Calvinistic branches, in the character of the peoples who accepted it, reveals a totally different relationship—*a causal relationship between the most ascetic branches of Protestantism and the economic activities of its subjects.* For, as it has been aptly said, the Calvinistic diaspora during the wars of religion became the missionaries of skilled labor and the nursery of a capitalistic spirit.

It is a matter of common knowledge among historical investigators that the universal and consuming preoccupation with business which, like a veritable giant, seemingly holds all men today in the hollow of its hand, is something decidedly novel in the experience of mankind. It was not so in the beginning, nor was it so until quite recently. The economic cosmos in which we today live and move and have our being goes back about two and a half centuries, though of course some of its elements are as old as human history. Already the seventeenth century, and still more the eighteenth, for obscure reasons which economic historians have not yet sufficiently explored, witnessed the beginnings of material progress first over small, then over wide areas in a most compelling and cumulative fashion for which the prior history of the race furnishes no analogy. This momentous event, known as the Industrial Revolution, was consummated in Great Britain about 1770 to 1825, whence it spread rapidly over the world.

The roots of this fateful revolution reach, of course, farther back. The immediate historical background for it was supplied primarily by the religious and political emancipation of the English people in the seventeenth century. It is noteworthy that no good economic reasons have ever been given for the late arrival of the Industrial Revolution. At a given point "England was ready for inventions," and "conditions were ripe," and something had set men to "thinking out better ways of doing things"; that is, upon a course of inventions.[12] Of this much the event itself is proof enough. England was evidently first ripe for it, because the revolution first occurred there. But why in the seventeenth and eighteenth centuries? The gainful spirit and activities of men are universal in time and place and among all sorts and conditions of men. And the natural advantages, such as climate, water power, coal, and iron, were always available, or ready to be made so. The secret lies elsewhere. An examination of the character, the social and political institutions of the English people before the revolution discloses the presence therein of certain high barriers which had first to be broken down. Now the English people came in the epoch of the Protestant Reformation under certain influences which impelled them not only to overturn all barriers, but also to blaze the way to industrial freedom. Under the operation of these forces, in spite of adversities that might have been fatal to a less resolute and resourceful people, they advanced to a distinct superiority in industrial and commercial energy. Under the impact of forces whose presence and operation remain obscure and invisible to the purely economic historian, the steadfast will to labor, to produce surplus values, and to accumulate wealth became almost a national trait.

[12] Hayes' *Modern Europe*, Vol. II, p. 674.

This resolute will to labor in an atmosphere of stern economy led on to a diligent search for inventions and for better organization, to a division of labor, to the making of machines and to the scientific control of natural forces—*in summa*, to improved ways of doing things generally. The motive forces to these mighty changes came not from the gainful spirit as such, for that is confessedly everywhere operative; nor did they come from the material factors of industry; for these factors were never lacking. The motive forces came out of the transformation of the national character by the tillage of human soil over a long stretch of time—several generations. The deeper reasons for the occurrence of the Industrial Revolution first, not in the Orient but in the Occident, not in Antiquity nor the Middle Ages, but in the modern world, and there primarily in seventeenth and eighteenth century England must be sought not only in the material conditions of life, but also in *the ideal aims and forces* by which men were guided in the utilization of the material conditions of life. And we are referred finally for a clue to this fateful revolution to *the interweaving of religious, political, and economic threads in the fabric of history*. In the great historic battle, fought and won, for the inestimable boon, the right, more precious than life itself, to worship God according to the dictates of one's own conscience, none daring to molest or make afraid, there was won, by inclusion and implication, especially for men whose conception of labor had a religious basis and motivation, for men who esteemed profitable industrial activity the best, the main part of that rational worship which embraces the whole of life—there was won also the right to work and eventually the right to vote according to the dictates of conscience, none daring to molest or make afraid.

The fountain of these deposits in the English national character, the indefeasible right of every man to life, liberty, and the pursuit of happiness, and the holy ordinance of God that every man shall labor, produce and increase in all values, spiritual and temporal, lies in the *vocational idealism* which is the offspring of Protestant Christianity and perhaps its most significant contribution to our western civilization. It is one of Weber's most thoughtful observations in his *Religionssoziologie* that only peoples whose religious life has been nurtured under the influence of the Protestant Bible have a word (Luther introduced it) to express the idea of a *calling* comprehending the sum total of life's interests and activities, civic and social, political and economic, as equally organic parts of that rational worship which every man owes to God. Non-Christian peoples do not have it, neither do peoples subject to Roman or Greek Catholicism. The full impact of religion upon the ethical conduct and practical activities of life was, after Protestantism had been established, no longer a distinction of the man set apart to the offices of the Church, but Protestantism poured the energies of religion into all the channels of secular activity. It became a potent article of belief that men are called of God in the day's work. Calvinism especially, still sternly ascetic, by giving the old ascetic self-restraint an extensive and intensive development hitherto unknown, did this in transcendent measure. In this achievement it stands unexcelled, unequaled in church history. No other branch of Christianity has developed so exalted a conception of work in this world as a divine appointment, propounding fruitfulness and efficiency as the normal and necessary test equally of being in a state of grace and of growth in grace. *Productive service* as the substance of one's calling, application and industry in worldly activity are made religious duties, lifted from the low plane of a pure means of subsistence, and given the highest rank *as the end and sign of active faith.* It is the most exalted religious evaluation of activity in the world to which Christianity has given birth. Whole communities permeated by this spirit which I have called vocational idealism were gradually molded by the discipline of godly labor. And the thing itself has had some remarkable economic and social consequences.

It is unnecessary to trace in all its ramifications the spread of this spirit in the Protestant world, especially the West European or Calvinistic branches. That has been done in a masterly and convincing manner by Weber, and in bold outline by Troeltsch, who has adopted Weber's thesis. The Belgian sociologist Laveleye was perhaps the first to develop the dynamic relations of Protestant ethics to industrial productivity and power. Following Laveleye's original conception, his point of view has been amplified and corrected by increasing numbers of investigators.

Only Protestants have a word for vocational idealism! The substance of it in all its sublimity and sanctified common sense, the thought, wondrous, deep, and rich, of life as a whole given over to activity in the world as a call of God, the spirit which made of religion a business and of useful labor a religion, found classic expression in Charles Wesley's immortal hymn rightly called the Marseillaise of Methodism. The author of it wrote the hymn not for priests and prelates, but for coal miners and carpenters, managers and merchants:

> A charge to keep I have,
>   A God to glorify;
> A never dying soul to save,
>   And fit it for the sky.

> To serve the present age,
>   My calling to fulfill;
> O! may it all my powers engage,
>   To do my Master's will.

> Arm me with jealous care,
>   As in thy sight to live,
> And O! thy servant, Lord, prepare
>   A strict account to give.

> Help me to watch and pray,
>   And on thyself rely,
> Assured if I my trust betray,
>   I shall forever die.

The Wesleys did not originate, but inherited this intense vocational idealism from their Nonconformist antecedents. It came to them from Baxter and the great Puritan divines, and from the deep impress of Bishop Taylor's *Holy Living*. Although Wesley in his early conferences [13] with his helpers taught them, in rather doubtful fashion for one who solemnly protested his belief in religious toleration, to repudiate the "Predestinarian poison" and to guard the flock against a doctrine worse than "all the devices of Satan," still he was careful to draw a line between the Calvinist emphasis on the electing love of Jehovah, and *the Calvinistic religious evaluation of activity in the world*. The latter, the idea of fidelity in vocational labor, he told his preachers was good solid Bible doctrine which we are bound to assert steadily "on the authority of our Lord himself. For God will not give true riches to a man not faithful in the unrighteous mammon." The Conference minutes on the subject of Calvinism reveal that Wesley recognized in its religious evaluation of "Man's faithfulness," that is, fidelity in vocational activity, something distinctly Calvinistic. And he couples his repudiation of Calvinism as a theory with a definite indorsement of Calvinistic ethics. It has been well said that Calvinism was primarily a system of conduct, a religious discipline of life, a church polity.[14] If so, Methodism was modeled after it. For Wesley is strong in emphasizing that the marks of Methodism are found in its strict religio-ethical regimentation of life, and only in its doctrine as a means to discipline. How frequently he pushes its strict stern discipline, its religio-ethical regimentation of life into the foreground! That is what first gave the movement its first name. Of course the re-

[13] I allow this overstatement of Wesley's doctrinal position to stand exactly as written some thirteen years ago, although it contains two inaccuracies. The language, "predestinarian poison," is genuinely Wesleyan. But the implication that Wesley broke his toleration principles in the way and manner he opposed "particular redemption" is contradicted by all the facts. The truth is he came to the brink of compromising his principles in order to placate evangelical Calvinists and prevent a final breach. Above all, I did not know thirteen years ago that the doctrinal minutes of the early Wesleyan Conferences mirror no concern at all to repudiate the "predestinarian poison," but do show an exclusive and profound concern to repudiate the humanistic poison in Anglican Arminianism. The key to Wesley's position and master purpose in the first years of the Revival is in the observation often made by him in the forties: "The truth is, the old doctrines of the Reformation are now quite new in the world." Letters, III, 391.

[14] *Cambridge Modern History*, Vol. II, pp. 357 f.

ligious dynamic which sustained the discipline counted supremely. "Having the form of godliness and seeking the power" locates the center of Methodism at its best. Even so it was not quietism nor mystical contemplation, but a religion of action that interested Wesley. A solitary religion, going out of the world or hiding oneself in it, he asserted, is repugnant to Christianity. The social, open, active Christians are the real ones.

The first Oxford Diary contains an entry dated October 1, 1726, of two words: *Idleness slays*. It introduces us to the beginnings of Wesley's lifelong battle against idleness. The process by which he trained himself and others in the habit of ceaseless diligence began in a fierce fight against the sin of ill-used time. The clue to this is found in a work by Bishop Taylor, who, as we know, was a great authority for Wesley and a principal fountain of his vocational idealism: "The first general Instrument of Holy Living is Care of our Time." All idleness is sin. *It is better to plow on Sunday than to do nothing.* The life of every man may and must be so ordered that it may be a perpetual serving of God. No man can complain that his calling takes him off from religion: his calling itself, i.e., his very worldly employment in honest trades and offices, is a serving of God. Plowmen, artisans, merchants are in their calling ministers of the Divine Providence. And God has given every man work enough to do, so that there shall be no idleness. In this conception of life, work and duty become synonyms.[15]

Wesley adopted thus early the fundamentals of Taylor's Holy Living and Dying, built his own life upon them and consecrated every moment and every faculty of his being to the high calling of inducing others to do the same. These fundamentals—they are the essentials of Calvinistic ethics—are three: stewardship, subordination of life, every detail of it, to the glory of God, and the practice of the presence of God, that is, every moment is lived under God's watchful eye. They comprise the means and the methods of a holy life. Holiness means that "all our labors and care, all our powers and faculties, must be wholly employed

[15] Taylor's *Holy Living*, etc., Bohn Ed., p. 3.

in the service of God, and even all the days of our life." Now among Taylor's twelve articles of a holy life and also the "twelve signs of grace and predestination" we find two of high import for our subject. There is enjoined an ascetic self-discipline of life as a means to an inner lordship over the world linked with a clear orientation of life on eternal values. Further, justice in dealings and diligence in one's calling are set down as one of the signs of grace and predestination. Therefore fruitful acquisitive activity or profitable productive industry and enterprise are a sign of active faith, are an assurance of one's calling and election. On this basis the production of surplus values and increase in goods become a religious duty. It is *the Puritan apotheosis of work* [16] as the most comprehensive human obligation from which there can be no exemption. The corollary of this principle, it may be noticed, is *the labor theory of values,* which appears to be also a deposit of Calvinistic ethics in economic thinking. "Work," says Petty, "is the father and active principle of wealth, as land (that is, natural resources) is the mother."

The several references to Richard Baxter in Wesley's Journals are sufficient to reveal an intimate knowledge of the great Puritan divine and a high appreciation of his qualities. Twice at least Wesley read his life, and his works were much studied. Wesley read Baxter's *History of the Councils* and was quite carried away with it. He eulogized his spirit, regarded him as one of the incomparable masters of the pastoral office, and incorporated his plans for religious education and pastoral visitation, into the Conference Minutes. Finally he laid on his preachers an injunction to study Baxter's plans and put them into practice. Wesley's knowledge of the *Saint's Everlasting Rest* (he quotes it in Sermon No. 70 of the *Christian Directory* and other masterpieces of Puritan piety and ethics) illuminates his very close affiliation with the Calvinistic branch of Christianity and ex-

---

[16] The Puritan religious evaluation of labor as the primary historical source of the famous labor theory of values is a relation which has not been, but should be, thoroughly investigated.

plains his energetic reaffirmation of the Puritan ethic of Labor in his own preaching, teaching and pastoral activities.

Wesley shared to the full the Puritan apotheosis of labor. He regarded work far more as a means of grace than as a means of making a living, and with it he shared all other essentials of Puritan ethics. A glance at the religio-ethical regimentation of life laid down for the Methodist Societies reveals elements of far-reaching social and economic significance. (a) Taste no spirituous liquor, no dram of any kind. (b) Be at a word in buying and selling. (c) Pawn nothing, no, not to save a life. (d) Wear no needless ornaments such as rings, ear-rings, necklaces, lace, ruffles. (e) Use no needless self-indulgence such as taking snuff or tobacco. (f) *Be patterns of diligence, frugality and self-denial.* (Italics mine.)

Wesley was a great preacher of stewardship, comprehensive of life, time, talent, money, everything. And he enforced it on his followers to the utmost. This appears both in his doctrine of work as a religious duty and the way he preached and enforced it. His own ideas are crystal clear: "Work is serving God. Idleness slays. Idleness is immorality. Idleness is sin. No idleness can consist with growth in grace, no, nor with the retention of grace received in justification. *The rising generation must be converted to the spirit and confirmed in habits of industry, if the revival is not to be an affair of one generation.* There is not one point in Methodism that is a distraction from work, every point of it is an incentive to rational industry. We hold our meetings at times when our people are free to come. If any are not, we enjoin them not to leave their work to do so. We severely condemn all who neglect their temporal concerns. *Let no one ever see a ragged Methodist.* So far am I from either causing or encouraging idleness, that an idle person, known to be such, is not suffered to remain in any of our societies. It is impossible that an idle man can be a good man. *We drive him out as we would a thief or a murderer.* To show all possible diligence (as well as frugality) is one of our standing rules, and one *concerning the observance of which we continually make the strictest inquiry."*

Profitable industry here is rated the first element of Christian prudence, something we owe to God, to our neighbors, and to ourselves. Work is so clearly of divine appointment that religion can not consist with the least degree of idleness.[17] The man who attains unto holiness is naturally not less but more efficient in his worldly business. In these precepts respecting work collected from Wesley's writings, partly verbatim, partly condensed, we find the genuinely Puritan ethics of work. It taught thousands to believe that to be useful, to render a service, to engage in pursuits affording financial profit had the high sanctions of heaven. It inculcated the idea that profit is Christian, and that the successful pursuit of it was a sign of active faith and continuance in grace.

The principle of stewardship received a unique application in the valuation and accounting of time. Life under God's watchful eye awoke in men a spirit of jealous carefulness and led many thoughtful minds into the practice of spiritual bookkeeping. Wesley himself gave a magnificent specimen of such a spiritual accounting, of putting conscience and calculation into every detail of life, in his diaries and journals. What a stewardship of time is there unfolded! But there was nothing exceptional in Wesley's practice, unless it was the intensity and thoroughness of his spiritual accounting. For sixty-six years the minutest details of the day are scrutinized under the piercing light of an active conscience sensitized by religion. Before such a tribunal moments take on the value of hours, hours of days, and days of destiny.

But Wesley, like the author of *Poor Richard's Almanac,* gave this principle a definite economic application. "Time is money," said the shrewd Yankee. But Wesley is not at all a stranger to this Yankee philosopher's economic maxim. "Suppose a man spends in sleep an hour a day more than nature requires. What is there serious about that? Why, first of all *it hurts your substance.* It is throwing away six hours a week which might turn to some temporal account. If you are of no trade, still you may

[17] Sermon 89.

so employ the time that it will bring money or money's worth to yourself or others." [18] There were for Wesley three points all told of Christian prudence: "Gain all you can, save all you can, and give all you can." The author of *Poor Richard's Almanac* and the great revivalist were very much agreed on the first and second points. But on Wesley's third point, "give all you can, and thou shalt have treasure in heaven," Franklin had another idea. "Remember that money is of the prolific generating nature. Money can beget money (this is a complete reversal of mediaeval economics—*Nummus nummum parere non potest*); its offspring can beget more, and so on." "In short, the way to wealth if you desire it, is as plain as the way to market. It depends on two words—industry and frugality. Waste neither time nor money, but make the best use of both. He that gets all he can honestly and saves all he gets (necessary expenses excepted) will certainly get rich." On this head Wesley from his semi-Franciscan attitude toward wealth would have said, "Quite true, he will get rich, but he will just as certainly go to hell." [19] Franklin recognized what Wesley was apparently a stranger to, namely, that vital element of the capitalist spirit, the will to invest or employ the surplus values produced by labor or accumulated wealth in promoting directly or indirectly further production for the sake of profit.

At another point, religion, through the Puritan ethic, made vital contact with economic functions. Before the spirit of capitalism can be acquired it is necessary that men be brought under an influence sufficient to put the bit into expenditure. Now the same magic which subdued communities to the discipline of work subjected them to the discipline of thrift. To industry, the first point, there was added frugality, the second point of Christian prudence. The stewardship of money impelled masses of men to put conscience and calculation into everything. Consider the tither. He must carefully scrutinize income and expenditure in relation to each other. Thus the keeping of accounts becomes a

[18] Sermon 93.
[19] Sermon 112.

religious duty. This practice has been for those engaged in
gainful pursuits the foundation of many a fortune. For although
tithing added nothing directly to income, as some have been
foolish enough to assert, nevertheless the rationalization of in-
comes and expenditure which the principle makes necessary does
disclose waste and stimulates carefulness in expenditure. Thus
what prudence often achieved, namely, a competence, piety was
free to interpret as the special blessing of the Lord. But tithing
is only a special case of a more comprehensive procedure. The
Puritan ethic on which Wesley insisted for all his followers in-
stilled a vigorous spirit of economy.

Attention has been directed to the society rules as a religio-
ethical regimentation of life along the lines of industry, frugality,
and charity. These rules were not bits of mild advice. They
were the axioms of admission and continued membership. The
observance of these rules has in these latter times of Methodism
passed into a state of "innocuous desuetude." But it was not
so then. On the duty of observing the society rules Wesley was
firm. He instructed his helpers to refuse tickets to all who were
known to violate the rules. They were to be ostracized, excluded
from the secret sessions of the elect. The signed ticket became a
certificate of good standing, not without its secular values. To
be denied a ticket was a total disgrace. Thus the Wesleyan discipline of work, thrift and charity was made thorough and
effective.

The economic aspects of his religio-ethical regimentation of life
were subjects of frequent comment. For the economic significance of various problems Wesley had a quick perception. The
economic consequences of alcoholism did not escape this sharp-
sighted observer. It was pictured as an intolerable tax on the
nation's food resources, as the cause of nervous disorders, laying
the foundations of numberless diseases and impairing the national
vigor. And tea drinking! We have a treatise on that too. The
use of tea was, so he came to think in August 1746, a source of
nervous disorder. It enfeebled vigor, impaired health, and (here
we have it!) "thereby it hurts their business also." People

would fare better without it and "would save just the price of tea." "And many a little, you know, put together, will make a great sum." Moreover, "nothing is small if it touches conscience," and "he who saves anything from the best motives, will lay it out to the best purpose." That is the essence of what has been called economic rationalism.

A striking instance of the way religious forces may by their operation be the forerunners of new economic formations of society is found in the motivation and bearing of Wesley's diatribes against fashion in dress among the Methodists. His fearless, at times furious, denunciations of fashion in dress and other needless expenditure could scarcely have won the applause of his more prosperous and wealthy adherents. But beyond doubt large numbers were sufficiently influenced thereby to keep the balance on the right side of the ledger and so were started right economically. Moreover, Wesley's objection to fashion in dress and similar luxuries was very little concerned about the appearances, but very much about the expensiveness of costly apparel. His *Appeal to Men of Reason and Religion* (1744) upbraids the Quakers for recreancy to their first principles. Under the influence of growing wealth they were showing signs of apostasy from their first ideals. "Multitudes of you are very jealous as to the color and form of your apparel, the least important of all the circumstances that relate to it, while in the most important you are without any concern at all. You now wear plain but still the costliest apparel. Surely you cannot be ignorant that *the sinfulness of fine apparel lies chiefly in the expensiveness.*"

Karl Marx makes the statement that the capitalist brands all consumption as a sin *against his function.* This statement reflects the *a priori,* unscientific exclusion or subordination of all other factors to the economic. It assumes that all *inductive reasoning* on the field of human history *must proceed from* the "material conditions of life" or "the *economic* structure of society" viewed as *causes to* the general character of the social, political, and *spiritual* processes of life viewed as *effects.* Under this dogmatic restriction of historical reasoning it was necessary to consider as a product of capitalism what was in reality a pre-supposition. He assumes that the exigencies of the capitalist procedure gave birth to thrift motives, as if the spirit of frugality could be acquired only by a man who was already a capitalist and was then imposed by him on others. The morale of modern business was not built up that way, at least not in all cases. In Wesley (and his case is typical of thousands) we have a mind utterly remote from the capitalistic procedure. It is wholly foreign to him. He advocated gaining and saving for absolutely non-economic ends. And yet he branded all needless consumption as sinful. I repeat, the sinfulness of needless consumption and the duty of thrift had for Wesley, Baxter, and men like them an exclusively religious orientation and motivation utterly foreign in its origin, though not in its effects, to the exigencies of the capitalistic procedure. The birthplace of thrift motives as here made clear must be sought not in the "modes of production" nor in the exigencies of the capitalist system, but in the genius of Protestant Christianity, in particular the Calvinistic branches. And Wesley's strictures on needless expenditure as sinful waste open up to view the operation of religio-ethical forces that have positively influenced economic outlook and contributed largely to the up-building of the morale of capitalism.

In one more particular, highly important, the operation of religious forces was productive of that "economic rationalism," as Sombart phrased it, which is the soul of modern business procedure. It is the spirit of enterprise and of constant improvement which had to be set on foot before capitalism as the deliberate, foreseeing organization of free labor could be developed. Economic traditionalism, *running on in the same dull track with the forefathers*, was the greatest barrier to this industrial revolution. There was no active quest of shorter and better, that is, more efficient ways of doing things, because few if any minds were awake to the possibility. Now the fact is that in the historical background of the Industrial Revolution some influence or other set hundreds of obscure workers to searching for improved ways of doing things. If we could locate *the fountain of this will to industrial progress* we should go a long way toward explaining historically the event of the Industrial Revolution. Undoubtedly it was not a simple but complex stream of influences which broke up the inert conservatism of industry and awakened a spirit of enterprise in masses of workers, and presumably it will be some time yet before the deeper reasons and motives for this industrial expansion are discovered and defined. Ours is a simpler task, namely, to make clear the interweaving of religious, social, and economic threads in that fateful transformation.

Wesley was a very practically minded man. Lecky says of him that he wielded the widest constructive influence in the sphere of practical religion since Luther. We commonly and rightly think of him as a very conservative man, and so he was. But within the bounds set by his conservatism he was exceedingly progressive. I pass over numerous sentences of his which scintillate with radicalism. But certainly in things ecclesiastical he was something of an *entrepreneur*. He might vow his intention to live and die a member of the Church of England. But that could not alter the fact that as a master-builder he had created an ecclesiastical system which has secured him a place among the world's great organizers. "He had a genius for government not inferior to that of Richelieu." Not only in the affairs of the church, but in practical ways Wesley displayed this spirit of true enterprise. Witness the measures to provide remunerative work for people who otherwise must needs be subjects of charity. Witness the employment of a man to "superintend my printing," out of which he made and gave away a small fortune. Instances abound. No better description of the spirit in which he did his work can be found than his own words: *"We are always open to instruction; willing to be wiser every day than we were before, and to change whatever we can change for the better."* [20]

In that remarkable sermon on "The Use of Money" he recommended this practical gospel of the open mind, the spirit of constant progress, and of steady improvement, to men engaged in business pursuits. He goes over as usual his three points of

[20] Wesley, *A Plain Account of People Called Methodists.*

Christian prudence, gain, save, and give all you can. Gain all you can by honest industry, using all possible diligence in your calling. Here we notice that profitable industry, *gainful pursuits with a view to profit* (the profit motive), *are accounted a part of one's God-given calling.* And the utmost application, energy, dispatch should be put into gainful business. But above all

"use in your business all the understanding which God has given you. It is amazing to observe how few do this, how men run on in the same dull track with their forefathers. But whatever they do who know not God, this is no rule for you. It is a shame for a Christian not to improve upon them in whatever he takes in hand. You should be continually learning from the experience of others or from your own experience, reading and reflection, to do everything you have to do better than you did yesterday. And see that you practice whatever you learn that you may make the best use of all that is in your hands."

We might search far and wide without finding a more apt description of the psychology of the modern business man at his best.

Let us suppose this economic gospel (Wesley designated it as a peculiar offspring of Christianity) of constant and strenuous improvement should be put into practice by only a percentage of those engaged in commercial and industrial pursuits. What would happen to the thousand and one who failed to keep step with the most progressive spirits? Wesley in the same discourse sets up a barrier to lawless acquisition and insists further that it is never allowable to gain in ways that "hurt any one in his substance." "Underselling a competitor, any expedient to injure his trade to advance your own, enticing his workmen away, etc., none can gain thus by swallowing up his neighbor's substance, without gaining the damnation of hell!" This sounds quite altruistic. But suppose a man by "using all his understanding" invents an improvement; it may be a machine to make the same article at half the cost, or some ingenious improvement in the organization, direction, or training of labor, whether employed in the production or distribution of goods, or any other device affording a decisive economic superiority. Is the inventor or discoverer to hide his invention under a bushel and keep to the old paths in order to be economically harmless and not hurt any man's substance; or is he in duty bound resolutely to put this philosophy of strenuous improvement into practice? If the latter alternative is chosen, then a process commonly known as the survival of the fittest lieth at the door. Fatalities like this make up a considerable part of the store of so-called free enterprise and its evolution. The idea that a group of men in any society could pursue a course of strenuous industrial improvement without inconvenience to those who failed to follow suit is somewhat naïve.

The conception of painless economic progress is on a par with Wesley's amazing statement that to put money into the Bank of England was in effect to throw it away. It might just as well be buried in the earth, he thought, or cast into the sea. Charity, he said, is the only true use for what remains over and above the necessities of life. Wesley has abandoned "subsistence ethics" in his view of the production, but not in his view of the use of wealth. Here he remains traditionalistic. He of course had no occasion and still less the equipment to think economic principles through into their practical consequences. But this aloofness from the realities of industrial procedure does not diminish the value of his observations and insight into the bearing of religion upon the economic activities of men. It does but augment their accuracy. He saw religious forces subduing men to the discipline of labor and of thrift and making their minds active in the search for improved ways of doing things. All this took place, of course, in cooperation with other forces and other influences. For the warp and woof of the fabric of history is a complex of many threads and the work of many weavers. Our thesis goes no farther than that religious forces have been powerful factors and that economic agents have often obeyed religious mandates in their conception and execution of economic activities.

The conclusion yielded by this brief study—it might be amplified many times by similar materials out of various Calvinistic communities—is obvious. A people having a thoroughgoing religious orientation of life, taking the issues of religion seriously as the supreme practical concern of life, brought under the Puritan ethics of work, taught to look on vocational activity or the day's work as essential not only to keep valid their primary acceptance with God, but also as necessary for perseverance in grace or going on to perfection, feeling thus an enduring religious incentive to industrial effort, mingling the high sanctions of heaven with the experience speedily forthcoming of rapidly improving circumstances, investing all useful activity, all honest toil with the aroma of saving faith—such a people, we can readily understand, advanced rapidly in industrial energy and economic capacities. Religious forces helped to impart new labor capacities, mental and manual. The will to work became strong and steady in whole communities. It put the bit into expenditure. It taught multitudes for whom life had been from hand to mouth on an animal level, to look a long way ahead and to try to see life, and see it whole. It taught a man humility before God, but in so doing made him the child of a King. It linked the highest spiritual prizes with vocational fruitfulness, lifting men up from the lower levels of instinct and passion to the higher altitudes of vision and purpose, reaching out into the eternities. This religious culture flowered out into the thought of pressing forward to some worthy goal in this life as well as that which is to come. With this psychological approach, we would be more than surprised to miss the important social and economic consequences already referred to in any given community.

The rapid rise in economic status of the early Methodists accords, therefore, with similar social and economic phenomena in other religious communities, notably the early Puritans, Quakers, Baptists, Mennonites, etc. Whereas formerly the people called Methodists recklessly squandered time, money, strength of body and mind in drink, gambling, wild barbaric sports, or vicious wasteful forms of pleasure, they became under the influence of the Revival *paradigms of sobriety, industry, and frugality.* Temperance, labor, and thrift followed the Revival. "You seem a very temperate people here and in comfortable circumstances," said Cardinal Newman on a walking tour in Cornwall to a miner whom he met on the way. "How do you account for it?" The miner, slowly lifting his hat, made answer: "There came a man amongst us once. His name was John Wesley."

In addition to this direct influence of the Revival we must not overlook its vast indirect influence. There were above all the contagion of example, the magic of an intensive and expansive group influence, and the compulsion of competition. Perhaps the sudden and steady improvement in the economic status of the early Methodist workers may throw light on the very hostile feelings they excited in their former associates and therewith upon the destruction of their tools. In any event Wesley wrote already in the twentieth year of the Revival that multitudes of the Methodists who in times past had scarce food to eat or raiment to put on have now "all things needful for life and godliness," for their families as well as themselves, and in addition were becoming dispensers of extensive charities. "I went to Macclesfield, and found a people *still alive to God, in spite of swiftly increasing riches.* If they continue so it will be the only instance I have known in above half a century." [21]

It is a thesis often put forward from the economic or sociological standpoint that Christianity was a class movement and that Protestantism in particular was a middle-class movement. There is enough truth in this to make it thoroughly specious. But while it remains uncertain whether Christianity ever has been in any sense a class movement, we may be sure that Christianity has been a perennial and powerful factor in the development of the Western world. Whether the capitalistic economic formation and structure of our western civilization, which is now spreading rapidly through the Orient, is a passing phase or a permanent formation is a question the solution of which is not yet accomplished. Its foes have distilled from their contemplation of its crying evils and abuses a confidence in its speedy destruction about as extravagant as the assurance of the early Christians that the end of the world was knocking at the doors. It is doubtful whether human

[21] Journal, VII, 256.

societies will ever prefer essential communism, with its fatal gravitation toward laziness, waste and stagnation, to a system which adds the fuel of interest to the fire of genius and puts a premium on industry, thrift, and man's energetic foreseeing thoughtfulness. Perhaps the avenue of social progress will be neither labor for pure profit nor for pure service, but the search for profit through service and for service through profit. In any event to condemn that intense feeling as to the duty and dignity of productive labor or the industrial spirit which gave birth to capitalism as the "sickness of an acquisitive society," is to condemn the most distinctive deposit of Christianity in the psychology of Western peoples. And so we reach a conclusion that may be expressed in one of Abraham Lincoln's wisest observations: "While man exists it is his duty to improve not only his own condition but to assist in ameliorating mankind." This position, like the religious ethic of Jesus, given in his résumé of law and prophets (Matthew XXII, 40) and his statement of the Golden Rule (Matthew VII, 12) is neither that of pure individualism nor of pure communism, but calls for a clear distinction, full recognition, and sound correlation of the indispensable truth-values in both principles. Above all, history nowhere speaks for the idea of morality without religion. New active powers of mind and will have always been given to men from having the right God in their experience. So, then, all men need now supremely the Luther-Calvin-Wesley faith in God that carries in itself victory over the world and thoroughly furnishes for every good work in the world.

WESLEY'S PUBLISHED SERMONS

1. Salvation by Faith.
2. The Almost Christian.
3. Awake, thou that sleepest.
4. Scriptural Christianity.
5. Justification by Faith.
6. The Righteousness of Faith.
7. The Way to the Kingdom.
8. The First Fruits of the Spirit.
9. The Spirit of Bondage and of Adoption.
10. The Witness of the Spirit.
11. The Witness of Our Own Spirit.
12. The Means of Grace.
13. The Circumcision of the Heart.
14. The Marks of the New Birth.
15. The Great Privilege of those that are Born of God.
16. Sermon on the Mount—1.
17. Sermon on the Mount—2.
18. Sermon on the Mount—3.
19. Sermon on the Mount—4.
20. Sermon on the Mount—5.
21. Sermon on the Mount—6.
22. Sermon on the Mount—7.
23. Sermon on the Mount—8.
24. Sermon on the Mount—9.
25. Sermon on the Mount—10.
26. Sermon on the Mount—11.
27. Sermon on the Mount—12.
28. Sermon on the Mount—13.
29. The Original, Nature, Property, and use of the Law.
30. The Law Established through Faith; Discourse I.
31. The Law Established through Faith; Discourse II.
32. The Nature of Enthusiasm.

415

111. On the Omnipresence of God.
112. The Rich Man and Lazarus.
113. Walking by Sight, and Walking by Faith.
114. The Unity of the Divine Being.
115. The Ministerial Office.
116. Causes of the Inefficacy of Christianity.
117. On Knowing Christ after the Flesh.
118. On a Single Eye.
119. On Worldly Folly.
120. On the Wedding Garment.
121. Human Life a Dream.
122. On Faith.
123. On the Deceitfulness of the Human Heart.
124. The Heavenly Treasure in Earthen Vessels.
125. On Living Without God.
126. On the Danger of Increasing Riches.
127. The Trouble and Rest of Good Men.
128. Free Grace.
129. The Cause and Cure of Earthquakes.
130. National Sins and Miseries.
131. Some Account of the late Work of God in North America.
132. On the Foundation of City-Road Chapel.
133. On the Death of the Rev. Mr. John Fletcher.
134. True Christianity Defended.
135. On Mourning for the Dead.
136. On Corrupting the Word of God.
137. On the Resurrection of the Dead.
138. On Grieving the Holy Spirit.
139. On Love.
140. On Public Diversions.
141. On the Holy Spirit.

INDEX OF NAMES

419

S